T0309483

# NETS, TERMS AND FORMULAS

# NETS, TERMS AND FORMULAS

Three views of Concurrent Processes and Their Relationship

E.-R. OLDEROG
*Professor of Computer Science*
*Fachbereich Informatik, Universität Oldenburg*

The right of the
University of Cambridge
to print and sell
all manner of books
was granted by
Henry VIII in 1534.
The University has printed
and published continuously
since 1584.

CAMBRIDGE UNIVERSITY PRESS

*Cambridge*

*New York   Port Chester   Melbourne   Sydney*

CAMBRIDGE UNIVERSITY PRESS
Cambridge, New York, Melbourne, Madrid, Cape Town, Singapore, São Paulo

Cambridge University Press
The Edinburgh Building, Cambridge CB2 2RU, UK

Published in the United States of America by Cambridge University Press, New York

www.cambridge.org
Information on this title: www.cambridge.org/9780521400442

First published 1991
This digitally printed first paperback version 2005

*A catalogue record for this publication is available from the British Library*

ISBN-13 978-0-521-40044-2 hardback
ISBN-10 0-521-40044-9 hardback

ISBN-13 978-0-521-01845-6 paperback
ISBN-10 0-521-01845-5 paperback

# PREFACE

The stepwise development of complex systems through various levels of abstraction is good practice in software and hardware design. However, the semantic link between these different levels is often missing. This book is intended as a detailed case study how such links can be established. It presents a theory of concurrent processes where three different semantic description methods are brought together in one uniform framework. Nets, terms and formulas are seen as expressing complementary views of processes, each one describing processes at a different level of abstraction.

- Petri nets are used to describe processes as concurrent and interacting machines which engage in internal actions and communications with their environment or user.

- Process terms are used as an abstract concurrent programming language. Due to their algebraic structure process terms emphasise compositionality, i.e. how complex terms are composed from simpler ones.

- Logical formulas of a first-order predicate logic, called trace logic, are used as a specification language for processes. Logical formulas specify safety and liveness aspects of the communication behaviour of processes as required by their users.

At the heart of this theory are two sets of transformation rules for the top-down design of concurrent processes. The first set can be used to transform logical formulas stepwise into process terms, and the second set can be used to transform process terms into Petri nets. These rules are based on novel techniques for the operational and denotational semantics of concurrent processes.

This book grew out of my research work in the area of concurrent processes which started during my visit to the Programming Research Group in Oxford. The text is based on the my habilitation thesis – a kind of second doctoral thesis – completed at the University of Kiel, and on graduate courses on the subject given at the Universities of Kiel, Saarbrücken and Oldenburg. Parts of the material have also been presented at international summer schools in France, The Netherlands and Germany.

What I found most difficult when designing the structure of this book was to choose the definitions and concepts in such a way that everything fits together smoothly: Petri nets, process terms, logical formulas, and the transformations. Various subtletees that do not come to surface when writing short research papers had to solved.

# How to use this Book

This book is intended for graduate students and researchers interested in concurrency theory. The emphasis is on the relationship between Petri nets, algebraic process terms and logical formulas in the systematic construction of concurrent processes. This book does not contain material on Petri nets or process algebra that is covered by other books.

The prerequisites for this book are fluency in the mathematical concepts of sets, relations and functions; familiarity with the basic concepts around automata and regular languages; some practice in reading formulas in predicate logic; and a background in programming. In some parts also basic knowledge from decidability theory is assumed. Apart from these assumptions I have presented the central concepts of this book in a self-contained manner.

A large part of this book is appropriate for a one-semester course on concurrent processes for graduate studies. For a course with emphasis on process construction I suggest the following structure:

| | |
|---|---|
| Introduction: | 1.1, |
| Petri Nets: | 2.1 – 2.2, A, 2.4, |
| Process Terms: | 3.1 – 3.4, 3.5 and 3.8 without proofs, B, |
| Logical Formulas: | 4.1 – 4.5, |
| Process Construction: | 5.1, 5.3 – 5.6. |

The figures refer to the sections in the list of contents, and the letters A and B to possible additions from other sources:

- A: More on Petri nets, e.g. from [Rei85]. In particular, verification of net properties using S-invariants and illustrated by mutual exclusion examples fits well to rest of the book.

- B: Introduction to process algebra, e.g. from [BW90b]. The axiomatic view of process algebra should be explained. Also simple examples of process verification using algebraic laws are recommended.

The remaining sections of this book, in particular 2.3, 3.6, 3.7, 4.6, 4.7, 5.2 and 5.7, are advanced. They are suitable for study groups or seminar work. Extensions of the theory and directions for further research are stated in the sections 6.1 – 6.5.

# Acknowledgements

H. Langmaack carefully introduced me to computer science and all there is around it, and directed my interest towards program correctness and verification. During a summer school, F.L. Bauer and H. Wössner gave me the bad conscience that program construction by transformation is much better than a posteriori verification. But how to put their advice into practice, I began to see only at Oxford where C.A.R. Hoare introduced me to the exiting world of communicating processes.

My understanding of this subject broadened during visits to Amsterdam with joint work with J.W. de Bakker, J.A. Bergstra, J.W. Klop, J.-J. Ch. Meyer and J.I. Zucker and to Edinburgh with discussions with M. Hennessy, G. Milne, R. Milner, G.D. Plotkin and C. Stirling. My technical interest in nets originates from the work of P. Degano, R. DeNicola and U. Montanari. Invitations by G. Rozenberg to a course on Petri nets and by G. Hotz to his VLSI group in Saarbrücken have been very helpful.

Moreover, I have greatly benefitted from discussions with K.R. Apt, E. Best, M. Bretschneider, M. Broy, R. van Glabbeek, U. Goltz, B. Jonsson, M. Nielsen, A. Pnueli, W. Reisig, W.P. de Roever, P.S. Thiagarajan, B.A. Trakhtenbrot, B. Steffen, F. Vaandrager and J. Zwiers. I am grateful for detailed comments on draft versions of this book from M. Broy, H. Langmaack, S. Rössig, M. Schenke, J. Zwiers, from the participants of a seminar organised by J. Loeckx and A. Schmitt, in particular A. Heckler and M. Hell, and from D. Tranah of Cambridge University Press. Thanks go also to R. Marzinkewitsch and P. Pichol who have critically assisted my lectures on the subject of this book.

Finally, I would like to thank M. Engels, O. Mehlberg, A. Mengel, C. Schier and A. Wallaschek who have – very often concurrently – transformed various fragments of my manuscripts into this LaTeX typescript.

# CONTENTS

# 1

# INTRODUCTION

Many computing systems consist of a possibly large number of components that not only work independently or concurrently, but also interact or communicate with each other from time to time. Examples of such systems are operating systems, distributed systems and communication protocols, as well as systolic algorithms, computer architectures and integrated circuits.

Conceptually, it is convenient to treat these systems and their components uniformly as *concurrent processes*. A process is here an object that is designed for a possibly continuous interaction with its user, which can be another process. An interaction can be an input or output of a value, but we just think of it abstractly as a *communication*. In between two subsequent communications the process usually engages in some *internal actions*. These proceed autonomously at a certain speed and are not visible to the user. However, as a result of such internal actions the process behaviour may appear *nondeterministic* to the user. Concurrency arises because there can be more than one user and inside the process more than one active subprocess. The behaviour of a process is unsatisfactory for its user(s) if it does not communicate as desired. The reason can be that the process stops too early or that it engages in an infinite loop of internal actions. The first problem causes a *deadlock* with the user(s); the second one is known as *divergence*. Thus most processes are designed to communicate arbitrarily long without any danger of deadlock or divergence.

Since the behaviour of concurrent processes has so many facets, it is not surprising that their description has been approached from rather different angles. In particular, Petri nets [Pet62, Rei85], algebraic process terms [Mil80, BHR84, BK86, BW90b] and logical formulas of temporal or ordinary predicate logic [Pnu77, CH81, MC81] have been used. One may regret such a diversity, but we claim that these different

1

descriptions can be seen as expressing complementary views of concurrent processes, each one serving its own purpose.

To support this claim we present a theory where nets, terms and formulas represent processes at three levels of abstraction: Petri nets are used to describe processes as concurrent and interacting machines with all details of their operational machine behaviour; process terms are used as an abstract concurrent programming language that stresses compositionality, i.e. how complex processes are composed from simpler ones by a small set of process operators; and logical formulas are used to describe or *specify* the communication behaviour of processes as required by their users. The main emphasis and technical contribution of this theory are transformations for a top-down design of concurrent processes starting with formulas and ending in nets:

The top arrow refers to transformation rules for a systematic construction and verification of process terms from logical formulas and the bottom arrow refers to the transition rules of an operational net semantics of process terms. Apart from defining the transformations the theory will carefully develop its concepts. To show that they fit together well, we explore their relationship by establishing various properties.

It seems that our theory is the first approach which brings together nets, terms and formulas in one uniform framework, viz. that of process construction. We hope that it will contribute to a better understanding of these different description methods. On the more ambitious side, this theory is intended as one detailed case study for an essential topic in computer science: provably correct system construction through various levels of abstraction.

To achieve a coherent theory, we have concentrated on a simple setting, but one where a number of interesting process constructions are possible. The main decision was to leave communications as atomic or unstructured objects. This has freed us from several notational and conceptual problems (such as dealing with infinitely many values or assignable variables) and enabled us to concentrate more deeply on the rest. The remaining decisions concern various details such as the class and representation of nets, the operators allowed in process terms, the class of logical formulas and the notion of process correctness. When making such decisions our aim was definitions with pleasant consequences for all three views of concurrent processes.

## 1.1   Three Views: an Example

As a first contact with this theory let us discuss an example inspired by Hoare [Hoa85b]. We wish to describe a process that behaves like a counter, i.e. that stores a natural number which can be incremented and decremented.

More precisely, we shall describe a $k$-bounded counter where $k \geq 1$ is some given constant. A $k$-bounded counter

- stores at each moment an integer value $v$ within the range $0 \leq v \leq k$; initially this value is $v = 0$.

- allows two operations "up" and "dn" (shorthand for "down") to be performed as follows :

  - "up" is defined only if $v < k$ holds; it increments $v$ by 1.
  - "dn" is defined only if $v > 0$ holds; it decrements $v$ by 1.

The idea is to model the $k$-bounded counter as a process $C_k$ that can engage in communications $up$ and $dn$ with its user. This information may be despicted as a connection diagram showing two communication lines between the user and the process named $up$ and $dn$ :

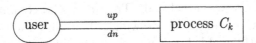

The effect of $C_k$ engaging in a communication $up$ or $dn$ should be the same as performing the operations "up" or "dn" on the value $v$ stored by the counter. To describe this dynamic aspect of $C_k$ we now present three different views.

*Logical Formulas.* The most abstract view is a specification of what the process $C_k$ is supposed to do, i.e. of its intended communication behaviour with the user, but not of its internal structure. We represent the communication behaviour of a process simply as a set of finite communication sequences, usually called *histories* of *traces*. This set is described by a formula of a predicate logic with variables ranging over traces. We therefore talk of *trace formulas* and *trace logic*.

For a fixed $k \geq 1$ the process $C_k$ can be specified by the trace formula

$$S_k = 0 \leq up\#h - dn\#h \leq k$$

where we use $up\#h$ to denote the number of $up$'s in a trace $h$ and $dn\#h$ to denote the number of $dn$'s. The difference $up\#h - dn\#h$ represents the value $v$ stored in $C_k$ after a trace $h$ has occured. Formally, $S_k$ describes the set of all traces $h$ of communications $up$ and $dn$ such that for $h$ and all its prefixes the value $v = up\#h - dn\#h$ is kept within the range $0 \leq v \leq k$.

For example, taking $k = 2$ we see that

$$\epsilon,\ up,\ up.dn \text{ and } up.up.dn$$

are all in the set of traces described by $S_2$, but

$$dn,\ dn.up,\ up.dn.dn$$

are not. Note that $h = dn.up$ itself satisfies the condition $0 \leq up\#h - dn\#h \leq 2$ but not its prefix $dn$. That is why $h$ is not in the set of traces described by $S_2$.

We say a process $C_k$ satisfies the specification $S_k$ if the following two conditions hold:

(1)  the process $C_k$ may only engage in traces that occur in the set
     described by $S_k$,

(2)  if the user insists on, the process $C_k$ must engage in every trace that
     occurs in the set described by $S_k$.

The first condition is a so-called *safety property* of $C_k$ because it prevents $C_k$ from
doing something wrong, viz. engaging in a trace not allowed by $S_k$. The second
condition is a so-called *liveness property* of $C_k$ because it requires $C_k$ to be responsive
to certain communication requests from the user.

*Process Terms.* This view is more detailed; it describes how a process $C_k$ satisfying
$S_k$ can be expressed as an abstract concurrent program. We call these programs
*process terms* because they are generated by a small set of process operators.

Let us start with the case $k = 1$. According to $S_1$ the intended behaviour of $C_1$
is as follows. Initially, $C_1$ stores the value 0. Then only the communication *up* is
possible. We picture the states of $C_1$ by drawing a box with the currently stored
value inside and the currently enabled communication as lines outside:

After performing *up* the process $C_1$ stores the value 1. Then only the communication
*dn* is possible:

Performing now *dn* brings $C_1$ back to its initial state:

A process $C_1$ exhibiting this behaviour can be expressed by the recursive equation

$$C_1 = up.dn.C_1. \tag{1.1}$$

For any process $P$ the term $up.P$ denotes a process that first communicates *up* and
then behaves like $P$. Similarly, for any process $Q$ the term $dn.Q$ denotes a process that
first communicates *dn* and then behaves like $Q$. Thus $up.dn.C_1$ denotes a process that
first communicates *up* then *dn* and then behaves like $C_1$. By the recursive equation
for $C_1$, this actually means that after the communication *dn* the process is ready for
a communication *up* and then *dn* again etc. Thus $C_1$ denotes a process that can
engage in the traces

$$\epsilon,\ up,\ up.dn,\ up.dn.up,\ up.dn.up.dn,\ \ldots$$

with its user. This is exactly the communication behaviour specified by the trace
formula $S_1$.

In the syntax of process terms we shall use an explicit recursive construct instead of the recursive equation (1.1): viz.

$$C_1 = \mu X.up.dn.X. \qquad (1.2)$$

Here $X$ is a process identifier which stands for a recursive call of the term $up.dn.X$ prefixed by $\mu X$.

One of the objectives of this book is to show how a process term like $C_1$ can be constructed systematically from a trace formula like $S_1$. To this end, we shall develop *transformation rules* that transform trace formulas stepwise into process terms. In case of $S_1$ the construction consists of three main steps which we shall represent as a chain of three equalities:

$$
\begin{array}{c}
S_1 \qquad\qquad\qquad (1.3)\\
|||\\
up.S_{1,up}\\
|||\\
up.dn.S_1\\
|||\\
\mu X.up.dn.X
\end{array}
$$

Each step corresponds to the application of one or more transformation rules. The initial step of the construction (1.3) starts with the trace formula $S_1$ and the last step ends with the process term $C_1$. In between we see two so-called *mixed terms*, i.e. syntactic constructs mixing process terms with trace formulas. Intuitively, the mixed term $up.S_{1,up}$ denotes a process that first communicates $up$ and then behaves as specified by the trace formula $S_{1,up}$. Here $S_{1,up}$ is a variant of the formula $S_1$ which is obtained by performing a certain substitution on $S_1$. The details are given by a corresponding transformation rule.

Let us now turn to the case $k = 2$. According to $S_2$ the intended behaviour of $C_2$ is as follows. Initially, $C_2$ stores the value 0 and only allows the communication $up$ to take place:

After performing $up$ the process $C_2$ stores the value 1. Now both the communication $up$ and $dn$ are enabled:

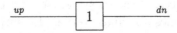

If the user chooses to engage in the communication $up$, the process $C_2$ changes its internal value to 2. Then only the communication $dn$ is possible:

After performing $dn$ the process $C_1$ is back in the state where 1 is the stored value and both communications $up$ and $dn$ are enabled:

If now the user chooses to engage in the communication $dn$, the process $C_2$ returns to its initial state

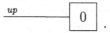

How can we represent this communication behaviour as a process term? Let us first explain a simple direct construction. We introduce three process identifiers named *ZERO*, *ONE* and *TWO* to represent the process $C_2$ being in a state where its internal value is 0,1 or 2. For each of these states we explore the next possible communication. This leads to the following system of recursive equations:

$$
\begin{aligned}
C_2 &= ZERO \\
ZERO &= up.ONE \\
ONE &= up.TWO + dn.ZERO \\
TWO &= dn.ONE
\end{aligned}
\tag{1.4}
$$

For any processes $P$ and $Q$ the term $P+Q$ represents a choice between $P$ and $Q$. More precisely, $P + Q$ denotes a process that behaves like $P$ or $Q$ depending on whether the first communication is one of $P$ or one of $Q$. Thus the process *ONE* behaves like process $up.TWO$ if $up$ is communicated and like $dn.ZERO$ if $dn$ is communicated. Whether $up$ or $dn$ is chosen depends on the user of the process *ONE*.

By a simple substitution we can simplify (1.4) into the following system:

$$
\begin{aligned}
C_2 &= ZERO \\
ZERO &= up.ONE \\
ONE &= up.dn.ONE + dn.ZERO
\end{aligned}
\tag{1.5}
$$

By introducing two nested recursive $\mu$-constructs, we express (1.5) in the syntax of process terms:

$$
C_2 \;=\; \mu X.up.\mu Y.(up.dn.X + dn.Y)
\tag{1.6}
$$

Later we shall construct this process term $C_2$ systematically from the trace formula $S_2$ by applying transformation rules on mixed terms. Essentially, this construction will first discover the system (1.5) of recursive equations from $S_2$ and then express this as the process term (1.6).

Let us now present a second, rather different construction of $C_2$. The idea is to combine two copies of the 1-bounded counter $C_1$ such that the communication line for $dn$ of the first counter is linked to the communication line for $up$ of the second counter. A communication on the link between $dn$ and $up$ is enabled if it is enabled on both communication lines *dn* and *up* simultaneously. When enabled such a communication occurs as an internal action, i.e. without participation and even observation of the user. For the user only the external communications *up* and *dn* are visible.

We picture this construction of $C_2$ as a big box with two smaller boxes inside, one for each copy of $C_1$. A state of $C_2$ is represented by putting the values that are currently stored in the copies of $C_1$ inside the smaller boxes and by drawing the (external and internal) communications as lines to or between the smaller boxes. For example, the initial state of $C_2$ is pictured as follows:

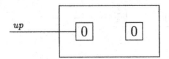

This picture shows that only the communication *up* is enabled and that it will effect the first copy of $C_1$. After performing *up* the first copy of $C_1$ stores the value 1 whereas the second stays at 0. At this state no external communication is possible because neither the first copy of $C_1$ can engage in *up* nor the second one in *dn*. This is undesirable from the user's point of view. However, now an internal communication on the link between the two copies of $C_1$ is possible because at the first copy the communication *dn* is enabled and at the second copy the communication *up*. Following Milner, we use the letter $\tau$ to indicate internal actions. Hence we picture the current state of $C_2$ as follows:

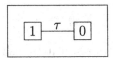

This is a so-called *instable* and *transient* state of $C_2$ because the internal communication $\tau$ is enabled and will proceed autonomously at a certain speed. This brings $C_2$ into the following stable state:

Now the communications *up* and *dn* are both enabled as the user would expect from a 2-bounded counter after having performed the initial communication *up*.

If the user chooses to engage in the comminication *up*, the process $C_2$ gets into a state where both copies of $C_1$ store the value 1. Then only the communication *dn* is enabled:

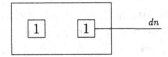

After performing $dn$ the process $C_2$ enters the same instable state as above:

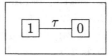

Again the internal communication $\tau$ proceeds automatically, which brings $C_2$ into the following stable state:

If now the user chooses to engage in the communication $dn$, the process $C_2$ returns to its initial state:

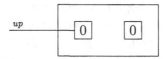

Here we have used pictures to describe the dynamic behaviour of this second construction of $C_2$. Now we explain how this construction can be expressed in the syntax of process terms.

We start from the process term

$$C_1 = \mu X.up.dn.X \tag{1.2}$$

constructed earlier and produce two copies of it by using a new communication $lk$ (shorthand for *link*) and a renaming operator:

$$C_1[lk/dn] \text{ and } C_1[lk/up]. \tag{1.7}$$

For any process $P$ and any two communications $a,b$ the term $P[b/a]$ denotes a process that behaves like $P$ but with all communications $a$ renamed to $b$. Next, we apply parallel composition to these two copies yielding

$$C_1[lk/dn] \parallel C_1[lk/up]. \tag{1.8}$$

For any two processes $P$ and $Q$ the term $P\|Q$ denotes a process that behaves like $P$ and $Q$ working independently or concurrently except that all communications that occur in both $P$ and $Q$ have to be synchronised. For (1.8) this means that both copies of $C_1$ have to synchronise on the new communication $lk$. Note that (1.8) denotes a process that can engage in three communications, viz. $up$, $dn$ and $lk$.

To transform the communication $lk$ into an internal action that proceeds autonomously and invisibly for the user, we finally apply a hiding operator to $lk$. This brings us to a process term $C_2{}^*$ expressing the second construction of the 2-bounded counter:

$$C_2{}^* = (C_1[lk/dn]\| C_1[lk/up])\backslash lk.$$

In general, for any process $P$ and any communication $b$, the term $P \backslash b$ denotes a process that behaves like $P$ but with all communications $b$ transformed into internal actions.

*Petri Nets.* The most detailed view describes the operational machine behaviour of a process. To this end, we use Petri nets or, more precisely, *labelled place/transition nets*. Petri nets are easy to understand because they are a simple extension of the classical notion of an automaton. This extension deals with the explicit representation of concurrency.

Like automata, Petri nets have a graphical representation. We draw a box subdivided into an upper part displaying a set of communications, the *alphabet* of the net, and a lower part displaying the *flow graph* of the net. This is a directed graph with two types of nodes: *places*, some of them marked by one or more so-called tokens, and *transitions*, all of them labelled either by a communication of the alphabet of the net or by the symbol $\tau$. Places are represented as circles and transitions as boxes.

The 1-bounded counter can be represented by the following Petri net $\mathcal{N}_1$:

$$\mathcal{N}_1 = \quad \boxed{\{\, up, dn \,\}} \qquad (1.9)$$

In a Petri net a transition $t$ is *enabled* if all places that are connected with $t$ via an ingoing arc are marked by at least one token. In $\mathcal{N}_1$ the transition labelled with the communication $up$ is enabled. *Executing* an enabled transition $t$ results in removing one token from each place connected with $t$ via an ingoing arc and adding one token to each place connected with $t$ via an outgoing arc.

Thus executing the transition labelled with $up$ in $\mathcal{N}_1$ yields the following new Petri net:

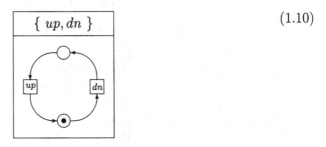

$$(1.10)$$

It has the same overall structure as $\mathcal{N}_1$ only that now the lower place is marked. Hence the transition labelled with $dn$ is now enabled. Its execution brings us back to the Petri net $\mathcal{N}_1$.

The distribution of tokens in a Petri net is called a *marking*. We say that the Petri net (1.10) exhibits $\mathcal{N}_1$ at a different marking. Thus $\mathcal{N}_1$ has two markings: the initial marking shown in (1.9) represents the 1-bounded counter in a state where it stores the value 0 and where only the communication *up* is possible, and the second marking shown in (1.10) represents the counter in a state where it stores the value 1 and where only the communication *dn* is possible. Thus the Petri net $\mathcal{N}_1$ realises exactly the communication behaviour as described by the process term $C_1$.

One of the objectives of this book is to show how a Petri net like $\mathcal{N}_1$ can be constructed systematically from a process term like $C_1$. This will be done with the help of a so-called *Petri net semantics* for process terms. Combining the construction of $\mathcal{N}_1$ from $C_1$ with the construction of $C_1$ from the trace formula $S_1$ considered in (1.3), we obtain a construction of $\mathcal{N}_1$ from $S_1$ so that $\mathcal{N}_1$ realises exactly the communication behaviour specified by $S_1$.

Using the Petri net semantics, we can also construct Petri nets for the process terms $C_2$ and $C_2{}^*$. These nets describe two different realisations of a 2-bounded counter. For $C_2$ we obtain the following Petri net $\mathcal{N}_2$:

$$\mathcal{N}_2 = \qquad\qquad\qquad\qquad\qquad\qquad (1.11)$$

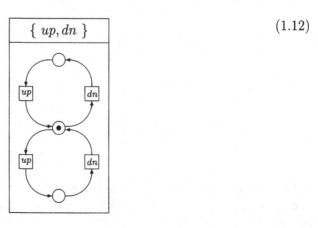

In this initial marking the upper transition labelled with *up* is enabled. Its execution yields the following marking of $\mathcal{N}_2$:

$$(1.12)$$

Now two transitions are enabled: the lower one labelled with *up* and the upper one labelled with *dn*. However, since there is only one token available, only one of these transitions can be executed, which one depends on the choice between the two communications *up* and *dn* by the user of the process modelled by $\mathcal{N}_2$. If the user chooses to communicate *dn*, we get back to the initial marking (1.11) of $\mathcal{N}_2$. If the user chooses to communicate *up*, we arrive at the following new marking of $\mathcal{N}_2$:

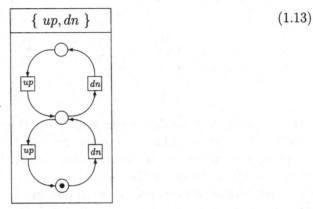

(1.13)

Now only the transition *dn* is enabled. Its execution brings us back to the marking (1.12). These three markings of $\mathcal{N}_2$ correspond to the 2-bounded counter being in a state where it stores the value 0,1 or 2.

Let us now turn to the process term $C_2{}^*$. It denotes the following Petri net $\mathcal{N}_2^*$:

$$\mathcal{N}_2^* =$$ 
{ *up, dn* }

(1.14)

In contrast to all previously discussed Petri nets this one carries two tokens in its initial markings. This is how Petri nets can represent *concurrency*. In general, two transitions can be executed independently or concurrently if they are both enabled and if all places that are connected to both transitions via ingoing arcs carry at least two tokens. At the initial marking (1.14) of $\mathcal{N}_2^*$, however, only the *up*-transition is enabled. Its execution yields the following marking of $\mathcal{N}_2^*$:

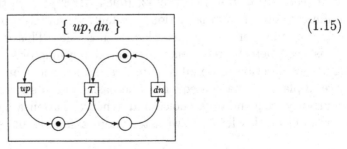

(1.15)

Now the transition labelled with $\tau$ is enabled. This transition corresponds to the internal action encountered in the construction of $C_2{}^*$. Thus the idea is that the above marking is unstable because the $\tau$-transition will occur autonomously without participation of a user. This results in the following marking of $\mathcal{N}_2^*$:

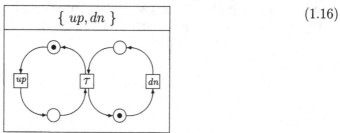

$(1.16)$

Now the *up*-transition and the *dn*-transition are both enabled and can be executed concurrently. This is quite different from the marking (1.12) discussed for the Petri net $\mathcal{N}_2$. There also an *up*- and a *dn*-transition were enabled but only one of them could be chosen for execution by the user.

Here the concurrent execution of the two transitions brings us back to the unstable marking (1.15). Executing only the *dn*-transition brings us back to the initial marking (1.14) of $\mathcal{N}_2^*$ where the upper two places are marked by a token. Executing only the *up*-transition yields the following marking of $\mathcal{N}_2^*$:

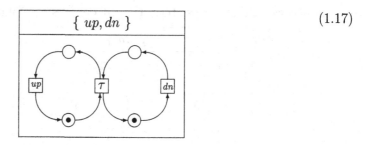

$(1.17)$

Note that the *dn*-transition remains enabled. Its execution leads again to the unstable marking (1.15).

## 1.2   Outline of this Book

Our presentation in this book is organised as follows. In Chapter 2 on Petri nets we start from *place/transition nets* [Pet62, Rei84, BF86] where transitions are *labelled* by communications or internal actions. In fact, we mainly work in the class of *safe* nets where at most one token per place is possible. This is the simplest class of nets; it is used here to represent a low level machine-like view of processes. In particular, we describe in detail how process states and transitions are distributed over several places. As a consequence, the basic concepts of process behaviour such as concurrency, sequentiality, choice and synchronisation are clearly distinguished. However, even at this level we wish to ignore a few details such as the names of places. To this end, we introduce *abstract* nets which are equivalence classes of nets modulo a notion of *weak isomorphism*.

We use *causal nets* [Pet77] as a formalisation of the concurrent computations of a safe net. Thus to show that safe nets with a different structure admit the same concurrent computations we prove that these nets are *causally equivalent*, that is, have the same causal nets. As a proof method we introduce a new notion of *strong bisimilarity* for safe nets which extends Park's original definition for automata [Par81]. The main idea is to define the underlying strong bisimulation as a relation on places. When lifted to the reachable markings it preserves their token game and distribution over the places.

We show that strong bisimilarity on safe nets implies causal equivalence. Our notion of strong bisimilarity allows the expansion of cycles and the sharing of common substructures just as in the case of automata. On the other hand, it is not an equivalence relation; it is reflexive and symmetric but not transitive as noticed in [ABS91]. It is therefore suitable only as an auxiliary notion in proving that structurally different nets are causally equivalent.

Place/transition nets serve very well to represent all the details of the process behaviour, but their drawback is the lack of compositionality and abstraction. To deal with these two problems, we take terms and formulas as complementary views.

In Chapter 3 on process terms we start from operators taken from Lauer's COSY [LTS79], Milner's CCS [Mil80, Mil83] and Hoare's CSP [BHR84, Hoa85b]. The choice of operators is influenced by the aim of obtaining simple transition and transformation rules later on. Each operator represents a high level composition principle on processes. For example, the term $P \parallel Q$ represents the parallel composition of two processes $P$ and $Q$. By using such terms, we describe the architecture of a process and do not think at the level of machine transitions. Process terms invite an algebraic treatment of processes. The aim is to rewrite given process terms into other, more desirable process terms by using algebraic laws which are valid for the process operators. We do not pursue this approach any further in our presentation because it has been dealt with extensively in numerous publications, e.g. [Mil80, BK86, Hen88, RH88].

Our aim here is the *link* between different description methods of processes corresponding to different levels of abstraction in process design. The link between process terms and nets is given by a Petri net semantics which assigns an abstract net to every process term. This semantics is defined by extending the *structured operational approach* as advocated by Plotkin [Plo81, Plo82] from automata to nets. Our definition owes much to the work of Degano, DeNicola and Montanari [DDM87, DDM88b], but the details are different. In particular, our transition rules are simpler than theirs. However, the price for this simplicity is a more complicated analysis of the resulting net semantics.

This analysis is guided by the following question [Old87]: What is a good net semantics ? This question arises because for process terms, which traditionally have only an interleaving semantics yielding automata, many different net semantics are conceivable. We suggest two principles that a good net semantics should satisfy. The *Retrievability Principle* requires that by forgetting about concurrency we should get back the original interleaving semantics, at least modulo Park's strong bisimilarity on automata. The *Concurrency Principle* requires that modulo strong bisimilarity on nets, the operational net semantics should be compositional with respect to the standard compositional net operators. This allows some flexibility for the operational net semantics, but ensures that it admits exactly the same concurrent computations as the standard compositional net semantics.

We prove that our operational net semantics satisfies these two principles. The strong bisimulation relation needed to prove the Retrievabilty Principle reveals that every global state of the automaton generated by the interleaving semantics is related to *more than one* distributed marking of the net semantics. We conjecture that such a difference between the global and distributed view of concurrent processes is unavoidable. Additionally, we deal with other properties of our net semantics, viz. safeness, finiteness and basic algebraic properties.

In Chapter 4 on logical formulas we consider a many-sorted first-order predicate logic which is essentially taken from Zwiers [Zwi89]. Since its main sort is "trace", standing for finite communication sequences, it is called *trace logic*. We use the formulas of this logic to specify the communication behaviour of processes. The communication behaviour is given by the set of traces in which the process can engage in. This is a simple but widely applicable definition which abstracts both from internal actions and possible concurrency in the process. Thus in our approach these two aspects of process behaviour are not part of its specification but its implementation by process terms and nets.

The link between trace formulas and process terms is given by a novel notion of *process correctness*. It defines when a process term $P$ satisfies a trace formula $S$, abbreviated

$$P \text{ sat } S ,$$

using Hoare's *sat* notation [Hoa85b]. In most approaches trace formulas are only used to express *safety* properties or *partial correctness* [CH81, MC81, Oss83, WGS87, Zwi89]. Partial correctness is insensitive against divergence and deadlock. As a consequence, there exists a single process term which satisfies every trace specification; it is called a *miracle* after Dijkstra [Dij76]. With miracles the task of process construction becomes trivial and meaningless. Therefore we shall be more demanding and use trace formulas to express also a simple type of *liveness* property implying *total correctness*. Essentially, $P$ sat $S$ requires the following:

- Safety: $P$ *may* only engage in traces satisfying $S$;

- Liveness: $P$ *must* engage in every trace satisfying $S$.

The notions of "may" and "must" are inspired by DeNicola and Hennessy [DH84, Hen88], but defined here by looking at the operational net semantics of $P$. The liveness condition is due to [OH86] and implies that every process $P$ that satisfies a trace specification $S$ is divergence free and *externally* deterministic. That is: in every run of $P$ the user has exactly the same communication possibilities, no matter which actions $P$ has pursued internally. Thus in our approach only a subset of processes can be specified by trace formulas. We are interested in this subset because it has many applications and yields simple compositional transformation rules for process construction and verification.

The operational definition of "may" and "must" is very clear intuitively, but not helpful for discovering such rules. To simplify this task, we develop a second, more abstract semantics for process terms and specifications. It is a *modified* version $\mathcal{R}^*$ of the *readiness semantics* $\mathcal{R}$ introduced in [OH86]. For process terms, $\mathcal{R}^*$ is defined by filtering out certain information about the process behaviour as described by the net semantics. Amongst this information are pairs consisting of a trace and a so-called *ready* set. This is a set of communications in which the process is ready to engage when after that trace all its internal activity has ceased [Hoa81, FLP84]. Ready sets are used to explain the liveness requirement of process correctness $P$ *sat* $S$.

By these modifications with respect to the original readiness semantics, we obtain a semantics which is tailored just to help us dealing with the satisfaction relation *sat*. Firstly, in $\mathcal{R}^*$ process correctness boils down to a *semantic equation* between $P$ and $S$:

$$P \text{ sat } S \text{ iff } P \equiv S.$$

This is a clear conceptual simplification. Secondly, $\mathcal{R}^*$ can be proved equivalent to a *denotational semantics* in the sense of Scott and Strachey [Sco70, Sto77, Bak80]. This implies that it is compositional with respect to the process operators and uses fixed point techniques when dealing with recursion. Therefore $\mathcal{R}^*$ serves well as a stepping stone for developing compositional transformation rules for process construction.

Thirdly, $\mathcal{R}^*$ is *fully abstract* for our notion of process correctness [Mil77]. This means that any two process terms $P$ and $Q$ are equivalent under $\mathcal{R}^*$ if and only if no replacement of $P$ by $Q$ within any larger process term can be discovered by the satisfaction relation *sat*. Thus $\mathcal{R}^*$ records no more information about the process behaviour than is motivated by our notion of process correctness. Full abstraction implies that the *modified readiness equivalence* is uniquely determined by that notion. We observe that this equivalence is closely related, but different from two other well-known equivalences for processes, viz. *failure equivalence* [BHR84] and *strong testing equivalence* [DH84]. However, for divergence free and stable process terms all three equivalences coincide.

In Chapter 5 we combine all three views of concurrent processes in a top-down fashion:

formulas
↓
terms
↓
nets

The bottom arrow refers to the Petri net semantics of process terms, as defined in Chapter 3. The top arrow refers to the contribution of Chapter 5: a systematic approach to top-down construction and verification of process terms from trace formulas, based on the modified readiness semantics of Chapter 4. Such a construction is presented as a sequence

$$S \; \equiv \; Q_1$$
$$|||$$
$$\vdots$$
$$|||$$
$$Q_n \; \equiv \; P$$

of semantic equations where $Q_1$ is the given trace specification and $Q_n$ is the constructed process term $P$. By the transitivity of $\equiv$, it follows that $P \equiv S$ which means $P$ *sat* $S$. Thus by construction, $P$ satisfies the safety and liveness requirements of $S$.

But what are the terms $Q_i$ in between $S$ and $P$ ? We choose them to be *mixed terms*, i.e. syntactic constructs mixing process terms with trace formulas. The idea of mixing programming notation (here represented by process terms) with specification parts (here represented by trace formulas) stems from the work of Dijkstra and Wirth on program development by stepwise refinement [Dij76, Wir71]. It has been utilised by many researchers, but its application to concurrent processes is a most recent activity [Heh84, Hoa85a, Old85, Old86, Bro87].

The sequence of equations in the top-down construction is obtained by applying the principle of *transformational programming* as for example advocated in the Munich Project CIP [Bau85, Bau87]. Thus each equation $Q_i \; \equiv \; Q_{i+1}$ is justified by applying a transformation rule on mixed terms. We present a system of such transformation rules and prove their soundness using the modified readiness semantics $\mathcal{R}^*$. Most rules are extremely simple. For example, parallel composition $P \parallel Q$ of terms $P$ and $Q$ is reflected by the logical conjunction of trace formulas. Only two process operators which can completely restructure the communication behaviour of a process need transformation rules which are difficult to apply. These operators are *hiding* and *renaming with aliasing*.

We use the transformation rules in a series of example process constructions. For each constructed process term we examine the Petri net that it denotes according to the operational net semantics. This gives us further information about the suitability of the terms as an implementation, e.g. about the possible concurrency or communication delays through internal actions. For a particularly good illustration of our method we refer to Section 5.5 where three different process terms and hence nets are constructed from the trace specification of a scheduling problem due to Milner [Mil80, Mil89].

For each system of rules we can pose the question: Are these rules complete? We distinguish two types of completeness. *Verification completeness* means that for every process term $P$ and every trace formula $S$, whenever $P$ *sat* $S$ holds, i.e. $P \equiv S$, then this equation can be deduced with the transformation rules. We observe that our rules are incomplete in this sense. The reason for this incompleteness is that some rules check semantic properties of processes dealing with liveness by sufficient, but not neccessary, syntactic conditions. By contrast, Zwiers has shown verification completeness for a similar but simpler setting where only the safety condition of $P$ *sat* $S$ (partial correctness) is considered [Zwi89]. We conjecture that our transformation rules are verification complete for a suitably restricted set of process terms.

In any case, we believe that verification completeness will provide little insight into how to do process construction. Therefore we also consider *construction completeness*. By this we mean that for (a certain subset of) trace formulas $S$ there is a strategy describing *how to apply* the transformation rules to construct a process term $P$ (of a certain form) with $P \equiv S$. We present such a completeness result for the simplest strategy for process construction: the *expansion strategy*. We show that when starting with a formula $S$ specifying a regular set of traces this strategy will always, and under certain conditions mechanically, produce a process term $P$ satisfying $S$. This term $P$ denotes a finite Petri net, though one without any concurrency. In fact, the constructed net just corresponds to a deterministic automaton which satisfies the safety and liveness conditions required by $S$. This result resembles the synthesis of finite-state automata from formulas of propositional temporal logic [EC82, MW84].

In Chapter 6 we sketch possible extensions of the theory presented here and indicate various directions for future research. In more detail, we outline how our approach to process construction and verification can be extended to deal with non-determinism at the level of specification. We also explain basic ideas on how to handle fairness and concurrency at this level. A key for scaling up the present theory to be able to deal with realistic applications will be the incorporation of structured communication into all three views of concurrent processes. A very interesting topic would be the development of more general strategies for process construction.

# 2
# PETRI NETS

Our first view of a concurrent process is that of a machine where every detail of its behaviour is explicit. We could take as our machine model *automata* in the sense of classical automata theory [RS59], also known as *transition systems* [Kel76]. Automata are fine except that they cannot represent situations where parts of a machine work independently or concurrently. Since we are after such a representation, we use *Petri nets* [Pet62, Rei85] instead. This choice is motivated by the following advantages of nets:

(1) *Concepts.* Petri nets are based on a simple extension of the concepts of state and transition known from automata. The extension is that in nets both states and transitions are distributed over several places. This allows an explicit distinction between concurrency and sequentiality.

(2) *Graphics.* Petri nets have a graphical representation that visualises the different basic concepts about processes like sequentiality, choice, concurrency and synchronisation.

(3) *Size.* Since Petri nets allow cycles, a large class of processes can be represented by finite nets. Also, as a consequence of (1), parallel composition will be additive in size rather than multiplicative.

An attractive alternative to Petri nets are *event structures* introduced in [NPW81] and further developed by Winskel [Win80, Win87]. Event structures are more abstract than nets because they do not record states, only events, i.e. the occurences of transitions. But in order to forget about states, event structures must not contain cycles. This yields infinite event structures even in cases where finite (but cyclic) nets suffice. We prefer finite objects whenever possible, and thus Petri nets, as our basic machine-like view of processes.

Another alternative to Petri nets could be Harel's formalism of *state charts* [Har87]. Like nets state charts extend the classical notion of an automaton, but that extension models only fully synchronous parallelism. Since we aim here at modelling asynchronous parallelism with synchronous communication, state charts cannot replace Petri nets for our machine-like view of processes.

However, Petri nets as discussed in [Pet62, Rei85] are not sufficient for this purpose. We need to express the effect of a transition as seen by the user of the process. For example, a transition can represent a communication between user and process or an internal action not controllable by the user. Therefore we will use *labelled* Petri nets where labels attached to the transitions express their effect.

To make explicit the conceptual roots of nets, we begin by recalling the basic notions of automata.

## 2.1  Automata

We start from an infinite set *Comm* of *communications* and an element $\tau \notin Comm$ to build the set

$$Act = Comm \cup \{\tau\}$$

of *actions*. The intuition is that a transition labelled by a communication requires the participation of both the user and the process whereas a transition labelled by the action $\tau$ occurs spontaneously inside the process without participation of the user. Therefore the element $\tau$ is called *internal* action and the communications are called *external* actions. We let $a, b, c$ range over *Comm* and $u, v, w$ over *Act*.

In applications communications often possess a structure. For example, they may be pairs $(ch, m)$ consisting of a channel name $ch$ and a message $m$ [Hoa85b, Mil80], or the set *Comm* may have an algebraic structure as in [BK86, Mil83]. For simplicity we shall not consider such structures here.

By a *communication alphabet* or simply *alphabet* we mean a finite subset of *Comm*. We let $A, B$ range over alphabets. Every process will have a communication alphabet associated with it. This alphabet describes the interface through which the process communicates with its user(s) or with other processes.

The following notion of an automaton is taken from classical automata theory [RS59] and the work on labelled transition systems [Kel76].

**Definition 2.1.1** An *automaton* is a structure

$$\mathcal{A} = (A, St, \longrightarrow, q_0)$$

where

(1)  $A$ is a communication alphabet;

(2)  $St$ is a possibly infinite set of *states*;

(3) $\longrightarrow \subseteq St \times (A \cup \{\tau\}) \times St$ is the *transition relation*;

(4) $q_0 \in St$ is the *initial state*. □

We let $p$, $q$, $r$ range over $St$. An element $(p, u, q) \in \longrightarrow$ is called a *transition* (*labelled with the action u*) and usually written as

$$p \xrightarrow{\ u\ } q.$$

In automata theory, the set $A$ corresponds to the input alphabet and $\tau$ to a spontaneous $\varepsilon$-move of an automaton. For processes Milner's symbol $\tau$ (instead of $\varepsilon$) is common [Mil80].

Every automaton $\mathcal{A} = (A, St, \longrightarrow, q_0)$ has a graphical representation which is often easier to understand. We draw a rectangular box subdivided into an upper part displaying the alphabet $A$ and a lower part displaying the *state transition diagram*. This is a directed, rooted graph with edges labelled by actions in $A \cup \{\tau\}$ which represents in an obvious way the remaining components $St$, $\longrightarrow$ and $q_0$ of $\mathcal{A}$. We mark the root of a state diagram by an additional ingoing arc.

**Example 2.1.2**

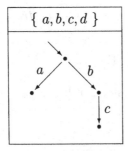

alphabet

state transition diagram

Intuitively, this automaton describes a process with a communication interface consisting of $a$, $b$, $c$ and $d$. Thus the process can at most engage in these communications with its user.

The state transition diagram tells us that initially the process is ready to engage in the communications $a$ or $b$ but not in $c$ or $d$. Which of the communications $a$ or $b$ occurs is the user's choice. If the user chooses $a$, the transition labelled with $a$ occurs, after which no further communication is possible. If the user chooses $b$, the transition labelled with $b$ occurs, after which the process is ready for a communication $c$.

Note that the communication $d$ of the alphabet does not appear as a label of any transition. Consequently, the process described by this automaton can never engage in $d$. □

Mostly we wish to ignore the identity of states in an automaton. To this end, we use the concept of an isomorphism. It is convenient to restrict its definition to the reachable states; we shall therefore talk of *weak* isomorphism.

A *reachable state* of an automaton $\mathcal{A} = (A, St, \longrightarrow, q)$ is a state $q \in St$ for which there exist intermediate states $q_1,\ldots,q_n \in St$ and actions $u_1,\ldots,u_n \in A \cup \{\tau\}$ with

$$q_0 \overset{u_1}{\longrightarrow} q_1 \overset{u_2}{\longrightarrow} \ldots \overset{u_n}{\longrightarrow} q_n = q.$$

Let *reach*$(\mathcal{A})$ denote the set of reachable states of $A$.

**Definition 2.1.3** Two automata $\mathcal{A}_i = (A_i, St_i, \longrightarrow_i, q_{0i})$, $i$=1,2, are *weakly isomorphic*, abbreviated

$$\mathcal{A}_1 =_{isom} \mathcal{A}_2,$$

if $A_1 = A_2$ and there exists a bijection

$$\beta : reach(\mathcal{A}_1) \longrightarrow reach(\mathcal{A}_2)$$

such that

$$\beta(q_{01}) = q_{02}$$

and for all $p,q \in reach(\mathcal{A})$ and all $u \in A_1 \cup \{\,\tau\,\}$

$$p \overset{u}{\longrightarrow}_1 q \text{ iff } \beta(p) \overset{u}{\longrightarrow}_2 \beta(q).$$

The bijection $\beta$ is called a *weak isomorphism between* $\mathcal{A}_1$ and $\mathcal{A}_2$.                    □

Clearly, $=_{isom}$ is an equivalence relation on automata. By an *abstract automaton* we mean the isomorphism class

$$[\mathcal{A}]_{=isom} = \{\mathcal{A}' \mid \mathcal{A} =_{isom} \mathcal{A}'\}$$

of an automaton $\mathcal{A}$. For brevity we shall write $[\mathcal{A}]$ instead of $[\mathcal{A}]_{=isom}$. Let

$$AAut$$

denote the set of all abstract automata. Graphically, abstract automata can be represented as automata; we have only to make sure that all states in the state transition diagram are reachable from the root and that nodes in this diagram do not carry particular names. Hence Example 2.1.2 represents an abstract automaton.

Often we are not interested in the exact structure of an automaton as given by its isomorphism class, but rather its transition behaviour. For example, the automata

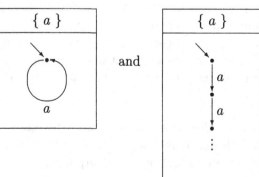

are not isomorphic (one resp. infinitely many states); but their transition behaviour is identical: both automata are always ready to engage in yet another communication $a$. The concept of having the same transition behaviour is captured elegantly by Park's notion of strong bisimilarity [Par81].

**Definition 2.1.4** Two automata $\mathcal{A}_i = (A_i,\ St_i,\ \longrightarrow_i,\ q_{0i})$, $i=1,2$, are *strongly bisimilar*, abbreviated

$$\mathcal{A}_1 \approx \mathcal{A}_2,$$

if $A_1 = A_2$ and there exists a relation

$$\mathcal{B} \subseteq St_1 \times St_2$$

satisfying the following conditions:

(1) initial states are related: $q_{01}\ \mathcal{B}\ q_{02}$;

(2) whenever $p\ \mathcal{B}\ q$ and $p \xrightarrow{\ u\ }_1 p'$ then, for some $q' \in St_2$, also $p'\ \mathcal{B}\ q'$ and $q \xrightarrow{\ u\ }_2 q'$;

(3) conversely, whenever $p\ \mathcal{B}\ q$ and $q \xrightarrow{\ u\ }_2 q'$ then, for some $p' \in St_1$, also $p'\ \mathcal{B}\ q'$ and $p \xrightarrow{\ u\ }_1 p'$.

The relation $\mathcal{B}$ is called a *strong bisimulation* between $\mathcal{A}_1$ and $\mathcal{A}_2$ , and the conditions (2) and (3) are called the *transfer property* of $\mathcal{B}$. □

Note that the same action $u$ is required for both transitions in (2) and (3). Intuitively, condition (2) means that, starting from any pair of related states, $\mathcal{A}_2$ can simulate $\mathcal{A}_1$ and (3) that analogously $\mathcal{A}_1$ can simulate $\mathcal{A}_2$. It is easy to see that $\approx$ is an equivalence relation on automata. Also

$$\mathcal{A}_1 =_{isom} \mathcal{A}_2 \text{ implies } \mathcal{A}_1 \approx \mathcal{A}_2$$

for any two automata $\mathcal{A}_1$ and $\mathcal{A}_2$ . Consequently, modulo strong bisimulation, we may rename states and remove unreachable ones in an automaton. In particular, we notice:

**Remark 2.1.5** The notion of strong bisimilarity does not change if in the definition of $\mathcal{A}_1 \approx \mathcal{A}_2$ we restrict ourselves to relations $\mathcal{B} \subseteq reach(\mathcal{A}_1) \times reach(\mathcal{A}_2)$. □

We may also lift strong bisimilarity to abstract automata by putting

$$[\mathcal{A}_1] \approx [\mathcal{A}_2] \text{ if } \mathcal{A}_1 \approx \mathcal{A}_2$$

Clearly, $\mathcal{A}_1 \approx \mathcal{A}_2$ does not in general imply $\mathcal{A}_1 =_{isom} \mathcal{A}_2$. The main differences are displayed in the following example.

**Example 2.1.6** The bisimulation relations are exhibited by drawing lines between related states.

(1) Modulo strong bisimilarity, cycles can be unfolded:

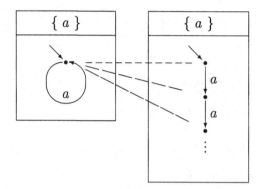

(2) Modulo strong bisimilarity, common substructures can be shared:

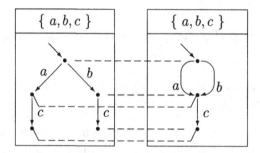

(3) On the other hand, strong bisimilarity preserves the forward branching structure of state transition diagrams:

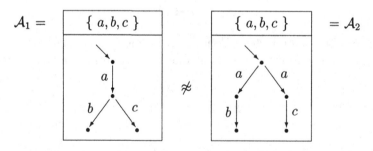

This puts strong bisimilarity into sharp contrast to the usual equivalence of automata where it matters only whether or not the automata accept the same communication sequences (see e.g. [HU69]). In process theory it is important to distinguish automata with a different forward branching structure of their state transition diagrams because they describe different processes.

Here $\mathcal{A}_1$ describes a *deterministic* process whereas $\mathcal{A}_2$ describes a *nondeterministic* one. Initially, both $\mathcal{A}_1$ and $\mathcal{A}_2$ are ready to engage in the communication

$a$ with their users. However, $\mathcal{A}_2$ contains two transitions labelled with $a$, and it is nondeterministic which one occurs when the user communicates $a$. If the left-hand transition occurs, only $b$ is possible as a next communication. If the right-hand transition occurs, only $c$ is possible as a next communication. Thus for the user it is nondeterministic whether $\mathcal{A}_2$ is ready fo a communication $b$ or $c$ after $a$.

By contrast, communicating $a$ with $\mathcal{A}_1$ leads to a state where $\mathcal{A}_1$ is ready for both $b$ and $c$, and it is the user who chooses which one to engage in. Later, in Chapter 4, such differences in the behaviour will be essential for the correctness of process with respect to given specifications. □

Automata provide a very simple machine-like model of processes. Their drawback is an inability to represent parts of a machine working independently or concurrently. For example, the diagram

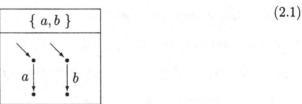

(2.1)

represents two machines operating concurrently, one capable of engaging in a communication $a$ and the other capable in engaging on $b$. However, (2.1) is no longer an automaton because the two initial states represent two independent loci of control. If we insist on using automata, (2.1) could at best be represented as the automaton

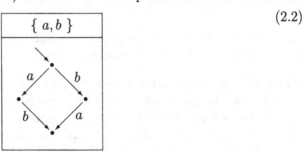

(2.2)

where we have used the *interleaving model of concurrency* whereby concurrency can be reduced to choice and sequentiality.

At the level of machines such a reduction is not appropriate because it hides whether components of the machine can work independently or not. Therefore we prefer representation (2.1) to (2.2). From (2.1) it seems that we just have to consider several instances of automata working in parallel. Unfortunately, this is the case only for disjoint parallelism. Since we wish also to model the case where concurrent machines have to synchronise from time to time, we need a real extension of automata. For the reasons explained in the beginning of this chapter we take Petri nets as this extension.

## 2.2   Place / Transition Nets

Within Petri net theory several different versions of nets are considered depending
on the detail with which one wishes to describe concurrent processes. Since we are
interested in a low level machine-like view, we shall use *place/transition nets* with
arc weight 1 and an unbounded capacity of places [Rei85, BF86]. For simplicity we
continue to use the term "Petri net" for this class of nets. In fact, we will be mainly
working in the subclass of safe Petri nets. Moreover, we will deviate slightly from the
standard definition and use the following one, inspired by [Gol88a, Gol88b].

**Definition 2.2.1** *A Petri net* or simply *net* is a structure

$$\mathcal{N} = (A, Pl, \longrightarrow, M_0)$$

where

(1)  $A$ is a communication alphabet;

(2)  $Pl$ is a possibly infinite set of *places*;

(3)  $\longrightarrow \subseteq \mathcal{P}_{nf}(Pl) \times (A \cup \{\tau\}) \times \mathcal{P}_{nf}(Pl)$ is the *transition relation*;

(4)  $M_0 \in \mathcal{P}_{nf}(Pl)$ is the *initial marking*.                                    □

We let $p$, $q$, $r$ range over $Pl$. The notation $\mathcal{P}_{nf}(Pl)$ stands for the set of all
non-empty, finite subsets of $Pl$. An element $(I, u, O) \in \longrightarrow$ with $I, O \in \mathcal{P}_{nf}(Pl)$
and $u \in A \cup \{\tau\}$ is called a *transition* (*labelled with the action u*) and will usually be
written as

$$I \xrightarrow{u} O.$$

For a transition $t = I \xrightarrow{u} O$ its *preset* or *input* is given by $pre(t) = I$, its *postset*
or *output* by $post(t) = O$ and its action by $act(t) = u$.

**Remark 2.2.2** The above definition of nets smoothly extends the previous definition of automata. Indeed, if we identify for a moment singleton sets of places with
states, automata are nets where the initial marking and the pre- and postsets of the
transitions are singleton sets. When comparing automata with nets we shall sometimes make use of this identification. In general, a net can be seen as distributing
the state of an automaton over several places.                                    □

The graphical representation of a net $\mathcal{N} = (A, Pl, \longrightarrow, M_0)$ is as follows. As for
automata we draw a rectangular box subdivided into an upper part displaying the
alphabet $A$ and a lower part displaying the remaining components $Pl, \longrightarrow$ and $M$
in the usual way for nets. Places $p \in Pl$ are represented as circles $\bigcirc$ with the name
$p$ outside and transitions

$$t = \{p_1, \ldots, p_m\} \xrightarrow{u} \{q_1, \ldots, q_n\}$$

as boxes $\boxed{u}$ carrying the label $u$ inside and connected via directed arcs to the places
in $pre(t)$ and $post(t)$:

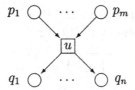

Since $pre(t)$ and $post(t)$ need not be disjoint, some of the outgoing arcs of $\boxed{u}$ may actually point back to places in $pre(t)$ and thus introduce *cycles*. The initial marking $M_0$ is represented by putting a token $\bullet$ into the circle of each $p \in M_0$.

**Example 2.2.3** The graphical representation of nets can clearly visualise the basic concepts of processes.

(1) Concurrency of two communications $a$ and $b$ is represented as follows:

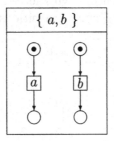

(2) Choice between $a$ and $b$ is represented by forward branching of places:

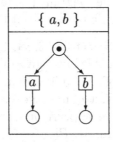

(3) Sequentiality of first $a$ and then $b$ is represented as follows:

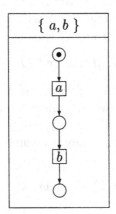

(4) Synchronisation of two concurrent processes (here seperated by a dashed line) on a communication $b$ is represented as follows:

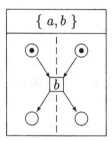

(5) As shown in the above nets, communications between user and processes are represented by labelling transitions with letters $a$, $b$, etc. Internal actions of processes are represented by labelling transitions with $\tau$:

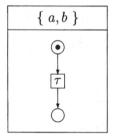

To understand why, for example, the diagram (1) represents concurrency and (2) choice, we have to explain the dynamic behaviour of Petri nets.                    □

The dynamic behaviour of a Petri net is defined by its *token game*; it describes which transitions are concurrently enabled at a given marking and what the result of their concurrent execution is. Though the initial marking of a net is defined to be a set of places, the token game can result in more general markings, viz. multisets.

Consider a net $\mathcal{N} = (A, Pl, \longrightarrow, M_0)$. A *marking* or *case* or *global* state of $\mathcal{N}$ is a *multiset* (*over* $Pl$), i.e. a mapping $M: Pl \longrightarrow \mathbb{N}_0$. Graphically, such a marking $M$ is represented by putting $M(p)$ tokens into the circle drawn for each $p \in Pl$. For simplicity any set $N \subseteq Pl$, for example the initial marking $M_0$, will be identified with the multiset given by the characteristic function of $N$: $N(p) = 1$ for $p \in N$ and $N(p) = 0$ otherwise. For multisets $M$ and $N$ let

$$M \subseteq N, M \sqcup N \text{ and } M - N$$

denote *multiset inclusion, union* and *difference*. If $M$ and $N$ are sets then $M \subseteq N$ and $M - N$ are just set inclusion and difference whereas $M \sqcup N$ in general differs from set-theoretic union. We write $p \in M$ if $M(p) \geq 1$.

A *global transition* of $N$ as above is any non-empty, finite set $\mathcal{T}$ of transitions of $\mathcal{N}$. Define by using multiset union

$$pre(\mathcal{T}) = \bigsqcup_{t \in \mathcal{T}} pre(t)$$

and analogously for $post(T)$ and $act(T)$.

**Definition 2.2.4** Let $\mathcal{N}$ be a net, $T$ be a global transition of $\mathcal{N}$ and $M$ be a marking of $\mathcal{N}$. Then

(1) the transitions in $T$ are *concurrently enabled at M* or simply $T$ is *enabled at M* if $pre(T) \subseteq M$,

(2) if enabled at $M$, the *concurrent execution* of the transitions in $T$ transforms $M$ into a new marking $M'$ of $N$; this is also called a *step from M to M' in (the token game of)* $\mathcal{N}$. In symbols:

$$M \xrightarrow{\;\;T\;\;} M' \text{ in } \mathcal{N}$$

if $pre(T) \subseteq M$ and $M' = (M - pre(T)) \sqcup post(T)$. For $T = \{t\}$ we write $M \xrightarrow{\;\;t\;\;} M'$ instead. □

States of automata have both a static and dynamic facet: statically they are part of the structure of the automaton and dynamically each state which is currently active solely determines the future behaviour of the automaton. In nets the static and dynamic facet of states are separated into places and markings. Therefore we will distinguish two notions of reachability for a net $\mathcal{N} = (\,A, Pl, \longrightarrow, M_0)$.

A *(dynamically) reachable marking* of $\mathcal{N}$ is a marking $M$ for which there exist intermediate markings $M_1, \ldots, M_n$ and global transitions $T_1, \ldots, T_n$ with

$$M_0 \xrightarrow{\;T\;} M_1 \xrightarrow{\;T_2\;} \cdots \xrightarrow{\;T_n\;} M_n = M. \qquad (2.3)$$

Let $mark(\mathcal{N})$ denote the set of *reachable* markings of $\mathcal{N}$. Note that the set $mark(\mathcal{N})$ does not change if in (2.3) we consider only singleton transitions $T_i = \{\,t_i\,\}$.

The set $place(\mathcal{N})$ of *statically reachable places* of $\mathcal{N}$ is the smallest subset of $Pl$ satisfying

(1) $M_0 \subseteq place(\mathcal{N})$,

(2) If $I \subseteq place(\mathcal{N})$ and $I \xrightarrow{\;\;u\;\;} O$ for some $u \in A \cup \{\,\tau\,\}$ and $O \subseteq Pl$ then also $O \subseteq place(\mathcal{N})$.

The term "statical" emphasises that, by (2), the set $place(\mathcal{N})$ is closed under the execution of any transition $t = I \xrightarrow{\;\;u\;\;} O$ independently of whether or not $t$ is enabled at some dynamically reachable marking of $\mathcal{N}$. Consequently,

$$place(\mathcal{N}) \supseteq \{p \mid \exists M \in mark(\mathcal{N}) : p \in M\}$$

and in general this inclusion is proper (see Example 2.2.7). However, we notice:

**Remark 2.2.5** If we identify for a moment, states with singleton sets of places, then for nets $\mathcal{N}$ which are automata (c.f. Remark 2.2.2) all notions of reachability coincide:

$$reach(\mathcal{N}) = mark(\mathcal{N}) = place(\mathcal{N}). \qquad \square$$

In the following we shall mainly work with safe nets where multiple tokens per place do not occur. Formally, a net $\mathcal{N}$ is *safe* if

$$\forall M \in mark(\mathcal{N}) \; \forall \, p \in Pl : M(p) \leq 1.$$

Thus in a safe net all reachable markings are sets.

Moreover, we mostly wish to ignore the identity of places and forget about places that are not statically reachable. As for automata, we do this by introducing suitable notions of isomorphism and abstract net.

**Definition 2.2.6** Two nets $\mathcal{N}_i = ( A_i, Pl_i, \longrightarrow_i, M_{0i})$, $i{=}1,2$, are *weakly isomorphic,* abbreviated

$$\mathcal{N}_1 =_{isom} \mathcal{N}_2,$$

if $A_1 = A_2$ and there exists a bijection

$$\beta : place(\mathcal{N}_1) \longrightarrow place(\mathcal{N}_2)$$

such that

$$\beta(M_{01}) = M_{02}$$

and for all $I,O \subseteq place(\mathcal{N}_1)$ and all $u \in A_1 \cup \{\, \tau \,\}$

$$I \xrightarrow{\;u\;}_1 O \text{ iff } \beta(I) \xrightarrow{\;u\;}_2 \beta(O)$$

where $\beta(M_{01})$, $\beta(I)$, $\beta(O)$ are understood elementwise. The bijection $\beta$ is called a *weak isomorphism between $\mathcal{N}_1$ and $\mathcal{N}_2$.*                                           □

For an illustration of this concept consider the following example.

**Example 2.2.7** Since $place(\mathcal{N}_1) = \{p_2, p_4, p_6\}$ and $place(\mathcal{N}_2) = \{q_1, q_2, q_3\}$, we have

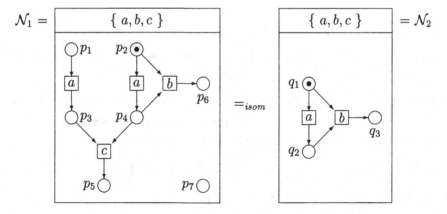

where the isomorphism maps $p_2$ onto $q_1$, $p_4$ onto $q_2$, and $p_6$ onto $q_3$. Note that the statically reachable place $q_3$ of $\mathcal{N}_2$ is not contained in any dynamically reachable marking of $\mathcal{N}_2$ because these are $M_0 = \{q_1\}$ and $M_1 = \{q_2\}$.                  □

Again, $=_{isom}$ is an equivalence relation. An *abstract net* is defined as the isomorphism class

$$[\mathcal{N}]_{=_{isom}} = \{N' \mid N =_{isom} N'\}$$

of a net $\mathcal{N}$; it will abbreviated as $[\mathcal{N}]$. Let

$$ANet$$

denote the set of all abstract nets. For abstract nets we use the same graphical representation as for nets; we have only to make sure that all places are statically reachable and eliminate their names. Most concepts for nets can be lifted in a straightforward way to abstract nets. For example, we shall call an abstract net $[\mathcal{N}]$ safe if $\mathcal{N}$ is safe.

The relationship between nets and automata is given by the following interleaving version of a case graph [Rei85].

**Definition 2.2.8** The *interleaving case graph* of a net $\mathcal{N} = (A, Pl, \longrightarrow, M_0)$ is the automaton

$$\mathcal{A}(\mathcal{N}) = (A, mark(\mathcal{N}), \longrightarrow_A, M_0)$$

where for all $M, N, \in mark(\mathcal{N})$ and $u \in A \cup \{\tau\}$

$$M \xrightarrow{\;u\;}_A N$$

if there exists a transition $t$ of $\mathcal{N}$ with $act(t) = u$ and $M \xrightarrow{\;t\;} N$ in $\mathcal{N}$. We extend this definition to abstract nets $[\mathcal{N}]$ by taking the abstract automaton.

$$\mathcal{A}([\mathcal{N}]) = [\mathcal{A}(\mathcal{N})]. \qquad \square$$

**Example 2.2.9** Consider the abstract net

$$[\mathcal{N}] = $$

of Example 2.2.3. The interleaving case graph of $[\mathcal{N}]$ is the abstract automaton

$$\mathcal{A}([\mathcal{N}]) = $$

discussed at the end of Section 2.1. It results from $[\mathcal{N}]$ by ignoring the possible concurrency. $\qquad \square$

## 2.3   Causal Nets

Except for the identity of (statically reachable) places, isomorphisms preserve all information about the net structure. Later in Chapter 3 we wish to ignore part of this information and state that safe nets with a different structure admit the same concurrent computations. To formalise this property, we employ an idea of Petri that the concurrent computations of a net can be described with the help of *causal nets* [Pet77, Rei85]. Informally, a causal net is an acyclic net where all choices have been resolved. It can be seen as a net-theoretic way of defining a partial order among the occurrences of transitions in a net to represent their causal dependency. Before we can give the formal definition we need some more notation.

Consider a net $\mathcal{N} = (A, Pl, \longrightarrow, M_0)$. We define *pre-* and *postsets of places* $p \in Pl$ by

$$pre(p) = \{t \in \longrightarrow \mid p \in post(t) \}$$

and

$$post(p) = \{t \in \longrightarrow \mid p \in pre(t) \}.$$

We also need the *flow relation* $\mathcal{F}_\mathcal{N} \subseteq Pl \times Pl$ of $\mathcal{N}$ given by

$$p \; \mathcal{F}_\mathcal{N} \; q \;\; \text{if} \;\; \exists t \in \longrightarrow : p \in pre(t) \text{ and } q \in post(t).$$

$\mathcal{F}_\mathcal{N}$ is *well-founded* if there are no infinite backward chains

$$\cdots p_3 \; \mathcal{F}_\mathcal{N} \; p_2 \; \mathcal{F}_\mathcal{N} \; p_1.$$

Now we can introduce:

**Definition 2.3.1** A *causal net* or *concurrent computation* is a net $\mathcal{N} = ( A, Pl, \longrightarrow, M_0)$ satisfying the following conditions:

(1) all places are unbranched, i.e.

$$\forall p \in Pl : |pre(p)| \leq 1 \text{ and } |post(p)| \leq 1,$$

(2) the flow relation $\mathcal{F}_\mathcal{N}$ is well-founded.

(3) the initial marking consists of all places without an ingoing arc, i.e.

$$M_0 = \{p \in Pl \mid pre(p) = \emptyset\}. \qquad \qquad \square$$

Condition (1) implies that there are no choices left in $\mathcal{N}$ (cf. Example 2.2.3(2)). Condition (2) implies that the transitive closure of $\mathcal{F}_\mathcal{N}$ is irreflexive. Thus a causal net $\mathcal{N}$ is acyclic so that each transition can occur only once. $\mathcal{N}$ induces a partial order $\leq$ on transitions where $t_1 \leq t_2$ means that $t_2$ can occur only after $t_1$ has occured. In other words : $t_2$ *causally depends* on $t_1$. If neither $t_1 \leq t_2$ nor $t_2 \leq t_1$ then $t_1$ and $t_2$ are *causally independent* and can occur *concurrently*. Conditions (1) – (3) together ensure that there are no superfluous places and transitions in causal nets (see Lemma 2.3.6).

Following Petri's intuition, causal nets should describe the concurrent computations of a net. Thus we have to explain how causal nets relate to ordinary (safe) nets. To this end, we use the following notion of embedding.

**Definition 2.3.2** Let $\mathcal{N}_1 = (A_1, Pl_1, \longrightarrow_1, M_{01})$ be a causal net and $\mathcal{N}_2 = (A_2, Pl_2, \longrightarrow_2, M_{02})$ be a safe net. $\mathcal{N}_1$ is a *causal net* or *concurrent computation of $\mathcal{N}_2$* if $A_1 = A_2$ and there exists a mapping

$$f : Pl_1 \longrightarrow Pl_2$$

such that

(1) $f(M_{01}) = M_{02}$

(2) $\forall\, M \in mark(\mathcal{N}_1) : f \downarrow M$ is injective,

(3) $\forall\, t \in \longrightarrow_1 : f(t) \in \longrightarrow_2$

where $f \downarrow M$ is the restriction of $f$ to $M$, where $f$ applied to sets of places is understood elementwise, and where $f(t) = (f(pre(t)), act(t), f(post(t)))$. The mapping $f$ is called an *embedding of $\mathcal{N}_1$ into $\mathcal{N}_2$*.                     □

In net theory an embedding is called a *process* [Pet77, Rei85]. We prefer to leave the notion of process more general and give meaning to it by looking at three complementary descriptions: nets, terms and formulas. The net-theoretic notion of process does not capture all our intentions, for example not the choices. But it is well suited as a formalisation of the concept of a concurrent computation [Bro86, DM87].

**Example 2.3.3** The following net $\mathcal{N}_1$ is a causal net of $\mathcal{N}_2$.

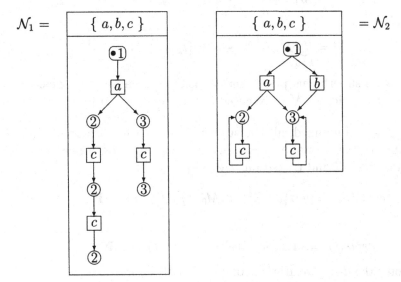

The embedding of $\mathcal{N}_1$ into $\mathcal{N}_2$ maps each place of $\mathcal{N}_1$ onto that place of $\mathcal{N}_2$ which is indicated by the corresponding number in $\mathcal{N}_1$.                     □

The following two lemmas investigate the properties of causal nets.

**Lemma 2.3.4** Let $\mathcal{N} = (A, Pl, \longrightarrow, M_0)$ be a causal net. Then every transition sequence

$$M_0 \xrightarrow{\ t_1\ } M_1 \xrightarrow{\ t_2\ } \cdots \xrightarrow{\ t_k\ } M_k \qquad\qquad (2.4)$$

of $\mathcal{N}$ satisfies

$$M_j \cap post(t_k) = \emptyset \qquad\qquad (2.5)$$

for all $j = 0, \ldots, k - 1$.

*Proof.* Consider a transition sequence (2.4) of $\mathcal{N}$ and suppose that

$$p \in M_j \cap post(t_k)$$

for some $p \in Pl$ and $j \in \{ 0, \ldots, k - 1 \}$.

This is impossible for $j = 0$ because by the definition of causal nets, $M_0$ has no ingoing arcs. Hence $j > 0$ and $p \in post(t_i)$ for some $i \in \{ 1, \ldots, j \}$. Thus $t_i, t_k \in pre(p)$ where $t_i \neq t_k$ because $\mathcal{F}_\mathcal{N}$ is well-founded. This is a contradiction because by the definition of causal nets, places are unbranched.                                                                                        $\square$

**Corollary 2.3.5** Every causal net is safe.

**Lemma 2.3.6** Let $\mathcal{N} = (A, Pl, \longrightarrow, M_0)$ be a causal net. Then there exists one possibly infinite transition sequence

$$M_0 \xrightarrow{\ t_1\ } M_1 \xrightarrow{\ t_2\ } \cdots \xrightarrow{\ t_k\ } M_k \xrightarrow{\ t_{k+1}\ } \cdots \qquad\qquad (2.6)$$

of $\mathcal{N}$ with

$$Pl = \bigcup_{k \geq 0} M_k \ \text{ and } \ \longrightarrow \ = \{t_k \,|k \geq 1\}. \qquad\qquad (2.7)$$

Thus $\mathcal{N}$ contains no superfluous places and transitions because every place of $\mathcal{N}$ is visited and every transition of $\mathcal{N}$ is executed in the sequence (2.6).

*Proof.* Since $\mathcal{F}_\mathcal{N}$ is well-founded, all transitions in $\longrightarrow$ have finite presets (cf. Definition 2.2.1) and $M_0$ consists of all places without ingoing arcs, we can associate a *depth* to all places $p \in Pl$ and transitions $t \in \longrightarrow$:

$$depth(p) \ = \ max\{d \mid \exists p_0 \in M_0 : p_0 \ \mathcal{F}_\mathcal{N}^d \ p \} \ \in \mathbb{N}_0$$

and

$$depth(t) \ = \ max\{ depth(p) \mid p \in pre(t) \} \ \in \mathbb{N}_0$$

where $\mathcal{F}_\mathcal{N}^d$ denotes the $d$-fold relational composition of $\mathcal{F}_\mathcal{N}$.

We construct now the transition sequence (2.6) as follows: Since in $M_0$ all transitions of depth 0 are enabled, we begin the construction of (2.6) by first executing in some order all of these transitions. This yields after intermediate markings $M_1$, $\ldots$, $M_{k-1}$ a new marking $M_k$, $k > 0$, in (2.6) where all transitions of depth 1 are enabled. We continue the construction of (2.6) by executing in some order all of these transitions. This yields a new marking $M_l$, $k \leq l$, in (2.6) where all transitions of depth 2 are enabled. By repeating this construction for all depths we make sure that all places in $Pl$ are visited and all transitions in $\longrightarrow$ are executed.

Note that this construction works because all places are unbranched. Thus whenever two transitions $t_1$ and $t_2$ are enabled at some marking $M$ and $t_1$ is executed, $t_2$ is still enabled. □

Based on causal nets we introduce the following equivalence relation on safe nets.

**Definition 2.3.7** Two safe nets $\mathcal{N}_1$ and $\mathcal{N}_2$ are *causally equivalent*, abbreviated

$$\mathcal{N}_1 \equiv_{caus} \mathcal{N}_2,$$

if $\mathcal{N}_1$ and $\mathcal{N}_2$ have the same causal nets. We say that two safe nets admit the *same concurrent computations* or exhibit the *same amount of concurrency* if they are causally equivalent. □

Note that

$$\mathcal{N}_1 =_{isom} \mathcal{N}_2 \text{ implies } \mathcal{N}_1 \equiv_{caus} \mathcal{N}_2$$

for all safe nets $\mathcal{N}_1$ and $\mathcal{N}_2$. Thus we can extend causal equivalence to abstract safe nets by putting

$$[\mathcal{N}_1] \equiv_{caus} [\mathcal{N}_2] \text{ if } \mathcal{N}_1 \equiv_{caus} \mathcal{N}_2.$$

This way we can compare the concurrency of abstract safe nets.

To prove causal equivalence of nets, we introduce now a new kind of structural relation on nets that is inspired by the notion of strong bisimilarity on automata [Par81].

Recall from Definition 2.1.4 that strong bisimilarity between two automata is shown by establishing a certain bisimulation relation $\mathcal{B}$ between the *states* of these automata. When lifting such a definition to nets, the question arises: what should replace the role of states ? Recently several versions of (strong and weak) bisimilarity on nets have been proposed and most definitions take *markings* as the right analogue for states [Pom85, GV87]. This works well as far as the dynamic behaviour (expressed by a transfer property as in Definition 2.1.4) is concerned.

However, one nice aspect of bisimulation on automata gets lost in this way, viz. the bisimulation relation $\mathcal{B}$ can be displayed on the static structure of the automata. We wish to preserve this static property of bisimulation in our definition for nets and therefore start from a relation $\mathcal{B}$ on *places* which will then be lifted to markings and transitions.

Consider safe nets $\mathcal{N}_i = (A_i, Pl_i, \longrightarrow_i, M_{0i})$, $i=1,2$, and a relation $\mathcal{B} \subseteq Pl_1 \times Pl_2$. Then *lifting* $\mathcal{B}$ to markings and transitions is done by the following very strong relation $\hat{\mathcal{B}}$.

(1) For sets $M_i \subseteq Pl_i$, $i=1,2$, we write

$$M_1 \; \hat{\mathcal{B}} \; M_2$$

if $\mathcal{B} \cap ( M_1 \times M_2)$ is a bijection.

(2) For transitions $t_i \in \longrightarrow_i$, $i=1,2$, we write

$$t_1 \ \hat{\mathcal{B}} \ t_2$$

if $pre(t_1) \ \hat{\mathcal{B}} \ pre(t_{12})$, $act(t_1) = act(t_2)$, $post(t_1) \ \hat{\mathcal{B}} \ post(t_2)$.

Now we can introduce the new notion of strong bisimilarity for safe nets.

**Definition 2.3.8** Two safe nets $\mathcal{N}_i = ( \ A_i, \ Pl_i, \ \longrightarrow_i, \ M_{0i})$, $i=1,2$, are *strongly bisimilar*, abbreviated

$$\mathcal{N}_1 \approx \mathcal{N}_2,$$

if $A_1 = A_2$ and there exists a relation

$$\mathcal{B} \subseteq Pl_1 \times Pl_2$$

satisfying the following conditions:

(1) $M_{01} \ \hat{\mathcal{B}} \ M_{02}$

(2) For all $M_1$, $N_1 \in \mathrm{mark}(\mathcal{N}_1)$, $M_2 \in \mathrm{mark}(\mathcal{N}_2)$ and all $t_1 \in \longrightarrow_1$ whenever

$$M_1 \ \hat{\mathcal{B}} \ M_2 \text{ and } M_1 \xrightarrow{\ t_1\ }_1 N_1$$

then there exists some $t_2 \in \longrightarrow_2$ with

$$t_1 \ \hat{\mathcal{B}} \ t_2$$

and some $N_2 \in \mathrm{mark}(\mathcal{N}_2)$ with

$$N_1 \ \hat{\mathcal{B}} \ N_2 \text{ and } M_2 \xrightarrow{\ t_2\ }_2 N_2.$$

(3) Conversely, for all $M_1 \in \mathrm{mark}(\mathcal{N}_1)$, $M_2$, $N_2 \in \mathrm{mark}(\mathcal{N}_2)$ and all $t_2 \in \longrightarrow_2$ whenever

$$M_1 \ \hat{\mathcal{B}} \ M_2 \text{ and } M_2 \xrightarrow{\ t_2\ }_2 N_2$$

then there exist some $t_1 \in \longrightarrow_1$ with

$$t_1 \ \hat{\mathcal{B}} \ t_2$$

and some $N_1 \in \mathrm{mark}(\mathcal{N}_1)$ with

$$N_1 \ \hat{\mathcal{B}} \ N_2 \text{ and } M_1 \xrightarrow{\ t_1\ }_1 N_1.$$

The relation $\mathcal{B}$ is called a *strong bisimulation* between $\mathcal{N}_1$ and $\mathcal{N}_2$ and the conditions (2) and (3) are called the *transfer property* of $\mathcal{B}$.                                        $\square$

As for automata, we have that

$$\mathcal{N}_1 =_{isom} \mathcal{N}_2 \text{ implies } \mathcal{N}_1 \approx \mathcal{N}_2$$

for all nets $\mathcal{N}_1$ and $\mathcal{N}_2$. Thus we can extend the definition of strong bisimilarity to abstract automata $[\mathcal{N}_1]$ and $[\mathcal{N}_2]$ by putting

$$[\mathcal{N}_1] \approx [\mathcal{N}_2] \text{ if } \mathcal{N}_1 \approx \mathcal{N}_2.$$

Moreover, by Remarks 2.1.5, 2.2.2 and 2.2.5, the new definition of $\approx$ coincides with the original Definition 2.1.4 when restricted to automata.

As noticed in [ABS91], the above notion of strong bisimilarity on safe nets is *not* an equivalence relation; $\approx$ is reflexive and symmetric but not transitive. While this is a serious shortcoming in general, it does not affect the purpose of the relation $\approx$ in this book. Here $\approx$ serves as an auxiliary notion in proving that structurally different nets are causally equivalent. This is the contents of the subsequent Causality Theorem 2.3.10.

The authors of [ABS91] have proposed another definition bisimilarity on nets which is an equivalence relation. Their idea is to consider general place/transition nets and then define lifting as a relation $\hat{\mathcal{B}}$ between multiset markings. Unfortunately, their definition forces them to consider also markings that are not reachable. We conclude here only that the idea of bisimilation on nets generated from relations on places requires further study.

A specific way of defining a strong bisimulation $\hat{\mathcal{B}}$ between two nets $\mathcal{N}_1$ and $\mathcal{N}_2$ is by giving *colours* to the places of $\mathcal{N}_1$ and $\mathcal{N}_2$. More precisely, we take a set $\mathcal{C}$ (of colours) and mappings $f_i \colon Pl_i \longrightarrow \mathcal{C}$, $i=1,2$, to define for all $p_i \in Pl_i$, $i=1,2$,

$$p_1 \ \mathcal{B} \ p_2 \ \text{ if } f_1(p_1) = f_2(p_2).$$

Thus $p_1$ and $p_2$ are related if they have the same colour. We make use of this technique in the following example.

**Example 2.3.9** The colours are natural numbers that appear inside the places of the following nets.

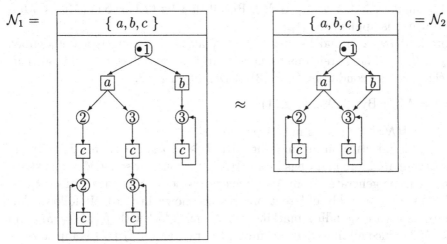

Note that we cannot further identify the places 2 and 3 because both appear in one reachable marking of $\mathcal{N}_1$ resp. $\mathcal{N}_2$ and the lifted relation $\hat{\mathcal{B}}$ is required to be a bijection on markings. Thus strong bisimilarity preserves the concurrency of the two cycles in $\mathcal{N}_2$.                                                                                  □

Using causal nets we can now state formally that strong bisimilarity preserves concurrency.

**Causality Theorem 2.3.10** Consider two strongly bisimilar safe nets $\mathcal{N}_1$ and $\mathcal{N}_2$. Then $\mathcal{N}$ is a causal net of $\mathcal{N}_1$ if and only if $\mathcal{N}$ is a causal net of $\mathcal{N}_2$. In other words,

$$\mathcal{N}_1 \approx \mathcal{N}_2 \text{ implies } \mathcal{N}_1 \equiv_{caus} \mathcal{N}_2.$$

*Proof.* Consider safe nets $\mathcal{N}_i = (A, Pl_i, \longrightarrow_i, M_{0i})$, $i=1,2$, and suppose that $\mathcal{N} = (A, Pl, \longrightarrow, M_0)$ is a causal net of $\mathcal{N}_1$ via the embedding $f_1 : Pl \longrightarrow Pl_1$ from $\mathcal{N}$ into $\mathcal{N}_1$ and let $\mathcal{N}_1 \approx \mathcal{N}_2$ via the strong bisimulation $\mathcal{B}$ between $\mathcal{N}$ and $\mathcal{N}_2$. We have to construct an embedding $f_2 : Pl \longrightarrow Pl_2$ from $\mathcal{N}$ into $\mathcal{N}_2$. The idea is to obtain $f_2$ by composing $f_1$ and $\mathcal{B}$.

More precisely, consider a transition sequence (2.6) of $\mathcal{N}$ satisfying (2.7), as in Lemma 2.3.6. Then, using $f_1$, there exists a transition sequence

$$M_{01} \xrightarrow{t_{11}} M_{11} \xrightarrow{t_{21}} \ldots \xrightarrow{t_{k1}} M_{k1} \xrightarrow{t_{k+1,1}} \ldots \tag{2.8}$$

of $\mathcal{N}_1$ with

$$f_1(M_k) = M_{k1} \text{ and } f_1(t_k) = t_{k1} \tag{2.9}$$

for every $k \geq 0$, and, using $\mathcal{B}$, there exists a transition sequence

$$M_{02} \xrightarrow{t_{12}} M_{12} \xrightarrow{t_{22}} \ldots \xrightarrow{t_{k2}} M_{k2} \xrightarrow{t_{k+1,2}} \ldots \tag{2.10}$$

of $\mathcal{N}_2$ with

$$M_{k1} \hat{\mathcal{B}} M_{k2} \text{ and } t_{k1} \hat{\mathcal{B}} t_{k2} \tag{2.11}$$

for every $k \geq 0$. Define now

$$f_2(p) = (\mathcal{B} \cap (M_{k1} \times M_{k2}))(f_1(p)) \tag{2.12}$$

where $k$ is the smallest index with $p \in M_k$. Recall that by (2.11), $\mathcal{B} \cap (M_{k1} \times M_{k2})$ is a bijection which is applied to $f_1(p)$.

First note that by (2.7) and Lemma 2.3.4, equation (2.12) yields a well-defined mapping $f_2 : Pl \longrightarrow Pl_2$. It remains to show that $f_2$ is indeed an embedding. This is done by checking the conditions (1) – (3) of Definition 2.3.2.

(1) $f_2(M_0) = M_{02}$ : By (2.9) and (2.11).

(2) $\forall\, M \in mark(\mathcal{N}) : f_2 \downarrow M$ is injective :
   Clearly, $f_2$ is injective on all markings $M_k$, $k \geq 0$, that occur in (2.6), but in general there are more markings in $mark(\mathcal{N})$. So consider some $M \in mark(\mathcal{N})$. Then $M$ can be generated from $M_0$ by executing some of the transitions $t_1$, $t_2$, ... of $\mathcal{N}$ in some possibly different order than shown in (2.6). It follows that there exists a corresponding marking $M_2 \in mark(\mathcal{N}_2)$ with $f_2(M) = M_2$ and $|M| = |M_2|$. Since all markings are finite, the restriction $f_2 \downarrow M$ is injective.

(3) $\forall \, t \in \longrightarrow : f_2(t) \in \longrightarrow_2 :$

Every transition $t$ of $\mathcal{N}$ occurs in (2.6), i.e. $t = t_k$ for some $k \geq 0$. By construction, $f_2(t_k) = t_{k2}$ is a transition of $\mathcal{N}_2$.

Thus $\mathcal{N}$ is a causal net of $\mathcal{N}_2$. Since $\approx$ is symmetric, this proves the theorem. □

Since $\equiv_{caus}$ is an equivalence relation, the Causality Theorem yields more generally that

$$\mathcal{N}_1 \approx^* \mathcal{N}_2 \text{ implies } \mathcal{N}_1 \equiv_{caus} \mathcal{N}_2$$

where $\approx^*$ is the reflexive, transitive closure of $\approx$. Thus to prove causal equivalence of nets $\mathcal{N}_1$ and $\mathcal{N}_2$, we shall exhibit a sequence of pairwise strongly bisimilar nets starting in $\mathcal{N}_1$ and ending in $\mathcal{N}_2$.

## 2.4 Problems with Nets

Petri nets are able to distinguish clearly the basic concepts in the behaviour of processes. The graphical representation of nets visualises these concepts. Therefore we selected nets for our very detailed, machine-like view of processes. But is this view of processes satisfactory ? The answer is "no" because there are at least two serious problems with it:

(1) *Compositionality.* Missing is a convenient way of composing or decomposing larger nets from or into smaller ones by a set of high level operators.

(2) *Abstraction.* Missing is a way of abstraction from internal actions $\tau$, i.e. processes are not yet treated as "black boxes" where only the communication behaviour is important.

Both compositionality and abstraction are necessary to manage with the behavioural complexity of processes.

**Example 2.4.1** For an illustration of these problems let us look at the abstract nets $\mathcal{N}_1$ and $\mathcal{N}_2$ on the next page. $\mathcal{N}_1$ achieves the *mutual exclusion* between the two critical sections marked by the actions $b_i$ and $e_i$ (*begin* and *end* of critical section), $i = 1, 2$, i.e. in every reachable marking of $\mathcal{N}_1$ at most one of the places inside the critical sections contains a token.

We would like to say $\mathcal{N}_1$ is *composed* out of three smaller nets : two cycles $n_i$ $p_i$ $b_i$ $e_i$ $v_i$, $i = 1,2$, modelling users that start with a non-critical action $n_i$ and then wish to enter their critical section $b_i.e_i$, and a *semaphore*, i.e. a synchronisation device enforcing a choice between the actions $p_1$, $v_1$ or $p_2$, $v_2$. But how to define such composition operators ?

$\mathcal{N}_1 =$    $\{\ n_i, p_i, b_i, e_i, v_i\ \mid\ i=1,2\ \}$

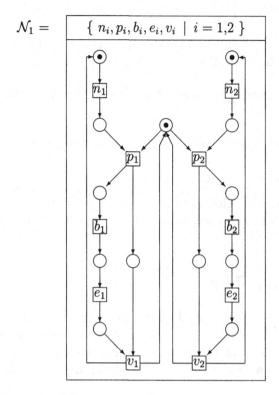

Much simpler is the following net $\mathcal{N}_2$.

$\mathcal{N}_2 =$    $\{\ b_i, e_i\ \mid\ i=1,2\ \}$

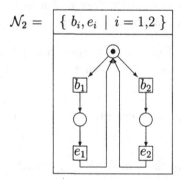

What is the relationship to $\mathcal{N}_1$ ? Intuitively, $\mathcal{N}_1$ is obtained from $\mathcal{N}_2$ by *abstracting* from the actions $n_i$, $p_i$, $v_i$, $i=1,2$, in $\mathcal{N}_1$, i.e. by transforming them into internal actions $\tau$ and then forgetting about the $\tau$' s. But how can we formalise this abstraction relation between $\mathcal{N}_1$ and $\mathcal{N}_2$ ?                                    □

To some extent the problems of compositionality and abstraction have been addressed within net theory. For example, to introduce abstraction, higher level places and transitions resulting in predicate/transition nets have been proposed [Gen87], and to introduce compositionality, notions like state-machine decomposition of nets have been defined [Ber87]. But in most cases nets are analyzed *as a whole* either conceptually with the help of graph-theoretic notions like synchronization graphs or partly automatically by using methods of linear algebra to determine invariants of the transition relation from which further desirable properties can be deduced. The disadvantage of analysing nets as a whole is of course that one has to redo the analysis whenever a part of the net changes. Overcoming this problem is the essence of compositionality.

We wish to approach compositionality and abstraction by bringing in ideas from outside net theory. This will equip us with new complementary views of concurrent processes.

# 3

# PROCESS TERMS

We now introduce a second view of concurrent processes whereby each process is a term over a certain signature of operator symbols. By interpreting these symbols on nets, we will solve the problem of compositionality. As interpretations we take a selection of the operators suggested in Lauer's COSY, Milner's CCS and Hoare's CSP.

Lauer's COSY (Concurrent Systems) is one of the first approaches to compositionality of processes on a schematic, uninterpreted level [LTS79]. It originates from path expressions [CH74] and can thus be seen as an extension of regular expressions to include parallelism. We use here COSY's operator for *parallel composition* because, as we shall see later in Chapter 4, it enjoys pleasant logical properties.

A significant step beyond COSY is Milner's CCS (Calculus of Communicating Systems) with its conceptual roots in algebra and the $\lambda$-calculus [Mil80, Mil83]. From CCS we take the idea that processes are *recursive terms* over certain operator symbols, i.e. they form the smallest set that is generated by the operator symbols and closed under parameterless recursion. In COSY only iteration is present as might be clear from its background in regular expressions. By using recursion we ensure that process terms are Turing powerful even on the schematic level without the help of interpreted values or variables. We also take CCS's *choice operator* because it allows a very clear treatment on the level of nets, and its notion of *action morphism* by which actions can be renamed. Intertwined with the development of CCS is that of Hoare's CSP (Communicating Sequential Processes). Originally, CSP referred to a programming notation extending Dijkstra's guarded commands [Dij76] with communication and parallelism [Hoa78]. On the one hand, this notation has motivated some of the operators in CCS. On the other, under the impact of CCS the original CSP has changed into a schematic and more abstract version, now often referred to as TCSP (Theory of Communicating Sequential Processes) [BHR84, Hoa85b]. We shall use its *hiding operator* which transforms communications between user and process into automatically occuring internal actions.

With nets hiding can be modelled easily as a specific action morphism in the sense of CCS. Only on the logical level where one deals with properties that are preserved under abstraction from internal actions, does hiding reveal its delicacy because it can easily result in processes exhibiting *divergence* (infinite internal looping). In CCS hiding is a part of its parallel composition. In our approach this would complicate its logical treatment; we therefore take COSY's parallel composition to achieve a separation of concerns between paralellism and hiding. An extension of COSY's parallel composition is also used in TCSP. We can model this extension with the help of action morphisms.

For a satisfactory treatment of COSY's parallel composition, every recursive term will have a *type* in the form of a communication alphabet. The typing constraints will be introduced a posteriori by enforcing certain context-sensitive restrictions on process terms, similarly to [Hoa85b]. Typing does create a certain notational overhead not needed in CCS, but we believe that in many applications types will be needed anyhow (see for example CADIC, a calculus for integrated circuits [BHK$^+$87]).

## 3.1   Syntax

The general scheme for recursive terms is very simple. Starting from a set of operator symbols $op$, each one with a certain arity $n \geq 0$, and a set of identifiers $X$, the context-free syntax of recursive terms $P$ is given by the following production rules:

$$P ::= op(P_1, \ldots, P_n) \text{ where } op \text{ has arity } n \mid X \mid \mu X.P.$$

Recursion is expressed in the $\mu$-notation of [Par76, Bak80]. The reason for separating recursion from the other operators $op$ is that semantically, recursion will get an extra treatment.

Let us now explain how this scheme is applied to yield process terms. Recall that *Comm* denotes the infinite set of communications and $Act = Comm \cup \{\tau\}$ the set of actions. As before, letters $a,b$ range over *Comm* and letters $A,B$ over communication alphabets, i.e. finite subsets of *Comm*. The set of (*process*) *identifiers* is denoted by *Idf*; it is partitioned into sets *Idf*:$A \subseteq Idf$ of *identifiers with alphabet A*, one for each communication alphabet $A$. We let $X,Y,Z$ range over *Idf*. By an *action morphism* we mean a mapping $\varphi : Act \longrightarrow Act$ with $\varphi(\tau) = \{\tau\}$ and $\varphi(a) \neq a$ for only finitely many $a \in Comm$. Communications $a$ with $\varphi(a) = \{\tau\}$ are said to be *hidden* via $\varphi$ and communications $a$ with $\varphi(a) = \{b\}$ for some $b \neq a$ are said to be *renamed* into $b$ via $\varphi$.

**Definition 3.1.1** The set *Rec* of (*recursive*) *terms*, with typical elements $P,Q,R$, consists of all terms generated by the following context-free production rules:

$$
\begin{array}{lll}
P ::= & stop{:}A & (\text{ deadlock }) \\
| & div{:}A & (\text{ divergence }) \\
| & a.P & (\text{ prefix }) \\
| & P + Q & (\text{ choice }) \\
| & P \parallel Q & (\text{ parallelism }) \\
| & P\,[\,\varphi\,] & (\text{ morphism }) \\
| & X & (\text{ identifier }) \\
| & \mu X.P & (\text{ recursion })
\end{array}
$$

The intended interpretation is given as a commentary.                    □

Formally, the signature of *Rec* consists of nullary operator symbols *stop*:$A$ and *div*:$A$ for each communication alphabet $A$, a unary prefix symbol $a.$ for each communication $a$, a unary postfix symbol $[\varphi]$ for each morphism $\varphi$, and binary infix symbols $+$ and $\parallel$ . Syntactic ambiguities are eliminated by using brackets and the following priorities among the operator symbols and recursion:

$$
\begin{array}{lll}
\text{priority } 0 & : & + \text{ and } \parallel, \\
\text{priority } 1 & : & a. \text{ and } \mu X., \\
\text{priority } 2 & : & [\varphi].
\end{array}
$$

Since $+$ and $\parallel$ turn out to be commutative and associative (Theorem 3.5.8), we sometimes use the abbreviations

$$
\sum_{i\in\{1,\ldots,n\}} P_i = \sum_{i=1}^{n} P_i = P_1 + \cdots + P_n
$$

and

$$
\|_{i\in\{1,\ldots,n\}} P_i = \|_{i=1}^{n} P_i = P_1 \| \cdots \| P_n .
$$

For action morphisms which purely rename or hide communications we use the following notations:

- *Renaming* : For distinct $a_1,\ldots,a_n$ and $n \geq 1$ let

$$
P[b_1,\ldots,b_n \,/\, a_1,\ldots,a_n] =_{df} P[\varphi]
$$

  where for $u \in Act$
$$
\varphi(u) = \begin{cases} b_i & \text{if } u = a_i \text{ for some } i \in 1,\ldots,n \\ u & \text{otherwise} \end{cases}
$$

- *Hiding* : $P \setminus B =_{df} P[\varphi]$
  where for $u \in Act$
$$
\varphi(u) = \begin{cases} \tau & \text{if } u \in B \\ u & \text{otherwise} \end{cases}
$$

  and $P \setminus b =_{df} P \setminus \{\, b \,\}$.

**Remark 3.1.2** Every action morphism $\varphi$ can be decomposed into a sequence of applications of renaming and hiding operators of the form $[b_1 \,/\, a_1]$ and $\setminus b$.                    □

We now introduce some auxiliary notions for terms. An occurrence of an identifier $X$ in a term $P$ is said to be *bound* if it occurs in $P$ within a subterm of the form $\mu X.Q$. Otherwise the occurrence is said to be *free*. Let *free*$(P)$ denote the set of identifiers that occur freely in a term $P$. A term without free occurrences of identifiers is called *closed*. For terms $P,Q$ and identifiers $X$ let $P\{Q/X\}$ denote the result of *substituting* $Q$ for every free occurrence of $X$ in $P$. As usual, by a preparatory renaming of bound identifiers in $P$ one has to ensure that no free identifier occurrences in $Q$ gets bound in $P\{Q/X\}$. Thus $P\{Q/X\}$ is unique up to renaming of bound identifiers. This notation readily extends to simultaneous substitution of lists of terms for lists of distinct identifiers: $P\{Q_1,\ldots,Q_n \ / \ X_1,\ldots,X_n\}$. Note that we use brackets $\{\ldots\}$ for evaluated substitutions and brackets $[\ldots]$ for unevaluated substitutions like the renaming operators above.

A term $P$ is called *action-guarded* if in every recursive subterm $\mu X.Q$ of $P$ every free occurrence of $X$ in $Q$ occurs within a subterm of the form

$$a.R$$

of $Q$. For example,

$$\mu X.a.X, \ \mu X.\mu Y.a.Y, \ (\mu X.a.X) \setminus a$$

are all action-guarded, but

$$a.\mu X.X$$

is not. The example $(\mu X.a.X)\backslash a$ shows that the guarding communication $a$ may well be within the scope of a hiding operator $\backslash a$. That's why we talk of *action*-guardedness; later in Chapter 5 we shall also introduce *communication*-guardedness (Definition 5.1.4).

The term "guardedness" is due to [Mil80]; it corresponds to the "Greibach condition" in formal language theory [Niv79] if we identify terminal symbols with actions, and nonterminal symbols with process identifiers. The Greibach condition requires that the right-hand side of every production rule of a context-free grammar starts with a terminal symbol. For example, the production $X ::= a.X$ satisfies this condition whereas $X ::= Y$ does not.

To every term $P$ we assign a communication alphabet $\alpha(P)$ defined inductively as follows :

$$
\begin{aligned}
\alpha(stop{:}A) &= \alpha(div{:}A) &&= A, \\
\alpha(a.P) &= \{a\} \cup \alpha(P), \\
\alpha(P{+}Q) &= \alpha(P \parallel Q) &&= \alpha(P) \cup \alpha(Q), \\
\alpha(P[\varphi]) &= \varphi(\alpha(P)) - \{\tau\}, \\
\alpha(X) &= A &&\text{if } X \in \mathit{Idf}{:}A, \\
\alpha(\mu X.P) &= \alpha(X) \cup \alpha(P).
\end{aligned}
$$

**Definition 3.1.3** A *process term* is a term $P \in \mathit{Rec}$ which satisfies the following context-sensitive restrictions:

(1) $P$ is action-guarded,

(2) every subterm $a.Q$ of $P$ satisfies $a \in \alpha(Q)$,

(3) every subterm $Q+R$ of $P$ satisfies $\alpha(Q) = \alpha(R)$,

(4) every subterm $\mu X.Q$ of $P$ satisfies $\alpha(X) = \alpha(Q)$.

Let *Proc* denote the set of all process terms and *CProc* the set of all closed process terms. □

The context-sensitive restrictions for process terms simplify their subsequent semantic treatment. Here we notice that the alphabet of a process term $P$ depends only on the alphabet of its subterms, not on their syntactic structure.

**Remark 3.1.4** For every $n$-ary operator symbol *op* of *Proc* there exists a set-theoretic operator $op_\alpha$ such that

$$\alpha(op(P_1, \ldots, P_n)) = op_\alpha(\alpha(P_1), \ldots, \alpha(P_n)).$$

Consequently, by context restriction (4),

$$\alpha(\mu X.P) = \alpha(P\{\mu X.P/X\})$$

for all recursive process terms $\mu X.P$. □

## 3.2 Informal Semantics

The intuitive meaning of process terms is as follows. *Deadlock stop:A* denotes a process which neither engages in any communication nor in any internal action. *Divergence div:A* denotes a process which pursues an infinite loop of internal actions. *Prefix a.P* first communicates $a$ and then behaves like $P$. Thus prefix is a restricted form of sequential composition. *Choice P+Q* behaves like $P$ or like $Q$ depending on whether the first action is one of $P$ or one of $Q$. If the first action belongs to both $P$ and $Q$, this choice is nondeterministic. *Parallel composition* combines concurrency and synchronisation: $P\|Q$ behaves like $P$ and $Q$ working independently or concurrently except that all communications which occur in the alphabet of both $P$ and $Q$ have to synchronise. *Morphism $P[\varphi]$* behaves like $P$, but with all actions $u$ changed into $\varphi(u)$. *Recursion $\mu X.P$* behaves like $P$, but with every occurrence of $X$ inside $P$ denoting a recursive call to $\mu X.P$.

In the original work on CCS and CSP these intuitions were made precise using an interleaving model of concurrency based on (abstractions from) automata [Mil80, BHR84, OH86].

Here we wish to be more detailed by mapping the term view of processes onto the net view presented in Chapter 2. To give an idea of this mapping, let us describe the abstract net $\mathcal{N}_1$ of Example 2.4.1 by a process term.

First consider the process term

$$SEM = \mu X.(p_1.v_1.X + p_2.v_2.X)$$

built up from an identifier $X$ with $\alpha(X) = \{p_i, v_i \mid i=1,2\}$, prefix, choice and recursion. It denotes the abstract net

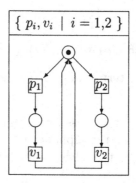

modelling a semaphore. Next consider the process term

$$CYCLE = \mu Y.n.p.b.e.v.Y$$

built up from an identifier $Y$ with $\alpha(Y) = \{n,p,b,e,v\}$, prefix and recursion. It denotes the abstract net

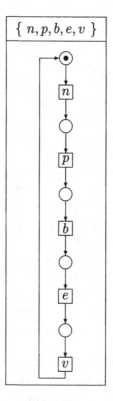

modelling a generic user cycle with non-critical action $n$ and critical section $b.e$ sheltered by semaphore communications $p$ and $v$.

Applying renaming morphisms we generate two copies of $CYCLE$:

$$CYCLE_1 = CYCLE \left[ \, n_1, \, p_1, \, b_1, \, e_1, \, v_1 \, / \, n, \, p, \, b, \, e, \, v \, \right],$$
$$CYCLE_2 = CYCLE \left[ \, n_2, \, p_2, \, b_2, \, e_2, \, v_2 \, / \, n, \, p, \, b, \, e, \, v \, \right].$$

$CYCLE_1$ denotes an abstract net with the same structure as $CYCLE$, but with the action labels $n$, $p$, $b$, $e$, $v$ renamed into $n_1$, $p_1$, $b_1$, $e_1$, $v_1$, and analogously for $CYCLE_2$.

To achieve mutual exclusion, we apply parallel composition to $CYCLE_1$, $SEM$ and $CYCLE_2$. This yields the process term

$$MUTEX = CYCLE_1 \parallel SEM \parallel CYCLE_2.$$

By definition of parallel composition, synchronisation is required for the communications $p_1$ and $v_1$ of $CYCLE_1$ and $SEM$, and for the communications $p_2$ and $v_2$ of $SEM$ and $CYCLE_2$. The remaining communications may occur asynchronously whenever they are enabled. Hence the process term $MUTEX$ denotes the abstract net $\mathcal{N}_1$ of Example 2.4.1:

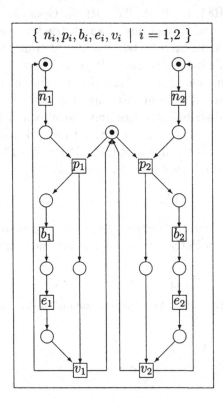

# 3.3 Operational Net Semantics

A semantics is a mapping which assigns to every element of a syntactic domain a meaning or interpretation, i.e. an element of a semantic domain. Here we wish to define a Petri net semantics which assigns to every process term $P$ a Petri net $\mathcal{N}[\![P]\!]$. The idea of linking the work around COSY, CCS and CSP with the world of Petri nets by giving a Petri net semantics to process terms is not new: a large number of papers is devoted to this aim (see e.g. [Bes87, Cza85, DDPS83, GV87, Gol88a, Gol88b, GM84, LC75, Rei84, Tau85, Win84, Win87]).

Interestingly, all these papers can be seen as providing a *compositional* Petri net semantics. Compositional refers to the way a semantics is defined and means that for every $n$-ary operator symbol $op$ on process terms a corresponding Petri net operator $op_\mathcal{N}$ is introduced satisfying the equation

$$\mathcal{N}[\![op(P_1,\ldots,P_n)]\!] = op_\mathcal{N}(\mathcal{N}[\![P_1]\!],\ldots,\mathcal{N}[\![P]\!]).$$

Some of these semantics are even *denotational*. This implies that their definitions are compositional and use fixed point techniques when dealing with recursion [Sco70, Sto77, Bac80]. (See Section 4.5 for more explanation.)

We pursue here an alternative approach which has been highly successful in providing lucid interleaving semantics to CCS, CSP and various other languages: structured *operational* semantics as advocated by Plotkin [Plo81, Plo82] and used by many others [Apt83, BMOZ88, BHR84, HP79, Mil80, OH86]. Operational means that for every process term the states and transitions of an abstract machine are described. Plotkin's idea is that states are denoted by terms and that transitions are defined by structural induction using a deductive system. It is well known how to apply this idea in the case of interleaving semantics where the machine is an automaton and hence states and transitions are global entities, but until recently it was a challenge to see how to apply it to the distributed states and transitions of Petri nets.

Degano, DeNicola and Montanari were the first to attack this problem and to propose an operational Petri net semantics of CCS [DDM87]. Their main idea was to decompose each process term $P$ syntactically into a set

$$\{C_1,\ldots,C_m\}$$

of *sequential components* which can be thought of as working concurrently. Sequential components denote the places of Petri nets. Consequently, net transitions are now of the form

$$\{C_1,\ldots,C_m\} \xrightarrow{\ u\ } \{D_1,\ldots,D_n\}$$

where $C_1,\ldots,C_m,D_1,\ldots,D_n$ are sequential components and $u$ is an action; represented graphically, this is:

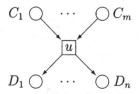

Whereas the semantics of Degano, DeNicola and Montanari models well the concurrency present in the parallel composition of CCS, it failed at first to master the subtleties of the interplay of concurrency with choice and recursion. Here the operational definition of [DDM87] exhibits less concurrency than the standard compositional semantics [GM84, Win84, GV87](see Section 3.6). These problems initiated our own work on operational Petri net semantics and stimulated further research of Degano, DeNicola and Montanari. As a result there are now two different and independently obtained solutions, viz. [DDM88b], and [Old87] on which our subsequent presentation is based. The difference is that [DDM88b] aim at a simple analysis of their semantics and therefore accept more complicated transition rules whereas we prefer simple transition rules and accept a more complicated analysis.

From [DDM87] we use the idea of decomposition, only we apply it here to the parallel operator of COSY not of CCS. For example, if $P$ and $Q$ do not contain any further symbol $\|$, the sequential components of $P \parallel Q$ are the subterms $P$ and $Q$ equipped with some information about their synchronisation set. We will write

$$P\|_A \text{ and } {}_A\|Q$$

where $A = \alpha(P) \cap \alpha(Q)$. By postfixing $P$ and prefixing $Q$ with $\|_A$ and ${}_A\|$ we generate distinct names for places which can be active concurrently. New is our treatment of recursion by an a priori expansion. This is how we solve the problem with recursion. Our solution for choice, however, cannot be so simple. Let us now explain the details of our approach. The set *Sequ* of *sequential components*, with typical elements $C,D$ , consists of all terms generated by the following production rules:

$$C ::= stop{:}A \mid div{:}A \mid a.P \mid C\|_A \mid {}_A\| D \mid C+D \mid C[\varphi]$$

where $P$ ranges over *CProc*. Note that every process term $a.P$ is also a sequential component regardless of whether $P$ contains any parallel composition. Thus sequentiality refers only to the set of initial actions; it states that this set does not contain any two actions that might occur concurrently.

We apply the operator symbols $\|_A$, ${}_A\|$, $+$, $[\varphi]$ also to *sets* of sequential components. Let $\mathbb{P}, \mathbb{Q}, \mathbb{R}$ range over $\mathcal{P}_{nf}(Sequ)$, the set of all non-empty, finite subsets of *Sequ*. Then

$$\mathbb{P}\|_A, \quad \|_A\mathbb{Q}, \quad \mathbb{P}+\mathbb{Q}, \quad \mathbb{P}[\varphi]$$

are understood element by element. For example,

$$\mathbb{P}\|_A = \{C\|_A | C \in \mathbb{P}\}.$$

This notation is used in the following definition.

**Definition 3.3.1** *Decomposition* and *expansion* of process terms into sequential components is achieved by a mapping

$$dex : CProc \longrightarrow \mathcal{P}_{nf}(Sequ)$$

defined as follows:

(1) $dex(stop{:}A) = \{ stop{:}A \}$,

(2) $dex(div{:}A) = \{ div{:}A \}$,

(3) $dex(a.P) = \{ a.P \}$,

(4) $dex(P\|Q) = dex(P) \|_A \cup {}_A\| dex(Q)$ where $A = \alpha(P) \cap \alpha(Q)$,

(5) $dex(P + Q) = dex(P) + \text{dex}(Q)$ ,

(6)  $dex(P[\varphi]) = dex(P)[\varphi]$ ,

(7)  $dex(\mu X.P) = dex(P \{ \mu X.P/X \} )$.

A set $\mathbb{P}$ of sequential components is called *complete* if there exists a closed process term $Q$ with $\mathbb{P}=dex(Q)$.                                                  □

In equation (7) the expanded term $P\{\mu X.P/X\}$ can be larger than $\mu X.P$ on the left-hand side. Thus well-definedness of $dex$ is not immediately obvious. We define the complexity $\gamma(P)$ of closed process terms $P$ by the following clauses:

$$\gamma(stop{:}A) = \ \ \gamma(div{:}A) \ = \gamma(a.P) = 0, \tag{3.1}$$
$$\gamma(P + Q) = \ \ \gamma(P\|Q) \ = 1 + max\{\gamma(P), \gamma(Q)\}, \tag{3.2}$$
$$\gamma(P[\varphi]) = \ \ \gamma(\mu X.P) \ = 1 + \gamma(P). \tag{3.3}$$

By action-guardedness of process terms, the following holds for the terms in equation (7) of Definition 3.3.1:

$$\gamma(\mu X.P) > \gamma(P) = \gamma(P\{\mu X.P/X\}).$$

We can now state:

**Proposition 3.3.2**

(1) The mapping $dex$ is well-defined.

(2) $dex$ is not injective.

(3) $dex(P) = dex(Q)$ implies $\alpha(P) = \alpha(Q)$.

*Proof.* Fact (1): By induction on the complexity of closed process terms.
Fact (2): For example, $dex(\mu X.aX) = \{a.\mu X.a.X\} = dex(a.\mu X.a.X)$.
Fact (3): Apply Remark 3.1.4.                                                  □

By part (3) of this proposition, we can define the alphabet of a complete set $\mathbb{P}$ of sequential components as follows :

$$\alpha(\mathbb{P}) = \alpha(Q) \text{ if } \mathbb{P} = dex(Q).$$

We extend the definition of complexity to sequential components by adding the following clauses:

$$\gamma(C\|_A) = \gamma(_A\|C) = \gamma(C[\varphi]) = 1 + \gamma(C), \tag{3.4}$$
$$\gamma(C + D) = 1 + max\{\gamma(C), \gamma(D)\}. \tag{3.5}$$

For finite sets $\mathbb{P}$ of sequential components we put

$$\gamma(\mathbb{P}) = \sum_{C \in \mathbb{P}} \gamma(C) \tag{3.6}$$

Now we can show:

**Proposition 3.3.3** For a given finite set $\mathbb{P}$ of sequential components the completeness of $\mathbb{P}$ is decidable and the alphabet $\alpha(\mathbb{P})$ is computable.

*Proof.* We proceed by induction on $n = \gamma(\mathbb{P})$.

$n = 0$: $\mathbb{P}$ is complete iff $\mathbb{P} = \{stop{:}A\}$ or $\mathbb{P} = \{div{:}A\}$ or $\mathbb{P} = \{a.P\}$ for some alphabet $A$, communication $a$ and closed process term $P$. Clearly, we have $\alpha(\mathbb{P}) = A$ in the first two cases of $\mathbb{P}$ and $\alpha(\mathbb{P}) = \{a\} \cup \alpha(P)$ if $\mathbb{P} = \{a.P\}$.

$n \longrightarrow n{+}1$: There exists some sequential component in $\mathbb{P}$ with top-level operator $\|_A$, $_A\|$, $+$ or $[\varphi]$. Suppose it is $\|_A$. Then $\mathbb{P}$ is complete iff all components in $\mathbb{P}$ have $\|_A$ or $_A\|$ as their top-level operator and the sets

$$\mathbb{L} = \{C \in Sequ \mid C\|_A \in \mathbb{P}\}$$

and

$$\mathbb{R} = \{D \in Sequ \mid {}_A\|D \in \mathbb{P}\}$$

of left-hand and right-hand side operands are complete and $A = \alpha(\mathbb{L}) \cap \alpha(\mathbb{R})$. By (3.4) and (3.6), we have $\gamma(\mathbb{L}) < \gamma(\mathbb{P})$ and $\gamma(\mathbb{R}) < \gamma(\mathbb{P})$. Thus by the induction hypothesis, completeness of $\mathbb{L}$ and $\mathbb{R}$ is decidable and the alphabets $\alpha(\mathbb{P})$ and $\alpha(\mathbb{R})$ are computable. If $\mathbb{P}$ is complete, we calculate $\alpha(\mathbb{P}) = \alpha(\mathbb{L}) \cup \alpha(\mathbb{R})$.

Similar arguments work for the operators $_A\|$, $+$ and $[\varphi]$. $\qquad\square$

Next we define a transition relation

$$\longrightarrow \subseteq \mathcal{P}_{nf}(Sequ) \times Act \times \mathcal{P}_{nf}(Sequ)$$

by induction on the syntactic structure of sequential components, using a deductive system. Thus transitions are now of the form

$$\mathbb{P} \overset{u}{\longrightarrow} \mathbb{Q}$$

with $\mathbb{P}, \mathbb{Q} \in \mathcal{P}_{nf}(Sequ)$ and $u \in Act$. The deductive system consists of *transition rules* of the form

$$\frac{T_1, \ldots, T_m}{T_{m+1}, \ldots, T_{m+n}} \text{ where } \ldots \tag{3.7}$$

with $T_1, \ldots, T_{m+n}$ denoting transitions ($m \geq 0$, $n \geq 1$). Rule (3.7) states that if $T_1, \ldots, T_m$ are transitions satisfying the condition "..." then also $T_{m+1}, \ldots, T_{m+n}$ are transitions. If $m{=}0$ and $n{=}1$, (3.7) is called an *axiom* and written as

$$T_1 \text{ where } \ldots$$

For the rules (3.7) to be effectively applicable, we require that the condition "..." is decidable.

**Definition 3.3.4** The *Petri net transition relation* $\longrightarrow$ consists of all transitions that are deducible by the following transition axioms and rules:
(Prefix)

$$\{a.P\} \overset{a}{\longrightarrow} dex(P)$$

(Divergence)

$$\{div{:}A\} \xrightarrow{\quad\tau\quad} \{div{:}A\}$$

(Parallel Composition)
   Asynchrony:

$$\frac{\mathbb{P} \xrightarrow{\quad u\quad} \mathbb{P}'}{\mathbb{P}\|_A \xrightarrow{\quad u\quad} \mathbb{P}'\|_A \ , \quad {}_A\|\mathbb{P} \xrightarrow{\quad u\quad} {}_A\|\mathbb{P}'} \quad \text{where } u \notin A$$

   Synchrony:

$$\frac{\mathbb{P} \xrightarrow{\quad a\quad} \mathbb{P}', \quad \mathbb{Q} \xrightarrow{\quad a\quad} \mathbb{Q}'}{\mathbb{P}\|_A \cup {}_A\|\mathbb{Q} \xrightarrow{\quad a\quad} \mathbb{P}'\|_A \cup {}_A\|\mathbb{Q}'} \quad \text{where } a \in A$$

(Choice)

$$\frac{\mathbb{P}_1 \cup \mathbb{P}_2 \xrightarrow{\quad u\quad} \mathbb{P}'}{\mathbb{P}_1 \cup (\mathbb{P}_2 + \mathbb{Q}) \xrightarrow{\quad u\quad} \mathbb{P}', \quad \mathbb{P}_1 \cup (\mathbb{Q} + \mathbb{P}_2) \xrightarrow{\quad u\quad} \mathbb{P}'} \quad \begin{array}{l} \text{where } \mathbb{P}_1 \cap \mathbb{P}_2 = \emptyset \\ \text{and } \mathbb{Q} \text{ is complete} \end{array}$$

(Morphism)

$$\frac{\mathbb{P} \xrightarrow{\quad u\quad} \mathbb{Q}}{\mathbb{P}[\varphi] \xrightarrow{\quad\varphi(u)\quad} \mathbb{Q}[\varphi]}$$

□

   Note that there are no transition rules for deadlock and recursion. For processes of the form *stop:A* this is as it should be. The transitions of recursive processes $\mu X.P$ are taken care of indirectly by the decomposition mapping *dex*, which by the clause

$$dex(\mu X.P) \; = \; dex(P\{\mu X.P/X\})$$

expands a recursive process term until each $\mu$ is guarded by an action occuring in a prefix operator.

   The essential new idea is embodied in the transition rule for choice. Firstly, only a part of the sequential components, viz. $\mathbb{P}_2$, need have an alternative $\mathbb{Q}$. Secondly $\mathbb{Q}$ needs to be complete. This condition is decidable and hence the rule is effectively applicable. Completeness ensures that no sequential component in $\mathbb{Q}$ has been active previously. There is no analogue to these conditions in the case of operational interleaving semantics for choice (cf. Definition 3.7.1) .

   For a given process term $P$ the transition relation of its net $\mathcal{N}[\![P]\!]$ is obtained by restricting the general relation $\longrightarrow$ of Definition 3.3.4 to the alphabet of $P$ and (via net isomorphism) to the places that are statically reachable from the decomposition of $P$ into its sequential components. Formally, this is expressed in the following definition.

**Definition 3.3.5** The operational Petri net semantics for process terms is a mapping

$$\mathcal{N}[\![\cdot]\!] : CProc \longrightarrow ANet$$

which assigns to every $P \in CProc$ the abstract net

$$\mathcal{N}[\![P]\!] = [(\alpha(P), Sequ, \longrightarrow \downarrow \alpha(P), dex(P))].$$

Here $\longrightarrow$ is the transition relation of Definition 3.3.4 and

$$\longrightarrow \downarrow \alpha(P) = \{\mathbb{P} \xrightarrow{u} \mathbb{Q} \mid u \in \alpha(P) \cup \{\tau\}\}$$

its restriction to the communications in $\alpha(P)$. □

To construct a particular abstract net $\mathcal{N}[\![P]\!]$ we start from $dex(P)$ as the initial marking and explore all transitions that are successively applicable. In this way, we will automatically restrict ourselves to communications in $\alpha(P)$ and the statically reachable places. Abstraction is introduced by finally removing all the names of places, here the sequential components.

**Example 3.3.6** In the following examples, however, these names are kept as an explanation of how the net was obtained.

(1) *stop*:{a}

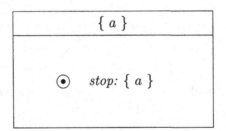

Since there is no transition with *stop*:{a} in its preset, we obtain the trivial net consisting of a single place.

(2) *div*:{a}

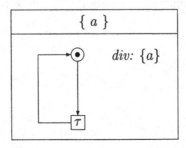

Divergence yields a simple $\tau$-loop.

(3)  $a.stop{:}\{a\} \parallel b.stop{:}\{b\}$

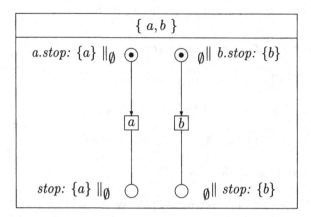

Since the synchronisation set is empty, the communications $a$ and $b$ can happen concurrently by the asynchrony clause in the rule of parallel composition.

(4)  $a.b.stop{:}\{a,b\} + b.a.stop{:}\{a,b\}$

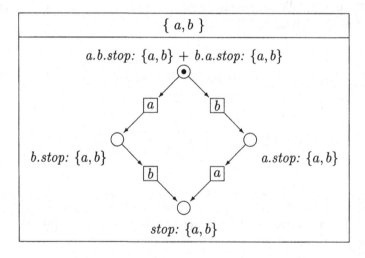

This is the result of "interleaving" two communications $a$ and $b$. Obviously, it is different from the concurrent execution of $a$ and $b$ represented above.

(5) $(a.stop{:}\{a,c\} \parallel b.stop{:}\{b,c\}) + c.stop{:}\{a,b,c\}$

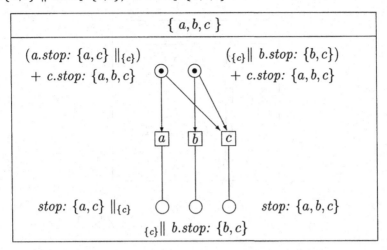

Here the preset of the transition labelled with $c$ is $\mathbb{Q} + c.stop{:}\{a,b,c\}$ where

$$\mathbb{Q} = \{a.stop{:}\{a,c\}\|_{\{c\}}, \,_{\{c\}}\|b.stop{:}\{b,c\}\}$$

is a complete set of sequential components. Note that by adding a choice of $c$ the concurrency of $a$ and $b$ is preserved.

(6) $\mu X.(a.stop{:}\{a\} \parallel b.stop{:}\{b\})$

Since there is no recursive call of $X$ in this process term, we obtain the same net as in (3) with exactly the same names of places.

(7) $a.b.c.stop{:}\{a,b,c\} \parallel d.b.e.stop{:}\{d,b,e\}$

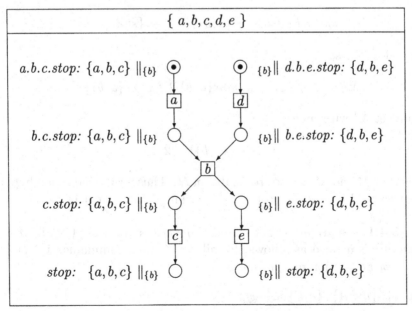

Synchronisation on $b$ results in a joint transition labelled with $b$.

(8) $\mu X.a.b.X$ with $\alpha(X) = \{a,b\}$

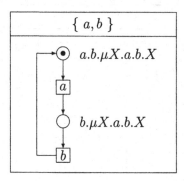

□

## 3.4   Safeness

As a first property and an example of the analysis of our operational semantics $\mathcal{N}[\![\cdot]\!]$, we wish to show that for every term $P \in CProc$ the abstract net $\mathcal{N}[\![P]\!]$ is safe. Our aim is an inductive proof showing that every reachable marking $M$ of the underlying concrete net

$$\mathcal{N} = (\alpha(P), Sequ, \longrightarrow \downarrow \alpha(P), dex(P))$$

is a set rather than a multiset. Clearly, $dex(P)$ is a set, but the property of being a set is not kept invariant under the execution of transitions.

For example, the transition

$$\{a.stop{:}\{a,b\} + b.stop{:}\{a,b\}\} \xrightarrow{\;\;a\;\;} \{stop{:}\{a,b\}$$

when executed at the set

$$M = \{stop{:}\{a,b\}, a.stop{:}\{a,b\} + b.stop{:}\{a,b\}\}$$

yields a multiset $M'$ with multiplicity

$$M'(stop{:}\{a,b\}) = 2$$

The point is that $M$ and $M'$ are not reachable in $\mathcal{N}$. Thus for the induction hypothesis of our proof we need a stronger property of markings than just being a set.

**Definition 3.4.1** A marking $M$ is called *well-formed*, abbreviated *wf*, if $M$ is a set and its structure is defined as follows: for all $a \in Comm$, communication alphabets $A,P,Q \in CProc$ and action morphisms $\varphi$

(1) $\{stop{:}A\}$, $\{div{:}A\}$, $\{a.P\}$ are *wf*,

(2) if $M_1$ and $M_2$ are *wf* then so is $M_1 \,\|_A\cup{}_A\| M_2$,

(3) if $M_1 \cup M_2$ is *wf* with $M_1 \cap M_2 = \emptyset$ then so are

$$M_1 \cup (M_2 + dex(Q)) \text{ and } M_1 \cup (dex(Q) + M_2),$$

(4) if $M$ is *wf* then so is $M[\varphi]$.                                          □

We first establish two lemmas about well-formedness.

**Lemma 3.4.2** Every complete set of sequential components is well-formed.

*Proof.* Complete sets $M$ satisfy the inductive structure of well-formedness, with additionally $M_1 = \emptyset$ in clause (3).                                □

**Lemma 3.4.3** For every transition $t$ and every well-formed marking $M$ with $pre(t) \subseteq M$ the marking

$$M' = (M - pre(t)) \sqcup post(t)$$

is also well-formed. Thus the property of well-formedness is kept invariant under the execution of transitions.

*Proof.* We use induction on the structure of $t$ as given by the Petri net transition rules of Definition 3.3.4.
*Induction Basis.*

(1) $t = \{a.P\} \xrightarrow{a} dex(P)$:
   Note that $pre(t) \subseteq M$ implies $M = \{a.P\}$. Thus $M' = dex(P)$ which is *wf* by Lemma 3.4.2.

(2) $t = \{div{:}A\} \xrightarrow{\tau} \{div{:}A\}$:
   This is trivial because $M = M'$.

*Induction step.*

(3.a) $t = \mathbb{P} \parallel_A \xrightarrow{u} \mathbb{P}' \parallel_A$:
   From $pre(t) \subseteq M$ we conclude that there exist two *wf* markings $\mathbb{P} \cup M_1$ and $M_2$ with $\mathbb{P} \cap M_1 = \emptyset$ and

$$M = \mathbb{P}\parallel_A \cup (\ldots + (M_1\parallel_A \cup {}_A\parallel M_2) + \ldots).$$

Here the notation $(\ldots + (M_1 \parallel_A \cup {}_A\parallel M_2) + \ldots)$ indicates that in addition to $M_1 \parallel_A \cup {}_A\parallel M_2$ there can be any number of applications of the choice operator according to clause (3) in the definition of well-formedness. By the transition rules,

$$t' = \mathbb{P} \xrightarrow{u} \mathbb{P}'$$

is also a transition. Applying the induction hypothesis to $t'$ and $\mathbb{P} \cup M_1$ yields:

$$((\mathbb{P} \cup M_1) - \mathbb{P}) \sqcup \mathbb{P}' = \mathbb{P}' \cup M$$

is *wf*. Since

$$M' = \mathbb{P}'\parallel_A \cup (\ldots + (M_1\parallel_A \cup {}_A\parallel M_2) + \ldots),$$

$M'$ is also *wf*.

(3.b) $t = {}_A\|\mathbb{P} \xrightarrow{\ u\ } {}_A\|\mathbb{P}'$:
   The situation is symmetric to (3.a).

(3.c) $t = \mathbb{P} \|_A\cup \|_A\mathbb{Q} \xrightarrow{\ a\ } \mathbb{P}' \|_A\cup \|_A\mathbb{Q}'$:
   We combine (3.a) and (3.b).

(4.a) $t = \mathbb{P}_1 \cup (\mathbb{P}_2 + dex(Q)) \xrightarrow{\ u\ } \mathbb{P}'$ with $\mathbb{P}_1 \cap \mathbb{P}_2 = \emptyset$ and $\mathbb{P}_2 \neq \emptyset$:
   By $pre(t) \subseteq M$, there exists a *wf* marking $M_1 \cup M_2$ with $M_1 \cap M_2 = \emptyset$,

$$M = M_1 \cup (M_2 + dex(Q)) \text{ and } \mathbb{P}_1 \subseteq M_1, \mathbb{P}_2 \subseteq M_2.$$

W.l.o.g. we can assume $\mathbb{P}_2 = M_2$. By the transition rules,

$$t' = \mathbb{P}_1 \cup \mathbb{P}_2 \xrightarrow{\ u\ } \mathbb{P}'$$

is also a transition. Applying the induction hypothesis to $t'$ and $M_1 \cup M_2$ yields:

$$M_1' = ((M_1 \cup M_2) - (\mathbb{P}_1 \cup \mathbb{P}_2)) \sqcup \mathbb{P}'$$

is *wf*. Exploiting $\mathbb{P}_2 = M_2$ we obtain

$$
\begin{aligned}
M' &= (M_1 \cup (M_2 + dex(Q))) - (\mathbb{P}_1 \cup (\mathbb{P}_2 + dex(Q))) \sqcup \mathbb{P}' \\
&= (M_1 - \mathbb{P}_1) \sqcup \mathbb{P}' = M_1'.
\end{aligned}
$$

Thus $M'$ is *wf*.

(4.b) $t = \mathbb{P}_1 \cup (dex(Q) + \mathbb{P}_2) \xrightarrow{\ u\ } \mathbb{P}'$ with $\mathbb{P}_1 \cap \mathbb{P}_2 = \emptyset$ and $\mathbb{P}_2 \neq \emptyset$:
   This is symmetric to (4.a).

(5) $t = \mathbb{P}[\varphi] \xrightarrow{\ \varphi(u)\ } \mathbb{Q}[\varphi]$:
   This is straighforward and similar to (3.a).                                       $\square$

Now we can prove the desired result.

**Safeness Theorem 3.4.4** For every closed process term $P$ the abstract net $\mathcal{N}[\![P]\!]$ is safe.

*Proof.* It suffices to show that the net

$$\mathcal{N} = (\alpha(P)), Sequ, \longrightarrow \downarrow \alpha P, dex(P))$$

is safe, i.e. all $M \in mark(\mathcal{N})$ are sets. We show more, viz. all $M \in mark(\mathcal{N})$ are *well-formed* sets. The proof is by induction on the number of singleton transition steps needed to reach $M$: Lemma 3.4.2 establishes the induction basis ($M = dex(P)$) and Lemma 3.4.3 the induction step.                                       $\square$

## 3.5 Finiteness and Algebraic Properties

Clearly, a net $\mathcal{N}=(A, Pl, \longrightarrow, M_0)$ is called finite if its set $Pl$ of places is finite. For abstract nets $[\mathcal{N}]$, however, we will look only at the set of statically reachable places because its cardinality is kept invariant under weak isomorphisms.

**Definition 3.5.1** An abstract Petri net $[\mathcal{N}]$ is called *finite* if $place(\mathcal{N})$ is a finite set.
□

So far we have seen only process terms denoting finite abstract nets. However, recursion in combination with parallel composition and/or morphism may easily yield infinite ones.

**Example 3.5.2** Consider the process term

$$P_\infty = \mu X.up.(X[lk/dn]\|\mu Y.dn.lk.Y) \setminus lk$$

where $\alpha(X)= \{up,dn\}$ and $\alpha(Y)= \{dn,lk\}$. Recall from Section 3.1 that $[lk/dn]$ and $\setminus lk$ are renaming and hiding morphisms. $P_\infty$ denotes the following infinite abstract net:

$\mathcal{N}[P_\infty] =$

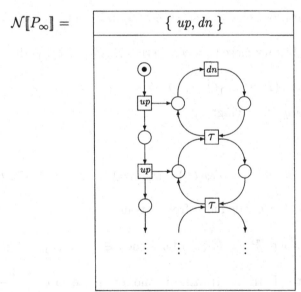

$\mathcal{N}[P]$ models an *unbounded counter* which can store an arbitrary natural number. This number can be manipulated by a user of the counter with the help of two communications *up* and *dn*. The communication *up* is always possible; its effect is to increment the number stored. The communication *dn* is possible only if the number stored is not zero; then its effect is to decrement this number. Note that after the $n$-th communication *up* the net will engage in $n-1$ internal actions $\tau$ before being ready for the corresponding $n$-th communication *dn*.
□

Our operational net semantics yields finite nets if we restrict the occurence of identifiers in recursions. Following the terminology used in the theory of formal languages and trees, we shall talk of regular process terms (cf. also [Mil84, Par85, Tau87]). Recall that *free*(P) denotes the set of free identifiers in a process term P.

**Definition 3.5.3** A *regular* process term is a term $P \in Proc$ which additionally satisfies the following context-sensitive restrictions:

(1) every subterm $Q \parallel R$ of P satisfies *free*(Q)=*free*(R)=$\emptyset$,

(2) every subterm $Q[\varphi]$ of P satisfies *free*(Q)=$\emptyset$.

Let *RegProc* denote the set of all regular process terms.                                   □

Note that by the definition of *Proc*, every term $P \in RegProc$ is action-guarded, but not necessarily closed. We wish to show that for every closed regular process term P the abstract net $\mathcal{N}[\![P]\!]$ is finite. In other words, we wish to show that for the underlying concrete net

$$\mathcal{N} = (\alpha(P), Sequ, \longrightarrow \downarrow \alpha(P), dex(P))$$

the set *place*($\mathcal{N}$) is finite. The proof employs an elaborate induction on non-closed regular terms.

First some notation: for arbitrary closed process terms $P, Q_1, \ldots, Q_r$ with $r \geq 0$ let

$$place(P) \; mod \; \{Q_1, \ldots, Q_r\}$$

denote the smallest set $M \subseteq Sequ$ satisfying:

(1) $dex(P) \subseteq M$,

(2) if $\mathbb{P} \overset{u}{\longrightarrow} \mathbb{Q}$ with $\mathbb{P} \subseteq M$ and $\mathbb{Q} \neq dex(Q_i)$ for all $i=1,\ldots,r$ then $\mathbb{Q} \subseteq M$,

(3) if $\mathbb{P} \overset{u}{\longrightarrow} \mathbb{Q}$ with $\mathbb{P} \subseteq M$ is *not* deduced from a transition

$$\mathbb{P}_0 \overset{u}{\longrightarrow} \mathbb{Q}, \text{ where } \mathbb{P}_0 \subseteq dex(Q_i) \text{ for some } i \in \{1, \ldots, r\},$$

by applying exclusively the Petri net transition rule for choice to $\mathbb{P}_0 \overset{u}{\longrightarrow} \mathbb{Q}$ so that $\mathbb{P}$ contains at least one symbol + in addition to $\mathbb{P}_0$, then $\mathbb{Q} \subseteq M$.

For $r=0$ we write *place*(P) instead of *place*(P) *mod* $\emptyset$. Note that

$$place(P) = place(\mathcal{N})$$

for $\mathcal{N} = (\alpha(P), Sequ, \longrightarrow \downarrow \alpha(P), dex(P))$ as above.

As an example consider

$$P = a.(b.\mu X.b.a.b.X + \mu X.b.a.b.X)$$

and

$$Q_1 = \mu X.b.a.b.X$$

where $\alpha(X) = \{a,b\}$. Then

$$place(P) \bmod \{Q_1\} = \{a.(b.Q_1 + Q_1), b.Q_1 + b.a.b.Q_1\}$$

Looking at the second component

$$b.Q_1 + b.a.b.Q_1$$

we see that every further Petri net transition would rewrite either $b.Q_1$ or $b.a.b.Q_1$ thus violating either condition (2) or (3) above.

Now we can state a lemma from which the desired finiteness result will follow immediately.

**Lemma 3.5.4** For every regular process term $P$ with precisely the free identifiers $X_1,\ldots,X_r$, $r \geq 0$, and all closed process terms $Q_1,\ldots,Q_r$ the set

$$place(P\{Q_1,\ldots,Q_r/X_1,\ldots,X_r\}) \bmod \{Q_1,\ldots,Q_r\}$$

is finite.

*Proof.* We proceed by induction on the structure of $P$. We abbreviate $P\{Q_1,\ldots,Q_r/X_1,\ldots,X_r\}$ by $\overline{P}$ and $\{Q_1,\ldots,Q_r\}$ by $\{\ldots\}$.

*Induction Basis.*

(1) $P = stop{:}A$: $place(stop{:}A) = \{stop{:}A\}$.

(2) $P = div{:}A$: $place(div{:}A) = \{div{:}A\}$.

(3) $P = a.X_1$: $place(a.Q_1) \bmod \{Q_1\} = \{a.Q_1\}$.

The case $P = X_1$ does not arise because every $P \in RegProc$ is action-guarded.

*Induction Step.*

(4) $P = a.Q$ with $Q \in RegProc$: Then $Q$ is action-guarded and the identifiers $X_1,\ldots,X_r$ appear in $Q$. Moreover,

$$place(a.\overline{Q}) \bmod \{\ldots\} \subseteq \{a.Q\} \cup place(Q) \bmod \{\ldots\}$$

which is finite by the induction hypothesis.

(5) $P = Q + R$: Then $Q,R \in RegProc$ and the identifiers $X_1,\ldots,X_r$ appear in $Q$ and $R$. We have

$$\begin{aligned}place(\overline{Q+R}) \bmod \{\ldots\} \ \subseteq \ & (dex(\overline{Q}) + dex(\overline{R})) \\ \cup \ & place(\overline{Q}) \bmod \{\ldots\} \cup place(\overline{R}) \bmod \{\ldots\}\end{aligned}$$

which is finite by the induction hypothesis. Note that $\subseteq$ holds because by the Petri net transition rule for choice, every transition in the context of a "+" throws away that "+".

(6) $P = Q \parallel R$: Then $r=0$ by the definition of *RegProc* and for $A = \alpha(Q) \cap \alpha(P)$

$$place(Q\|R) \subseteq place(Q)\|_A \cup {}_A\|place(R)$$

which is finite by induction hypothesis. Note that we cannot deal with $r > 1$ because in contrast to choice, every transition in the context of a "$\|_A$" or "${}_A\|$" keeps that symbol. Thus in general

$$place(\overline{Q\|R}) \bmod \{\ldots\}$$
$$\not\subseteq place(\overline{Q}) \bmod \{\ldots\}\|_A \cup {}_A\|place(\overline{R}) \bmod \{\ldots\}.$$

(7) $P = Q[\varphi]$: The proof is similar to (6).

(8) $P = \mu X.Q$: Then the identifiers $X_1,\ldots,X_r$ appear in $Q$. By the induction hypothesis,

$$M_0 = place(\overline{Q}\{\mu X.\overline{Q}/X\}) \bmod (\{\ldots\} \cup \{\mu X.\overline{Q}\})$$

is finite. Now consider

$$M_1 = place(\mu X.\overline{Q}) \bmod \{\ldots\}.$$

Clearly, $M_0 \subseteq M_1$. The difference between $M_0$ and $M_1$ is that in $M_1$ transitions

$$t = \mathbb{P}\overset{u}{\longrightarrow}\mathbb{Q}$$

with $\mathbb{P} \subseteq M_0$ could contribute new sets $\mathbb{Q} \subseteq M_1$. Then either

(i) $\mathbb{Q} = dex(\mu X.\overline{Q})$ or

(ii) $t$ is deduced from a transition

$$t_0 = \mathbb{P}_0\overset{u}{\longrightarrow}\mathbb{Q} \text{ where } \mathbb{P}_0 \subseteq dex(\mu X.\overline{Q})$$

by applying exclusively the Petri net transition rule for choice to $t_0$ so that $\mathbb{P}$ contains at least one symbol $+$ in addition to $\mathbb{P}_0$.

In case (i) the set $\mathbb{Q}$ is already in $M_0$ by clause (1) of the definition of place $\ldots$ *mod* $\ldots$, and in case (ii) the set $\mathbb{Q}$ can also be generated directly from $dex(\mu X.Q)$ and hence is already contained in $M_0$ because $t$ is possible only if $\mathbb{Q} \neq dex(Q_i)$ for all $i=1,\ldots,r$. Thus $M_1 = M_0$ so that $M_1$ is indeed finite.   □

We are now prepared for the desired result.

**Finiteness Theorem 3.5.5** For every closed regular process term $P$ the abstract net $\mathcal{N}[\![P]\!]$ is finite.

*Proof.* It suffices to show that for the net

$$\mathcal{N} = (\alpha(P), Sequ, \longrightarrow \downarrow \alpha(P), dex(P))$$

the set $place(\mathcal{N})$ is finite. Since $place(\mathcal{N}) = place(P)$, this is the statement of Lemma 3.5.4 when $r=0$.   □

Yielding finite nets is an important property of a workable net semantics. It is well-known that it is impossible to find a semantics which represents every process term by a finite place/transition net. This is because process terms, say, as described in the present operational net semantics, are Turing powerful whereas finite nets are not.

**Remark 3.5.6** The easiest way to show that process terms are Turing powerful is to simulate the moves of *2-counter machines* [Min67]. The simulating process terms have the structure

$$COUNT_1 \parallel COUNT_2 \parallel PROGRAM.$$

$COUNT_1$ and $COUNT_2$ are two copies of an unbounded counter similar to $P_\infty$ in Example 3.5.2, but with an additional communication *zero* which can test whether the stored number is zero. $PROGRAM$ is a process term representing the machine program of the given 2-counter machine; it consists of communications *up*, *down* and *zero* with the two counters $COUNT_1$ and $COUNT_2$.

A consequence of this simulation is that for the place/transition nets denoted by process terms the reachability problem (asking whether a given marking is reachable) is undecidable. On the other hand, *finite* place/transition nets have a decidable reachability problem [May84] and hence cannot be Turing powerful. □

Obviously, one can ask: are there net semantics which yield finite place/transition nets for larger classes of process terms than regular ones ?

Let us first look at restriction (2) in the Definition 3.5.3 of regularity. It is, for example, violated by the process term

$$P = \mu X.a.X[\varphi]$$

where $\alpha(X) = \{a,b\}$ and where the renaming operator $\varphi$ permutes $a$ and $b$ and is the identity otherwise. $P$ yields the infinite abstract net $\mathcal{N}[\![P]\!]$ displayed on the next page.

$\mathcal{N}[\![P]\!] =$

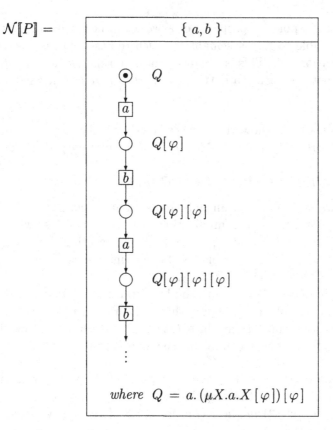

$$\{\,a,b\,\}$$

$Q$

$a$

$Q[\varphi]$

$b$

$Q[\varphi][\varphi]$

$a$

$Q[\varphi][\varphi][\varphi]$

$b$

$\vdots$

*where*  $Q = a.\,(\mu X.a.X\,[\,\varphi\,])\,[\,\varphi\,]$

Infinity arises because in our operational construction the operator symbols $[\varphi]$ are piling up. In this example, however, by evaluating the renaming operator one could observe the identity

$$Q[\varphi][\varphi] = Q$$

and thus obtain the finite abstract net

$$\mathcal{N}_{fin}[\![P]\!] =$$

$$\{\,a,b\,\}$$

$Q$

$Q[\varphi]$

which is strongly bisimilar to $\mathcal{N}[\![P]\!]$. Taubner uses the idea of evaluating renaming operators to define a compositional Petri net semantics that yields finite safe nets for all process terms $P$ satisfying restriction (1) in the Definition 3.5.3 of regularity [Tau89].

We conjecture that one can also define an operational Petri net semantics to that effect.

**Conjecture 3.5.7** One can define a variant $\mathcal{N}_{fin}[\![\cdot]\!]$ of the operational Petri net semantics $\mathcal{N}[\![\cdot]\!]$ such that for all closed process terms $P$:

(1) $\mathcal{N}_{fin}[\![P]\!]$ is safe and strongly bisimilar to $\mathcal{N}[\![P]\!]$ , and

(2) $\mathcal{N}_{fin}[\![P]\!]$ is finite provided $P$ satisfies the context-sensitive restriction (1) in the Definition 3.5.3 of regularity. □

What about dropping restriction (1)? U. Goltz has shown that by giving up safeness one can represent a class of CCS terms allowing any combination of recursion with the parallel composition of CCS by finite place/transition nets [Gol88a, Gol88b]. Unfortunately, the construction critically depends on the total absence of action morphisms (thus trivially satisfying restriction (2)) and does not extend to COSY's parallel composition used in our approach.

We now turn to another aspect of process terms. Following Milner's pioneering work in [Mil80], the representation of processes by terms over a signature of operator symbols allows us to reason algebraically about processes. Algebraic reasoning means: in order to show that different terms $P$ and $Q$ denote the same process behaviour one transforms $P$ into $Q$ by applying the algebraic laws satisfied by the operator symbols. In our present setting, these laws are determined by the Petri net semantics $\mathcal{N}[\![\cdot]\!]$ of process terms. For example, we shall see that parallel composition is commutative and associative. Note that associativity was already anticipated in Section 3.2 when we were writing

$$MUTEX \ = \ CYCLE_1 \parallel SEM \parallel CYCLE_2$$

without using brackets. Since by intention the Petri net semantics is very discriminating, rather few algebraic laws will hold in this semantics.

Often the algebraic approach to processes starts the other way round: first the desirable algebraic laws of the operators are stated and then a semantic model is sought in which these laws are valid [BBK87, BW90b]. Algebraic laws obtain a particular relevance if they completely axiomatise the equality of process terms in a given semantic model (see e.g. [DH84, Mil84]). Since process terms are Turing powerful (cf. Remark 3.5.6), finite axiomatisations are possible only for subclasses, e.g. the class of closed regular process terms (see [Mil84]).

We shall not pursue the algebraic approach any further and restrict ourselves with stating the most basic algebraic properties of process terms when interpreted on Petri nets.

**Theorem 3.5.8** For all closed process terms $P,P_1,P_2,P_3$ the following laws hold:

(1) $\mathcal{N}[\![\mu X.P]\!] = \mathcal{N}[\![P\{\mu X.P/X\}]\!]$

(2) $\mathcal{N}[\![P_1 \parallel P_2]\!] = \mathcal{N}[\![P_2 \parallel P_1]\!]$

(3) $\mathcal{N}[\![P_1 \parallel (P_2 \parallel P_3)]\!] = \mathcal{N}[\![(P_1 \parallel P_2) \parallel P_3]\!]$

(4) $\mathcal{N}[\![P_1 + P_2]\!] = \mathcal{N}[\![P_2 + P_1]\!]$

(5) $\mathcal{N}[\![P_1 + (P_2 + P_3)]\!] = \mathcal{N}[\![(P_1 + P_1) + P_3]\!]$

*Proof.* We verify the laws (1),(3) and (5).

Fact (1): This law follows immediately from the definition of $\mathcal{N}[\![\cdot]\!]$.

Fact (3): Let $A_i = \alpha(P_i)$, for $i$=1,2,3, and $A = A_1 \cup A_2 \cup A_3$ and

$$\mathcal{N}_l = (A, Sequ, \longrightarrow \downarrow A, dex(P_1\|(P_2\|P_3))),$$

$$\mathcal{N}_r = (A, Sequ, \longrightarrow \downarrow A, dex((P_1\|P_2)\|P_3)).$$

To show (3), we have to find a weak isomorphism

$$\beta : place(\mathcal{N}_l) \longrightarrow place(\mathcal{N}_r)$$

between $\mathcal{N}_l$ and $\mathcal{N}_r$. Since

$$dex((P_1\|P_2)\|P_3)$$

$$= (dex(P_1)\|_{A_1\cap A_2} \cup {}_{A_1\cap A_2}\| dex(P_2))\|_{(A_1\cup A_2)\cap A_3} \cup {}_{(A_1\cup A_2)\cap A_3}\| dex(P_3),$$

and

$$dex(P_1\|(P_2\|P_3))$$

$$= dex(P_1)\|_{A_1\cap(A_2\cup A_3)} \cup {}_{A_1\cap(A_2\cup A_3)}\|(dex(P_2))\|_{A_2\cap A_3} \cup {}_{A_2\cap A_3}\| dex(P_3)),$$

there is a partition $place(\mathcal{N}_r) = Pl_{r.1} \cup Pl_{r.2} \cup Pl_{r.3}$, where $Pl_{r.1}, Pl_{r.2}, Pl_{r.3}$ consist of components of the form

$(r.1)$  $(C\|_{A_1\cap A_2})\|_{(A_1\cup A_2)\cap A_3}$

$(r.2)$  $({}_{A_1\cap A_2}\|C)\|_{(A_1\cup A_2)\cap A_3}$

$(r.3)$  ${}_{(A_1\cup A_2)\cap A_3}\|C,$

and a partition $place(\mathcal{N}_l) = Pl_{l.1} \cup Pl_{l.2} \cup Pl_{l.3}$, where $Pl_{l.1}, Pl_{l.2}, Pl_{l.3}$ consist of components of the form

$(l.1)$  $C\|_{A_1\cap(A_2\cup A_3)}$

$(l.2)$  ${}_{A_1\cap(A_2\cup A_3)}\|(C\|_{A_2\cap A_3})$

$(l.3)$  ${}_{A_1\cap(A_2\cup A_3)}\|({}_{A_2\cap A_3}\|C).$

We take as mapping $\beta$ the one which maps every component of the form $(l.i)$ into the one of the form $(r.i)$, for $i = 1,2,3$. Clearly, $\beta$ is a bijection.

To see the isomorphism property we consider

$$\mathcal{N}_i = (A_i, Sequ, \longrightarrow \downarrow A_i, dex(P_i)),$$

and define projection mappings

$$\pi_{l.i} : Pl_{l.i} \longrightarrow place(\mathcal{N}_i),$$

$$\pi_{r.i} : Pl_{r.i} \longrightarrow place(\mathcal{N}_i)$$

from $\mathcal{N}_l$ and $\mathcal{N}_r$ into $\mathcal{N}_i$ which for every component of the form $(l.i)$ or $(r.i)$ yield the subcomponent $C$ as result, for $i=1,2,3$. Then by the Petri net transition rules for parallel composition,

$$\mathbb{P} \xrightarrow{u} \mathbb{Q} \text{ with } \mathbb{P} \subseteq place(\mathcal{N}_l)$$

iff     for $i=1,2,3$   if   $u \in A_i$ then $\pi_{l.i}(\mathbb{P} \cap Pl_{l.i}) \xrightarrow{u} \pi_{r.i}(\mathbb{P} \cap Pl_{l.i})$

iff     for $i=1,2,3$   if   $u \in A_i$ then $\pi_{r.i}(\beta(\mathbb{P}) \cap Pl_{l.i}) \xrightarrow{u} \pi_{r.i}(\beta(\mathbb{P}) \cap Pl_{l.i})$

iff     $\beta(\mathbb{P}) \xrightarrow{u} \beta(\mathbb{Q})$ with $\beta(\mathbb{P}) \subseteq place(\mathcal{N}_r)$.

Thus $\beta$ maps transitions in $\mathcal{N}_l$ and $\mathcal{N}_r$ onto each other if their projections into $\mathcal{N}_1$, $\mathcal{N}_2$ and $\mathcal{N}_3$ coincide. This is so if the action $u$ is in the corresponding alphabet $A_1$, $A_2$ and $A_3$.

Fact (5): Let $A_1 = \alpha(P_1) = \alpha(P_2) = \alpha(P_3)$ and

$$\mathcal{N}_l = (A, Sequ, \longrightarrow \downarrow A, dex(P_1 + (P_2 + P_3))),$$
$$\mathcal{N}_r = (A, Sequ, \longrightarrow \downarrow A, dex((P_1 + P_2) + P_3)),$$
$$\mathcal{N}_i = (A, Sequ, \longrightarrow \downarrow A, dex(P_i)), i = 1, 2, 3.$$

To show (5), we have to find a weak isomorphism

$$\beta : place(\mathcal{N}_l) \longrightarrow (\mathcal{N}_r)$$

between $\mathcal{N}_l$ and $\mathcal{N}_r$. Since

$$place(\mathcal{N}_l) \subseteq \; place(\mathcal{N}_1) + (place(\mathcal{N}_2) + place(\mathcal{N}_3))$$
$$\cup \; place(\mathcal{N}_1) \cup place(\mathcal{N}_2) \cup place(\mathcal{N}_3)$$

and

$$place(\mathcal{N}_r) \subseteq \; (place(\mathcal{N}_1) + place(\mathcal{N}_2)) + place(\mathcal{N}_3)$$
$$\cup \; place(\mathcal{N}_1) \cup place(\mathcal{N}_2) \cup place(\mathcal{N}_3),$$

we consider the mapping $\beta$ which changes bracketing, i.e.

$$\beta(C_1 + (C_2 + C_3)) = (C_1 + C_2) + C_3$$

for $C_i \in place(\mathcal{N}_i)$, $i=1,2,3$, and $\beta(C) = C$ otherwise. Obviously, $\beta$ is a bijection. Suppose now that

$(l)$                    $\mathbb{P} \xrightarrow{u} \mathbb{Q}$ with $\mathbb{P} \subseteq place(\mathcal{N}_l)$.

Then there exist disjoint sets $\mathbb{R}_1, \mathbb{R}_2 \subseteq Sequ$ with $\mathbb{R}_1 \cup \mathbb{R}_2 \xrightarrow{u} \mathbb{Q}$ such that $\mathbb{P}$ is of the form (l.1)  $\mathbb{R}_1 \cup (\mathbb{R}_2 + (dex(P_2) + dex(P_3)))$ with $\mathbb{R}_1 \cup \mathbb{R}_2 \subseteq place(\mathcal{N}_1)$, or

(l.2)  $\mathbb{R}_1 \cup (dex(P_1) + (\mathbb{R}_2 + dex(P_3)))$ with $\mathbb{R}_1 \cup \mathbb{R}_2 \subseteq place(\mathcal{N}_2)$, or

(l.3)  $\mathbb{R}_1 \cup (dex(P_1) + (dex(P_2) + \mathbb{R}_2))$ with $\mathbb{R}_1 \cup \mathbb{R}_2 \subseteq place(\mathcal{N}_3)$.

Consequently, $\beta(\mathbb{R})$ is of the form

(r.1)  $\mathbb{R}_1 \cup ((\mathbb{R}_2 + dex(P_2)) + dex(P_3))$ with $\mathbb{R}_1 \cup \mathbb{R}_2 \subseteq place(\mathcal{N}_1)$, or

(r.2)  $\mathbb{R}_1 \cup ((dex(P_1) + \mathbb{R}_2) + dex(P_3))$ with $\mathbb{R}_1 \cup \mathbb{R}_2 \subseteq place(\mathcal{N}_2)$, or

(r.3)  $\mathbb{R}_1 \cup ((dex(P_1) + dex(P_2)) + \mathbb{R}_2)$ with $\mathbb{R}_1 \cup \mathbb{R}_2 \subseteq place(\mathcal{N}_3)$,

for the same $\mathbb{R}_1, \mathbb{R}_2 \subseteq Sequ$. Since $\beta(\mathbb{Q})=\mathbb{Q}$, the Petri net transition rule for choice also implies that

(r)  $$\beta(\mathbb{P}) \xrightarrow{u} \beta(\mathbb{Q}) \text{ with } \beta(\mathbb{P}) \subseteq place(\mathcal{N}_r).$$

Analogously, $(r)$ also implies $(l)$. Thus $\beta$ is a weak isomorphism between $\mathcal{N}_l$ and $\mathcal{N}_r$.
□

## 3.6   What is a Good Net Semantics ?

We have defined a Petri net semantics for process terms and investigated its basic properties. But since there are so many possibilities of defining such a semantics, we posed the following question in [Old87]:

What is a good Petri net semantics ?

In agreement with [DDM88b] we suggest adopting the following two principles:

- *Retrievability*. The standard interleaving semantics for process terms (to be defined in Section 3.7) should be retrievable from the net semantics.

- *Concurrency*. The net semantics should represent the intended concurrency of process terms.

Of course, the point is now to define the notions of "retrievability" and "intended concurrency". For retrievability we propose to use Park's notion of strong bisimilarity for automata (Definition 2.1.4). By constrast, [DDM88b] use an *ad hoc* notion of a transition-preserving homomorphism. We prefer Park's notion for its conceptual clarity and greater flexibility and leave any further investigation of the *kind of* bisimilarity as a secondary issue.

**Definition 3.6.1** An interleaving semantics $\mathcal{A}[\![\cdot]\!]$: $CProc \longrightarrow AAut$ is *retrievable* from a net semantics $\mathcal{N}[\![\cdot]\!]$: $CProc \longrightarrow ANet$ if the interleaving case graph (Definition 2.2.8) of $\mathcal{N}[\![P]\!]$ is strongly bisimilar to $\mathcal{A}[\![P]\!]$, i.e.

$$\mathcal{A}(\mathcal{N}[\![P]\!]) \equiv \mathcal{A}[\![P]\!]$$

for every $P \in CProc$.
□

Under strong bisimilarity the state representations of $\mathcal{A}(\mathcal{N}[\![P]\!])$ and $\mathcal{A}[\![P]\!]$ may differ, but the transition behaviour must coincide. In other words: the net $\mathcal{N}[\![P]\!]$ must neither contain fewer transitions than the automaton $\mathcal{A}[\![P]\!]$ nor new "auxiliary transitions" not present in $\mathcal{A}[\![P]\!]$, even no "hidden" $\tau$-transitions. This is a very strong requirement which several of the proposed net semantics fail to satisfy (e.g [GM84, Tau87]). In fact, the statement and proof of the relationship between net and interleaving semantics appears only in the most recent publications on this topic. Retrievability in the above sense is shown in [DDM87, DDM88b, Gol88a, Gol88b]; we will show it for our operational net semantics using a completely different proof strategy.

However, since retrievability deals only with individual transitions, it does not reject net semantics that exhibit "too little" concurrency. As an illustration of this point we consider the original operational net semantics in [DDM87], called here $\mathcal{N}^*[\![\cdots]\!]$. As expected, the process term

$$P_0 = a.stop{:}\{a,c\} \| b.stop{:}\{b,c\}$$

denotes the abstract net

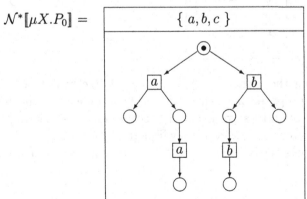

Now consider $P_0$ in the context of the (trivial) recursion

$$\mu X.P_0.$$

Surprisingly, the semantics of [DDM87] produces the following:

Thus initially, $a$ and $b$ cannot happen concurrently. As a consequence, this semantics does not satisfy the $\mu$-expansion law for recursion

$$\mathcal{N}^*[\![\mu X.P]\!] = \mathcal{N}^*[\![P\{\mu X.P/X\}]\!]$$

because this would imply $\mathcal{N}^*[\![\mu X.P_0]\!] = \mathcal{N}^*[\![P_0]\!]$.

A similar restriction on concurrency occurs in [DDM87] if $P_0$ is considered in the context of a choice, say

$$P_0 + c.stop:\{a, b, c\}.$$

Then the semantics of [DDM87] yields the following net:

$$\mathcal{N}^*[\![P_0 + \ldots]\!] = $$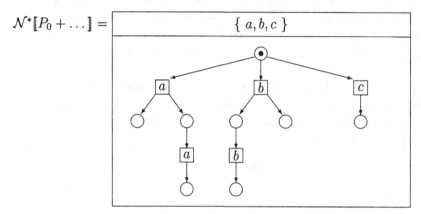

where the initial concurrency of $a$ and $b$ within $P_0$ is lost. As a consequence, this semantics does not satisfy the compositionality law for choice:

$$\mathcal{N}^*[\![P_1 + P_2]\!] = \mathcal{N}^*[\![P_1]\!] +_{\mathcal{N}} \mathcal{N}^*[\![P_2]\!].$$

Here $+_{\mathcal{N}}$ is the standard compositional net operator for choice [GM84, Win84, Win87, GV87, Gol88b]; it requires that $\mathcal{N}^*[\![P_0 + \ldots]\!]$ should be as follows:

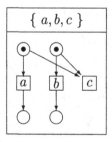

Thus we suggest formalising the Concurrency Principle indirectly by requiring algebraic laws that relate the proposed net semantics to the standard composition operators $op_{\mathcal{N}}$ on nets. These operators are generally accepted as representing the intended concurrency of process terms. However, we will require the laws to hold only modulo strong bisimilarity on nets (Definition 2.3.8). This allows a greater flexibility for the proposed net semantics.

**Definition 3.6.2** A net semantics $\mathcal{N}[\![\cdot]\!]$: *CProc* $\longrightarrow$ *ANet represents the intended concurrency* of *CProc* if, modulo strong bisimilarity, it is *compositional* with respect to the standard net operators $op_{\mathcal{N}}$ (to be defined in Section 3.8). That is,

(1) $\mathcal{N}[\![op(P_1,\ldots,P_n)]\!] \approx op_{\mathcal{N}}(\mathcal{N}[\![P_1]\!],\ldots,\mathcal{N}[\![P_n]\!])$

(2) $\mathcal{N}[\![\mu X.P]\!] \approx \mathcal{N}[\![P\{\mu X.P/X\}]\!]$

for all operator symbols *op* of *CProc* and all terms $P_1, \ldots, P_n, \mu X.P \in CProc$. $\square$

By the Causality Theorem 2.3.10, the conditions (1) and (2) of this definition imply the causal equivalence of the nets:

$$\mathcal{N}[\![op(P_1, \ldots, P_n)]\!] \equiv_{caus} op_{\mathcal{N}}(\mathcal{N}[\![P_1]\!], \ldots, \mathcal{N}[\![P_n]\!])$$

and

$$\mathcal{N}[\![\mu X.P]\!] \equiv_{caus} \mathcal{N}[\![P\{\mu X.P/X\}]\!]$$

Thus the net semantics $\mathcal{N}[\![\cdot]\!]$ indeed admits the same concurrent computations as the standard compositional net semantics.

An advantage of our definition is that we stay within the framework of nets. By contrast, Degano, DeNicola and Montanari have suggested two other formalisations of the Concurrency Principle both of which leave this framework. One refers to the so-called *step semantics* of process terms [DDM88b] and the second to *event structure semantics* [Win82, DDM88a]. Step semantics is not sufficient because it can represent only a restricted form of concurrency, viz. clocked or synchronous. Event structure semantics nicely covers all aspects of choice and concurrency, but it would require the introduction of yet another formalism.

## 3.7 Retrievability

In this section we wish to show that our operational Petri net semantics satisfies the Retrievability Principle. As a point of reference we first introduce a standard operational interleaving semantics for process terms. It assigns to every closed process term $P$ an abstract automaton $\mathcal{A}[\![P]\!]$ and is based on an interleaving transition relation

$$\longrightarrow \subseteq CProc \times Act \times CProc$$

consisting of interleaving transitions of the form

$$P \xrightarrow{\ u\ } Q$$

with $P, Q \in CProc$ and $u \in Act$. Since these transitions can be clearly distinguished from Petri net transitions

$$\mathbb{P} \xrightarrow{\ u\ } \mathbb{Q}$$

where $\mathbb{P}, \mathbb{Q}$ are sets of sequential components, we will use the symbol $\longrightarrow$ for both types of transitions.

**Definition 3.7.1** The *interleaving transition relation* $\longrightarrow$ consists of all transitions that are deducible by the following transition axioms and rules:
(Prefix)

$$a.P \xrightarrow{\ a\ } P$$

(Divergence)

$$div{:}A \xrightarrow{\ \tau\ } div{:}A$$

(Parallel Composition)
   Asynchrony :

$$\frac{P \xrightarrow{\ u\ } P'}{P\|Q \xrightarrow{\ u\ } P'\|Q \ , \ Q\|P \xrightarrow{\ u\ } Q\|P'} \qquad \text{where } u \notin \alpha(P) \cap \alpha(Q)$$

   Synchrony :

$$\frac{P \xrightarrow{\ a\ } P', Q \xrightarrow{\ a\ } Q'}{P\|Q \xrightarrow{\ a\ } P'\|Q'} \qquad \text{where } a \in \alpha(P) \cap \alpha(Q)$$

(Choice)

$$\frac{P \xrightarrow{\ u\ } P'}{P+Q \xrightarrow{\ u\ } P', \ Q+P \xrightarrow{\ u\ } P'}$$

(Morphism)

$$\frac{P \xrightarrow{\ u\ } Q}{P[\varphi] \xrightarrow{\ \varphi(u)\ } Q[\varphi]}$$

(Recursion)

$$\frac{P\{\mu X.P/X\} \xrightarrow{\ u\ } Q}{\mu X.P \xrightarrow{\ u\ } Q}$$

□

The above transition rules are all standard [Mil80, Mil86, OH86]. In particular, Milner's recursion rule [Mil80] is used in contrast to the a priori expansion via the mapping *dex* in the Petri net transition rules. The transition rule for parallel composition can be found in [Mil86]. However, there and also in [Mil83] a difficulty arises in knowing whether $\alpha(P) \cap \alpha(Q)$ always determines the right synchronisation set. Indeed, whereas the above rules determine the synchronisation set anew at each step, the Petri net transition rules fix this set at the very beginning when decomposing $P\|Q$.

To relate these different treatments of parallel composition and recursion, we will need the following two lemmas.

**Static Alphabet Lemma 3.7.2** For all $P,Q \in$ *CProc* and $u \in$ *Act*

$$P \xrightarrow{\ u\ } Q \text{ implies } \alpha(P) = \alpha(Q).$$

*Proof.* We use induction on the structure of interleaving transitions, thereby using the context restrictions (2) – (4) in Definition 3.1.3 and Remark 3.1.4.      □

By the Static Alphabet Lemma, the synchronisation set $\alpha(P) \cap \alpha(Q)$ of $P\|Q$ is invariant under transitions of $P$ and $Q$. This resolves the difficulties mentioned in [Mil83, Mil86]. Turning now to recursion, an inspection of the above transition rules shows that

$$\mu X.P \xrightarrow{\ u\ } Q \text{ iff } P\{\mu X.P/X\} \xrightarrow{\ u\ } Q. \tag{3.8}$$

We generalise this observation by introducing a *μ-expansion operator*

$$exp : CProc \longrightarrow CProc$$

defined as follows:

(1) $exp(stop{:}A) = stop{:}A$,

(2) $exp(div{:}A) = div{:}A$,

(3) $exp(a.P) = a.P$,

(4) $exp(P\|Q) = exp(P) \| exp(Q)$,

(5) $exp(P + Q) = exp(P) + exp(Q)$,

(6) $exp(P[\varphi]) = exp(P)[\varphi]$,

(7) $exp(\mu X.P) = exp(P\{\mu X.P/X\})$.

The operator *exp* is well-defined because process terms are action-guarded (cf. the context restriction (1) in Definition 3.1.3). The proof is analogous to that of Proposition 3.3.2 (1) stating the well-definedness of the mapping *dex*.

**μ-Expansion Lemma 3.7.3** For all $P$, $Q \in CProc$ and $u \in Act$

$$P \xrightarrow{\ u\ } Q \text{ iff } exp(P) \xrightarrow{\ u\ } Q$$

*Proof.* We use induction on the complexity $\gamma(P)$ as introduced by (3.1) – (3.3) in Section 3.3, thereby using observation (3.8) above. □

Analogously to the definition of $\mathcal{N}[\![P]\!]$, the interleaving semantics $\mathcal{A}[\![P]\!]$ of a closed process term $P$ is obtained by restricting the general transition relation $\longrightarrow$ of Definition 3.7.1 to the alphabet of $P$ and (modulo isomorphism) to the states that are reachable from $P$.

**Definition 3.7.4** The *operational interleaving semantics* for process terms is a mapping

$$\mathcal{A}[\![\cdot]\!] : CProc \longrightarrow AAut$$

which assigns to every $P \in CProc$ the abstract automaton

$$\mathcal{A}[\![P]\!] = [(\alpha(P), CProc, \longrightarrow \downarrow \alpha(P), P)].$$

Here $\longrightarrow$ is the transition relation of 3.7.1 and

$$\longrightarrow \downarrow \alpha(P) = \{P \xrightarrow{\ u\ } Q \mid u \in \{\tau\} \cup \alpha(P)\}$$

its restriction to ($\tau$ and) the communications in $\alpha(P)$. □

To construct a particular abstract automaton $\mathcal{A}[\![P]\!]$, we start from $P$ and explore all transitions that are successively applicable. In this way, we will automatically restrict ourselves to the communications in $\alpha(P)$ and the reachable states. Abstraction is introduced by finally removing all the names of states, here the process terms.

**Example 3.7.5** As an illustration let us construct the interleaving view of the process term of Example 3.3.6 (5):

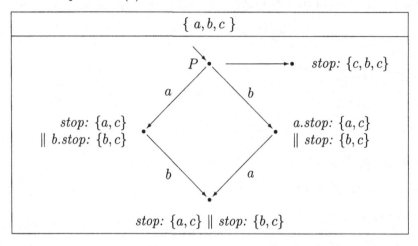

To explain the construction, we retain terms as names of the states. Note that parallel composition ‖ is not decomposed in the interleaving view.                                    □

To prove the retrievability of the semantics $\mathcal{A}[\![P]\!]$ from the net semantics $\mathcal{N}[\![P]\!]$, we have to prove the strong bisimilarity $\mathcal{A}(\mathcal{N}[\![P]\!]) \equiv \mathcal{A}[\![P]\!]$. This requires a detailed analysis of the reachable markings of the underlying concrete net $\mathcal{N} = (\alpha(P), Sequ, \longrightarrow\!\downarrow \alpha(P), dex(P))$ - much more detailed than was necessary for proving safeness.

In the original paper of Degano, DeNicola and Montanari [DDM87] this analysis was quite simple because every reachable marking was a *complete set* of sequential components. This would allow us to set up a strong bisimulation $\mathcal{B} \subseteq mark(\mathcal{N}) \times CProc$ as follows:

$$M \; \mathcal{B} \; Q \text{ if } M = dex(Q).$$

In other words, every global state $Q$ of the interleaving semantics is related to *exactly* one distributed state of $\mathcal{A}(\mathcal{N})$, viz. the reachable marking $M = dex(Q)$ of $\mathcal{N}$. The price for this simplicity was an inadequate treatment of the interplay of concurrency and choice in [DDM87] (cf. Section 3.6).

In our approach, and also in the new [DDM88b], reachable markings of $\mathcal{N}$ need not be complete. As an illustration, consider once more the term

$$P = (a.stop{:}\{a,c\}\|b.stop{:}\{b,c\}) + c.stop{:}\{a,b,c\},$$

of Example 3.3.6(5). The initial marking

$$
\begin{aligned}
M_0 \;\; &= \;\; dex(P) \\
&= \;\; \{(a.stop{:}\{a,c\}\|_{\{c\}}) + c.stop{:}\{a,b,c\}, (_{\{c\}}\|b.stop{:}\{b,c\}) + c.stop{:}\{a,b,c\}\}
\end{aligned}
$$

is complete by definition, but execution of the transition labelled with a yields an incomplete marking, viz.

$$M_1 = \{stop\text{:}\{a,c\}\|_{\{c\}}, (_{\{c\}}\|b.stop\text{:}\{b,c\}) + c.stop\text{:}\{a,b,c\}\}.$$

Incompleteness results from the alternative "$+ c.stop\text{:}\{a,b,c\}$" in the second component. This alternative is redundant, i.e. it cannot be taken any more because the transition rule for choice would require a complete set $\mathbb{Q}$ such that

$$\mathbb{Q} + c.stop\text{:}\{a.b.c\}$$

is contained in $M_1$. In this case, removing the redundant alternative yields a complete set of components, viz.

$$M_2 = \{stop\text{:}\{a,c\}\|_{\{c\}}, {}_{\{c\}}\|stop\text{:}\{b,c\}\}.$$

Both $M_1$ and $M_2$ are related to the same global state

$$\mathbb{Q} = stop\text{:}\{a,c\}\|stop\text{:}\{b,c\}$$

of the interleaving semantics. This observation is typical of our approach and also [DDM88b]: every global state $Q$ of the interleaving semantics is related to *more than one* marking of the net semantics. It is this difference between the global and distributed views of processes which makes the proof of retrievability difficult. One might think that this difference is of a purely technical nature and could be avoided by another set-up of the operational net semantics, but we conjecture that it is a fundamental difference.

**Conjecture 3.7.6** It is impossible to find an operational Petri net semantics which represents all the intended concurrency of process terms and for which the reachable markings are in $1-1$ correspondence with the global states of the standard operational interleaving semantics. $\qquad\Box$

The conjecture is supported by similar observations of Bednarczyk stated for so-called asynchronous systems (see [Bed87], Section 9.1). However, it remains to be investigated how these observations translate into the present framework.

To cope with incomplete markings, we introduce an update operation *upd*. When applied to a marking $M$, it yields a set $upd(M)$ of components where all redundant alternatives are removed. For $M_1$ and $Q$ as above, we obtain

$$upd(M_1) = \{stop\text{:}\{a,c\}\|_{\{c\}}, {}_{\{c\}}\|stop\text{:}\{b,c\}\} = dex(Q).$$

In the subsequent Transfer Lemmas 3.7.13 and 3.7.15 we shall show that every reachable marking can be updated into a complete set of components. From these lemmas retrievability will follow.

The key to the lemmas lies in finding a suitable invariance property for reachable markings. We need here a slightly stronger property than the well-formedness introduced in Section 3.4 when proving safeness.

**Definition 3.7.7** A marking $M$ is *strongly well-formed*, abbreviated *swf*, if $M$ is a set and its structure is defined as follows: for all $a \in Comm$, communication alphabets $A,P,Q \in CProc$ and action morphisms $\varphi$

(1) $\{stop{:}A\}$, $\{div{:}A\}$, $\{a.P\}$ are *swf*,

(2) if $M_1$ and $M_2$ are *swf* then so is $M_1 \, \|_A \cup {}_A\| \, M_2$,

(3) if $M_1 \cup M_2$ is *swf* such that $M_1 \cap M_2 = \emptyset$ and either $M_1 = \emptyset$ or not all components in $M_1$ contain $+$ as their top-level operator symbol then

$$M_1 \cup (M_2 + dex(Q)) \text{ and } M_1 \cup (dex(Q) + M_2)$$

are also *swf*,

(4) if $M$ is *swf* then so is $M[\varphi]$. $\qquad\qquad\qquad\qquad\qquad\qquad\qquad\square$

**Remark 3.7.8** All strongly well-formed markings generated by clause (3) satisfy the following disjointness condition:

$$M_1 \cap (M_2 + dex(Q)) = M_1 \cap (dex(Q) + M_2) = \emptyset. \qquad\qquad\square$$

Compared with the Definition 3.4.1 of well-formedness, only clause (3) for choice has been strengthened; note that the phrase "not all components in $M_1$ contain $+$ as their top-level operator symbol" is here equivalent to "at least one component in $M_1$ contains an operator symbol $\|_A$or ${}_A\|$or $[\varphi]$ at its top-level". Analogously to Lemma 3.4.2 we show:

**Lemma 3.7.9** Every complete set of sequential components is strongly well-formed.
$$\square$$

We can now introduce:

**Definition 3.7.10** The *update operation upd* assigns to every strongly well-formed marking $M$ a set $upd(M)$ of sequential components defined as follows:

$$upd(M) = \begin{cases} M & \text{if } M \text{ is complete} & (1) \\ upd(M_1)\|_A \cup {}_A\| upd(M_2) & \text{if } M = M_1 \, \|_A \cup {}_A\| \, M_2 & (2) \\ & \text{is incomplete} \\ upd(M_1 \cup M_2) & \text{if } M = M_1 \cup (M_2 + dex(Q)) & (3) \\ & \text{is incomplete} \\ upd(M_1 \cup M_2) & \text{if } M = M_1 \cup (dex(Q) + M_2) & (4) \\ & \text{is incomplete} \\ upd(M_1)[\varphi] & \text{if } M = M_1[\varphi] & (5) \\ & \text{is incomplete} \end{cases}$$

$$\square$$

Thus in $upd(M)$ all redundant alternatives of $M$ have been eliminated. More formally, we state:

**Proposition 3.7.11** For every strongly well-formed marking $M$ the update operation is well-defined and yields a complete set $upd(M)$.

*Proof. Well-definedness*: Every computation of $upd(M)$ using the equations (1) – (5) above will terminate. This is easily shown by induction on the structure of $M$ as given in Definition 3.7.10 of strong well-formedness. However, there may be more than one computation of $upd(M)$ because for an incomplete marking $M$ containing a component with top-level symbol $+$, the application of the clauses (3) and (4) above is not unique and may even overlap.

We show that for every such $M$ there exists a unique structurally simpler $M_0$ such that each computation of $upd(M)$ will hit the equation

$$upd(M) = upd(M_0).$$

Using this observation, we can complete the inductive proof of well-definedness. So suppose $M = M_1 \cup (M_2 + dex(Q))$ with $M_2 \neq \emptyset$.

*Case 1*: $M_1 = \emptyset$.
Then $M_2$ is incomplete and only clause (3) is applicable. It eliminates the alternative "$+ \ dex(Q)$" for some non-empty subset of $M_2$. Clause (3) remains applicable until no component of $M_2$ with "$+ \ dex(Q)$" as alternative is left. Thus every evaluation of $upd(M)$ will hit the equation

$$upd(M) = upd(M_2).$$

Clearly, $M_2$ is uniquely determined by $M$ and structurally simpler than $M$.

*Case 2*: $M_1 \neq \emptyset$.
Since $M$ is *swf*, $M_1$ contains a component with a symbol $\|_A$ or $_A\|$ or $[\varphi]$ at its top. Thus there exist *swf* $M_0$, $N_1$ and $N_2$ such that

$$M_0 = N_1 \|_A \cup _A\| N_2 \text{ or } M_0 = N_1[\varphi]$$

and $M$ is generated from $M_0$ by successive applications of clause (3) in the Definition 3.7.7 of strong well-formedness. As long as $M$ is of this form, only clauses (3) and (4) are applicable when computing $upd(M)$. Though these applications are not unique and may overlap, they will always hit the equation

$$upd(M) = upd(M_0).$$

Again $M_0$ is uniquely determined by $M$ and structurally simpler than M. An analogous argument works for $M = M_1 \cup (dex(Q) + M_2)$.

*Completeness*: Once well-definedness of $upd(M)$ is shown, completeness is established by a simple induction on the structure of $M$. $\square$

**Remark 3.7.12** When applied to well-formed markings, the operation *upd* does not yield unique results. Take e.g.

$$M = \{(a.stop{:}\{a\}\|\emptyset) + a.stop{:}\{a,b\}, ((\emptyset\|b.stop{:}\{b\}) + a.stop{:}\{a,b\}) + b.stop{:}\{a,b\}\}.$$

By Definition 3.4.1, $M$ is *wf*, but not *swf*. Then depending on whether clause (3) of the definition of *upd* is at first applied to "$+ a.stop:\{a,b\}$" or to "$+ b.stop:\{a,b\}$", we obtain

$$upd(M) = \{a.stop:\{a\}\|_\emptyset, \ _\emptyset\|b.stop:\{b\}\}$$

or

$$upd(M) \ = \ \{ \ (a.stop:\{a\}\|_\emptyset) + a.stop:\{a,b\},$$
$$(_\emptyset\|b.stop:\{b\}) + a.stop:\{a,b\}\}. \qquad\qquad \square$$

Using *upd* we can formulate the desired strong bisimulation

$$\mathcal{B} \subseteq mark(\mathcal{N}) \times CProc$$

between $\mathcal{A}(\mathcal{N})$ and $\mathcal{A}$ (see above) as follows:

$$M \ \mathcal{B} \ Q \ \text{if} \ upd(M) = dex(Q).$$

To prove that $\mathcal{B}$ enjoys the transfer property, we need two lemmas.

**First Transfer Lemma 3.7.13** Consider a closed process term $Q$, a strongly well-formed marking $M$, a Petri net transition $t$ with $act(t) = u$, and another marking $M'$ with

$$upd(M) = dex(Q) \ \text{and} \ M \xrightarrow{\ t\ } M'.$$

Then $post(t) = M'$ or not all components in $post(t)$ contain $+$ as their top-level symbol. Moreover, $M'$ is strongly well-formed and there exists some closed process term $Q'$ with

$$Q \xrightarrow{\ u\ } Q' \ \text{and} \ upd(M') = dex(Q').$$

*Proof.* We use induction on the structure of $t$ as given by the Petri net transition rules of Definition 3.3.4. This induction is a much more elaborate version of the proof of Lemma 3.4.3 used to show safeness of our nets. Recall that by definition

$$M \xrightarrow{\ t\ } M'$$

if $pre(t) \subseteq M$ and $M' = (M - pre(t)) \sqcup post(t)$.

*Induction Basis.*

  (1) $t = \{a.P\} \xrightarrow{\ a\ } dex(P)$:

     Then $pre(t) \subseteq M$ implies $M = \{a.P\}$. Thus $M' = post(t) = dex(P)$ is complete and hence *swf* by Lemma 3.7.9. Note that $upd(M) = dex(Q)$ does not imply $Q = a.P$, but only $exp(Q) = a.P$. Thus taking $Q' = P$ yields

$$exp(Q) \xrightarrow{\ a\ } Q' \ \text{and} \ upd(M') = M' = dex(Q').$$

     Finally, the $\mu$-Expansion Lemma 3.7.3 yields $Q \xrightarrow{\ a\ } Q'$

(2) $t = \{div{:}A\} \xrightarrow{\;\tau\;} \{div{:}A\}$: Simpler than (1).

*Induction Step.*

(3.a) $t = \mathbb{P} \,\|_A \xrightarrow{\;u\;} \mathbb{P}' \,\|_A$ where $u \notin A$:

By $pre(t) \subseteq M$, there exist two *swf* markings $\mathbb{P} \cup M_1$ and $M_2$ with $\mathbb{P} \cap M_1 = \emptyset$ and

$$M = \mathbb{P}\|_A \cup (\ldots + (M_1\|_A \cup _A\|M_2) + \ldots).$$

Analogously to the proof of Lemma 3.4.3 for the Safeness Theorem 3.4.4, the notation $(\ldots + (M_1 \|_A\cup _A\|M_2) + \ldots)$ indicates that in addition to $M_1 \|_A\cup _A\|M_2$ there can be any number of applications of the choice operator according to clause (3) in the definition of strong well-formedness. Thus

$$upd(M) = upd(M_1)\|_A \cup _A\|upd(M_2),$$

so that $upd(M) = dex(Q)$ implies

$$exp(Q) = Q_1\|Q_2$$

for some closed process terms $Q_1$ and $Q_2$ with $A = \alpha(Q_1) \cap \alpha(Q_2)$, and

$$upd(\mathbb{P} \cup M_1) = dex(Q_1) \text{ and } upd(M_2) = dex(Q_2).$$

By the Petri net transition rules,

$$t' = \mathbb{P} \xrightarrow{\;u\;} \mathbb{P}'$$

is also a transition. Applying the induction hypothesis to $t'$ and $\mathbb{P} \cup M$ yields:

$$M_1' = (\mathbb{P} \cup M_1 - \mathbb{P}) \sqcup \mathbb{P}' = \mathbb{P}' \cup M$$

is *swf* and there exists a closed process term $Q_1'$ with

$$Q_1 \xrightarrow{\;u\;} Q_1' \text{ and } upd(M_1') = dex(Q_1').$$

Since

$$M' = \mathbb{P}'\|_A \cup (\ldots + (M_1\|_A \cup _A\|M_2) + \ldots),$$

$M'$ is also *swf*. Obviously, none of the components in $post(t) = \mathbb{P}' \,\|_A$ contains $+$ as its top-level symbol. Moreover, taking

$$Q' = Q_1'\|Q_2$$

yields $exp(Q) \xrightarrow{\;u\;} Q'$ because $u \notin A$ and $A = \alpha(Q_1') \cap \alpha(Q_2)$ by the Static Alphabet Lemma 3.7.2. The $\mu$-Expansion Lemma 3.7.3 implies $Q \xrightarrow{\;u\;} Q'$. Moreover,

$$upd(M') = upd(M_1')\|_A \cup _A\|upd(M) = dex(Q').$$

(3.b) $t = {}_A \| \mathbb{P} \xrightarrow{\ u\ } {}_A \| \mathbb{P}'$ where $u \notin A$:
The proof is symmetric to (3.a).

(3.c) $t = \mathbb{P} \|_A \cup {}_A \| \mathbb{Q} \xrightarrow{\ a\ } \mathbb{P}' \|_A \cup {}_A \| \mathbb{Q}'$ where $a \in A$:
We combine (3.a) and (3.b).

(4.a) $t = \mathbb{P}_1 \cup (\mathbb{P}_2 + dex(Q_2)) \xrightarrow{\ u\ } \mathbb{P}'$ with $\mathbb{P}_1 \cap \mathbb{P}_2 = \emptyset$ and $\mathbb{P}_2 \neq \emptyset$:
By $pre(t) \subseteq M$, there exists a *swf* marking $M_1 \cup M_2$ with $M_1 \cap M_2 = \emptyset$ such that
$$M = M_1 \cup (M_2 + dex(Q_2)), \mathbb{P}_1 \subseteq M_1 \text{and} \mathbb{P}_2 \subseteq M_2.$$

Note that in contrast to the proof of Lemma 3.4.3 used for the Safeness Theorem 3.4.4 we cannot always assume $\mathbb{P}_2 = M_2$. This is due to the additional constraints for *swf* markings which, for complete $M$, require $M_1 = \emptyset$.

We first observe the following : if $M$ is incomplete then
$$upd(M) = upd(M_1 \cup M_2);$$

otherwise $M$ is complete and for some $M_1'$ we have $M_1 = M_1' + dex(Q_2)$ and
$$upd(M) = M = (M_1 \cup M_2) + dex(Q_2).$$

Thus in either case $upd(M) = dex(Q)$ implies that there exists some closed process term $Q_1$ with
$$upd(M_1 \cup M_2) = dex(Q_2)$$
and either
$$exp(Q) = Q_1 \text{ or } exp(Q) = Q_1 + Q_2. \tag{3.9}$$

Now looking at $t$, the Petri net transition rule for choice implies that
$$t' = \mathbb{P}_1 \cup \mathbb{P}_2 \xrightarrow{\ u\ } \mathbb{P}'$$

is also a transition.  Applying the induction hypothesis to $t'$ and $M_1 \cup M_2$ yields:
$$M_1' = ((M_1 \cup M_2) - (\mathbb{P}_1 \cup \mathbb{P}_2)) \sqcup \mathbb{P}'$$
is *swf* and $\mathbb{P}' = M_1'$ or not all components in $\mathbb{P}'$ contain $+$ as their top-level symbol.  Moreover, there exists a closed process term $Q_1'$ with
$$Q_1 \xrightarrow{\ u\ } Q_1' \text{ and } upd(M_1') = dex(Q_1').$$

We can rewrite the *swf* $M_1'$ as
$$M_1' = (M_1 - \mathbb{P}_1) \cup (M_2 - \mathbb{P}_2) \cup \mathbb{P}'$$

where all the unions are disjoint.  By the above properties of $\mathbb{P}'$,
$$M_1'' = (M_1 - \mathbb{P}_1) \cup ((M_2 - \mathbb{P}_2) + dex(Q_2)) \cup \mathbb{P}'$$

is also *swf* and satisfies

$$upd(M_1'') = upd(M_1') = dex(Q_1').$$

By Remark 3.7.8, all unions of $M_1''$ are also disjoint. Thus the marking $M'$ with $M \xrightarrow{\ t\ } M'$ satisfies

$$
\begin{aligned}
M' &= (M - (\mathbb{P}_1 \cup (\mathbb{P}_2 + dex(Q_2)))) \sqcup \mathbb{P}' \\
&= ((M_1 - \mathbb{P}_1) \cup ((M_2 - \mathbb{P}_2) + dex(Q_2))) \sqcup \mathbb{P}' \\
&= M_1''.
\end{aligned}
$$

Taking $Q' = Q_1'$ and considering (3.9) above yields

$$exp(Q) \xrightarrow{\ u\ } Q' \text{ and } upd(M') = dex(Q').$$

By the $\mu$-Expansion Lemma 3.7.3, $Q \xrightarrow{\ u\ } Q'$.

(4.b) $t = \mathbb{P}_1 \cup (dex(Q_2) + \mathbb{P}_2) \xrightarrow{\ u\ } \mathbb{P}'$ with $\mathbb{P}_1 \cap \mathbb{P}_2 = \emptyset$ and $\mathbb{P} \neq \emptyset$:
The proof is symmetric to (4.a).

(5) $t = \mathbb{P}[\varphi] \xrightarrow{\ \varphi[u]\ } \mathbb{Q}[\varphi]$:
The proof is straightforward, and easier than (3.a). □

**Remark 3.7.14** The Safeness Theorem 3.4.4 can also be proved with the help of Lemma 3.7.9 and the First Transfer Lemma, but we prefer the simpler direct proof given in Section 3.4. □

**Second Transfer Lemma 3.7.15** For all closed process terms $Q$ and $Q'$, all actions $u$, and all strongly well-formed markings $M$ with

$$upd(M) = dex(Q) \text{ and } Q \xrightarrow{\ u\ } Q', \tag{3.10}$$

there exists a Petri net transition $t$ with $act(t) = u$ and a strongly well-formed marking $M'$ satisfying

$$M \xrightarrow{\ t\ } M' \text{ and } upd(M') = dex(Q').$$

We decompose the lemma into two sublemmas, one dealing with *dex* and one with *upd*.

**Lemma 3.7.16** The same statement as in the Second Transfer Lemma, but with the stronger assumption $M = dex(Q)$ in line (3.10).

*Proof.* We use induction on the structure of $Q \xrightarrow{\ u\ } Q'$ as given by the interleaving transition rules of Definition 3.7.1.

*Induction Basis.*

(1) $Q \xrightarrow{u} Q'$ is $a.P \xrightarrow{a} P$:

Then $Q' = P$ and $M = \{a.P\}$. Take the Petri net transition $t = \{a.P\} \xrightarrow{a} dex(P)$ and $M' = dex(P)$. By Lemma 3.7.9, $M'$ is *swf*. Clearly,

$$M \xrightarrow{t} M' \text{ and } upd(M') = dex(Q').$$

(2) $Q \xrightarrow{u} Q'$ is $div{:}A \xrightarrow{\tau} div{:}A$:

Trivial.

*Induction Step.*

(3) $Q \xrightarrow{u} Q'$ is $Q_1 \parallel Q_2 \xrightarrow{u} Q_1' \parallel Q_2'$:

Thus $Q = Q_1 \parallel Q_2$, $Q' = Q_1' \parallel Q_2'$ and

$$M = dex(Q_1)\|_A \cup {}_A\| dex(Q_2)$$

where $A = \alpha(Q_1) \cap \alpha(Q_2)$. By the interleaving transition rules, $Q \xrightarrow{u} Q'$ can be deduced as follows.

(3.a) $Q_1 \xrightarrow{u} Q_1'$ where $u \notin A$ and $Q_2' = Q_2$:

Then the induction hypothesis applies to $M_1 = dex(Q_1)$ and yields a Petri net transition $t'$ with $act(t) = u$ and a *swf* marking $M_1'$ with

$$M_1 \xrightarrow{t'} M_1' \text{ and } upd(M_1') = dex(Q_1').$$

By the Petri net transition rules,

$$t = pre(t')\|_A \xrightarrow{u} post(t')\|_A$$

is also a transition with

$$M \xrightarrow{t} M' \text{ where } M' = M_1'\|_A \cup {}_A\| dex(Q_2).$$

Thus $M'$ is *swf* and satisfies

$$upd(M') = upd(M_1')\|_A \cup {}_A\| dex(Q_2) = dex(Q').$$

(3.b) $Q_2 \xrightarrow{u} Q_2'$ where $u \notin A$ and $Q_1' = Q_1$:

The proof is symmetric to (3.a).

(3.c) $Q_1 \xrightarrow{u} Q_1'$ and $Q_2 \xrightarrow{u} Q_2'$ where $u \in A$:

We combine (3.a) and (3.b).

(4) $Q \xrightarrow{\ u\ } Q'$ is $Q_1 + Q_2 \xrightarrow{\ u\ } Q'$:

Thus $Q = Q_1 + Q_2$ and $M = dex(Q_1) + dex(Q_2)$. By the interleaving transition rules, $Q \xrightarrow{\ u\ } Q'$ can be deduced as follows.

(4.a) $Q_1 \xrightarrow{\ u\ } Q'$:

Then the induction hypothesis applies to $M_1 = dex(Q_1)$ and yields a Petri net transition $t'$ with $act(t') = u$ and a *swf* marking $M_1'$ with

$$M_1 \xrightarrow{\ t'\ } M_1' \text{ and } upd(M_1') = dex(Q').$$

Since $M_1'$ is *swf*, we have

$$M_1' = (M_1 - pre(t')) \cup post(t')$$

where the union is disjoint. By the Petri net transition rules,

$$t = pre(t') + dex(Q_2) \xrightarrow{\ u\ } post(t')$$

is also a transition yielding

$$M \xrightarrow{\ t\ } M'$$

for some $M'$. By the First Transfer Lemma, $M'$ is *swf* and thus of the form

$$M' = ((M_1 - pre(t')) + dex(Q_2)) \cup post(t').$$

This implies

$$upd(M') = upd(M_1') = dex(Q').$$

(4.b) $Q_2 \xrightarrow{\ u\ } Q'$:

The proof is symmetric to (4.a).

(5) $Q \xrightarrow{\ u\ } Q'$ is $P[\varphi] \xrightarrow{\ \varphi(u)\ } Q[\varphi]$:

This is straightforward, and easier than (3.a).

(6) $Q \xrightarrow{\ u\ } Q'$ is $\mu X.P \xrightarrow{\ u\ } Q'$:

Thus $Q = \mu X.P$ and

$$M = dex(Q) = dex(P\{\mu X.P/X\}).$$

By the interleaving transition rules, $Q \xrightarrow{\ u\ } Q'$ is deduced from

$$P\{\mu X.P/X\} \xrightarrow{\ u\ } Q'.$$

Then the induction hypothesis applies to $M$ and yields a Petri net transition $t$ with $act(t) = u$ and a *swf* marking $M'$ with

$$M \xrightarrow{\ t\ } M' \text{ and } upd(M') = dex(Q'). \qquad \square$$

**Lemma 3.7.17** Consider strongly well-formed markings $M$, $N$ and $N'$ where $N$ is complete, and a Petri net transition $t'$ with $act(t') = u$ such that

$$upd(M) = N \text{ and } N \xrightarrow{\ t'\ } N'.$$

Then there exists a Petri net transition $t$ with $act(t) = u$ and a strongly well-formed marking $M'$ satisfying

$$M \xrightarrow{\ t\ } M' \text{ and } upd(M') = upd(N').$$

*Proof.* We use induction on the structure of $M$ as distinguished in Definition 3.7.10 of $upd(M)$.

*Induction Basis.*

(1)  $M$ is complete:

Then $N = upd(M) = M$ and the claim follows trivially.

*Induction Step.*

(2)  $M = M_1 \|_A \cup {}_A\| M_2$ is incomplete:

Then $N = upd(M) = upd(M_1) \|_A \cup {}_A\| upd(M_2)$. Consider $t'$ with $N \xrightarrow{\ t'\ } N'$.

(2.a)  $t' = \mathbb{P} \|_A \xrightarrow{\ u\ } \mathbb{P}' \|_A$:

For $t'' = \mathbb{P} \xrightarrow{\ u\ } \mathbb{P}'$ we have

$$upd(M_1) \xrightarrow{\ t''\ } N_1',$$

where $N_1'$ satisfies

$$N' = N_1'\|_A \cup {}_A\| upd(M_2).$$

By the induction hypothesis applied to $M_1$, there exists a Petri net transition $t'''$ with $act(t''') = u$ and a *swf* marking $N_1''$ satisfying

$$M_1 \xrightarrow{\ t'''\ } N_1'' \text{ and } upd(N_1'') = upd(N_1').$$

By the Petri net transition rules,

$$t = pre(t''')\|_A \xrightarrow{\ u\ } post(t''')\|_A$$

is a transition with

$$M \xrightarrow{\ t\ } M' \text{ where } M' = N_1''\|_A \cup {}_A\| M_2.$$

$M'$ is *swf* and satisfies

$$
\begin{aligned}
upd(M') &= upd(N_1'')\|_A \cup {_A}\|upd(M_2) \\
&= upd(N_1')\|_A \cup {_A}\|upd(M_2) \\
&= upd(N').
\end{aligned}
$$

(2.b) $t' = {_A}\|\mathbb{P} \xrightarrow{\ u\ } {_A}\|\mathbb{P}'$:
The proof is symmetric to (2.a).

(2.c) $t' = \mathbb{P}_1\|_A\cup {_A}\|\mathbb{P}_2 \xrightarrow{\ u\ } \mathbb{P}_1'\|_A\cup {_A}\|\mathbb{P}_2'$:
We combine (2.a) and (2.b).

(3) $M = M_1 \cup (M_2 + dex(Q))$ is incomplete:
Then $M_1 \cup M_2$ is *swf* with $M_1 \cap M_2 = \emptyset$ and $upd(M_1 \cup M_2) = upd(M) = N$. By the induction hypothesis applied to $M_1 \cup M_2$, there exists a Petri net transition $t''$ with $act(t'') = u$ and a *swf* marking $N''$ with

$$
M_1 \cup M_2 \xrightarrow{\ t''\ } N'' \text{ and } upd(N'') = upd(N').
$$

Let $\mathbb{P}_1 = M_1 \cap pre(t'')$ and $\mathbb{P}_2 = M_2 \cap pre(t'')$. Then

$$
N'' = (M_1 - \mathbb{P}_1) \cup (M_2 - \mathbb{P}_2) \cup post(t'')
$$

where all unions are disjoint. By the Petri net transition rule for choice,

$$
t = \mathbb{P}_1 \cup (\mathbb{P}_2 + dex(Q)) \xrightarrow{\ u\ } post(t'')
$$

is a transition yielding

$$
M \xrightarrow{\ t\ } M'
$$

for some marking $M'$. By the First Transfer Lemma, $M'$ is *swf* so that

$$
M' = (M_1 - \mathbb{P}_1) \cup ((M_2 - \mathbb{P}_2) + dex(Q)) \cup post(t'')
$$

and

$$
upd(M') = upd(N'') = upd(N).
$$

(4) $M = M_1 \cup (dex(Q) + M_2)$ is incomplete:
The proof is symmetric to (3).

(5) $M = M_1[\varphi]$ is incomplete:
This is straightforward. $\qquad\square$

We now return to the main lemma.

*Proof of the Second Transfer Lemma 3.7.15.* Suppose

$$upd(M) = dex(Q) \text{ and } Q \xrightarrow{u} Q'$$

for $M$, $Q$, $Q'$ and $u$ as stated in the lemma. By Lemma 3.7.16, there exists a Petri net transition $t'$ with $act(t') = u$ and a *swf* marking $N'$ satisfying

$$dex(Q) \xrightarrow{t'} N' \text{ and } upd(N') = dex(Q'). \tag{3.11}$$

Furthermore, by Lemma 3.7.17, there exists a Petri net transition $t$ with $act(t) = u$ and a *swf* marking $M'$ satisfying

$$M \xrightarrow{t} M' \text{ and } upd(M') = upd(N'). \tag{3.12}$$

Combining (3.11) and (3.12) yields

$$M \xrightarrow{t} M' \text{ and } upd(M') = dex(Q')$$

as desired.                                                                                      □

The two Transfer Lemmas enable us to show that our operational Petri net semantics satisfies the Retrievability Principle put forward in Section 3.6.

**Retrievability Theorem 3.7.18** For every closed process term $P$ we have the strong bisimilarity

$$\mathcal{A}(\mathcal{N}[\![P]\!]) \equiv \mathcal{A}[\![P]\!]$$

between the interleaving case graph $\mathcal{A}(\mathcal{N}[\![P]\!])$ of the net semantics $\mathcal{N}[\![P]\!]$ and the direct interleaving semantics $\mathcal{A}[\![P]\!]$.

*Proof.* It suffices to show the strong bisimilarity

$$\mathcal{A}(\mathcal{N}) \equiv \mathcal{A}$$

of the automaton $\mathcal{A}(\mathcal{N})$ associated with the net $\mathcal{N} = (\alpha(P), Sequ, \longrightarrow \downarrow \alpha(P), dex(P))$ and the automaton $\mathcal{A} = (\alpha(P), CProc, \longrightarrow \downarrow \alpha(P), P)$. Recall that the states of $\mathcal{A}(\mathcal{N})$ are the reachable markings of $\mathcal{N}$. Consider the relation

$$\mathcal{B} \subseteq mark(\mathcal{N}) \times CProc$$

between the states of $\mathcal{A}(\mathcal{N})$ and $\mathcal{A}$ defined by

$$M \mathrel{\mathcal{B}} Q \text{ if } M \text{ is } swf \text{ and } upd(M) = dex(Q)$$

for all $M \in mark(\mathcal{N})$ and $Q \in CProc$. We show that $\mathcal{B}$ is a strong bisimulation in the sense of Park (cf. Definition 2.1.4). Since trivially $dex(P) \mathrel{\mathcal{B}} P$, the initial states of $\mathcal{A}(\mathcal{N})$ and $\mathcal{A}$ are related by $\mathcal{B}$. Moreover , by the two Transfer Lemmas, $\mathcal{B}$ satisfies the transfer property.                                                                         □

## 3.8 Compositionality

To show that our operational Petri net semantics satisfies the Concurrency Principle, we will show that it is compositional w.r.t. the standard net operators $op_N$ which we now introduce.

**Definition 3.8.1** Given an $n$-ary operator symbol $op$ of *CProc* the corresponding net operator $op_N$ is a mapping

$$op_N : \underbrace{ANet \times \ldots \times ANet}_{n \ times} \longrightarrow ANet$$

on abstract nets which is defined with the help of certain representatives in the isomorphism classes of abstract nets:

(1) *Deadlock.* For an arbitrary place $p$ let

$$stop{:}A_N = [(A, \{p\}, \emptyset, \{p\})].$$

(2) *Divergence.* For an arbitrary place $p$ let

$$div{:}A_N = [(A, \{p\}, \{((\{p\}, \tau, \{p\})\}, \{p\})].$$

(3) *Prefix.* For $N_0 = (A_0, Pl_0, \longrightarrow_0, M_0)$ and $p \notin Pl_0$ let

$$a._N[N_0] = [(A_0 \cup \{a\}, Pl_0 \cup \{p\}, \longrightarrow, \{p\})]$$

where

$$\longrightarrow \ = \ \longrightarrow_0 \cup \{((\{p\}, a, M_0)\}.$$

(4) *Parallelism.* For $N_i = (A_i, Pl_i, \longrightarrow_i, M_{0i})$, $i = 1,2$, with $Pl_1 \cap Pl_2 = \emptyset$ let

$$[N_1]\|_N[N_2] = [(A_1 \cup A_2, Pl_1 \cup Pl_2, \longrightarrow, M_{01} \cup M_{02})]$$

where

$$\begin{aligned}
\longrightarrow \ = \quad &\{ \quad (I, u, O) \in \longrightarrow_1 \cup \longrightarrow_2 \mid u \notin A_1 \cap A_2 \quad \} \\
\cup \ &\{ \quad (I_1 \cup I_2, a, O_1 \cup O_2) \mid a \in A_1 \cap A_2 \text{ and} \\
&\quad (I_1, a, O_1) \in \longrightarrow_1 \text{ and } (I_2, a, O_2) \in \longrightarrow_2 \quad \}.
\end{aligned}$$

(5) *Choice.* For $N_i = (A_i, Pl_i, \longrightarrow_i, M_{0i})$, $i = 1,2$, with $Pl_i \cap Pl_2 = \emptyset$ let

$$[N_1] +_N [N_2] = [(A_1 \cup A_2, Pl_1 \cup Pl_2 \cup (M_{01} \times M_{02}), \longrightarrow, M_{01} \times M_{02})]$$

where

$$\begin{aligned}
\longrightarrow \ = \quad &\{ \quad ((I_1 \times M_{02}) \cup I_2, u, O) \mid I_1 \subseteq M_{01} \text{ and } I_1 \cap I_2 = \emptyset \\
&\qquad\qquad\qquad \text{and } (I_1 \cup I_2, u, O) \in \longrightarrow_1 \quad \} \\
\cup \ &\{ \quad (I_1 \cup (M_{01} \times I_2)), u, O) \mid I_2 \subseteq M_{02} \text{ and } I_1 \cap I_2 = \emptyset \\
&\qquad\qquad\qquad \text{and } (I_1 \cup I_2, u, O) \in \longrightarrow_2 \quad \}.
\end{aligned}$$

(6) *Morphism.* For $\mathcal{N}_0 = (A_0, Pl_0, \longrightarrow_0, M_0)$ let

$$[\mathcal{N}_0][\varphi]_{\mathcal{N}} = [(\varphi A_0) - \{\tau\}, Pl_0, \longrightarrow, M_0)]$$

where

$$\longrightarrow = \{(I, \varphi(u), O)|(I, u, O) \in \longrightarrow_0\}. \qquad \square$$

The operators are well-defined because for every abstract net we can find a representative satisfying the disjointness requirement and because the resulting abstract net is independent of the particular choice of this representative. Except for choice, the effect of these operators should be easy to understand. For example, prefix $a._{\mathcal{N}}$ creates a new place as initial marking and links it via an $a$-transition to all the places of the old initial marking. Parallel composition $\|_{\mathcal{N}}$ puts the nets side by side and for transitions with the same action label takes the union of their individual pre- and postsets. In this way synchronisation is enforced.

The definition of $+_{\mathcal{N}}$ is new and inspired by the transition rule for choice in Section 3.3: it combines the standard choice operator of [GM84, Win84] with the idea of *root unwinding* due to [GV87]. Root unwinding ensures that there are no cycles left at initially marked places. Only for such nets is the operator of [GM84, Win84] applicable; it then uses a cartesian product construction to introduce choices between all pairs of initial transitions of the two nets involved. For example, we obtain:

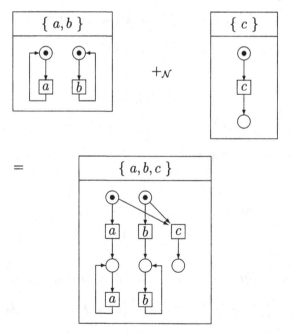

Actually, the definition of $+_{\mathcal{N}}$ creates statically unreachable places which can be ignored modulo weak isomorphism. Hence they are not shown in the resulting net above.

We first show that the above net operators respect strong bisimilarity on safe nets as introduced in Definition 2.3.8.

## Theorem 3.8.2

(1) The net operators $a._{\mathcal{N}}$, $\|_{\mathcal{N}}$, $+_{\mathcal{N}}$ and $[\varphi]_{\mathcal{N}}$ preserve safeness of abstract nets.

(2) The above net operators respect strong bisimilarity $\approx$ on safe abstract nets, i.e. whenever $[\mathcal{N}_1] \approx [\mathcal{N}_1'], \ldots, [\mathcal{N}_n] \approx [\mathcal{N}_n']$ for safe abstract nets, then

$$op_{\mathcal{N}}([\mathcal{N}_1], \ldots, [\mathcal{N}_n]) \approx op_{\mathcal{N}}([\mathcal{N}_n'], \ldots, [\mathcal{N}_n']).$$

for these operators.

*Proof.* Fact (1): The claim is obvious for $a._{\mathcal{N}}$ and $[\varphi]_{\mathcal{N}}$, and for $\|_{\mathcal{N}}$ and $+_{\mathcal{N}}$ it is true because the places of their arguments are kept disjoint.

Fact (2): For pairwise disjoint sets of places $Pl_i$ and $Pl_i'$ let

$$\mathcal{N}_i = (A_i, Pl_i, \longrightarrow_i, M_{0i}) \text{ and } \mathcal{N}_i' = (A_i', Pl_i', \longrightarrow_i', M_{0i}'),$$

and suppose that $\mathcal{N}_i \approx \mathcal{N}_i'$ via the strong bisimulation

$$\mathcal{B}_i \subseteq Pl_i \times Pl_i',$$

$i = 1, \ldots, n$. Recall that $\mathcal{N}_i \approx \mathcal{N}_i'$ implies $A_i = A_i'$.

*Prefix $a._{\mathcal{N}}$:* Take some $p \notin Pl_1$ and $p' \notin Pl_2$ and consider

$$\mathcal{N} = (A_1 \cup \{a\}, Pl_1 \cup \{p\}, \longrightarrow, M_0),$$

and

$$\mathcal{N}' = (A_1 \cup \{a\}, Pl_1' \cup \{p'\}, \longrightarrow', M_0')$$

where $\longrightarrow$ and $\longrightarrow'$ are as in the definition of $a._{\mathcal{N}}$ so that

$$a._{\mathcal{N}}[\mathcal{N}_1] = [\mathcal{N}] \text{ and } a._{\mathcal{N}}[\mathcal{N}_1'] = [\mathcal{N}'].$$

Then $\mathcal{N} \approx \mathcal{N}'$ via $\mathcal{B} = \mathcal{B}_1 \cup \{(p,p')\}$. Checking that $\mathcal{B}$ is a strong bisimulation between $\mathcal{N}$ and $\mathcal{N}'$ is straightforward. Thus

$$a._{\mathcal{N}}[\mathcal{N}_1] \approx a._{\mathcal{N}}[\mathcal{N}_1'].$$

*Parallelism $\|_{\mathcal{N}}$:* Consider

$$\mathcal{N} = (A_1 \cup A_2, Pl_1 \cup Pl_2, \longrightarrow, M_{01} \cup M_{02})$$

and

$$\mathcal{N}' = (A_1 \cup A_2, Pl_1' \cup Pl_2', \longrightarrow', M_{01}' \cup M_{02}')$$

where $\longrightarrow$ and $\longrightarrow'$ are as in the definition of $\|_{\mathcal{N}}$ so that

$$[\mathcal{N}_1]\|_{\mathcal{N}}[\mathcal{N}_2] = [\mathcal{N}] \text{ and } [\mathcal{N}_1']\|_{\mathcal{N}}[\mathcal{N}_2'] = [\mathcal{N}'].$$

Then $\mathcal{N} \approx \mathcal{N}'$ via $\mathcal{B} = \mathcal{B}_1 \cup \mathcal{B}_2$. Disjointness of $Pl_1$ and $Pl_2$ and $Pl_1{}'$ and $Pl_2{}'$ ensures that $\mathcal{B}$ is indeed a strong bisimulation between $\mathcal{N}$ and $\mathcal{N}'$. It follows

$$[\mathcal{N}_1] \|_{\mathcal{N}} [\mathcal{N}_2] \approx [\mathcal{N}_1{}'] \|_{\mathcal{N}} [\mathcal{N}_2{}'].$$

*Choice* $+_{\mathcal{N}}$: Consider

$$\mathcal{N} = (A_1 \cup A_2, Pl_1 \cup Pl_2 \cup (M_{01} \times M_{02}), \longrightarrow, M_{01} \times M_{02})$$

and

$$\mathcal{N}' = (A_1 \cup A_2, Pl_1{}' \cup Pl_2{}' \cup (M_{01}{}' \times M_{02}{}'), \longrightarrow', M_{01}{}' \times M_{02}{}')$$

where $\longrightarrow$ and $\longrightarrow'$ are as in the definition of $+_{\mathcal{N}}$ so that

$$[\mathcal{N}_1] +_{\mathcal{N}} [\mathcal{N}_2] = [\mathcal{N}] \quad \text{and} \quad [\mathcal{N}_1{}'] +_{\mathcal{N}} [\mathcal{N}_2{}'] = [\mathcal{N}'].$$

Then $\mathcal{N} \approx \mathcal{N}'$ via

$$\mathcal{B} = \mathcal{B}_1 \cup \mathcal{B}_2 \cup \{ \ ((p_1, p_2), (p_1{}', p_2{}')) \mid p_1 \in M_{01}, p_2 \in M_{02},$$
$$p_1{}' \in M_{01}{}', p_2{}' \in M_{02}{}', p_1 \mathcal{B}_1 p_1{}' \text{ and } p_2 \mathcal{B}_2 p_2{}' \}.$$

This time verifying that $\mathcal{B}$ is indeed a strong bisimulation between $\mathcal{N}$ and $\mathcal{N}'$ gets more complicated. We omit the details and conclude only

$$[\mathcal{N}_1] +_{\mathcal{N}} [\mathcal{N}_2] \approx [\mathcal{N}_1{}'] +_{\mathcal{N}} [\mathcal{N}_2{}'].$$

*Morphism* $[\varphi]_{\mathcal{N}}$: This case is particularly simple because we can take $\mathcal{B} = \mathcal{B}_1$ to show

$$[\mathcal{N}_1][\varphi]_{\mathcal{N}} \approx [\mathcal{N}_1{}'][\varphi]_{\mathcal{N}}. \qquad \square$$

We now turn to the main theorem of this section.

**First Compositionality Theorem 3.8.3** For all $n$-ary operator symbols $op$ of $CProc$ and all process terms $P_1, \ldots, P_n, \mu X.P \in CProc$,

(1) $\mathcal{N}[\![op(P_1, \ldots, P_n)]\!] \approx op_{\mathcal{N}}(\mathcal{N}[\![P_1]\!], \ldots, \mathcal{N}[\![P_n]\!])$,

(2) $\mathcal{N}[\![\mu X.P]\!] \approx \mathcal{N}[\![P\{\mu X.P/X\}]\!]$.

In fact, equality holds in (2) and in (1) except for $op = a.$ and $op = + $.

*Proof.* The $\mu$-expansion law (2) with equality is stated in Theorem 3.5.8. The compositionality laws (1) with equality obviously hold for

$$op \in \{ stop{:}A, div{:}A, [\varphi] \mid A \text{ communication alphabet}, \ \varphi \text{ action morphism } \}.$$

Thus we are left with the following cases:

*Prefix:* $op = a.$
We wish to show $\mathcal{N}[\![a.P]\!] \approx a._{\mathcal{N}} \mathcal{N}[\![P]\!]$ for every $P \in CProc$. Consider

$$\mathcal{N}_P = (\alpha(P), Sequ, \longrightarrow \downarrow \alpha(P), der(P)),$$

and

$$\mathcal{N} = (\alpha(P), Sequ, \longrightarrow \downarrow \alpha(P), \{a.P\}).$$

Then because of $a \in \alpha(P)$

$$\mathcal{N}[\![a.P]\!] = [\mathcal{N}] \text{ and } \mathcal{N}[\![P]\!] = [\mathcal{N}_P].$$

Since $a.P \in place(\mathcal{N}_P)$ is possible, e.g. for $P = \mu X.a.X$, we have in general

$$\mathcal{N}[\![a.P]\!] \neq a._{\mathcal{N}}\mathcal{N}[\![P]\!].$$

To construct $a._{\mathcal{N}} \mathcal{N}[\![P]\!]$, we need a completely new place. Let it be $a*P \notin Sequ$ and define

$$\mathcal{N}_0 = (\alpha(P), Sequ \cup \{a * P\}, \longrightarrow_0, \{a * P\})$$

where $\longrightarrow_0 = (\longrightarrow \downarrow \alpha(P)) \cup \{(\{a * P\}, a, dex(P))\}$. Then

$$[\mathcal{N}_0] = a._{\mathcal{N}}[\mathcal{N}_P].$$

It remains to show that

$$\mathcal{N} \approx \mathcal{N}_0.$$

To this end, consider the relation $\mathcal{B} \subseteq Sequ \times (Sequ \cup \{a * P\})$ defined by

$$\mathcal{B} = \text{id}_{Sequ} \cup \{(a.P, a * P)\}$$

with $\text{id}_{Sequ}$ denoting the identity on $Sequ$. $\mathcal{B}$ is a strong bisimulation between $\mathcal{N}$ and $\mathcal{N}_0$. This is easily established by observing that every reachable marking of $\mathcal{N}_0$ is either of the form $\{a*P\}$ or does not contain $a*P$ at all; then it is also a reachable marking of $\mathcal{N}$. Thus we obtain

$$\mathcal{N}[\![a.P]\!] = [\mathcal{N}] \approx [\mathcal{N}_0] = a._{\mathcal{N}}[\mathcal{N}_P] = a._{\mathcal{N}}\mathcal{N}[\![P]\!].$$

*Parallelism: op = ||*
We show $\mathcal{N}[\![P_1\|P_2]\!] = \mathcal{N}_1[\![P_1]\!] \|_{\mathcal{N}} \mathcal{N}_2[\![P_2]\!]$ for all $P_1, P_2 \in CProc$. Let $A = \alpha(P_1) \cap \alpha(P_2)$ and consider

$$\mathcal{N}_i = (\alpha(P_i), Sequ, \longrightarrow \downarrow \alpha(P_i), dex(P_i))$$

for $i = 1,2$ and

$$\mathcal{N} = (\alpha(P_1) \cup \alpha(P_2), Sequ, \longrightarrow \downarrow A, dex(P\|Q)).$$

Then

$$\mathcal{N}[\![P_1\|P_2]\!] = [\mathcal{N}] \text{ and } \mathcal{N}[\![P_i]\!] = [\mathcal{N}_i]$$

for $i = 1,2$. Since the places of $\mathcal{N}_1$ and $\mathcal{N}_2$ are not disjoint, we need other representatives in their isomorphism classes before applying the operator $\|_{\mathcal{N}}$. We take

$$\mathcal{N}_{11} = (\alpha(P_1), Sequ\|_A, \longrightarrow_{11}, dex(P_1)\|_A),$$

where
$$\longrightarrow_{11} = \{(\mathbb{P}\|_A, u, \mathbb{P}'\|_A) \mid \mathbb{P} \xrightarrow{u} \mathbb{P}' \text{ and } u \in \alpha(P_1) \cup \{\tau\}\},$$

and
$$\mathcal{N}_{21} = (\alpha(P_2), Sequ\|_A, \longrightarrow_{21}, dex(P_2)\|_A),$$

where
$$\longrightarrow_{21} = \{({}_A\|\mathbb{P}, u, {}_A\|\mathbb{P}') \mid \mathbb{P} \xrightarrow{u} \mathbb{P}' \text{ and } u \in \alpha(P_2) \cup \{\tau\}\}.$$

Then $\mathcal{N}_{11}$ and $\mathcal{N}_{21}$ are disjoint copies of $\mathcal{N}_1$ and $\mathcal{N}_2$ so that obviously

$$[\mathcal{N}_1] = [\mathcal{N}_{11}] \text{ and } [\mathcal{N}_2] = [\mathcal{N}_{21}].$$

Comparing the Petri net transition rules for parallel composition and the definition of $\|_\mathcal{N}$ yields:
$$[\mathcal{N}] = [\mathcal{N}_{11}]\|_\mathcal{N}[\mathcal{N}_{21}].$$

Putting everything together we obtain

$$\mathcal{N}[\![P_1\|P_2]\!] = [\mathcal{N}] = [\mathcal{N}_{11}]\|_\mathcal{N}[\mathcal{N}_{21}] = [\mathcal{N}_1]\|_\mathcal{N}[\mathcal{N}_2] = \mathcal{N}[\![P_1]\!]\|_\mathcal{N}\mathcal{N}[\![P_2]\!].$$

*Choice:* $op = +$
We wish to show $\mathcal{N}[\![P_1 + P_2]\!] \approx \mathcal{N}[\![P_1]\!] +_\mathcal{N} \mathcal{N}[\![P_2]\!]$ for all $P_1, P_2 \in CProc$. Let $A = \alpha(P_1) = \alpha(P_2)$ and consider

$$\mathcal{N}_i = (A, Sequ, \longrightarrow \downarrow A, dex(P_i))$$

for $i = 1,2$ and
$$\mathcal{N} = (A, Sequ, \longrightarrow \downarrow A, dex(P_1 + P_2)).$$

Since $place(\mathcal{N}_1) \cap place(\mathcal{N}_2) \neq \emptyset$ is possible, e.g. for $P_1 = a.c.stop:\{a,b,c\}$ and $P_2 = b.c.stop:\{a,b,c\}$, we have in general

$$\mathcal{N}[\![P_1 + P_2]\!] \neq \mathcal{N}[\![P_1]\!] +_\mathcal{N} \mathcal{N}[\![P_2]\!],$$

but we will show that this difference is only modulo $\approx$. To this end, we combine the proof ideas for the previous two cases. First we create for every sequential component $C$ two new copies denoted by $C+$ and $+C$. As in the case of parallelism, these are used to build two disjoint copies of $\mathcal{N}_1$ and $\mathcal{N}_2$ as required for applying $+_\mathcal{N}$, viz.

$$\mathcal{N}_{11} = (A, Sequ+, \longrightarrow_{11}, dex(P_1)+),$$

where
$$\longrightarrow_{11} = \{(\mathbb{P}+, u, \mathbb{Q}+) \mid \mathbb{P} \xrightarrow{u} \mathbb{Q} \text{ and } u \in A \cup \{\tau\}\},$$

and
$$\mathcal{N}_{21} = (A, +Sequ, \longrightarrow_{21}, +dex(P_2)),$$

where
$$\longrightarrow_{21} = \{(+\mathbb{P}, u, +\mathbb{Q}) \mid \mathbb{P} \xrightarrow{u} \mathbb{Q} \text{ and } u \in A \cup \{\tau\}\}.$$

Obviously
$$[\mathcal{N}_1] = [\mathcal{N}_{11}] \text{ and } [\mathcal{N}_2] = [\mathcal{N}_{21}].$$

Second, we introduce a version $\mathcal{N}_0$ of the net $\mathcal{N}$ containing completely new transitions, similarly to the case of prefix:

$$\mathcal{N}_0 = (A, Sequ \cup Sequ+ \cup +Sequ, \longrightarrow_0, dex(P+Q))$$

where

$$\begin{aligned}
\longrightarrow_0 = \quad & \{(\mathbb{Q}_1 + \cup (\mathbb{Q}_2 + dex(P_2)), u, \mathbb{R}+) \mid \mathbb{Q}_1 \cup \mathbb{Q}_2 \xrightarrow{u} \mathbb{R} \text{ with} \\
& \qquad\qquad\qquad \mathbb{Q}_1 \cap \mathbb{Q}_2 = \emptyset \text{ and } u \in A \cup \{\tau\} \ \} \\
\cup \ & \{((dex(P_1) + \mathbb{Q}_1) \cup +\mathbb{Q}_2, u, +\mathbb{R}) \mid \mathbb{Q}_1 \cup \mathbb{Q}_2 \xrightarrow{u} \mathbb{R} \text{ with} \\
& \qquad\qquad\qquad \mathbb{Q}_1 \cap \mathbb{Q}_2 = \emptyset \text{ and } u \in A \cup \{\tau\} \ \}.
\end{aligned}$$

In $\longrightarrow_0$ the transitions for choice keep track whether the left-hand or right-hand side of $+$ was chosen. By the definition of $+_\mathcal{N}$ and weak isomorphism, we realise:

$$[\mathcal{N}_0] = [\mathcal{N}_{11}] +_\mathcal{N} [\mathcal{N}_{21}].$$

It remains to show
$$\mathcal{N} \approx \mathcal{N}_0.$$

Consider the relation $\mathcal{B} \subseteq Sequ \times (Sequ \cup Sequ+ \cup +Sequ)$ defined as follows:

$$\mathcal{B} = \mathrm{id}_{Sequ} \cup \{(C, C+), (C, +C) \mid C \in Sequ\}.$$

$\mathcal{B}$ is a strong bisimulation between $\mathcal{N}$ and $\mathcal{N}_0$. This is easily established by observing that every reachable marking of $\mathcal{N}_0$ is either of the form

$$\{C_1+, \ldots, C_m+\} \cup (\{C_{m+1}, \ldots, C_{m+n}\} + dex(P_2))$$

or

$$\{+C_1, \ldots, +C_m\} \cup (dex(P_1) + \{C_{m+1}, \ldots, C_{m+n}\}).$$

The corresponding markings of $\mathcal{N}$ are obtained by dropping the unary $+$'s. By the transition relation of $\mathcal{N}$ and $\mathcal{N}_0$, every transition of $\mathcal{N}$ can be matched by a corresponding transition of $\mathcal{N}_0$ and vice versa as required for the transfer property of $\mathcal{B}$. Summarising, we obtain

$$\mathcal{N}[\![P_1 + P_2]\!] = [\mathcal{N}] \approx [\mathcal{N}_0] = [\mathcal{N}_{11}] +_\mathcal{N} [\mathcal{N}_{21}] = \mathcal{N}[\![P_1]\!] +_\mathcal{N} \mathcal{N}[\![P_2]\!].$$

This finishes the proof of the First Compositionality Theorem. $\qquad\qquad\square$

A Second Compositionality Theorem will be stated later in Section 4.6. It may seem as a shortcoming of our operational Petri net semantics that we can show compositionality only modulo strong bisimilarity. But in fact, it is an advantage because only by this deviation from the standard net operators does our semantics yield finite nets for all regular process terms (Finiteness Theorem 3.5.5). For example, equality

$$\mathcal{N}[\![\mu X.a.X]\!] = \mathcal{N}[\![a.\mu.X.a.X]\!] = a._{\mathcal{N}}\mathcal{N}[\![\mu X.a.X]\!]$$

would force $\mathcal{N}[\![\mu X.a.X]\!]$ to be infinite because the operator $a._{\mathcal{N}}$ always creates a completely new initial place.

Thus strong bisimilarity allows a greater flexibility for the net semantics. On the other hand, it is strong enough to preserve concurrency. We have shown this in the Causality Theorem 2.3.10 stating that strongly bisimilar nets have exactly the same causal nets. Recall from Section 2.3 that strong bisimilarity on nets is not transitive. Therefore reasoning about the net semantics of process terms with several operators has to be done stepwise. We illustrate this with an example similar to the one studied in Section 3.6.

**Example 3.8.4** Consider a process term of the form $(a.P \parallel b.Q)+c.R$ with $P, Q, R \in$ *CProc*. We wish to show that operational and compositional net semantics of this term admit the same concurrent computations. In other words, we wish to show that the nets

$$\mathcal{N}[\![(a.P \parallel b.Q) + c.R]\!]$$

and

$$(a._{\mathcal{N}}\mathcal{N}[\![P]\!] \parallel_{\mathcal{N}} b._{\mathcal{N}}\mathcal{N}[\![Q]\!]) +_{\mathcal{N}} c._{\mathcal{N}}\mathcal{N}[\![R]\!].$$

are causally equivalent.

Using the above Theorems 3.8.2 and 3.8.3, we obtain the following:

$$\mathcal{N}[\![(a.P \parallel b.Q) + c.R]\!] \approx \tag{3.13}$$
$$\mathcal{N}[\![a.P \parallel b.Q]\!] +_{\mathcal{N}} \mathcal{N}[\![c.R]\!],$$

$$\mathcal{N}[\![a.P \parallel b.Q]\!] +_{\mathcal{N}} \mathcal{N}[\![c.R]\!] \approx \tag{3.14}$$
$$(\mathcal{N}[\![a.P]\!] \parallel_{\mathcal{N}} \mathcal{N}[\![b.Q]\!]) +_{\mathcal{N}} \mathcal{N}[\![c.R]\!],$$

$$(\mathcal{N}[\![a.P]\!] \parallel_{\mathcal{N}} \mathcal{N}[\![b.Q]\!]) +_{\mathcal{N}} \mathcal{N}[\![c.R]\!] \approx \tag{3.15}$$
$$(a._{\mathcal{N}}\mathcal{N}[\![P]\!] \parallel_{\mathcal{N}} b._{\mathcal{N}}\mathcal{N}[\![Q]\!]) +_{\mathcal{N}} c._{\mathcal{N}}\mathcal{N}[\![R]\!].$$

By the Causality Theorem 2.3.10, we can replace in (3.13) – (3.15) strong bisimilarity $\approx$ by causal equivalence $\equiv_{caus}$. Since $\equiv_{caus}$ is an equivalence relation and thus transitive, we obtain

$$\mathcal{N}[\![(a.P \parallel b.Q) + c.R]\!] \equiv_{caus}$$
$$(a._{\mathcal{N}}\mathcal{N}[\![P]\!] \parallel_{\mathcal{N}} b._{\mathcal{N}}\mathcal{N}[\![Q]\!]) +_{\mathcal{N}} c._{\mathcal{N}}\mathcal{N}[\![R]\!]$$

as desired.                                                                                    □

# 4

# LOGICAL FORMULAS

Our third view of a process is that of a logical formula specifying the intended communication behaviour between user and process. This view brings about the necessary level of abstraction because we will apply the following principle:

> The internal structure of a process is irrelevant as long
> as it exhibits the specified communication behaviour.

But what exactly *is* the communication behaviour? Many answers are possible and meaningful. We aim at a simple, but widely applicable definition and therefore let it be a set of finite communication sequences

$$tr \in Comm^*,$$

known as *histories* or *traces* [Hoa80]. Since traces are insensitive to intervening internal actions $\tau$ or concurrent process activities, this definition is independant of both internal activity and concurrency. Our viewpoint is here that internal activity and concurrency are only part of the process construction, not of the specified communication behaviour. Of course, other viewpoints are possible. For example, in the work of Mazurkiewicz [Maz77] even the word "trace" is used for something more elaborate, viz. the equivalence class of finite communication sequences modulo an independence relation on communications expressing concurrency. To avoid confusion, we call these equivalence classes "Mazurkiewicz-traces" and reserve the word "trace" for finite sequences.

As specification language for trace sets we will use a *many-sorted first-order predicate logic*. Since its main sort is "trace", it is called *trace logic* and its formulas are called *trace formulas*. Informal use of trace logic appears in a number of papers (e.g. [CH81, MC81, Oss83, Sne85, Rem87, WGS87]). Precise syntax and semantics, however, is given only in the work of Zwiers [ZRE85, Zwi89]. We shall adopt Zwiers' proposal, but we need only a simplified version of it because we deal here only with atomic communications instead of messages sent along channels (cf. Section 2.1).

An important point of departure from the papers above is our novel way of linking process terms with trace formulas. It is given in the definition of when a process term $P$ *satisfies* a trace formula $S$, abbreviated

$$P \; sat \; S.$$

In [CH81, MC81, Oss83, ZRE85, Zwi89] trace formulas express only *safety properties* or *partial correctness* (cf. [OL82]): $P \; sat \; S$ if every trace of $P$ satisfies the formula $S$. This does not exclude the possibility that $P$ diverges or deadlocks. As a consequence, there exists a single process term which satisfies every trace specification with the same alphabet, viz. *div:A* but also *stop:A*. Such a process term is called a *miracle*, following Dijkstra [Dij76]. With miracles the task of process construction becomes trivial and meaningless. Therefore we shall be more demanding and use trace formulas also to express a simple type of *liveness property* implying *total correctness* (cf. [OL82]). Essentially, $P \; sat \; S$ if the following two conditions hold:

(1) *Safety.* $P$ may only engage in traces satisfying $S$.

(2) *Liveness.* $P$ must engage in every trace satisfying $S$.

The liveness condition is due to [OH86] and will be explained in detail in Section 4.3. It is related to the idea of Misra and Chandy of using so-called *quiescent* infinite trace specifications to express liveness in the setting of asynchronous communication (see [Jon87]). Here we remark only that it rules out processes $P$ with divergence and unwanted deadlocks. In fact, $P \; sat \; S$ implies that $P$ is *externally deterministic*, i.e. in every run of the process the user has exactly the same possibilities of communication, no matter which actions the process has pursued internally. Thus in our approach trace formulas can specify only a subset of processes. We are interested in this subset because, as we shall see in Chapter 5, it has many applications, and it allows us to formulate particularly simple *transformation rules* for the stepwise transformation of a given trace specification $S$ into a process term $P$ satisfying $S$. We believe that in computing it is essential to identify subclasses of problems or programs where things work better than in the general case.

Of course, trace logic is not the only specification language for processes. More common is *temporal logic* [Pnu77, Pnu86] because it can express more general safety and liveness properties. Often the *propositional subset* of temporal logic is used because it enjoys the finite model property and hence has a decidable validity problem. This result has been exploited for a fully automatic verification and even synthesis of finite-state processes from propositional temporal logic specifications [EC82, MW84].

We cannot use propositional temporal logic because processes need not be finite-state (cf. Section 3.5), but we could use first-order temporal logic since trace specifications can be translated into a fragment of it (see Section 4.3). The translation shows that trace specifications can be viewed as compact representations of larger temporal formulas. We prefer to work with this representation because it allows us, in Chapter 5, to formulate the transformation rules for process construction and verification in a *compositional* fashion (cf. [Roe85]).

Other approaches to the specification of processes use *modal logics* [HM85, GS86, Sti87, Ste89, BS90]. These logics mix logical operators with process operators like prefix and $\mu$-recursion. Since at present there does not exist any generally accepted approach to the specification of concurrent processes, we found it best to develop one particular approach as far as we can, viz. trace logic. We hope that at a later stage this work can then be used as a firm basis for evaluating advantages and disadvantages of the various approaches.

## 4.1 Trace Logic

We adopt syntax and semantics of trace logic from Zwiers [Zwi89]. However, since we do not consider channels, messages and termination signals, simplified definitions suffice so that in our case trace logic is a many-sorted predicate logic with the following sorts:

| | |
|---|---|
| *trace* | (finite sequences of communications) |
| *nat* | (natural numbers) |
| *comm* | (communications) |
| *log* | (logical values) |

*Trace logic* then consists of sorted expressions built up from sorted constants, variables and operator symbols. For notational convenience, trace formulas count here as expressions of sort *log*.

We use the following notation. All communications $a$, $b$ appear as constants of sort *trace* and of sort *comm*, and all natural numbers $k > 0$ appear as constants of sort *nat*. The set *Var* of *variables* is partitioned into a set *Var:trace* of variables $t$ of sort *trace* and a set *Var:nat* of variables $n$ of sort *nat*. For all communication alphabets $A$ and all communications $a$, $b$ there are unary operator symbols $\bullet{\downarrow}A$ and $\bullet[b/a]$ of sort

$$\bullet{\downarrow}A \;:\; trace \longrightarrow trace \quad \text{(projection)}$$
$$\bullet[b/a] \;:\; trace \longrightarrow trace \quad \text{(renaming)}$$

Further on, there are binary operator symbols $\bullet.\bullet$ and $\bullet[\bullet]$ of sort

$$\bullet.\bullet \;:\; trace \times trace \longrightarrow trace \quad \text{(concatenation)}$$
$$\bullet[\bullet] \;:\; trace \times nat \longrightarrow comm \quad \text{(selection)}$$

and a unary operator symbol $|\bullet|$ of sort

$$|\bullet| : trace \longrightarrow nat \quad \text{(length)}$$

The intended interpretation is given as a commentary. The remaining symbols used in trace logic are all standard.

**Definition 4.1.1** The syntax of trace logic is given by a set

$$Exp = Exp : trace \cup Exp : nat \cup Exp : comm \cup Exp : log$$

of *expressions* ranged over by $xe$. The constituents of $Exp$ are defined as follows.

(1) The set $Exp$:*trace* of *trace expressions* consists of all expressions $te$ that are generated by the production rules

$$te ::= \varepsilon \mid a \mid t \mid te_1.te_2 \mid te{\downarrow}A \mid te[b/a]$$

and that satisfiy the following context-sensitive restriction: every trace variable $t$ in a trace expression $te$ occurs within a subexpression of the form $te_0{\downarrow}A$ of $te$.

(2) The set $Exp$:*nat* of *natural number expressions* consists of the following expressions $ne$:

$$ne ::= k \mid n \mid ne_1 + ne_2 \mid ne_1 * ne_2 \mid |te|$$

(3) The set $Exp$:*comm* of *communication expressions* consists of the following expressions $ce$:

$$ce ::= a \mid te[ne]$$

(4) The set $Exp$:*log* of *trace formulas* or *logical expressions* consists of the following expressions $le$:

$$le ::= true \mid te_1 \leq te_2 \mid ne_1 \leq ne_2 \mid ce_1 = ce_2 \mid \neg le \mid le_1 \wedge le_2 \mid \exists t : le \mid \exists n : le$$

$$\square$$

Examples of trace expressions are

$$t{\downarrow}\{up\} \text{ and } ((up.t){\downarrow}\{up\}).dn \; ;$$

counterexamples are

$$t \text{ and } up.t.dn$$

because the context-sensitive restriction on trace expressions is not satisfied. This restriction is needed to prove some important properties of trace and other expressions like the Value Lemma 4.1.5, the Coincidence Lemma 4.1.6, and the Renaming Theorem 4.1.7.

*Free* and *bound* (occurrences of) variables in an expression $xe$ are defined as usual. Let $free(xe)$ denote the set of free variables in $xe$. The notation $xe\{te/t\}$ denotes the result of *substituting* the trace expression $te$ for every free occurrence of the trace variable $t$ in $xe$. As for process terms, substitution requires a preparatory renaming of the bound variables in $xe$ to avoid clashes with the free variables in $te$. Simultaneous substitution of a list $te_1,\ldots,te_n$ of trace expressions for a list of distinct trace variables $t_1,\ldots,t_n$ is denoted by $xe\{te_1,\ldots,te_n/t_1,\ldots,t_n\}$.

Furthermore, let $xe\{b/a\}$ denote the result of *renaming* every occurrence of the communication $a$ in $xe$ into $b$. Simultaneous renaming of a list of distinct communications $a_1,\ldots,a_n$ in $xe$ into the list $b_1,\ldots,b_n$ is denoted by $xe\{b_1,\ldots,b_n/a_1,\ldots,a_n\}$.

The *standard semantics* or *interpretation* $\Im$ *of trace logic* is introduced along the lines of Tarski's semantic definition for predicate logic. As a preparation, we fix for each sort a set of values, called the semantic domain of that sort. The definitions are mostly as expected:

- The semantic domain of sort *trace* is $Comm^*$, the set of finite sequences of communications, called here *communication traces* or just *traces*. We let *tr* range over $Comm^*$. The empty trace is denoted by $\varepsilon$. In a non-empty trace we separate the individual communications by the symbol "." denoting *concatenation*. For example,

$$up.up.dn$$

is the trace consisting of two communications *up* followed by one communication *dn*. In general, the concatenation of two traces $tr_1$ and $tr_2$ is denoted by $tr_1.tr_2$. Note that for every trace *tr* we have $\varepsilon.tr = tr.\varepsilon = tr$.

We often refer to the prefix relation between traces. A trace $tr_1$ is a *prefix* of a trace *tr*, abbreviated $tr_1 \le tr$, if there exists a trace $tr_2$ with $tr_1.tr_2 = tr$. For example,

$$up.dn \le up.dn.up.$$

Note that the empty trace is a prefix of every other trace.

- The semantic domain of sort *nat* is $\mathbb{N}_0$, the set of natural numbers including 0. As stated above, we let *k* range over $\mathbb{N}_0$.

- The semantic domain of sort *comm* is $Comm \cup \{\bot\}$, the set consisting of all communications and the special value $\bot$, called *bottom*. This value is needed to interpret communication expressions that do not yield a proper communication value. An example is

$$(up.up.dn)[5],$$

the fifth value of a trace $up.up.dn$ ; it yields $\bot$.

- The semantic domain of sort *log* is {true, false}, the set of Boolean values.

Note that by Definition 4.1.1, we have the following inclusions:

$$Comm \subseteq Comm^* \subseteq Exp : trace \qquad (4.1)$$

and

$$\mathbb{N}_0 \subseteq Exp : nat. \qquad (4.2)$$

Thus every trace is also a trace expression. Hence we may write substitutions of the form $xe\{tr/t\}$ or $xe\{tr_1,\ldots,tr_n/t_1,\ldots,t_n\}$. Note that throughout this book we carefully distinguish traces, ranged over by *tr*, from trace variables, ranged over by *t*.

The *semantic domain of* $\Im$ is now defined as the union of the semantic domains of sort *trace, nat, comm* and *log* :

$$DOM_\Im = Comm^* \cup \mathbb{N}_0 \cup Comm \cup \{\bot\} \cup \{\text{true, false}\}.$$

The standard semantics of logic is a mapping

$$\Im : Exp \longrightarrow (Env_\Im \longrightarrow DOM_\Im)$$

that assigns to every expression in $Exp$ a value in the semantics domain $DOM_\Im$ with the help of so-called *environments*. These are mappings

$$\rho : Var \longrightarrow DOM_\Im$$

that assign values to the free variables in expressions. The set $Env_\Im$ consists of all environments $\rho$ that respect sorts, i.e. where trace variables $t$ get values $\rho(t) \in Comm^*$ and natural number variables $n$ get values $\rho(n) \in \mathbb{N}_0$.

**Definition 4.1.2** With the above conventions the standard semantics $\Im$ of trace logic is defined as follows.

(1) *Semantics of trace expressions* yielding values in $Comm^*$:

$\Im[\![\varepsilon]\!](\rho) = \varepsilon$

$\Im[\![a]\!](\rho) = a$

$\Im[\![t]\!](\rho) = \rho(t)$

$\Im[\![te_1.te_2]\!](\rho) = \Im[\![te_1]\!](\rho)._\Im\Im[\![te_2]\!](\rho),$
> the concatenation of the traces $\Im[\![te_1]\!](\rho)$ and $\Im[\![te_2]\!](\rho)$.

$\Im[\![te{\downarrow}A]\!](\rho) = \Im[\![te]\!](\rho){\downarrow}_\Im A,$
> the projection of the trace $\Im[\![te]\!](\rho)$ onto $A$, i.e. $\Im[\![te]\!](\rho)$ with all communications outside $A$ removed.

$\Im[\![te[b/a]]\!](\rho) = \Im[\![te]\!](\rho)\{b/a\},$
> i.e. the trace $\Im[\![te]\!](\rho)$ with every occurrence of $a$ replaced by $b$. As for process terms, brackets $[\dots]$ denote an unevaluated renaming operator and brackets $\{\dots\}$ its evaluation.

(2) *Semantics of natural number expressions* yielding values in $\mathbb{N}_0$:

$\Im[\![k]\!](\rho) = k$

$\Im[\![n]\!](\rho) = \rho(n)$

$\Im[\![ne_1+ne_2]\!](\rho) = \Im[\![ne_1]\!](\rho) +_\Im \Im[\![ne_2]\!](\rho),$
> the standard interpretation of addition on $\mathbb{N}_0$.

$\Im[\![ne_1 * ne_2]\!](\rho) = \Im[\![ne_1]\!](\rho) *_\Im \Im[\![ne_2]\!](\rho),$
> the standard interpretation of multiplication on $\mathbb{N}_0$.

$\Im[\![|te|]\!](\rho) = |\Im[\![te]\!](\rho)|_\Im,$
> the length of the trace $\Im[\![te]\!](\rho)$.

(3) *Semantics of communication expressions* yielding values in $Comm \cup \{\bot\}$:

$$\Im[\![a]\!](\rho) = a$$

$$\Im[\![te[ne]]\!](\rho) = \Im[\![te]\!](\rho)[\Im[\![ne]\!](\rho)]_\Im,$$
the $\Im[\![ne]\!](\rho)$-th element of the trace $\Im[\![te]\!](\rho)$ if it exists and the value $\bot$ otherwise.

(4) *Semantics of trace formulas* yielding values in {true, false}:

$$\Im[\![true]\!](\rho) = \text{true}$$

$$\Im[\![te_1 \leq te_2]\!](\rho) = \text{true} \ \text{ iff } \ \Im[\![te_1]\!](\rho) \leq_\Im \Im[\![te_2]\!](\rho),$$
where $\leq_\Im$ is the reflexive prefix relation on $Comm^*$.

$$\Im[\![ne_1 \leq ne_2]\!](\rho) = \text{true} \ \text{ iff } \ \Im[\![ne_1]\!](\rho) \leq_\Im \Im[\![ne_2]\!](\rho),$$
where $\leq_\Im$ is the standard reflexive ordering relation on $\mathbb{N}_0$.

$$\Im[\![ce_1 = ce_2]\!](\rho) = \text{true} \ \text{ iff } \ \Im[\![ce_1]\!](\rho) =_\Im \Im[\![ce_2]\!](\rho),$$
where $=_\Im$ is the equality on $DOM_\Im$. Note that the value $\bot$, which is possible for a communication expression, is treated as any other value. Thus $\bot =_\Im \bot$ is the only true equality involving $\bot$.

$$\Im[\![\neg le]\!](\rho) = \text{true} \ \text{ iff } \ \Im[\![le]\!](\rho) = \text{false}$$

$$\Im[\![le_1 \wedge le_2]\!] = \text{true} \ \text{ iff } \ \Im[\![le_1]\!](\rho) = \text{true and } \Im[\![le_2]\!](\rho) = \text{false}$$

$$\Im[\![\exists t : le]\!] = \text{true} \ \text{ iff } \ \Im[\![le]\!](\rho[tr/t]) = \text{true}$$
for some $tr \in Comm^*$. Here $\rho[tr/t]$ is the environment that agrees with $\rho$ except for the trace variable $t$ where its value is $tr$.

$$\Im[\![\exists n : le]\!](\rho) = \text{true} \ \text{ iff } \ \Im[\![le]\!](\rho[k/n]) = \text{true}$$
for some $k \in \mathbb{N}_0$. Here $\rho[k/n]$ is the environment that agrees with $\rho$ except for the natural number variable $n$ where its value is $k$.

(5) A trace formula *le* is called *valid*, abbreviated

$$\models le,$$

if $\Im[\![le]\!](\rho) = \text{true}$ for all environments $\rho$.                    $\square$

If the context avoids ambiguities, we will drop the subscript $\Im$ in the above semantic operators and thus use the same symbols in both syntax and semantics.

In the remainder of this section we investigate the basic semantic properties of trace logic; it may be skipped at the first reading. To simplify proofs, we consider only expressions in a certain normal form where all trace projections $\bullet{\downarrow}A$ are adjacent to the trace variables [Old86, Zwi89].

**Definition 4.1.3** A trace expression $te$ is called *normal* if it can be generated by the following syntax rules:

$$te ::= \varepsilon \mid a \mid t{\downarrow}A \mid te_1.te_2 \mid te[b/a].$$

An arbitrary expression $xe$ is normal if every maximal trace expression $te$ in $xe$ is normal. Maximal means that $te$ is not contained in a larger trace expression in $xe$.

□

Thanks to the context-sensitive restriction imposed on trace expressions by Definition 4.1.1, every expression $xe$ can be converted into a unique normal expression, called its *normal form* and denoted by

$$xe_{norm}.$$

This conversion is done by applying from left to right the following algebraic laws which move all projections $\bullet{\downarrow}A$ in the trace expressions of $xe$ down to the trace variables.

(1) $\varepsilon{\downarrow}A = \varepsilon$

(2) $a{\downarrow}A = a$ if $a \in A$

(3) $a{\downarrow}A = \varepsilon$ if $a \notin A$

(4) $(te{\downarrow}B){\downarrow}A = te{\downarrow}(B \cap A)$

(5) $(te_1.te_2){\downarrow}A = (te_1{\downarrow}A).(te_2{\downarrow}A)$

(6) $(te[b/a]){\downarrow}A = te{\downarrow}(A - \{a\})$ if $b \notin A$

(7) $(te[b/a]){\downarrow}A = (te{\downarrow}(A \cup \{a\}))[b/a]$ if $b \in A$

Obviously, these laws preserve the semantics of trace expressions:

**Proposition 4.1.4** Let $LHS = RHS$ be one of the above equations $(1) - (7)$. Then

$$\Im[\![LHS]\!](\rho) = \Im[\![RHS]\!](\rho)$$

for every environment $\rho$.

□

Equipped with these techniques, we can determine the semantic values of expressions more precisely. Let the *extended alphabet*

$$\alpha\alpha(xe) \tag{4.3}$$

of an expression $xe$ be the set of all communications appearing somewhere in $xe$. By convention, whenever $te{\downarrow}A$ is a subexpression in $xe$ then $A \subseteq \alpha\alpha(xe)$. For example,

$$xe =_{df} (lk.t){\downarrow}\{dn\} \le (lk.t){\downarrow}\{up\}$$

yields $\alpha\alpha = \{lk, dn, up\}$. We can now state:

**Value Lemma 4.1.5** For all trace expressions $te$, communication expressions $ce$ and environments $\rho$ the values are as follows:

$$\Im[\![te]\!](\rho) \subseteq \alpha\alpha(te)^* \text{ and } \Im[\![ce]\!](\rho) \in \alpha\alpha(ce) \cup \{\bot\} \,.$$

*Proof.* We use Proposition 4.1.4, the observation that $\alpha\alpha(te_{norm}) \subseteq \alpha\alpha(te)$ and $\alpha\alpha(ce_{norm}) \subseteq \alpha\alpha(ce)$, and straightforward induction on the structure on the normal forms $te_{norm}$ and $ce_{norm}$. $\square$

Note that the context-sensitive restriction imposed on trace expressions by Definition 4.1.1 is needed for the Value Lemma. For example, if we considered $te = t$, we would obtain $\alpha\alpha(t) = \emptyset$ but not $\Im[\![t]\!](\rho) \subseteq \emptyset$. An analogous problem would arise if we considered $ce = t[1]$. In the above proof of the Value Lemma, the existence of the normal forms $te_{norm}$ and $ce_{norm}$ relies on that restriction. The restriction is also needed for the following lemma.

**Coincidence Lemma 4.1.6** Consider an expression $xe$. If two environments $\rho_1$ and $\rho_2$ agree on all free natural number variables in $xe$ and, within the extended alphabet $\alpha\alpha(xe)$, also on all free trace variables $t$, i.e. if

$$\rho_1(t){\downarrow}\alpha\alpha(xe) = \rho_2(t){\downarrow}\alpha\alpha(xe)$$

for all such $t$, then the values of $xe$ at $\rho_1$ and $\rho_2$ coincide:

$$\Im[\![xe]\!](\rho_1) = \Im[\![xe]\!](\rho_2).$$

*Proof.* We use Proposition 4.1.4, the observation that $\alpha\alpha(te_{norm}) \subseteq \alpha\alpha(te)$, and straightforward induction on the structure of $xe$. $\square$

We need these lemmas in the proof of the next theorem, on renaming. Recall that renaming $xe\{b/a\}$ has already been explained for expressions $xe$ and thus, as part of expressions, for traces $tr$, communications $c$ and communication alphabets $A$:

$$tr\{b/a\}, c\{b/a\}, A\{b/a\}.$$

It is convenient to extend this notation to elements $d \in \mathbb{N}_0 \cup \{\bot\} \cup \{\text{true}, \text{false}\}$, simply by putting

$$d\{b/a\} =_{df} d. \tag{4.4}$$

Then $d\{b/a\}$ is defined for every element $d \in DOM_\Im$, the semantic domain of the interpretation $\Im$. Now we can lift renaming to environments $\rho \in Var \longrightarrow DOM_\Im$ by defining $\rho\{b/a\}$ pointwise:

$$\rho\{b/a\}(n) =_{df} \rho(n)\{b/a\} = \rho(n) \tag{4.5}$$
$$\rho\{b/a\}(t) =_{df} \rho(t)\{b/a\}, \tag{4.6}$$

for all variables $n$ of sort *nat* and $t$ of sort *trace*.

With these conventions, we can now state the announced theorem.

**Renaming Theorem 4.1.7** Consider an expression $xe$, communications $a$, $b$ and an environment $\rho$ satisfying the following two conditions:

$$b \notin \alpha\alpha\{xe\} \tag{4.7}$$

and for all trace variables $t \in \mathit{free}(te)$

$$\rho(t) \in \alpha\alpha(xe)^*. \tag{4.8}$$

Then renaming $\bullet\{b/a\}$ behaves compositionally, i.e. the equation

$$(\Im[\![xe]\!](\rho))\{b/a\} = (\Im[\![xe\{b/a\}]\!](\rho\{b/a\})$$

holds.

*Proof.* We proceed by induction on the structure of $xe$, distinguishing the sort of $xe$.

*Case 1: $xe$ is a trace expression $te$.*
The argument is straightforward except for the following two subcases.

- $te = te_1{\downarrow}A$: By definition,

$$(\Im[\![te]\!](\rho))\{b/a\} = ((\Im[\![te_1]\!](\rho)){\downarrow}_{\Im}A)\{b/a\}.$$

Now observe that $A \subseteq \alpha\alpha(te)$ and $\Im[\![te]\!](\rho) \in \alpha\alpha(te)^*$ either by the Value Lemma 4.1.5 or, if $te_1 = t$ for some trace variable $t$, by condition (4.8). Thus by (4.7), the communication $b$ neither occurs in $A$ nor in the trace $\Im[\![te_1]\!](\rho)$. Therefore

$$((\Im[\![te_1]\!](\rho)){\downarrow}_{\Im}A\{b/a\} = ((\Im[\![te_1]\!](\rho))\{b/a\}){\downarrow}_{\Im}A\{b/a\}.$$

Using the induction hypothesis, we continue to calculate:

$$((\Im[\![te_1]\!](\rho))\{b/a\}){\downarrow}_{\Im}A\{b/a\}$$
$$= (\Im[\![te_1\{b/a\}]\!]((\rho\{b/a\})){\downarrow}_{\Im}A\{b/a\}$$
$$= \Im[\![te_1\{b/a\}{\downarrow}A\{b/a\}]\!](\rho\{b/a\})$$
$$= \Im[\![te\{b/a\}]\!](\rho\{b/a\}).$$

- $te = te_1[b_1/a_1]$: By definition,

$$(\Im[\![te]\!](\rho))\{b/a\} = ((\Im[\![te_1]\!](\rho))\{b_1/a_1\})\{b/a\}.$$

Next, by an exhaustive case analysis considering in turn:

(i)  $a = a_1 = b_1$

(ii) $a = a_1, a \neq b_1$

(iii) $a \neq a_1, a = b_1$

(iv) $a \neq a_1, a \neq b_1$

and by noticing, for case (iv), that $b \neq a_1$ since $a_1 \in \alpha\alpha(te)$ and condition (4.7) on $b$, we see that

$$((\Im[\![te_1]\!](\rho))\{b_1/a_1\})\{b/a\} = ((\Im[\![te_1]\!](\rho))\{b/a\})\{b_1\{b/a\}/a_1\{b/a\}\}.$$

Finally, using the induction hypothesis and by simple calculation, we find:

$$((\Im[\![te_1]\!](\rho))\{b/a\})\{b_1\{b/a\}/a_1\{b/a\}\}$$
$$= \Im[\![(te_1\{b/a\})\{b_1\{b/a\}/a_1\{b/a\}\}]\!](\rho\{b/a\})$$
$$= \Im[\![te\{b/a\}]\!](\rho\{b/a\}).$$

*Case 2: xe is a natural number expression ne.*
By (4.4), we have $\Im[\![ne]\!](\rho) = (\Im[\![ne]\!](\rho))\{b/a\}$. Thus it suffices to show inductively that

$$\Im[\![ne]\!](\rho) = \Im[\![ne\{b/a\}]\!](\rho\{b/a\}).$$

The argument is straightforward or, in the subcase $ne = |te|$, by reduction to Case 1.

*Case 3: xe is a communication expression ce.*
This case can be reduced to Cases 1 and 2.

*Case 4: xe is a logical expression le.*
By (4.4), we have $\Im[\![le]\!](\rho) = (\Im[\![le]\!](\rho))\{b/a\}$. Thus it suffices to show inductively that

$$\Im[\![le]\!](\rho) = \Im[\![le\{b/a\}]\!](\rho\{b/a\}).$$

Most subcases are straightforward or by reduction to Cases 1 – 3. The only interesting subcase is quantification:

- $le = \exists t : le_1$: Consider some $b$ and $\rho$ satisfying conditions (4.7) and (4.8), i.e. $b \notin \alpha\alpha(le)$ and $\rho(t') \in \alpha\alpha(le)^*$ for all $t' \in \mathit{free}(le)$. Suppose that

$$\Im[\![le\{b/a\}]\!](\rho\{b/a\}) = \text{true}.$$

Then

$$\Im[\![\exists t : (le_1\{b/a\})]\!](\rho\{b/a\}) = \text{true}.$$

By the Coincidence Lemma 4.1.6, we may assume that

$$\Im[\![le_1\{b/a\}]\!](\rho_1) = \text{true}$$

for some environment $\rho_1$ that coincides with $\rho\{b/a\}$ except at $t$ where $\rho_1(t) \in \alpha\alpha(le_1\{b/a\})^*$. Since $\alpha\alpha(le_1) = \alpha\alpha(le)$, we have $b \notin \alpha\alpha(le_1)$. Hence there exists an environment $\rho_2$ that coincides with $\rho$ except at $t$, where $\rho_2(t) \in$

$\alpha\alpha(le_1)^*$, and which satisfies $\rho_1 = \rho_2\{b/a\}$. Thus $\rho_2(t') \in \alpha\alpha(le_1)^*$ for all $t' \in free(le_1)$ and

$$\Im[\![le_1\{b/a\}]\!](\rho_2\{b/a\}) = \text{true}.$$

By the induction hypothesis,

$$\Im[\![le_1]\!](\rho_2) = \text{true}.$$

Consequently,

$$\Im[\![le]\!](\rho) = \text{true}.$$

Showing the converse, that $\Im[\![le]\!](\rho) = \text{true}$ implies $\Im[\![le\{b/a\}]\!](\rho\{b/a\}) = \text{true}$, uses a similar, but slightly simpler argument.

This completes the proof of the Renaming Theorem.                               □

Consider once more the expression

$$xe =_{df} (lk.t)\!\!\downarrow\!\!\{dn\} \le (lk.t)\!\!\downarrow\!\!\{up\}$$

yielding $\alpha\alpha(xe) = \{lk, dn, up\}$ as its extended alphabet. By the Coincidence Lemma 4.1.6, for any two environments $\rho_1$ and $\rho_2$ that agree at $t$ within $\alpha\alpha(xe)$, i.e. with

$$\rho_1(t)\!\!\downarrow\!\!\{lk, dn, up\} = \rho_2(t)\!\!\downarrow\!\!\{lk, dn, up\}.$$

the values of $xe$ at $\rho_1$ and $\rho_2$ coincide:

$$\Im[\![xe]\!](\rho_1) = \Im[\![xe]\!](\rho_2). \tag{4.9}$$

On the other hand, it is easy to see that the communication $lk$ is irrelevant for the value of $xe$ because the trace variable $t$ is accessed only via the trace projections $t\!\!\downarrow\!\!\{dn\}$ and $t\!\!\downarrow\!\!\{up\}$. Thus already

$$\rho_1(t)\!\!\downarrow\!\!\{dn, up\} = \rho_2(t)\!\!\downarrow\!\!\{dn, up\}$$

implies (4.9) above.

This observation brings us to a more restricted notion of alphabet: for a given trace variable $t$ we wish to define the *projection alphabet* $\alpha_t(xe)$ of an expression $xe$ as the smallest subset of $\alpha\alpha(xe)$ such that $t$ is accessed only via trace projections within $\alpha_t(xe)$. The definition is not straightforward because expressions allow an arbitrary nesting of projection and renaming operators. Consider for example

$$xe_1 =_{df} (lk.t)\!\!\downarrow\!\!\{dn\} \le ((lk.t)\{dn/lk\})\!\!\downarrow\!\!\{lk, up\}.$$

Should the communication $lk$ appear in $\alpha_t(xe_1)$ or not? To answer this question, we follow [Zwi89] and first convert every expression into normal form. Then the alphabet can be determined easily.

**Definition 4.1.8** Let $t$ be a trace variable. For normal trace expressions $te$ the *projection alphabet* or simply *alphabet* $\alpha_t(te)$ is defined inductively as follows:

$$\alpha_t(\varepsilon) = \alpha_t(a) = \emptyset$$
$$\alpha_t(t{\downarrow}A) = A$$
$$\alpha_t(t_0{\downarrow}A) = \emptyset \text{ if } t \neq t_0$$
$$\alpha_t(te_1.te_2) = \alpha_t(te_1) \cup \alpha_t(te_2)$$
$$\alpha_t(te[b/a]) = \alpha_t(te)$$

For arbitrary trace expressions $te$ the alphabet is given by

$$\alpha_t(te) = \alpha_t(te_{norm}).$$

For arbitrary expressions $xe$ the alphabet is

$$\alpha_t(xe) = \bigcup \alpha_t(te),$$

where the union is taken over all maximal trace expressions $te$ in $xe$ that contain an occurrence of $t$ that is free in $xe$. If such a trace expression does not exist, the alphabet $\alpha_t(xe)$ is empty. □

**Example 4.1.9** We determine the projection alphabet $\alpha_t(xe_1)$ of the expression

$$xe_1 =_{df} (lk.t){\downarrow}\{dn\} \leq ((lk.t)[dn/lk]){\downarrow}\{lk, up\}$$

considered earlier. The maximal trace expressions of $xe_1$ are

$$te1 =_{df} (lk.t){\downarrow}\{dn\}$$

and

$$te2 =_{df} ((lk.t)[dn/lk]){\downarrow}\{lk, up\}.$$

Using the projection laws, they are transformed into normal form:

$$te1_{norm} = \varepsilon.t{\downarrow}\{dn\}$$

and

$$te2_{norm} = \varepsilon.t{\downarrow}\{up\}.$$

Thus we obtain

$$\alpha_t(xe_1) = \alpha_t(te1) \cup \alpha_t(te2) = \alpha_t(te1_{norm}) \cup \alpha_t(te2_{norm}) = \{dn, up\}. \qquad \square$$

For projection alphabets we can now state the following stronger version of the Coincidence Lemma 4.1.6.

**Projection Lemma 4.1.10** Consider an expression $xe$. If two environments $\rho_1$ and $\rho_2$ agree on all free natural number variables in $xe$ and, within their projection alphabet $\alpha_t(xe)$, on all free trace variables $t$ as well, i.e. if

$$\rho_1(t){\downarrow}\alpha_t(xe) = \rho_2(t){\downarrow}\alpha_t(xe)$$

for all such $t$, then the values of $xe$ at $\rho_1$ and $\rho_2$ coincide:

$$\Im[\![xe]\!](\rho_1) = \Im[\![xe]\!](\rho_2).$$

*Proof.* We use induction on the structure of $xe_{norm}$, thereby relying on Proposition 4.1.4. □

This finishes our investigation of the basic semantic properties of trace logic.

## 4.2   Trace Specifications

In this section we consider the question: How can we use trace logic for the specifica-tion of trace sets? The answer is that we shall use a certain subset of trace formulas. To this end, we introduce a distinguished trace variable called $h$ standing for *history*.

**Definition 4.2.1** The set *Spec* of *trace specifications*, ranged over by $S$, $T$, $U$, con-sists of all trace formulas where at most the distinguished variable $h$ of sort *trace* is free. For a trace specification $S$ the *projection alphabet*, or simply *alphabet*, $\alpha(S)$ is defined by referring to Definition 4.1.8: $\alpha(S) = \alpha_h(S)$. The *extended alphabet* $\alpha\alpha(S)$ is defined as in (4.3), i.e. as the set of all communications appearing somewhere in $S$.

The logical value $\Im[\![S]\!](\rho)$ of a trace specification $S$ depends only on the trace value $\rho(h)$. We therefore say that a trace $tr \in Comm^*$ *satisfies* $S$ and write

$$tr \models S$$

if $\Im[\![S]\!](\rho) = \text{true}$ for $\rho(h) = tr$. Note the following relationship between satisfaction and validity:

$$tr \models S \text{ iff } \models S\{tr/h\}.$$

Recall that $S\{tr/h\}$ is the result of substituting the trace $tr$ for every free occurence of the trace variable $h$ in $S$. By (4.1), $S\{tr/h\}$ is a well-defined trace formula whose validity is expressed by $\models S\{tr/h\}$. Thus a trace specification $S$ specifies the set of all traces satisfying $S$. In fact, whether or not a trace satisfies a trace specification $S$ depends only on the trace value within the projection alphabet $\alpha(S)$. This is an immediate consequence of the Projection Lemma 4.1.10.

**Projection Corollary 4.2.2** Let $S$ be a trace specification. Then

$$tr \models S \text{ iff } tr{\downarrow}\alpha(S) \models S$$

for all traces $tr \in Comm^*$.                                                                    □

We shall frequently apply this corollary in Chapter 5 when proving the soundness of various transformation rules dealing with trace specifications. Then we will also need the following consequence of the Renaming Theorem 4.1.7.

**Renaming Corollary 4.2.3** Consider a trace specification $S$ and communications $a$, $b$ with $b \notin \alpha\alpha(S)$. Then

$$tr \models S \text{ iff } tr\{b/a\} \models S\{b/a\}$$

for all traces $tr \in \alpha(S)$.                                                                    □

Let us exercise the above concepts in an example.

**Example 4.2.4** Consider the trace specification

$$S =_{df} |\ (lk.h)\!\downarrow\!\{dn\}\ | \ \leq \ |\ (lk.h)\!\downarrow\!\{up\}\ |.$$

Using Definition 4.1.1, we see that for example,

$$\varepsilon \ \models \ S$$
$$up \ \models \ S$$
$$up.dn \ \models \ S$$
$$up.up.dn \ \models \ S,$$

but that $dn \models S$ does not hold.

The projection alphabet of $S$ is $\alpha(S) = \{up, dn\}$. By the Projection Corollary 4.2.2,

$$up.happy.up.birth.dn.day \models S$$

because

$$(up.happy.up.birth.dn.day)\!\downarrow\!\alpha(S) = up.up.dn$$

and $up.up.dn \models S$ as stated above.

The extended alphabet of $S$ is $\alpha\alpha(S) = \{up, dn, lk\}$. Consider the renaming of the communication $dn$ into $out$. Then

$$S\{out/dn\} = |\ (lk.h)\!\downarrow\!\{out\}\ | \ \leq \ |\ (lk.h)\!\downarrow\!\{up\}\ |$$

and

$$(up.up.dn)\{out/dn\} = up.up.out\ .$$

Since $out \notin \alpha\alpha(S)$ and $up.up.dn \models S$, the Renaming Corollary 4.2.3 yields

$$up.up.out \models S\{out/dn\}\ .$$

To see that the condition of the Renaming Corollary is needed, consider the renaming of $dn$ into $lk$. Since $lk \notin \alpha(S)$, the Renaming Corollary 4.2.3 is not applicable. Indeed, we have $up.dn \models S$ but not

$$(up.dn)\{lk/dn\} \models S\{lk/dn\}. \qquad \square$$

Since trace logic includes the standard interpretation of Peano arithmetic, viz. the model $(\mathbb{N}_0, 0, 1, +_\Im, *_\Im, =_\Im)$, trace specifications are very expressive. The following theorem is essentially stated in Zwiers' book ([Zwi89], pp. 203-205).

**Expressiveness Theorem 4.2.5** Let $\mathcal{L} \subseteq A^*$ be a recursively enumerable set of traces over the alphabet $A$. Then there exists a trace specification $TRACE(\mathcal{L})$ with projection alphabet $\alpha(TRACE(\mathcal{L})) = A$ such that

$$tr \in \mathcal{L} \ \text{iff} \ tr \models TRACE(\mathcal{L})$$

for all traces $tr \in A^*$. The same is true for sets $\mathcal{L} \subseteq A^*$ whose complement in $A^*$ is recursively enumerable.

*Proof idea.* Using coding functions and standard techniques from recursion theory, every recursively enumerable set $\mathcal{L} \subseteq A^*$ can be represented by a first order formula $le$ in Peano arithmetic [Sho67]. From $le$ the trace specification $TRACE(\mathcal{L})$ can be constructed easily. Obviously, negation deals with the complements of recursively enumerable sets.                                                                    □

For practical specification, such a general expressiveness result is not very helpful, and a concise and clear notation is important. For this purpose, we make use of several abbreviations, most of which are self-explanatory.

(1) Natural number expressions *counting* the number of communications in a trace:

$$a\#te =_{df} |te\downarrow\{a\}|.$$

(2) Communication expressions *selecting specific* elements of a trace:

$$first\ te\ =_{df}\ te[1]$$
$$last\ te\ =_{df}\ te[|te|].$$

(3) Extended syntax for logical expressions:

$$ne_1 = ne_2\ =_{df}\ ne_1 \leq ne_2 \wedge ne_2 \leq ne_1$$
$$te_1 = te_2\ =_{df}\ te_1 \leq te_2 \wedge te_2 \leq te_1$$
$$le_1 \vee le_2\ =_{df}\ \neg(\neg le_1 \wedge \neg le_2)$$
$$le_1 \longrightarrow le_2\ =_{df}\ \neg le_1 \vee le_2$$
$$le_1 \longleftrightarrow le_2\ =_{df}\ (le_1 \longrightarrow le_2) \wedge (le_2 \longrightarrow le_1)$$
$$\forall t : le\ =_{df}\ \neg \exists t : \neg le$$
$$\forall n : le\ =_{df}\ \neg \exists n : \neg le$$
$$\exists t \in A^* : le\ =_{df}\ \exists t : (le\{t\downarrow A/t\})$$
$$\forall t \in A^* : le\ =_{df}\ \forall t : (le\{t\downarrow A/t\}).$$

We may also use any other convenient notation, e.g. for $k \geq 2$,

$$\bigwedge_{j=1}^{1} le_j\ =_{df}\ le_1$$

$$\bigwedge_{j=1}^{k} le_j\ =_{df}\ (\bigwedge_{j=1}^{k-1} le_j) \wedge le_k$$

$$ne_1 \leq \ldots \leq ne_k\ =_{df}\ \bigwedge_{j=1}^{k-1} ne_j \leq ne_{j+1}.$$

(4) *Regular expressions* denoting sets of traces: we use the standard syntax for regular expressions (see e.g. [HU69]) augmented by the symbol *pref* denoting *prefix closure*. Thus in our case the set *Reg* of regular expressions consists of the following expressions *re*:

$$
\begin{array}{lll}
re ::= & \varepsilon & \text{(empty trace)} \\
\mid & a & \text{(communication)} \\
\mid & pref\, re & \text{(prefix closure)} \\
\mid & re_1 \cup re_2 & \text{(union)} \\
\mid & re_1.re_2 & \text{(concatenation)} \\
\mid & re^* & \text{(Kleene star)}.
\end{array}
$$

Let $\alpha(re)$ denote the set of all communications occuring in $re$. Then the standard semantics of $Reg$ is a mapping that assigns to every regular expression $re$ a set or *language*

$$\mathcal{L}[\![re]\!] \subseteq \alpha(re)^*$$

of traces. As usual this set is defined by induction on the structure of $re$:

$$
\begin{aligned}
\mathcal{L}[\![\varepsilon]\!] &= \{\varepsilon\} \\
\mathcal{L}[\![a]\!] &= \{a\} \\
\mathcal{L}[\![pref\, re]\!] &= \{tr \mid \exists t(h.t \in \Im[\![re]\!])\} \\
\mathcal{L}[\![re_1 \cup re_2]\!] &= \mathcal{L}[\![re_1]\!] \cup \mathcal{L}[\![re_2]\!] \\
\mathcal{L}[\![re_1.re_2]\!] &= \{tr_1.tr_2 \mid tr_1 \in \mathcal{L}[\![re_1]\!] \wedge tr_2 \in \mathcal{L}[\![re_2]\!]\} \\
\mathcal{L}[\![re^*]\!] &= \mathcal{L}[\![re]\!]^*.
\end{aligned}
$$

Relying on the Expressiveness Theorem 4.2.5, we introduce as an abbreviation the following trace specification:

$$h{\downarrow}\alpha(re) \in re =_{df} TRACE(\mathcal{L}[\![re]\!]).$$

Note that for all traces $tr \in Comm^*$

$$tr \models TRACE(\mathcal{L}[\![re]\!]) \text{ iff } tr{\downarrow}\alpha(re) \in \mathcal{L}[\![re]\!].$$

We shall give below a direct construction of $TRACE(\mathcal{L}[\![re]\!])$ following the syntactic structure of $re$. This provides us with information about the extended alphabet of $TRACE(\mathcal{L}[\![re]\!])$.

Syntactic ambiguities in trace specifications are resolved by using brackets and some priorities among the operator symbols. Within trace expressions the unary symbols $\bullet{\downarrow}A$ and $\bullet[\rho]$ have a higher priority than the binary concatenation $\bullet.\bullet$; within natural number expressions $*$ has a higher priority than $+$; within logical expressions we stipulate the following priorities:

priority 0 : $\longrightarrow$ and $\longleftrightarrow$
priority 1 : $\wedge$ and $\vee$
priority 2 : $\neg$ and $\exists$ and $\forall$.

Additionally, we save brackets by relying on the associativity of $\wedge$ and $\vee$. When writing sequences of quantifiers, we drop inner occurences of the symbol ":". For example, we write

$$\exists t_1 \in A_1^* \ \exists t_2 \in A_2^* : le$$

instead of $\exists t_1 \in A_1^* : \exists t_2 \in A_2^* : le$.

**Example 4.2.6** As an exercise in the use of the above conventions we now give a direct construction of a trace specification $TRACE(re)$ for each regular expression $re$. We proceed by induction on the structure of $re$; the only difficult case is of course the Kleene star $re^*$:

$$
\begin{aligned}
TRACE(\varepsilon) \quad &=_{df} \quad h{\downarrow}\emptyset = \varepsilon \\
TRACE(a) \quad &=_{df} \quad a\#h = 1 \\
TRACE(pref\, re) \quad &=_{df} \quad \exists t : TRACE(re)\{h.t/h\} \\
TRACE(re_1 \cup re_2) \quad &=_{df} \quad TRACE(re_1) \vee TRACE(re_2) \\
TRACE(re_1.re_2) \quad &=_{df} \quad \exists t_1 \in \alpha(re_1)^* \, \exists t_2 \in \alpha(re_2)^* : (h{\downarrow}\alpha(re_1.re_2) = t_1.t_2 \wedge \\
&\qquad\qquad TRACE(re_1)\{t_1/h\} \wedge TRACE(re_2)\{t_2/h\}) \\[6pt]
TRACE(re^*) \quad &=_{df} \quad \exists t_1 \in (\alpha(re) \cup \{\&\})^* : (h{\downarrow}\alpha(re) = t_1{\downarrow}\alpha(re) \wedge \\
&\qquad \forall t_2 \in (\alpha(re) \cup \{\&\})^* \, \forall t_3 \in \alpha(re)^* \, \forall t_4 \in (\alpha(re) \cup \{\&\})^* : \\
&\qquad (t_1 = t_2.\&.t_3.\&.t_4 \longrightarrow TRACE(re)\{t_3/h\})),
\end{aligned}
$$

where $\&$ is a fresh communication symbol not occuring in $re$. The idea of this construction is as follows. By definition, every trace $h$ described by $re^*$ is the concatenation of a number of traces $t_3$ of $re$. In order to recognize the concatenation points more easily, $h$ is expanded into a trace $t_1$ where at least one symbol $\&$ is inserted at the beginning and the end, and at all concatenation points of traces $t_3$ of $re$.

With these definitions we have

$$tr \in \mathcal{L}[\![re]\!] \text{ iff } tr \models TRACE(re)$$

for all traces $tr \in \alpha(re)^*$. Thus we can take $TRACE(re)$ instead of the "anonymous" specification $TRACE(\mathcal{L}[\![re]\!])$ which exists by virtue of the Expressiveness Theorem 4.2.5. Note that we have

$$
\begin{aligned}
\alpha(TRACE(re)) \quad &= \quad \alpha(re) \\
\alpha\alpha(TRACE(re)) \quad &\subseteq \quad \alpha(re) \cup \{\&\}
\end{aligned}
$$

for all regular expressions $re$ not themselves involving the symbol $\&$.                     $\square$

## 4.3   Process Correctness

In this section we relate process terms to trace specification by introducing a novel notion of process correctness. It defines when a process term $P$ *satisfies* a trace specification $S$, abbreviated

$$P \; sat \; S.$$

Let us begin with an informal explanation. We stipulate a rudimentary user interface of the process P which may be pictured as follows:

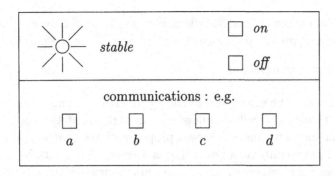

The ingredients are:

(1) a power switch for starting and halting the process (on or off switch);

(2) a stability light that indicates when the internal process activity has ceased;

(3) communication buttons, one for each communication symbol in the alphabet $\alpha(P)$. Communication between user and process is possible only when the stability light is on. A particular communication is performed by depressing the corresponding communication button. If this button cannot be depressed, the process is not ready for that communication.

There do exist more comfortable user interfaces, but we will make do with the above.

Consider now a communication trace $tr = a_1 \ldots a_n$ over $\alpha(P)$. We say that $P$ *may engage* in $tr$ if there exists a transition sequence of the process where the user was able to depress the communication buttons $a_1 \ldots a_n$ in that order. We say that $P$ *must engage* in $tr$ if the following holds: When started the process eventually becomes stable. Then it is possible for the user to communicate $a_1$ by depressing the corresponding communication button. Now the process may engage in some internal activity, but eventually it becomes stable again. Then it is ready for the next communication $a_2$ with the user, and so on for $a_3, \ldots, a_n$. Moreover, after the last communication $a_n$ the process eventually becomes stable again. Summarising, in every transition sequence of the process the user is able to depress the communication buttons $a_1, \ldots, a_n$ in that order, after which the process eventually becomes stable. Stability can be viewed as an acknowledgement by the process for a successful communication with the user. We say that $P$ is *stable immediately* if the stability light goes on immediately after switching on the process.

These explanations should suffice for appreciating the following definition of process correctness [Old89].

**Definition 4.3.1** Consider a closed process term $P$ and a trace specification $S$. We say that $P$ is *correct* with respect to $S$, or $P$ *satisfies* $S$, abbreviated

$$P \; sat \; S,$$

if $\alpha(P) = \alpha(S)$ and the following conditions hold:

(1) *Safety.* For every trace $tr \in \alpha(P)^*$ whenever $P$ may engage in $tr$ then $tr \models S$.

(2) *Liveness.* For every trace $tr \in \alpha(S)^*$ whenever *pref tr* $\models S$ then $P$ must engage in $tr$. The notation *pref tr* $\models S$ means that $tr$ and all its prefixes satisfy $S$.

(3) *Stability.* $P$ is stable immediately.                                                □

The distinction between the safety and liveness properties of concurrent processes is due to Lamport (see e.g. [OL82]). Following Lamport, a safety property states that nothing bad ever happens and a liveness property states that something good eventually happens. In our context, a bad thing is a trace $tr$ not satisfying $S$ and a good thing is the successful engagement in all communications of a trace $tr$. Note that the notion of safety is different from safeness defined for nets in Section 2.2: safeness can be viewed as a specific safety property of the token game of a net. Stability is also a safety property, but it is singled out here because its rôle is more technical. Its presence allows a more powerful transformation rule for the choice operator later in Chapter 5. For mathematical characterisations of safety and liveness properties see [AS85].

In what follows we give formal definitions of the notions of "may" and "must engage" and of initial stability by looking at the Petri net denoted by $P$. The intuition behind these definitions is as follows. Whereas transitions labelled by a communication occur only if the user participates in them, transitions labelled by $\tau$ occur autonomously at an unknown, but positive speed. Thus $\tau$-transitions give rise to unstability and divergence.

**Definition 4.3.2** Consider a net $\mathcal{N} = (A, Pl, \longrightarrow, M_0)$ and let $M, M' \in mark(\mathcal{N})$ and $tr \in A^*$.

(1) *Progress properties.* The set of *next possible actions* at $M$ is given by

$$next(M) = \{u \in Act | \exists t \in \longrightarrow : pre(t) \subseteq M \text{ and } Act(t) = u\}.$$

$M$ is called *stable* if $\tau \notin next(M)$ otherwise it is called *unstable*. $M$ is *ready* for a communication $b$ if $M$ is stable and $b \in next(M)$. $M$ is ready for the communication set $A$ if $M$ is stable and $next(M) = A$. $\mathcal{N}$ *is stable immediately* if $M_0$ is stable. We write

$$M \overset{tr}{\Longrightarrow} M'$$

if there exists a finite transition sequence

$$M \overset{t_1}{\longrightarrow} M_1 \dots M_{n-1} \overset{t_n}{\longrightarrow} M_n = M'$$

such that

$$tr = (act(t_1) \dots act(t_n)) \backslash \tau,$$

i.e. $tr$ results from the sequence of actions $act(t_1) \dots act(t_n)$ by deleting all internal actions $\tau$.

(2) *Divergence properties.* $\mathcal{N}$ can *diverge* from $M$ if there exists an infinite transition sequence

$$M \xrightarrow{\;t_1\;} M_1 \xrightarrow{\;t_2\;} M_2 \xrightarrow{\;t_3\;} \ldots$$

such that

$$\tau = act(t_1) = act(t_2) = act(t_3) = \ldots$$

$\mathcal{N}$ can *diverge immediately* if $\mathcal{N}$ can diverge from $M_0$. $\mathcal{N}$ can *diverge after tr* if there exists a marking $M$ with

$$M_0 \overset{tr}{\Longrightarrow} M$$

such that $\mathcal{N}$ can diverge from $M$. $\mathcal{N}$ can *diverge only after tr* if whenever $\mathcal{N}$ can diverge after some trace $tr'$ then $tr \leq tr'$. $\mathcal{N}$ can *diverge* if there is a marking $M \in mark(\mathcal{N})$ from which $\mathcal{N}$ can diverge. $\mathcal{N}$ is *divergence free* if $\mathcal{N}$ cannot diverge.

(3) *Deadlock properties.* $\mathcal{N}$ *deadlocks* at $M$ if $next(M) = \emptyset$. $\mathcal{N}$ *deadlocks immediately* if $\mathcal{N}$ deadlocks at $M_0$. $\mathcal{N}$ can *deadlock after tr* if there exists a marking $M$ with

$$M_0 \overset{tr}{\Longrightarrow} M$$

such that $\mathcal{N}$ deadlocks at $M$. $\mathcal{N}$ can *deadlock only after tr* if whenever $\mathcal{N}$ can deadlock after some trace $tr'$ then $tr \leq tr'$. $\mathcal{N}$ can *deadlock* if there is a marking $M \in mark(\mathcal{N})$ at which $\mathcal{N}$ deadlocks. $\mathcal{N}$ is *deadlock free* if $\mathcal{N}$ cannot deadlock.

$\square$

We now turn to process terms.

**Definition 4.3.3** Consider a closed process term $P$, a representative $\mathcal{N}_0 = (\alpha(P), Pl, \longrightarrow, M_0)$ of the abstract net $\mathcal{N}[\![P]\!]$, and a trace $tr \in \alpha(P)^*$

(1) $P$ *is stable immediately* if $\mathcal{N}_0$ is so.

(2) $P$ *can diverge* (*immediately* or *after tr* or *only after tr*) if $\mathcal{N}_0$ can do so. $P$ *is divergence free* if $\mathcal{N}_0$ is so.

(3) $P$ *deadlocks immediately* if $\mathcal{N}_0$ does so. $P$ *can deadlock* (*after tr* or *only after tr*) if $\mathcal{N}_0$ can do so. $P$ *is deadlock free* if $\mathcal{N}_0$ is so.

(4) $P$ *may engage* in $tr$ if there exists a marking $M \in mark(\mathcal{N}_0)$ such that

$$M_0 \overset{tr}{\Longrightarrow} M.$$

(5) $P$ *must engage* in $tr = a_1 \ldots a_n$ if the process term

$$P \parallel a_1 \ldots a_n.stop{:}\alpha(P)$$

is divergence free and can deadlock only after $tr$.

$\square$

Clearly, the above definitions are independent of the choice of the representative $\mathcal{N}_0$. The formalisations of immediate stability and "may engage" capture the intuitions mentioned earlier, but the formalisation of "must engage" requires some explanation. The process term $a_1 \ldots a_n.stop{:}\alpha(P)$ models a user wishing to communicate the trace $tr = a_1 \ldots a_n$ to $P$ and then stop. Communication is enforced by making the alphabet of user and process identical. Thus the parallel composition $P \parallel a_1 \ldots a_n.stop{:}\alpha(P)$ can behave only as follows: it can engage in some prefix $a_1 \ldots a_k$ of $tr$ with $0 \leq k \leq n$ and then either diverge (i.e. never become stable again), or deadlock (i.e. become stable, but unable to engage in any further communication). The user's wish to communicate $tr$ is realised if and only if $P \parallel a_1 \ldots a_n.stop{:}\alpha(P)$ never diverges and if it deadlocks only after $tr$. A final deadlock is unavoidable because the user wishes to stop. This is how we formalise the notion of "must engage".

The terminology of "may" and "must engage" originates from DeNicola and Hennessy's work on testing of processes [DH84, Hen88]. There it is used to define several so-called testing equivalences on processes, among them one for the "may" case and one for the "must" case. Our definition of "may engage" is equivalent to the one given in [DH84, Hen88] but our definition of "must engage" is stronger. We require that $P \parallel a_1 \ldots a_n.stop{:}\alpha(P)$ cannot diverge whereas [DH84, Hen88] allows divergence after the final communication $a_n$. We consider here divergence as an undesirable process behaviour no matter where it occurs. This approach simplifies the design of the transformation rules from trace specifications to correct process terms in Chapter 5.

Next we prove some basic properties of the above notions. To this end, we need the following general result about trees due to König.

**König's Infinity Lemma 4.3.4** Every finitely branching tree is either finite or it has an infinite path.

*Proof.* See [Kön27] or [Knu68], p. 381. $\qquad\qquad\qquad\qquad\qquad\qquad\square$

**Proposition 4.3.5** Consider a closed process term $P$, traces $tr, tr' \in \alpha(P)^*$ and a representative $\mathcal{N}_0 = (\alpha(P), Pl, \longrightarrow, M_0)$ of $\mathcal{N}[\![P]\!]$. Then the following holds:

(1) *Prefix closure.* If $P$ may engage in $tr$ then also in every prefix of $tr$.

(2) "Must" implies "may", i.e. if $P$ must engage in $tr$ then $P$ may engage in $tr$, but in general not vice versa.

(3) If for some fixed trace $tr$ there are infinitely many transition sequences

$$ M \xrightarrow{\;t_1\;} M_1 \ldots \xrightarrow{\;t_n\;} M_n $$

with

$$ tr = (act(t_1) \ldots act(t_n)) \backslash \tau $$

then there exists a prefix $tr'$ of $tr$ such that $P$ can diverge after $tr'$.

*Proof.* Properties (1) and (2) are straightforward. To prove (3), consider a trace $tr$ for which the assumption of (3) holds. By the Petri net transition rules given in Definition 3.3.4, the finite transition sequences

$$M_0 \xrightarrow{t_1} M_1 \ldots \xrightarrow{t_n} M_n$$

of $\mathcal{N}_0$, for which $(act(t_1) \ldots act(t_n))\backslash\tau$ is a prefix of $tr$, constitute the finite paths of a finitely branching tree. By the assumption of (3), this tree is infinite. Thus König's Infinity Lemma 4.3.4 implies that it contains an infinite path corresponding to an infinite transition sequence

$$M_0 \xrightarrow{t_1} M_1 \xrightarrow{t_2} M_2 \xrightarrow{t_3} \ldots$$

where for some $n \geq 1$ the trace

$$tr' = (act(t_1) \ldots act(t_n))\backslash\tau$$

is a prefix of $tr$ and where otherwise

$$\tau = act(t_{n+1}) = act(t_{n+2}) = \ldots$$

holds. Thus $P$ can diverge after $tr$. □

We shall also need a notion of external determinism. Intuitively, a process is externally deterministic if the user cannot detect any nondeterminism by communicating with it. Formally, we define this notion as follows:

**Definition 4.3.6** Consider a divergence free, closed process term $P$ and some representative $\mathcal{N}_0 = (\alpha(P), Pl, \longrightarrow, M_0)$ of $\mathcal{N}[\![P]\!]$. Then $P$ is called *externally deterministic* if for all traces $tr \in \alpha(P)^*$, all communications $b \in Comm$ and all markings $M_1, M_2 \in mark(\mathcal{N}_0)$, whenever

$$M_0 \overset{tr.b}{\Longrightarrow} M_1 \text{ and } M_0 \overset{tr}{\Longrightarrow} M_2$$

such that $M_2$ is stable, then

$$b \in next(M_2).$$

That is: every communication $b$ after a trace $tr$ is possible also when stability has occurred after $tr$. □

For externally deterministic processes every comunication trace $tr$ uniquely determines the next stable set of communications, i.e. whenever

$$M_0 \overset{tr}{\Longrightarrow} M_1 \text{ and } M_0 \overset{tr}{\Longrightarrow} M_2$$

such that $M_1$ and $M_2$ are stable then

$$next(M_1) = next(M_2).$$

With the above definitions at hand, let us now have a closer look at our notion of process correctness. We will show that $P$ *sat* $S$ has very strong consequences for $P$.

**Proposition 4.3.7** Consider a closed process term $P$ and a trace specification $S$. Then $P$ *sat* $S$ implies the following:

(1) "May" is equivalent to "must", i.e. for every trace $tr \in \alpha(P)^*$ the process $P$ may engage in $tr$ if and only if $P$ must engage in $tr$.

(2) $P$ is divergence free.

(3) $P$ is externally deterministic.

*Proof.*  Let $\mathcal{N} = (\alpha(P), Pl, \longrightarrow, M_0)$ be a representative of $\mathcal{N}[\![P]\!]$.

Fact (1): Assume that $P$ may engage in some trace $tr$. By Proposition 4.3.5(1), $P$ may also engage in every prefix of $tr$. Then the safety condition of $P$ *sat* $S$ implies *pref tr* $\models S$ which by the liveness requirement implies that $P$ must engage in $tr$. For the converse see Proposition 4.3.5(2).

Fact (2): Suppose $P$ can diverge. Then there exists a trace $tr = a_1 \ldots a_n$ and a marking $M \in mark(\mathcal{N}_0)$ with $M_0 \overset{tr}{\Longrightarrow} M$ such that $\mathcal{N}_0$ can diverge from $M$. $M_0 \overset{tr}{\Longrightarrow} M$ implies that $P$ may engage in $tr$. By (1), $P$ must engage in $tr$, which is a contradiction because $P \parallel a_1 \ldots a_n.stop{:}\alpha(P)$ is not divergence free.

Fact (3): Suppose $M_0 \overset{tr.b}{\Longrightarrow} M_1$ and $M_0 \overset{tr}{\Longrightarrow} M_2$ where $M_2$ is stable, but $b \notin next(M_2)$. Then $P$ may engage in the trace $tr.b$, but it is not the case that $P$ must engage in $tr.b$, contradicting (1). Indeed, consider

$$P \parallel tr.b.stop{:}\alpha(P).$$

By the Petri net transition rules,

$$dex(P) \parallel_{\alpha(P)} \cup_{\alpha(P)} \parallel \{tr.b.stop{:}\alpha(P)\} \overset{tr}{\Longrightarrow} M_2 \parallel_{\alpha(P)} \cup_{\alpha(P)} \parallel \{b.stop{:}\alpha(P)\}$$

where the set of next possible markings of the latter marking is empty because $M_2$ is stable and $b \notin next(M_2)$ . Thus $P \parallel tr.b.stop{:}\alpha(P)$ can deadlock too early.  □

By Proposition 4.3.7, trace formulas specify only divergence free and externally deterministic processes. This is a clear restriction of the approach presented in this chapter, but it yields an interesting class of processes with many applications and the simplest verification rules. It is possible to extend our approach to deal with nondeterministic processes as well (see Chapter 6), but at the expense of more complicated verification rules.

**Examples 4.3.8** Let us consider the trace specification

$$S =_{df} 0 \le up\#h - dn\#h \le 2$$

which is an abbreviation for $dn\#h \le up\#h \le 2 + dn\#h$, and examine how a process $P$ satisfying $S$ should behave. Since $P$ *sat* $S$ implies

$$\alpha(P) = \alpha(S) = \{up, dn\},$$

$P$ should engage only in the communications $up$ and $dn$. By the safety condition, for every communication trace $tr$ that $P$ may engage in, the difference between the number of $up$'s and $dn$'s is $0, 1$, or $2$. If $P$ has engaged in such a trace $tr$ and the extension $tr.dn$ still satisfies $S$, the liveness condition of $P$ *sat* $S$ requires that after $tr$ the process $P$ must engage in the communication $dn$. The same is true for $up$.

Thus $S$ specifies that $P$ should behave like a bounded counter of capacity 2 which can internally store a natural number $n$ with $0 \le n \le 2$. After a communication trace $tr$, the number stored is

$$n = up\#tr - dn\#tr.$$

Initially, when $tr$ is empty, $n$ is zero. Communicating $up$ increments $n$ and communicating $dn$ decrements $n$. Of course, these communications are possible only if the resulting changes of $n$ do not exceed the counter bounds.

A process term satisfying $S$ is

$$P =_{df} \mu X.up.\mu Y.(dn.X + up.dn.Y) ;$$

it denotes the following abstract net:

$$\mathcal{N}[\![P]\!] =$$

This net is purely sequential, i.e. every reachable marking contains at most one token, and there are no internal actions involved.

Another process term satisfying $S$ is

$$Q =_{df} ((\mu X.up.dn.X)[lk/dn] \parallel (\mu X.up.dn.X)[lk/up]) \backslash lk ;$$

it denotes the following abstract net:

$$\mathcal{N}[\![Q]\!] =$$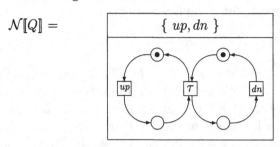

Here, after each *up*-transition, the net has to engage in an internal action $\tau$ before it is ready for the corresponding *dn*-transition. Since $\tau$-actions occur autonomously, readiness for the next *dn* is guaranteed, as required by the specification $S$. This leads in fact to the marking

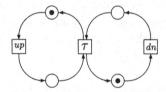

where *up* and *dn* are concurrently enabled.

The examples of $P$ and $Q$ demonstrate that presence or absence of concurrency or intervening internal activity are treated here as properties of the implementation (process term and net), not of the specification.

It is easy to generalise the above trace specification. For $k \geq 1$ a bounded counter of capacity $k$ is specified by

$$S_k =_{df} 0 \leq up\#h - dn\#h \leq k.$$

If we drop the upper bound $k$, we obtain a trace specification $S_\infty$ of an unbounded counter that can store an arbitrary large natural number:

$$S_\infty =_{df} dn\#h \leq up\#h.$$

In a process satisfying $S_\infty$ the communication *up* may and must occur after every trace. One such process is given by the term

$$P_\infty =_{df} \mu X.up.(X[lk/dn] \parallel \mu Y.dn.lk.Y) \backslash lk$$

considered in Example 3.5.2. Recall that $P_\infty$ denotes the infinite abstract net

$\mathcal{N}[\![P_\infty]\!] =$

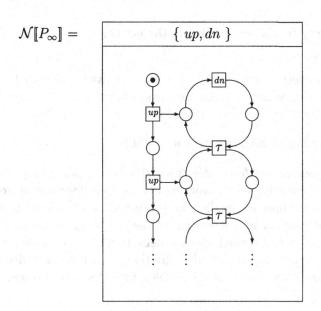

After the $n$-th communication $up$ the net will engage in $n-1$ internal actions $\tau$ before being ready for the corresponding $n$-th communication $dn$. But again, these intervening internal actions do not impair the user's view of the specified behaviour.

$\square$

Trace specifications $S$ are formulas of ordinary predicate logic, but the notion of process correctness, $P$ *sat* $S$, refers to operational or temporal properties of $P$. It is common to express such properties in *temporal logic* initiated by Pnueli [Pnu77]. It is instructive to look briefly at a translation of trace specifications into temporal logic.

Given a trace specification $S$, the corresponding temporal logic formula is

$$T(S) \quad =_{df} \quad \square S \tag{4.10}$$

$$\wedge \square \lozenge (stable \wedge ready = \{b \in \alpha(S) | S\{h.b/h\}\}) \tag{4.11}$$

$$\wedge stable \tag{4.12}$$

which is to be interpreted over transition sequences

$$M_0 \xrightarrow{\ t_1\ } M_1 \xrightarrow{\ t_2\ } M_2 \dots \xrightarrow{\ t_n\ } M_n = M$$

of Petri nets $\mathcal{N}_0 = (A, Pl, \longrightarrow, M_0)$. As usual, the temporal operators $\square$ and $\lozenge$ stand for "always" and "eventually". In $T(S)$ we stipulate that at every marking $M \in mark(\mathcal{N}_0)$ the following variables are observable:

- the distinguished trace variable "$h$",

- the Boolean variable "$stable$", and

- the set-valued variable "$ready$".

Then the lines of $T(S)$ read as follows:

- (4.10) states that in every reachable marking of the net the value of $h$ satisfies the formula $S$.

- (4.11) states that from every reachable marking the net eventually reaches a (possibly different) marking which is stable and ready for the set of communications $b$ allowed by $S$ after the present value of $h$.

- (4.13) states that at the initial marking the net is stable.

Now $P$ *sat* $S$ iff the representatives $\mathcal{N}_0$ of $\mathcal{N}[\![P]\!]$ satisfy the temporal properties expressed by $T(S)$. Thus conceptually, we are working in a certain fragment of first-order temporal logic, but in our approach explicit knowledge of this fragment is not needed. We can view $S$ as a compact representation of the temporal formula $T(S)$. The temporal operators of $T(S)$ are absorbed into our definition of $P$ *sat* $S$ and into the compositional verification rules based on this definition. We leave any deeper analysis of this and other fragments of temporal logic as a topic for future research.

## 4.4   Modified Readiness Semantics

The liveness condition of the satisfaction relation $P$ *sat* $S$ is difficult to check when only the net semantics of $P$ is available. To simplify matters, we introduce now a second, more abstract semantics for process terms. It is a variation of the readiness semantics $\mathcal{R}$ introduced in [OH86]. The main idea of $\mathcal{R}$ is to record information about the process behaviour in the form of pairs $(tr, \mathcal{F})$ consisting of a trace $tr$ and a so-called *ready set* $\mathcal{F}$. This is a set of communications in which the process is ready to engage when it has become stable after the trace $tr$ [Hoa81, FLP84]. In $\mathcal{R}$, nondeterminism is represented by associating more than one ready set with the trace $tr$. Additionally, $\mathcal{R}$ records information about divergence, and applies a certain closure operator due to [BHR84] known as "chaotic closure". The semantics $\mathcal{R}$ is modified here in three aspects:

(1) Information about initial instability is recorded. This is needed because we use here Milner's choice operator $+$ instead of Hoare's two operators $\square$ and *or*, which distinguish external and internal choice as in [OH86].

(2) The "acceptance closure" due to [DH84] is enforced on the ready sets.

(3) A new "radiation closure" on ready sets is enforced; it will be explained below.

With these modifications the readiness semantics is in complete harmony with the satisfaction relation $P$ *sat* $S$. We explain this in Example 4.4.4 and prove it later in Section 4.7.

To avoid confusion, we shall write $\mathcal{R}^*$ for the modified readiness semantics. Formally, it is a mapping

$$\mathcal{R}^*[\![\,\cdot\,]\!] : CProc \longrightarrow DOM_{\mathcal{R}}$$

which assigns to every $P \in CProc$ an element $\mathcal{R}^*[\![P]\!]$ in the so-called *readiness domain* $DOM_{\mathcal{R}}$. This domain consists of pairs

$$(A, \Gamma)$$

where $A$ is a communication alphabet and $\Gamma$ is a set of *process information*. We consider three types of process information:

(1) The element $\tau$ indicating initial *unstability*.

(2) *Ready pairs* $(tr, \mathcal{F})$ consisting of a trace $tr \in A^*$ and a ready set $\mathcal{F} \subseteq A$.

(3) *Divergence points* $(tr, \uparrow)$ consisting of a trace $tr \in A^*$ and a special symbol $\uparrow$ standing for divergence.

Formally the set of process information can be expressed as follows:

$$Info_{\mathcal{R}} : A = \{\tau\} \cup (A^* \times \mathcal{P}(A)) \cup (A^* \times \{\uparrow\}).$$

Define

$$DOM_{\mathcal{R}} : A = \{(A, \Gamma) \mid \Gamma \subseteq Info_{\mathcal{R}} : A\}.$$

The readiness domain is then given by

$$DOM_{\mathcal{R}} = \bigcup DOM_{\mathcal{R}} : A$$

where the union is taken over all communication alphabets $A$.

We define the alphabet of a pair $(A, \Gamma) \in DOM_{\mathcal{R}}$ by

$$\alpha(A, \Gamma) = A$$

and its set of process information by

$$\pi(A, \Gamma) = \Gamma$$

We adopt the following notational conventions: letters $\gamma, \delta$ range over $Info_{\mathcal{R}} : A$; letters $\Gamma, \Delta$ over subsets of $Info_{\mathcal{R}} : A$ and hence pairs $(A, \Gamma)$, $(B, \Delta)$ over $DOM_{\mathcal{R}}$; letters $\mathcal{F}, \mathcal{G}, \mathcal{H}$ range over ready sets and the letter $\mathcal{X}$ can either be a ready set or the symbol $\uparrow$.

The mapping $\mathcal{R}^*[\![\cdot]\!]$ retrieves the relevant process information from the operational Petri net semantics. Hence we talk of an operational readiness semantics. First we consider individual nets.

**Definition 4.4.1** The *readiness semantics* of a Petri net $\mathcal{N} = (A, Pl, \longrightarrow, M_0)$ is given by

$$\begin{aligned}
\mathcal{R}^*(\mathcal{N}) = \quad & close(A, \{\tau \mid M_0 \text{ is unstable }\} \\
& \cup \{(tr, \mathcal{F}) \mid \exists M \in mark(\mathcal{N}) : M_0 \overset{tr}{\Longrightarrow} M \text{ and } M \text{ is stable} \\
& \qquad\qquad\qquad\qquad\qquad\qquad\quad \text{and } \mathcal{F} = next(M)\} \\
& \cup \{(tr, \uparrow) \mid \exists M \in mark(\mathcal{N}) : M_0 \overset{tr}{\Longrightarrow} M \text{ and } \mathcal{N} \text{ can diverge from } M\}),
\end{aligned}$$

where the closure operator $close: DOM_{\mathcal{R}} \longrightarrow DOM_{\mathcal{R}}$ is defined as follows:

$$close(A, \Gamma) = (A, \Gamma \quad \cup \quad \{(tr, \mathcal{G}) \mid \exists \mathcal{F} : (tr, \mathcal{F}) \in \Gamma \text{ and } \mathcal{F} \subseteq \mathcal{G} \subseteq succ(tr, \Gamma)\}$$
$$\cup \quad \{(tr', \mathcal{X}) \mid \exists tr \leq tr' : (tr, \uparrow) \in \Gamma \text{ and } tr' \in A^*$$
$$\text{and } (\mathcal{X} \subseteq A \text{ or } \mathcal{X} = \uparrow)\}$$
$$\cup \quad \{(tr, \mathcal{G}) \mid \exists a : (tr.a, \uparrow) \in \Gamma \text{ and } \mathcal{G} \subseteq succ(tr, \Gamma)\}).$$

Here $succ(tr, \Gamma)$ denotes the set of all *successor communications* of $tr$ in $\Gamma$:

$$succ(tr, \Gamma) = \{a \mid \exists \mathcal{X} : (tr.a, \mathcal{X}) \in \Gamma\}.$$

The *readiness semantics of an abstract net* $[\mathcal{N}]$ is given by

$$\mathcal{R}^*([\mathcal{N}]) = \mathcal{R}^*(\mathcal{N})$$

and the (*operational*) *readiness semantics of a closed process term* $P$ is given by

$$\mathcal{R}^*[\![P]\!] = \mathcal{R}^*(\mathcal{N}[\![P]\!]).\qquad\qquad \square$$

The readiness semantics enjoys a number of structural properties which we summarise under the notion of being well-structured.

**Definition 4.4.2** An element $(A, \Gamma) \in DOM_{\mathcal{R}}$ is called *well-structured* if it enjoys the following properties:

(1)  *Initial ready pair:* $\exists \mathcal{G} \subseteq A : (\varepsilon, \mathcal{G}) \in \Gamma$.

(2)  *Prefix closure:* $(tr.a, \mathcal{F}) \in \Gamma$ implies $\exists \mathcal{G} \subseteq A : (tr, \mathcal{G}) \in \Gamma$ and $a \in \mathcal{G}$.

(3)  *Extensibility:* $(tr, \mathcal{F}) \in \Gamma$ and $a \in \mathcal{F}$ imply $\exists \mathcal{G} \subseteq A : (tr.a, \mathcal{G}) \in \Gamma$.

(4)  *Acceptance closure:* $(tr, \mathcal{F}) \in \Gamma$ and $\mathcal{F} \subseteq \mathcal{G} \subseteq succ(tr, \Gamma)$ imply $(tr, \mathcal{G}) \in \Gamma$.

(5)  *Chaotic closure:* $(tr, \uparrow) \in \Gamma$ and $tr \leq tr'$ and $tr' \in A^*$ and $(\mathcal{X} \subseteq A$ or $\mathcal{X} = \uparrow)$ imply $(tr', \mathcal{X}) \in \Gamma$.

(6)  *Radiation closure:* $(tr.a, \uparrow) \in \Gamma$ and $\mathcal{G} \subseteq succ(tr, \Gamma)$ imply $(tr, \mathcal{G}) \in \Gamma$.

(7)  *Unstability closure:* $(\varepsilon, \uparrow) \in \Gamma$ implies $\tau \in \Gamma$.                    $\square$

**Proposition 4.4.3** For every closed process term $P$ the readiness semantics $\mathcal{R}^*[\![P]\!] \in DOM_{\mathcal{R}}$ is well-structured.

*Proof.* Properties (1) - (3) and (7) follow from the underlying net semantics $\mathcal{N}[\![P]\!]$ and the closure operator incorporated in the definition of $\mathcal{R}^*[\![P]\!]$. Moreover, the three clauses of this closure operator yield properties (4) - (6).                    $\square$

Properties (1), (3), (5) and (2) without the condition "and $a \in \mathcal{G}$" are as in the original readiness semantics $\mathcal{R}$ in [OH86]. Property (4) stems from the semantic models studied by DeNicola and Hennessy [DH84, Hen88]; it implies the condition "and $a \in \mathcal{G}$" in (2). Property (7) is motivated by [DH84] and [BKO87]. Property (6) is completely new: it states that divergence affects the ready sets one level up; we therefore say that divergence "radiates up". Note that the closure properties (4) - (6) add ready sets and divergence points to $\mathcal{R}^*[\![\cdot]\!]$ which are not justified by the token game of the underlying net $\mathcal{N}[\![\cdot]\!]$.

These additions make the semantics $\mathcal{R}^*[\![\cdot]\!]$ more abstract so that fewer process terms can be distinguished under $\mathcal{R}^*[\![\cdot]\!]$. In Section 4.7 we shall see that the resulting level of abstraction is in perfect match with the distinctions that we can make among process terms under the satisfaction relation $P$ *sat* $S$. Technically speaking, $\mathcal{R}^*[\![\cdot]\!]$ is *fully abstract* with respect to this relation. We now explain this delicate point more intuitively by means of some examples.

**Example 4.4.4** In the following we examine five pairs of process terms from the viewpoint of their readiness semantics. We argue that the identifications and distinctions made under the readiness semeantics are exactly the ones that are desirable from the viewpoint of the satisfaction relation $P$ *sat* $S$. In this way we motivate the acceptance, chaotic and radiation closures.

(1) Consider the process terms

$$P_1 = a.(b.stop{:}\{a, b, c\} + c.stop{:}\{a, b, c\})$$

and

$$Q_1 = a.b.stop{:}\{a, b, c\} + a.c.stop{:}\{a, b, c\}.$$

They denote the following abstract nets:

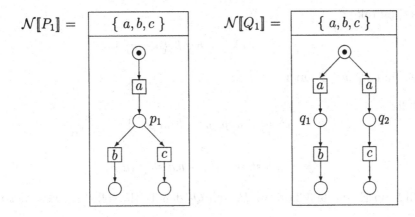

For an easy reference we have marked three places in the nets by $p_1$, $q_1$ and $q_2$.

Applying Definition 4.4.1, we obtain from $\mathcal{N}[\![P_1]\!]$ and $\mathcal{N}[\![Q_1]\!]$ the following readiness semantics of $P_1$ and $Q_1$:

$$\mathcal{R}^*[\![P_1]\!] = (\{a,b,c\},\{\quad (\varepsilon,\{a\}),$$
$$(a,\{b,c\}),$$
$$(a.b,\emptyset),(a.c,\emptyset)\})$$

and

$$\mathcal{R}^*[\![P_1]\!] = (\{a,b,c\},\{\quad (\varepsilon,\{a\}),$$
$$(a,\{b\}),(a,\{c\}),(a,\{b,c\}),$$
$$(a.b,\emptyset),(a.c,\emptyset)\}).$$

$\mathcal{N}[\![P_1]\!]$ contains only one ready pair with the trace $a$, namely the pair $(a,\{b,c\})$ retrieved from the marking $\{p_1\}$ of $\mathcal{N}[\![P_1]\!]$. By contrast $\mathcal{R}^*[\![Q_1]\!]$ contains three ready pairs with the trace $a$, namely the pairs $(a,\{b\})$ and $(a,\{c\})$ retrieved from the markings $\{q_1\}$ and $\{q_2\}$ of $\mathcal{N}[\![P_2]\!]$, and the pair $(a,\{b,c\})$ generated from the first two by the acceptance closure. We examine the effect of this closure more carefully under point (3) below. Here we are interested only in the fact that $P_1$ and $Q_1$ are distinguished under the readiness semantices: $\mathcal{R}^*[\![P_1]\!] \neq \mathcal{R}^*[\![Q_1]\!]$.

How can this distinction be explained from the perspective of the satisfaction relation *sat* defined in terms of "may" and "must" ? Well, $P_1$ and $Q_1$ may engage in the traces $a.b$ and $a.c$, but only $P_1$ must engage in both of them. By contrast, the communication $a$ performed with $Q_1$ nondeterministically moves the token of $\mathcal{N}[\![Q_1]\!]$ either into the place $q_1$ or into $q_2$. If it is put into $q_1$ only $b$ is possible as a next communication. If it is put into $q_2$, only $c$ is possible as a next communication. These two cases violate the conditions for "$Q_1$ must engage in $a.b$" and "$Q_1$ must engage in $a.c$".

In fact, by taking

$$S =_{df} h{\downarrow}\{a,b,c\} \leq a.b \vee h{\downarrow}\{a,b,c\} \leq a.c$$

we see that $P_1$ *sat* $S$ but not $Q_1$ *sat* $S$.

(2) Consider

$$P_2 = a.stop{:}\{a\} \parallel b.stop{:}\{b\}$$

and

$$Q_2 = a.b.stop{:}\{a,b\} + b.a.stop{:}\{a,b\}.$$

Recall from Example 3.3.6 that $P_2$ and $Q_2$ denote the following abstract nets:

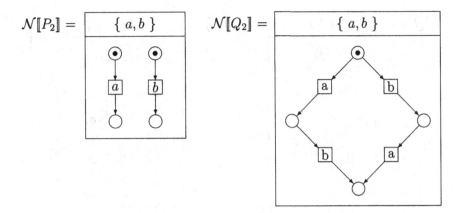

Thus by Definition 4.4.1, the readiness semantics of $P_2$ and $Q_2$ coincide:

$$\mathcal{R}^*[\![P_2]\!] = \mathcal{R}^*[\![Q_1]\!] = (\{a,b\}, \{ \quad (\varepsilon, \{a,b\}),$$
$$(a, \{b\}), (b, \{a\}),$$
$$(a.b, \emptyset)\}).$$

Since $\mathcal{R}^*$ records only traces augmented with ready sets or information about divergence, it is insensitive against concurrency. Therefore $\mathcal{R}^*$ is classified as an interleaving semantics. However, compared with the operational interleaving semantics $\mathcal{A}$ introduced in Definition 3.7.4, the readiness semantics $\mathcal{R}^*$ identifies many more process terms. For instance, for all subsequent process terms $P_i$ and $Q_i$ with $i \in \{3, 4, 5\}$ we shall find $\mathcal{N}[\![P_i]\!] \neq \mathcal{N}[\![Q_i]\!]$ and $\mathcal{A}[\![P_i]\!] \neq \mathcal{A}[\![Q_i]\!]$ but $\mathcal{R}^*[\![P_i]\!] = \mathcal{R}^*[\![Q_i]\!]$.

How can the identification of $P_2$ and $Q_2$ be explained from the viewpoint of the satisfaction relation *sat* ? The answer is easy: the "may" and "must" conditions of *sat* check only traces. These conditions hold for $P_2$ if and only if they hold for $Q_2$. Thus $P_2$ *sat* $S$ if and only if $Q_2$ *sat* $S$ for all trace specifications $S$.

(3) Consider now

$$P_3 = Q_1 = a.b.stop{:}\{a, b, c\} + a.c.stop{:}\{a, b, c\}$$

and

$$Q_3 = P_1 + Q_1 = a.(b.stop{:}\{a, b, c\} + c.stop{:}\{a, b, c\}) + P_3.$$

Then the abstract nets of $P_3$ and $Q_3$ differ from each other:

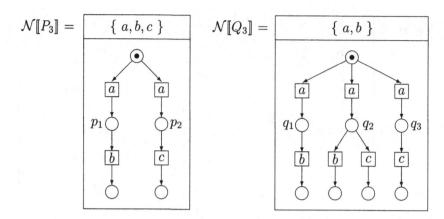

However the readiness semantics of $P_3$ and $Q_3$ coincide:

$$\mathcal{R}^*[\![P_3]\!] = \mathcal{R}^*[\![Q_3]\!] = (\{a, b, c\}, \{ \quad (\varepsilon, \{a\}),$$
$$(a, \{b\}), (a, \{c\}), (a, \{b, c\}),$$
$$(a.b, \emptyset), (a.c, \emptyset)\}).$$

Let us examine how the ready pairs with the trace $a$ come about. In $\mathcal{R}^*[\![Q_3]\!]$ the ready pairs $(a, \{b\}), (a, \{c\}), (a, \{b, c\})$ are retrieved directly from the markings $\{q_1\}, \{q_2\}, \{q_3\}$ of the net $\mathcal{N}[\![q_3]\!]$. In $\mathcal{R}^*[\![P_3]\!]$ only the pairs $(a, \{b\})$ and $(a, \{c\})$ are retrieved directly from the markings $\{p_1\}$ and $\{p_2\}$ of $\mathcal{N}[\![q_3]\!]$. The ready pair $(a, \{b, c\})$ in $\mathcal{R}^*[\![P_3]\!]$ is added by the acceptance closure. Indeed, take

$$\Gamma = \{(a, \{b\}), (a, \{c\})\}.$$

Then $succ(a, \Gamma) = \{b, c\}$. Thus by Definition 4.4.1,

$$\{b\} \subseteq \{b, c\} \subseteq succ(a, \Gamma)$$

implies that the ready pair $(a, \{b, c\})$ is to be included in $\mathcal{R}^*[\![P_3]\!]$ as well.

We argue that a user trying to communicate with $P_3$ and $Q_3$ cannot distinguish between these process terms by means of the "may" and "must" conditions. Indeed both $P_3$ and $Q_3$ may engage in the traces $\varepsilon, a, a.b$ and $a.c$, and both $P_3$ and $Q_3$ must engage in the traces $\varepsilon$ and $a$ but no other trace. Consequently $P_3$ and $Q_3$ are indistinguishable from the viewpoint of the satisfaction relation: $P_3$ *sat* $S$ if and only if $Q_3$ *sat* $S$ for all trace specifications $S$. It was to achieve this desirable identification of $P_3$ and $Q_3$ under the readiness semantics as well, that we included the acceptance closure in its definition.

(4) Consider the process terms

$$P_4 = a.a.div{:}\{a, b\}$$

and

$$Q_4 = a.a.(div{:}\{a, b\} + b.stop{:}\{a, b\}).$$

They denote the following bastract nets:

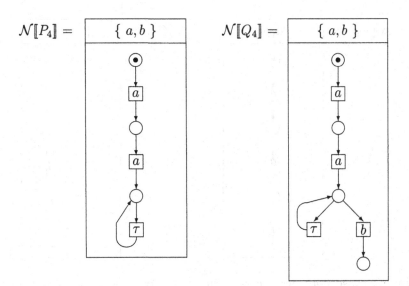

$\mathcal{N}[\![P_4]\!] =$ { $a, b$ }

$\mathcal{N}[\![Q_4]\!] =$ { $a, b$ }

Looking at these nets, we see that the ready pair $(a.a.b, \emptyset)$ is retrievable from $\mathcal{N}[\![Q_4]\!]$ but not from $\mathcal{N}[\![P_4]\!]$. Thus we might expect that $P_4$ and $Q_4$ are distinguished under the readiness semantics.

However, the divergence point $(a.a, \uparrow)$ is retrievable from both nets. Applying now the chaotic closure to $(a.a, \uparrow)$ makes the readiness semantics of $P_4$ and $Q_4$ identical. Indeed, the presence of $(a.a, \uparrow)$ in $\mathcal{R}^*[\![P_4]\!]$ and $\mathcal{R}^*[\![Q_4]\!]$ implies that for any trace $tr \in \{a, b\}^*$ and any ready set $\mathcal{F} \subseteq \{a, b\}$, all ready pairs of the form $(a.a.tr, \mathcal{F})$ and all divergence points of the form $(a.a.tr, \uparrow)$ are also included in $\mathcal{R}^*[\![P_4]\!]$ and $\mathcal{R}^*[\![Q_4]\!]$. In particular, the ready pair $(a.a.b, \emptyset)$ gets included in $\mathcal{R}^*[\![P_4]\!]$ this way.

What about a user trying to communicate with $P_4$ and $Q_4$ ? Clearly, $Q_4$ may engage in the trace $a.a.b$ whereas $P_4$ cannot do so. However, since $Q_4$ can diverge after the trace $a.a$, a user of $Q_4$ cannot rely on $Q_4$ engaging in the communication $b$ after $a.a$. In fact, neither $P_4$ nor $Q_4$ must engage in the trace $a.a.b$. Thus a user cannot distinguish between $P_4$ and $Q_4$ by means of the "must" condition. In fact, since both $P_4$ and $Q_4$ can diverge, there is no trace specification $S$ with $P_4$ *sat* $S$ or $Q_4$ *sat* $S$. Thus divergence is considered as catastrophic for the satisfication relation. It was to model this point of view in the readiness semantics, that we included the chaotic closure in its definition.

(5) Let us examine $P_4$ more closely by comparing now the process terms

$$P_5 = P_4 \text{ and } Q_5 = P_5 + a.stop:\{a, b\}.$$

They denote the following abstract nets:

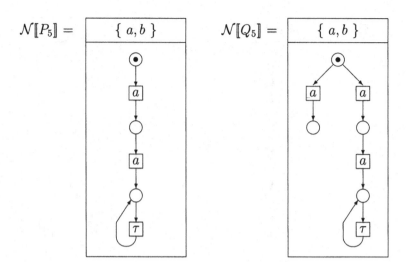

Looking at these nets, we see that the ready pair $(a, \emptyset)$ its retrievable from $\mathcal{N}[\![Q_5]\!]$ but not from $\mathcal{N}[\![P_5]\!]$. Thus we might expect that $P_5$ and $Q_5$ are distinguished under the readiness semantics.

However, the divergence point $(a.a, \uparrow)$ is also retrievable from both nets. By the radiation closure, $(a.a, \uparrow)$ "radiates up" and implies that the missing ready pair $(a, \emptyset)$ gets included in $\mathcal{R}^*[\![Q_5]\!]$. In fact, the readiness semantics of $P_5$ and $Q_5$ coincide:

$$\mathcal{R}^*[\![P_5]\!] = \mathcal{R}^*[\![Q_5]\!] = (\{a, b\}, \quad \{(\varepsilon, \{a\}), (a, \emptyset), (a, \{a\})\}$$

$$\cup \{(a.a.tr, \mathcal{F}) \mid tr \in \{a, b\}^* \text{ and } \mathcal{F} \subseteq \{a, b\}\}$$

$$\cup \{(a.a.tr, \uparrow) \mid tr \in \{a, b\}^*\})$$

Think now of a user trying to communicate with $P_5$ and $Q_5$. At first sight it seems that $P_5$ is "better" than $Q_5$ because after engaging in a first communication $a$ the process $P_5$ is always ready to engage in a second communication $a$. By contrast, $Q_5$ can deadlock after a first communication $a$. However, $P_5$ can diverge after the trace $a.a$. Therefore it is not the case that $P_5$ must engage in the trace $a.a$. Indeed, Definition 4.3.3 (5) of "must engage" would imply that $P_5$ cannot diverge after $a.a$.

In fact, both $P_5$ and $Q_5$ may engage in the traces $\varepsilon$, $a$ and $a.a$, and must engage in $\varepsilon$ and $a$ but in no other trace. Thus a user cannot distinguish $P_5$ and $Q_5$ by the means of the "may" and "must" conditions. Moreover, since both $P_5$ and $Q_5$ can diverge, there is no trace specification $S$ with $P_5$ *sat* $S$ or $Q_5$ *sat* $S$. It was to achieve the identification of $P_5$ and $Q_5$ in the readiness semantics, that we included the radiation closure in its definition.

$\square$

In the following proposition we show that using the readiness semantics we can easily express the process properties relevant for the satisfaction relation $P$ *sat* $S$. Recall that $\pi(\mathcal{R}^*[\![P]\!])$ is the set of process information collected by $\mathcal{R}^*[\![P]\!]$.

**Proposition 4.4.5** Consider a divergence free, closed process term $P$ and a trace $tr = a_1 \ldots a_n$. Then

(1) $P$ may engage in $tr$ iff $(tr, \mathcal{F}) \in \pi(\mathcal{R}^*[\![P]\!])$ for some ready set $\mathcal{F}$.

(2) $P$ can deadlock after $tr$ iff $(tr, \emptyset) \in \pi(\mathcal{R}^*[\![P]\!])$.

(3) $P$ must engage in $tr$ iff for every prefix $a_1 \ldots a_k$ of $tr$ with $0 < k < n$ and every ready set $\mathcal{F}$
$$(a_1 \ldots a_k, \mathcal{F}) \in \pi(\mathcal{R}^*[\![P]\!]) \text{ implies } a_{k+1} \in \mathcal{F}.$$

  i.e. whenever $P$ becomes stable, it is ready to engage in the next communication of $tr$.

(4) $P$ is externally deterministic iff for every trace $tr$ there is at most one ready set $\mathcal{F}$ with $(tr, \mathcal{F}) \in \pi(\mathcal{R}^*[\![P]\!])$.

*Proof.* Since $P$ is divergence free, the chaotic closure and the radiation closure do not contribute any ready pair in $\pi(\mathcal{R}^*[\![P]\!])$. Hence all ready pairs in $\pi(\mathcal{R}^*[\![P]\!])$ are justified by the token game of the net $\mathcal{N}[\![P]\!]$ and the acceptance closure. With this observation, the characterisations (1), (2) and (4) are easy to show.

It remains to prove (3). Consider the process term

$$Q = P \parallel a_1 \ldots a_n.stop : \alpha(P).$$

By the Compositionality Theorem 3.8.3,

$$\mathcal{N}[\![Q]\!] = \mathcal{N}[\![P]\!] \parallel_{\mathcal{N}} \mathcal{N}[\![a_1 \ldots a_n.stop : \alpha(P)]\!].$$

Let $\mathcal{N}_0 = (\alpha(P), \mathrm{Pl}, \longrightarrow, M_0)$ be a representative of the abstract net $\mathcal{N}[\![P]\!]$. Then we have the following chain of equivalences:

  $\quad P$ must engage in $tr$
iff $\quad$ { definition of "must" }
  $\quad Q$ is divergence free and can deadlock only after $tr$
iff $\quad$ {$P$ divergence free, definition of $\parallel_{\mathcal{N}}$}
  $\quad Q$ can deadlock only after $tr$
iff $\quad$ { definition of $\parallel_{\mathcal{N}}$}
  $\quad$ every stable marking $M \in mark(\mathcal{N}_0)$ with $M_0 \xrightarrow{a_1 \ldots a_k} M$
  $\quad$ and $0 < k < n$ satisfies $a_{k+1} \in next(M)$
iff $\quad$ { definition of $\mathcal{R}^*[\![\cdot]\!]$, $P$ divergence free }
  $\quad$ for every prefix $a_1 \ldots a_k$ of $tr$ with $0 \leq k < n$ and every ready set $\mathcal{F}$

  $\quad\quad (a_1 \ldots a_k, \mathcal{F}) \in \pi(\mathcal{R}^*[\![P]\!])$ implies $a_{k+1} \in \mathcal{F}$.

This proves (3). $\qquad\qquad\qquad\qquad\qquad\qquad\qquad\qquad\qquad\qquad\qquad\qquad\quad$ $\square$

With these preparations, we can now approach the main objective of this section: a direct comparison of process terms and trace specifications on the basis of the readiness domain. To this end, we extend now the readiness semantics $\mathcal{R}^*[\![\cdot]\!]$ to cover trace specifications as well, i.e. to a mapping

$$\mathcal{R}^*[\![\cdot]\!] : CProc \cup Spec \longrightarrow DOM_{\mathcal{R}}.$$

**Definition 4.4.6** The *readiness semantics of a trace specification* $S$ is given by

$$\mathcal{R}^*[\![S]\!] = (\alpha(S), \{(tr, \mathcal{F}) \mid tr \in \alpha(S)^* \quad \text{and} \quad pref\ tr \models S \\ \text{and}\ \mathcal{F} = \{a \in \alpha(S) \mid tr.a \models S\}\})$$

where, as before, $pref\ tr \models S$ means that $tr$ and all its prefixes satisfy $S$.          □

Since trace specifications $S$ specify only processes that are stable immediately and divergence free, it is understandable that $\mathcal{R}^*[\![S]\!]$ does not contain elements of the form $\tau$ and $(tr, \uparrow)$ which would indicate unstability and divergence. Note that $\mathcal{R}^*[\![S]\!]$ satisfies the properties (2) - (7) of being well-structured, but not (1) because $\mathcal{R}^*[\![S]\!]$ may be empty. Thus the readiness semantics of trace specifications $S$ is closed, i.e.

$$close(\mathcal{R}^*[\![S]\!]) = \mathcal{R}^*[\![S]\!]$$

but need not be well-structured. However, if $\varepsilon \models S$ then $\mathcal{R}^*[\![S]\!]$ is well-structured.

The main result of this section is the following theorem.

**Correctness Theorem 4.4.7** For every closed process term $P$ and trace specification $S$ we have

$$P\ sat\ S \quad \text{iff} \quad \mathcal{R}^*[\![P]\!] = \mathcal{R}^*[\![S]\!],$$

i.e. in the readiness semantics, process correctness reduces to semantics equality.

*Proof.* "if": Clearly $\mathcal{R}^*[\![P]\!] = \mathcal{R}^*[\![S]\!]$ implies $\alpha(P) = \alpha(S)$ and that $P$ is stable immediately and divergence free. It remains to verify the safety and liveness conditions required for $P\ sat\ S$. To this end, we consider the sets $\pi(\mathcal{R}^*[\![P]\!])$ and $\pi(\mathcal{R}^*[\![S]\!])$ of process information gathered by $P$ and $S$.

*Safety:* Suppose $P$ may engage in a trace $tr \in \alpha(P)^*$. By Proposition 4.4.5, there exists a ready set $\mathcal{F}$ with $(tr, \mathcal{F}) \in \pi(\mathcal{R}^*[\![P]\!])$ and hence $(tr, \mathcal{F}) \in \pi(\mathcal{R}^*[\![S]\!])$. Thus $tr \models S$ as required.

*Liveness:* Suppose $pref\ tr \models S$ for some trace $tr = a_1 \ldots a_n$. Then for every prefix $a_1 \ldots a_k$ of $tr$ with $0 \le k \le n$ and every ready set $\mathcal{F}$

$$(a_1 \ldots a_k, \mathcal{F}) \in \pi(R^*[\![S]\!]) \text{ implies } a_{k+1} \in \mathcal{F}.$$

(In fact, there exists exactly one ready set $\mathcal{F}$ with $(a_1 \ldots a_k, \mathcal{F}) \in \pi(\mathcal{R}^*[\![S]\!])$, but this is not important here.) Since $\mathcal{R}^*[\![P]\!] = \mathcal{R}^*[\![S]\!]$, Proposition 4.4.5 implies that $P$ must engage in $tr$.

"only if": The definition of $P$ *sat* $S$ and Proposition 4.3.7 imply $\alpha(P) = \alpha(S)$ and that $P$ is stable immediately, divergence free and externally deterministic. Thus

$$\pi(\mathcal{R}^*[\![P]\!]) \subseteq \alpha(P)^* \times \mathcal{P}(\alpha(P)).$$

We first show $\pi(\mathcal{R}^*[\![P]\!]) \subseteq \pi(\mathcal{R}^*[\![S]\!])$. To this end, consider a ready pair $(tr, \mathcal{F}) \in \pi(\mathcal{R}^*[\![P]\!])$. By Proposition 4.4.5 and 4.4.3 (the extensibility property), $P$ may engage, for every $a \in \mathcal{F}$, in the trace $tr.a$ and all its prefixes. Hence $(tr, \mathcal{G}) \in \pi(\mathcal{R}^*[\![S]\!])$ for some ready set $\mathcal{G} \supseteq \mathcal{F}$. Consider a communication $b \in \mathcal{G}$. By the definition of $P$ *sat* $S$, $P$ must and hence may engage in the extended trace $tr.b$. Thus there exists a ready set $\mathcal{F}_b$ with $b \in \mathcal{F}_b$ and $(tr, \mathcal{F}_b) \in \pi(\mathcal{R}^*[\![P]\!])$. Since $P$ is externally deterministic, it follows that $\mathcal{F} = \mathcal{F}_b$ and hence $b \in \mathcal{F}$. Thus in fact $\mathcal{G} = \mathcal{F}$ and hence $(tr, \mathcal{F}) \in \pi(\mathcal{R}^*[\![S]\!])$.

To show $\pi(\mathcal{R}^*[\![S]\!]) \subseteq \pi(\mathcal{R}^*[\![P]\!])$ consider a ready pair $(tr, \mathcal{G}) \in \pi(\mathcal{R}^*[\![S]\!])$. As shown above, for every communication $b \in \mathcal{G}$ there exists a ready set $\mathcal{F}_b$ with $b \in \mathcal{F}_b$ and $(tr, \mathcal{F}_b) \in \pi(\mathcal{R}^*[\![P]\!])$. Since $P$ is externally deterministic, all ready sets $\mathcal{F}_b$ are identical. Let $\mathcal{F}$ denote this ready set. Thus $\mathcal{F} \supseteq \mathcal{G}$. The safety condition of $P$ *sat* $S$ and the definition of $\mathcal{R}^*[\![S]\!]$ imply $\mathcal{F} = \mathcal{G}$ and hence $(tr, \mathcal{G}) \in \pi(\mathcal{R}^*[\![P]\!])$. $\square$

The Correctness Theorem simplifies, at least conceptually, the task of proving that a process term $P$ satisfies a trace specification $S$. Instead of laboriously checking the conditions required for $P$ *sat* $S$ we need only show that $\mathcal{R}^*[\![P]\!] = \mathcal{R}^*[\![S]\!]$ in the readiness semantics.

**Example 4.4.8** In Example 4.2.7 we considered the trace specification

$$S = 0 \leq up\#tr - dn\#tr \leq 2$$

and argued informally that the process terms

$$P = \mu X.up.\mu Y.(dn.X + up.dn.Y)$$

and

$$Q = ((\mu X.up.dn.X)[lk/dn] \parallel (\mu X.up.dn.X)[lk/up]) \setminus lk$$

both satisfy $S$. We can now prove this claim by comparing the readiness semantics of $S$ with $P$ and $Q$. Applying Definition 4.4.6 to $S$ above, we obtain

$$\mathcal{R}^*[\![S]\!] = \{ \ \{up, dn\},$$

$$\{(tr, \mathcal{F}) \mid \forall \ tr' \leq tr : 0 \leq up\#tr' - dn\#tr' \leq 2$$

$$\text{and ( if } 0 = up\#tr - dn\#tr \text{ then } \mathcal{F} = \{up\})$$

$$\text{and ( if } 0 < up\#tr - dn\#tr < 2 \text{ then } \mathcal{F} = \{up, dn\})$$

$$\text{and ( if } up\#tr - dn\#tr = 2 \text{ then } \mathcal{F} = \{dn\})\}).$$

By an exhaustive analysis of the reachable markings of the nets $\mathcal{N}[\![P]\!]$ and $\mathcal{N}[\![Q]\!]$ displayed in Example 4.3.8 we see that

$$\mathcal{R}^*[\![P]\!] = \mathcal{R}^*[\![S]\!] = \mathcal{R}^*[\![Q]\!].$$

Thus indeed $P$ *sat* $S$ and $Q$ *sat* $S$. $\square$

We referred above to the obvious way of determining the readiness semantics of a process term $P$, viz. by analysis of the underlying Petri net $\mathcal{N}[\![P]\!]$. The drawback of this method is that it is very inflexible: whenever a part of $P$ is exchanged, the analysis of $\mathcal{N}[\![P]\!]$ has to start again. Instead we would like to reuse the results established for those parts of $P$ which are left unchanged. To this end, we wish to determine the readiness semantics $\mathcal{R}^*[\![P]\!]$ by induction on the structure of $P$. This is the topic of the next section.

## 4.5   Denotational Approach

In this section we provide an alternative, denotational definition $\mathcal{R}^{**}[\![\cdot]\!]$ of the readiness semantics. Later, in Section 4.6 we show that on closed process terms, $\mathcal{R}^{**}[\![\cdot]\!]$ coincides with the previous operational definition $\mathcal{R}^*[\![\cdot]\!]$. In Chapter 5 this denotational definition will be the basis for developing verification rules for process correctness.

Following the approach of Scott and Strachey [Sco70, Sto77, Bak80, GMS89], a semantics of a programming language is called *denotational* if each phrase of the language is given a *denotation*; that is, a mathematical object that represents the contribution of the phrase to the meaning of any complete program in which it occurs. It is required that the denotation of each phrase is determined in a compositional fashion from the denotation of the subphrases. In general, the discipline of denotational semantics is concerned with giving mathematical models for programming languages, and with developing canonical techniques for constructing such models.

In our case the programming language is the set of process terms. The "phrases" of a process term are its subterms. As the denotations of process terms we wish to take elements of the readiness domain $DOM_{\mathcal{R}}$. A denotational definition of the semantic mapping from process terms into this domain should be compositional and use fixed point techniques when dealing with recursion. These techniques stipulate a certain structure of the composition operators and the semantic domain. We will use here the standard set-up and work with monotonic or continuous operators over complete partial orders (cpo's). Let us briefly recall the basic definitions and properties. Further details can be found in the literature, e.g. in [Bac80, LS84].

Let $DOM$ be a set of values, usually called a *semantic domain*, and $\sqsubseteq$ be a binary relation on $DOM$. Then $\sqsubseteq$ is called a *partial order* on $DOM$ if $\sqsubseteq$ is reflexive, antisymmetric and transitive. If $x \sqsubseteq y$ for some $x, y \in DOM$, we say that $x$ is *less than* $y$ and that $y$ is *greater* or *better than* $x$.

Suppose now that $\sqsubseteq$ is a partial order on $DOM$. Let $x \in DOM$ and $D \subseteq DOM$. Then $x$ is called the *least* element of $D$ if $x \in D$ and $x \sqsubseteq d$ for all $d \in D$. The element $x$ is called an *upper bound* of $D$ if $d \sqsubseteq x$ for all $d \in D$. Note that $x \in D$ is not required here. Let $U$ be the set of all upper bounds of $D$ and $x$ be the least element of $U$. Then we write $x = \bigsqcup D$.

A mapping $\Phi : DOM \longrightarrow DOM$ is called $\sqsubseteq$-*monotonic* if it preserves the partial order $\sqsubseteq$, i.e. if for all $x, y \in DOM$

$$x \sqsubseteq y \quad \text{implies} \quad \Phi(x) \sqsubseteq \Phi(y).$$

More generally, an $n$-ary mapping

$$\Phi : \underbrace{DOM \times \ldots \times DOM}_{n \text{ times}} \longrightarrow DOM$$

is $\sqsubseteq$-monotonic if it is $\sqsubseteq$-monotonic in every argument.

The partial order $\sqsubseteq$ on $DOM$ is called *chain-complete* or simply *complete* if $DOM$ contains a least element, often denoted by $\bot$, and if every ascending chain

$$x_0 \sqsubseteq x_1 \sqsubseteq x_2 \ldots \tag{4.13}$$

of elements $x_n \in DOM, n \geq 0$, has a *limit*

$$\bigsqcup_{n \geq 0} x_n$$

which is defined as the least upper bound of the set of elements in (4.13), i.e.

$$\bigsqcup_{n \geq 0} x_n = \bigsqcup \{x_0, x_1, x_2, \ldots\}.$$

If $\sqsubseteq$ is a complete partial order on $DOM$, we also say that $DOM$ is a complete order *under* $\sqsubseteq$.

Suppose now that $DOM$ is a complete partial order under $\sqsubseteq$. A mapping $\Phi : DOM \longrightarrow DOM$ is $\sqsubseteq$-*continuous* if it is $\sqsubseteq$-monotonic and if it preserves limits, i.e. if for every ascending chain (4.13) the equation

$$\Phi(\bigsqcup_{n \geq 0} x_n) = \bigsqcup_{n \geq 0} \Phi(x_n). \tag{4.14}$$

holds. Note that the limit on the right-hand side of (4.14) exists because the elements $\Phi(x_n)$ from an ascending chain

$$\Phi(x_0) \sqsubseteq \Phi(x_1) \sqsubseteq \Phi(x_2) \sqsubseteq \ldots$$

thanks to the $\sqsubseteq$-monotonicity of $\Phi$. More generally, an $n$-ary mapping

$$\Phi : \underbrace{DOM \times \ldots \times DOM}_{n \text{ times}} \longrightarrow DOM$$

is $\sqsubseteq$-continuous if it is $\sqsubseteq$-continuous in every argument.

Consider a mapping $\Phi : DOM \longrightarrow DOM$. An element $x \in DOM$ is called a *fixed point* of $\Phi$ if $\Phi(x) = x$. Let $FIX$ be the set of all fixed points of $\Phi$. An element $x \in DOM$ is called the *least fixed point* of $\Phi$ if it is the least element of $FIX$, i.e. if $x \in FIX$ and $x \sqsubseteq d$ for all $d \in FIX$. Then we write $x = fix\ \Phi$.

We wish to define the denotational readiness semantics of a recursive process term as the least fixed point of a certain mapping. To this end, we need sufficient conditions for the existence and representation of such fixed points. We use the following two theorems.

**Knaster-Tarski Fixed Point Theorem 4.5.1** Let $DOM$ be a complete partial order under $\sqsubseteq$ and $\Phi : DOM \longrightarrow DOM$ be a $\sqsubseteq$-monotonic mapping. Then $\Phi$ has at least one fixed point.

*Proof.* See [Tar55].          □

If $\Phi$ is not only monotonic but continuous, the least fixed point of $\Phi$ can be represented as the limit of its $n$-fold iterations $\Phi^n$ where $n \geq 0$. These are defined inductively as follows:

$$\Phi^0(x) = x,$$

$$\Phi^{n+1}(x) = \Phi(\Phi^n(x))$$

for every $x \in DOM$.

**Kleene's Fixed Point Theorem 4.5.2** Let $DOM$ be a complete partial order under $\sqsubseteq$ with least element $\bot$, and let $\Phi : DOM \longrightarrow DOM$ be a $\sqsubseteq$-continuous mapping. Then $\Phi$ has a least fixed point *fix* $\Phi$, and moreover,

$$fix\ \Phi = \bigsqcup_{n \geq 0} \Phi(\bot).$$

*Proof.* See [Kle52].          □

To apply this general fixed point theory to the specific format of our programming language, viz. recursive terms with alphabets as types, we need a few extra details which we explain now.

**Definition 4.5.3** A *denotational semantics for process terms* is a mapping

$$\mathcal{M} : Proc \longrightarrow (Env_{\mathcal{M}} \longrightarrow DOM_{\mathcal{M}})$$

which satisfies the following conditions:

(1) The semantic domain $DOM_{\mathcal{M}}$ is equipped with a partial order $\sqsubseteq$. For every alphabet $A \subseteq Comm$ there is a subdomain $DOM_{\mathcal{M}} : A \subseteq DOM_{\mathcal{M}}$ which is a complete partial order under $\sqsubseteq$.

(2) The set $Env_{\mathcal{M}}$ of *environments* consists of mappings

$$\rho : Idf \longrightarrow DOM_{\mathcal{M}}$$

which assign to every process identifier an element of the semantic domain and which respect alphabets, i.e. where $\alpha(X) = A$ implies $\rho(X) \in DOM_{\mathcal{M}} : A$.

(3) For every $n$-ary operator symbol $op$ of $Proc$ there exists a corresponding semantic operator

$$op_{\mathcal{M}} : \underbrace{DOM_{\mathcal{M}} \times \ldots \times DOM_{\mathcal{M}}}_{n \text{ times}} \longrightarrow DOM_{\mathcal{M}}$$

which is $\sqsubseteq$-monotonic and satisfies

$$op_{\mathcal{M}}((A_1, \Gamma_1), \ldots, (A_n, \Gamma_n)) \in DOM_{\mathcal{M}} : op_{\alpha}(A_1, \ldots, A_n).$$

Here $op_{\alpha}$ is the set-theoretic operator on alphabets that corresponds to $op$ (cf. Remark 3.1.4).

(4) The definition of $\mathcal{M}$ proceeds inductively and obeys the following principles:

- *Environment technique:*

$$\mathcal{M}[\![X]\!](\rho) = \rho(X)$$

- *Compositionality:*

$$\mathcal{M}[\![op(P_1, \ldots, P_n)]\!](\rho) = op_{\mathcal{M}}(\mathcal{M}[\![P_1]\!](\rho), \ldots, \mathcal{M}[\![P_n]\!](\rho))$$

- *Fixed point technique:*

$$\mathcal{M}[\![\mu X.P]\!](\rho) = fix\ \Phi_{P,\rho}$$

Here $fix\ \Phi_{P,\rho}$ denotes the least fixed point of the mapping

$$\Phi_{P,\rho} : DOM_{\mathcal{M}} : B \longrightarrow DOM_{\mathcal{M}} : B$$

defined by

$$\Phi_{P,\rho}(B, \Gamma) = \mathcal{M}[\![P]\!](\rho[(B, \Gamma)/X])$$

where $B = \alpha(X)$ and $\rho[(B, \Gamma)/X]$ is the environment that agrees with $\rho$ except for the identifier $X$ where its value is $(B, \Gamma)$. □

By the assumptions (1)-(3), and Knaster-Tarski Fixed Point Theorem 4.5.1, the inductive definition (4) of $\mathcal{M}$ is well-defined and yields a value

$$\mathcal{M}[\![P]\!](\rho) \in DOM_{\mathcal{M}} : \alpha(P)$$

for every process term $P$.

Environments $\rho$ assign values to the free identifiers in process terms, analogously to Tarski's semantic definition for predicate logic (cf. Definition 4.1.2). Thus for closed process terms $P$ the environment parameter $\rho$ of $\mathcal{M}$ is not needed; in that case we shall write $\mathcal{M}[\![P]\!]$ instead of $\mathcal{M}[\![P]\!](\rho)$.

**Remark 4.5.4** Note that the semantics $\mathcal{M}$ is uniquely determined by the domain $DOM_{\mathcal{M}}$, its partial order $\sqsubseteq$, and the semantic operators $op_{\mathcal{M}}$. □

Thus to provide a denotational definition of the readiness semantics, we need only introduce an appropriate partial order $\sqsubseteq$ and monotonic semantic operators $op_{\mathcal{R}}$ on the readiness domain $DOM_{\mathcal{R}}$ of Section 4.4. As partial ordering we take the following relation on pairs $(A, \Gamma), (B, \Gamma) \in DOM_{\mathcal{R}}$:

$$(A, \Gamma) \sqsubseteq (B, \Delta) \text{ if } A = B \text{ and } \Gamma \supseteq \Delta.$$

Intuitively, the reverse set inclusion $\Gamma \supseteq \Delta$ expresses that a process generating the set of process information $\Delta$ is *more controllable*, i.e. *more deterministic, less divergent* and *more stable* than a process generating $\Gamma$ [Hoa85b].

For every ascending chain

$$(A_1, \Gamma_1) \sqsubseteq (A_2, \Gamma_2) \sqsubseteq (A_3, \Gamma_3) \sqsubseteq \ldots$$

the alphabets are identical and the least upper bound in $DOM_{\mathcal{R}}$ exists, viz.

$$\bigsqcup_{i \geq 1}(A_i, \Gamma_i) = (A_1, \bigcap_{i \geq 1} \Gamma_i).$$

There is no least element in $DOM_{\mathcal{R}}$, but one in every subdomain $DOM_{\mathcal{R}} : A$, viz.

$$(A, Info_{\mathcal{R}} : A).$$

Hence we can state :

**Proposition 4.5.5** Every subdomain $DOM_{\mathcal{R}} : A$ is a complete partial order under the relation $\sqsubseteq$. □

We now introduce the semantic operators $op_{\mathcal{R}}$ on the readiness domain $DOM_{\mathcal{R}}$. For convenience, we shall separate the morphism operators into renaming and hiding. By Remark 3.1.2, this can be done without loss of generality.

**Definition 4.5.6** Consider $(A, \Gamma), (B, \Delta) \in DOM_{\mathcal{R}}$. Then:

(1) *Deadlock.*
$$stop{:}A_{\mathcal{R}} = close(A, \{(\varepsilon, \emptyset)\}) = (A, \{(\varepsilon, \emptyset)\}).$$

This process is stable immediately but never ready for any communication.

(2) *Divergence.*

$$div{:}A_{\mathcal{R}} = close(A, \{(\varepsilon, \uparrow)\}) = (A, Info_{\mathcal{R}} : A) = DOM_{\mathcal{R}} : A.$$

By the closure operator of Definition 4.3.1, a process that diverges immediately generates the full set of process information.

(3) *Prefix.*

$$a._{\mathcal{R}}(A, \Gamma) = close(A \cup \{a\}, \{(\varepsilon, \{a\})\} \cup \{(a.tr, \mathcal{X}) \mid (tr, \mathcal{X}) \in \Gamma\}).$$

Initially, this process can engage in the communication $a$ and after $a$ it behaves as described in $\Gamma$.

(4) *Choice.*

$$
\begin{aligned}
(A,\Gamma) +_{\mathcal{R}} (B,\Delta) = \quad & close(A \cup B, \{\tau \mid \tau \in \Gamma \cup \Delta\} \\
& \cup \{(\varepsilon, \mathcal{F} \cup \mathcal{G}) \mid (\varepsilon, \mathcal{F}) \in \Gamma \text{ and } (\varepsilon, \mathcal{G}) \in \Delta \\
& \qquad\qquad\qquad\qquad\qquad \text{and } \tau \notin \Gamma \cup \Delta\} \\
& \cup \{(tr, \mathcal{X}) \mid (tr, \mathcal{X}) \in \Gamma \text{ and} \\
& \qquad\qquad\qquad (tr \neq \varepsilon \text{ or } \mathcal{X} = \uparrow \text{ or } \tau \in \Gamma)\} \\
& \cup \{(tr, \mathcal{X}) \mid (tr, \mathcal{X}) \in \Delta \text{ and} \\
& \qquad\qquad\qquad (tr \neq \varepsilon \text{ or } \mathcal{X} = \uparrow \text{ or } \tau \in \Delta)\}).
\end{aligned}
$$

Initially, when the process is stable, it is ready for the union of the ready sets of $\Gamma$ and $\Delta$. Otherwise, the process can do what $\Gamma$ or $\Delta$ can.

(5) *Parallelism.*

$$
\begin{aligned}
(A,\Gamma) \parallel_{\mathcal{R}} (B,\Delta) = \quad & close(A \cup B, \{\tau \mid \tau \in \Gamma \cup \Delta\} \\
& \cup \{(tr, \mathcal{F}) \mid tr \in (A \cup B)^* \text{ and } \exists \mathcal{G}, \mathcal{H} \subseteq Comm : \\
& \quad ((tr{\downarrow}A, \mathcal{G}) \in \Gamma \text{ and } (tr{\downarrow}B, \mathcal{H}) \in \Delta \text{ and} \\
& \quad \mathcal{F} = (\mathcal{G} \cap \mathcal{H}) \cup ((\mathcal{G} \cup \mathcal{H}) - (A \cap B)))\} \\
& \cup \{(tr, \uparrow) \mid tr \in (A \cup B)^* \text{ and} \\
& \quad ((tr{\downarrow}A, \uparrow) \in \Gamma \text{ or } (tr{\downarrow}B, \uparrow) \in \Delta)\}),
\end{aligned}
$$

where $tr{\downarrow}A$ and $tr{\downarrow}B$ are the projections of the trace $tr$ onto the alphabets $A$ and $B$, respectively (cf. Definition 4.1.2 (1)). A parallel composition may engage in a trace $tr \in (A \cup B)^*$ if its components $\Gamma$ and $\Delta$ may engage in the projections $tr{\downarrow}A$ and $tr{\downarrow}B$. The ready set $\mathcal{F}$ after $tr$ is assembled from the individual ready sets $\mathcal{G}$ and $\mathcal{H}$ of $\Gamma$ and $\Delta$ after $tr{\downarrow}A$ and $tr{\downarrow}B$, respectively. In the equation

$$
\mathcal{F} = (\mathcal{G} \cap \mathcal{H}) \cup ((\mathcal{G} \cup \mathcal{H}) - (A \cap B))
$$

the first part $\mathcal{G} \cap \mathcal{H}$ collects all communications which require synchronous behaviour of $\Gamma$ and $\Delta$ and the second part $(\mathcal{G} \cup \mathcal{H}) - (A \cap B)$ collects all communications which may happen asynchronously because they do not occur in the synchronisation set $A \cap B$. The parallel composition can diverge after $tr$ if $\Gamma$ can diverge after $tr{\downarrow}A$ or $\Delta$ can diverge after $tr{\downarrow}B$.

(6) *Renaming.*

$$
\begin{aligned}
(A,\Gamma)[b/a]_{\mathcal{R}} = \quad & close(A\{b/a\}, \{\tau \mid \tau \in \Gamma\} \\
& \cup \{(tr\{b/a\}, \mathcal{F}\{b/a\}) \mid (tr, \mathcal{F}) \in \Gamma\} \\
& \cup \{(tr\{b/a\}, \uparrow) \mid (tr, \uparrow) \in \Gamma\})
\end{aligned}
$$

where $A\{b/a\}$, $tr\{b/a\}$ and $\mathcal{F}\{b/a\}$ result from $A$, $tr$ and $\mathcal{F}$ by replacing every occurrence of $a$ by $b$ (cf. Section 4.1) .

(7) *Hiding.*

$$
\begin{aligned}
(A, \Gamma) \setminus b_{\mathcal{R}} = \ & close(A - \{b\}, \{\tau \mid \tau \in \Gamma \text{ or } \exists \mathcal{G} \subseteq Comm : (b, \mathcal{G}) \in \Gamma\} \\
& \cup \ \{(tr{\downarrow}(A - \{b\}), \mathcal{F}) \mid (tr, \mathcal{F}) \in \Gamma \text{ and } b \notin \mathcal{F}\} \\
& \cup \ \{(tr{\downarrow}(A - \{b\}), \uparrow) \mid (tr, \uparrow) \in \Gamma \text{ or } \\
& \quad \forall n \geq 0 \ \exists \mathcal{G} \subseteq Comm : (tr.b^n, \mathcal{G}) \in \Gamma\})
\end{aligned}
$$

where $b^n$ stands for the $n$-fold concatenation of $b$. Thus in the readiness semantics hiding is more complicated than renaming. This contrasts with the Petri net semantics where both operators are treated uniformly as action morphisms. The reason for this difference is that hiding $(A, \Gamma) \setminus b_{\mathcal{R}}$ transforms the communication $b$ of $\Gamma$ into an internal action which may cause instability and divergence, i.e. phenomena to which the readiness semantics is sensitive. The process $(A, \Gamma) \setminus b_{\mathcal{R}}$ is stable if $\Gamma$ is at a ready pair $(tr, \mathcal{F})$ with $b \notin \mathcal{F}$, and it can diverge if $\Gamma$ can diverge or may engage in arbitrary long sequences of $b$'s. This motivates the clauses of the above definition. $\square$

Each of the definitions (1)-(7) involves the closure operator $close(A, \Gamma)$. As for (1) and (2) it is also possible to incorporate the effect of this operator in the clauses of (3)-(7), but we found the present set-up easier to explain and analyse. First, we notice:

**Proposition 4.5.7** The above operators $op_{\mathcal{R}}$ are all $\sqsubseteq$-monotonic.

*Proof.* Monotonicity is obvious from the form of the operator definitions: for smaller information sets as input the operators generate smaller information sets as output. $\square$

By instantiating the general Definition 4.5.3 with 4.5.5 - 4.5.7, we obtain a denotational readiness semantics

$$
\mathcal{R}^{**}[\![\cdot]\!] : Proc \longrightarrow (Env_{\mathcal{R}} \longrightarrow DOM_{\mathcal{R}}).
$$

To become familiar with this new semantics, let us compute it for a recursive process term.

**Example 4.5.8** Consider $\mu X.a.X$ where $\alpha(X) = \{a\}$. By Definition 4.5.3,

$$
\mathcal{R}^{**}[\![\mu X.a.X]\!] = \mathcal{R}^{**}[\![\mu X.a.X]\!](\rho) = fix \ \Phi_{a.X, \rho}
$$

where $\rho$ is an arbitrary environment and where the mapping

$$
\Phi_{a.X, \rho} : DOM_{\mathcal{R}} : \{a\} \longrightarrow DOM_{\mathcal{R}} : \{a\}
$$

is defined as follows: for any pair $(\{a\}, \Gamma) \in DOM_{\mathcal{R}} : \{a\}$

$$
\Phi_{a.X, \rho}(\{a\}, \Gamma) = \mathcal{R}^{**}[\![a.X]\!](\rho[(\{a\}, \Gamma)/X]).
$$

We calculate the left-hand side of this equation:

$$\mathcal{R}^{**}[\![a.X]\!](\rho[(\{a\},\Gamma)/X])$$

$= \quad \{ \text{ Definition 4.5.3: compositionality } \}$

$$a._{\mathcal{R}}(\mathcal{R}^{**}[\![X]\!](\rho[(\{a\},\Gamma)/X]))$$

$= \quad \{ \text{ Definition 4.5.3: environment technique } \}$

$$a._{\mathcal{R}}(\{a\},\Gamma)$$

$= \quad \{ \text{ Definition 4.5.6: prefix } \}$

$$close(\{a\},\{(\varepsilon,\{a\})\} \cup \{(a.tr,\mathcal{X}) \mid (tr,\mathcal{X}) \in \Gamma\}).$$

Thus $\mathcal{R}^{**}[\![\mu X.a.X]\!]$ is the least solution $(\{a\},\Gamma)$ with respect to the partial order $\sqsubseteq$ of the equation

$$\Phi_{a.X,\rho}(\{a\},\Gamma) = (\{a\},\Gamma).$$

By the definition of $\sqsubseteq$ and the above calculation, $\Gamma$ is the *largest* subset of $Info_{\mathcal{R}} : \{a\}$ satisfying the equation

$$(\{a\},\Gamma) = close(\{a\},\{(\varepsilon,\{a\})\} \cup \{(a.tr,\mathcal{X}) \mid (tr,\mathcal{X}) \in \Gamma\}). \tag{4.15}$$

It is easy to check that $\Gamma$ cannot contain certain types of process information. $\Gamma$ cannot contain $\tau$ because the right-hand side of (4.15) does not contain $\tau$. Also, $\Gamma$ cannot contain any divergence point $(a^n, \uparrow)$ or ready pair $(a^n, \emptyset)$ where $n \geq 0$ because the right-hand side of (4.15) would generate only $(a^{n+1}, \uparrow)$ or $(a^{n+1}, \emptyset)$.

Thus $\Gamma$ contains at most ready pairs of the form $(a^n, \{a\})$ where $n \geq 0$. Using induction on $n$, it is straightforward to show that every $\Gamma$ satisfying (4.15) contains at least all ready pairs $(a^n, \{a\})$ with $n \geq 0$. Summarizing, (4.15) has a *unique* solution which is

$$\Gamma = \{(a^n, \{a\}) \mid n \geq 0\}.$$

Thus we obtain

$$\mathcal{R}^{**}[\![\ \mu X.a.X]\!] = (\{a\},\{(a^n, \{a\}) \mid n \geq 0\}).$$

In Chapter 5 we generalize the observation that for the recursive process term $\mu X.a.X$ the corresponding semantic mapping $\Phi_{a.X,\rho}$ has a unique fixed point. We shall, in Definition 5.1.4, introduce the notion of a communication-guarded process term and show, in Corollary 5.2.2, that for every communication-guarded process term $\mu X.P$ the mapping $\Phi_{P,\rho}$ has a unique fixed point. $\qquad\square$

## 4.6 Equivalence

In this section we investigate the relationship between the denotational definition $\mathcal{R}^{**}[\![\cdot]\!]$ of the readiness semantics and the operational definition $\mathcal{R}^{**}[\![\cdot]\!]$ given in section 4.4. Our aim is to show that for closed process terms both definitions are equivalent. The proof is long and refines the strategy employed in [OH86] and [BMOZ88]. Thus we first show that the operational readiness semantics $\mathcal{R}^*[\![\cdot]\!]$ is compositional with respect to the operators $op_{\mathcal{R}}$ introduced in Section 4.5.

**Second Compositionality Theorem 4.6.1** For all $n$-ary operator symbols $op$ of *CProc* and all process terms $P_1, \ldots, P_n \in$ *CProc* the equation

$$\mathcal{R}^*[\![op(P_1, \ldots, P_n)]\!] = op_{\mathcal{R}}(\mathcal{R}^*[\![P_1]\!], \ldots, \mathcal{R}^*[\![P_n]\!])$$

holds.

The proof relies on the First Compositionality Theorem 3.8.3 dealing with the underlying net semantics and the following lemmas.

**Lemma 4.6.2** For all nets $\mathcal{N}_1$ and $\mathcal{N}_2$

$$\mathcal{N}_1 \approx \mathcal{N}_2 \text{ implies } \mathcal{R}^*(\mathcal{N}_1) = \mathcal{R}^*(\mathcal{N}_2)$$

and consequently all abstract nets $[\mathcal{N}_1]$ and $[\mathcal{N}_2]$

$$[\mathcal{N}_1] \approx [\mathcal{N}_2] \text{ implies } \mathcal{R}^*([\mathcal{N}_1]) = \mathcal{R}^*([\mathcal{N}_2]),$$

i.e. strong bisimilarity $\approx$ preserves the process information collected by the readiness semantics.

*Proof.* By Definition 2.3.1, strong bisimilarity $\approx$ preserves the transition behaviour of nets.                                                                                 □

**Lemma 4.6.3** For all $n$-ary operators $op_{\mathcal{R}}$ and all elements $(A_1, \Gamma_1), \ldots, (A_n, \Gamma_n) \in DOM_{\mathcal{R}}$

$$op_{\mathcal{R}}(close(A_1, \Gamma_1), \ldots, close(A_n, \Gamma_n)) = op_{\mathcal{R}}((A_1, \Gamma_1), \ldots, (A_n, \Gamma_n)),$$

i.e. the closure operator need only be applied at the topmost level within $op_{\mathcal{R}}$.

*Proof.* By inspection of the definitions of $op_{\mathcal{R}}$ and $close(A, \Gamma)$.                     □

Thus when proving 4.6.1 we need to consider only the composition operators $op_{\mathcal{N}}$ on nets and concentrate on the process information generated by the underlying nets, not by the closure operators.

*Proof of Theorem 4.6.1.* The claim is easily established for

$$op \in \{stop{:}A, div{:}A, a., [b/a] \mid a, b \in Comm \text{ and } A \text{ communication alphabet }\}.$$

Thus we are left with the following cases:

*Choice* : $op = +$
We wish to show $\mathcal{R}^*[\![P_1{+}P_2]\!] = \mathcal{R}^*[\![P_1]\!] +_{\mathcal{R}} \mathcal{R}^*[\![P_2]\!]$ for all $P_1, P_2 \in$ *CProc*. Let $A = \alpha(P_1) = \alpha(P_2)$ and consider nets

$$\mathcal{N}_i = (A, Pl_i, \longrightarrow_i, \mathcal{M}_{0i})$$

for $i = 1, 2$ with $Pl_1 \cap Pl_2 = \emptyset$ and $\mathcal{N}[\![P_i]\!] = [\mathcal{N}_i]$ for $i = 1, 2$. Put

$$\mathcal{N}_0 = (A, Pl_1 \cup Pl_2 \cup (M_{01} \times M_{02}), \longrightarrow, M_{01} \times M_{02})$$

where

$$\begin{aligned}
\longrightarrow = \quad & \{(I_1 \cup (I_2 \times M_{02}), act(t_1), post(t_1)) | t_1 \in \longrightarrow_1, \\
& pre(t_1) = I_1 \cup I_2 \text{ and } I_1 \cap I_2 = \emptyset \text{ and } I_2 \subseteq M_{01}\} \\[6pt]
\cup \quad & \{((M_{01} \times I_1) \cup I_2, act(t_2), post(t_2)) | t_2 \in \longrightarrow_2, \\
& pre(t_2) = I_1 \cup I_2 \text{ and } I_1 \cap I_2 = \emptyset \text{ and } I_1 \subseteq M_{02}\}.
\end{aligned}$$

By the First Compositionality Theorem 3.8.3,

$$\mathcal{N}[\![P_1 + P_2]\!] \approx \mathcal{N}[\![P_1]\!] +_\mathcal{N} \mathcal{N}[\![P_2]\!] = [\mathcal{N}_1] +_\mathcal{N} [\mathcal{N}_2] = [\mathcal{N}_0].$$

Then by Lemma 4.6.2,

$$\mathcal{R}^*[\![P_1 + P_2]\!] = \mathcal{R}^*(\mathcal{N}[\![P_1 + P_2]\!]) = \mathcal{R}^*(\mathcal{N}_0)$$

and

$$\mathcal{R}^*[\![P_i]\!] = \mathcal{R}^*(\mathcal{N}[\![P_i]\!]) = \mathcal{R}^*(\mathcal{N}_i)$$

for $i = 1, 2$ . Thus it suffices to show

$$\mathcal{R}^*(\mathcal{N}_0) = \mathcal{R}^*(\mathcal{N}_1) +_\mathcal{R} \mathcal{R}^*(\mathcal{N}_2).$$

This equation follows from the subsequent relationships between the token games of $\mathcal{N}_0$ and of $\mathcal{N}_1$ and $\mathcal{N}_2$.

(1) $M_{01} \times M_{02}$ of $\mathcal{N}_1$ is unstable iff $M_{01}$ of $\mathcal{N}_1$ is unstable or $M_{02}$ of $\mathcal{N}_2$ is unstable.

(2) If $M_{01} \times M_{02}$ of $\mathcal{N}_0$ is stable then

$$next(M_{01} \times M_{02}) = next(M_{01}) \cup next(M_{02}).$$

(3) For every action $u \in A \cup \{\tau\}$, trace $tr \in A^*$ and ready set $\mathcal{F} \subseteq A$ the following holds:

$$\begin{aligned}
& \exists M, M' \in mark(\mathcal{N}_0) \; \exists t \in \longrightarrow : \\
& M_{01} \times M_{02} \xrightarrow{\;t\;} M \text{ and } M \overset{tr}{\Longrightarrow} M' \text{ with} \\
& act(t) = u \text{ and } M' \text{ stable and } \mathcal{F} = next(M')
\end{aligned}$$

$$\begin{aligned}
\text{iff} \quad & \exists i \in \{1, 2\} \; \exists M_i, M_i' \in mark(\mathcal{N}_i) \; \exists t_i \in \longrightarrow_i : \\
& M_{0i} \xrightarrow{\;t_i\;} M_i \text{ and } M_i \overset{tr}{\Longrightarrow} M_i' \text{ with} \\
& act(t_i) = u \text{ and } M_i' \text{ stable and } \mathcal{F} = next(M_i')
\end{aligned}$$

Informally, after the first transition $t$ of $\mathcal{N}_0$ a choice has been made whether to continue as in $\mathcal{N}_1$ or in $\mathcal{N}_2$.

(4)  For every trace $tr \in A^*$ the following holds :

$$\exists M \in mark(\mathcal{N}_0) :$$

$$M_{01} \times M_{02} \xLongrightarrow{tr} M \text{ and } \mathcal{N}_0 \text{ can diverge from } M$$

$$\text{iff} \quad \exists i \in \{1, 2\} \ \exists M_i \in mark(\mathcal{N}_i) :$$

$$M_{0i} \xLongrightarrow{tr} M_i \text{ and } \mathcal{N}_i \text{ can diverge from } M_i.$$

*Parallelism:* $op = \|$

We wish to show $\mathcal{R}^*[\![P_1 \parallel P_2]\!] = \mathcal{R}^*[\![P_1]\!] \parallel_{\mathcal{R}} \mathcal{R}^*[\![P_2]\!]$ for all $P_1, P_2 \in CProc$. Let $A = \alpha(P_1) \cap \alpha(P_2)$ and consider nets

$$\mathcal{N}_i = (\alpha(P_i), Pl_i, \longrightarrow_i, M_{0i})$$

for $i = 1, 2$ with $Pl_1 \cap Pl_2 = \emptyset$ and $\mathcal{N}[\![P_1]\!]) = [\mathcal{N}_i]$ for $i = 1, 2$. Put

$$\mathcal{N}_0 = (\alpha(P_1) \cup \alpha(P_2), Pl_1 \cup Pl_2, \longrightarrow, M_{01} \cup M_{02})$$

where

$$\longrightarrow = \quad \{t | t \in \longrightarrow_1 \cup \longrightarrow_2 \text{ and } act(t) \notin A\}$$

$$\cup \quad \{(pre(t_1) \cup pre(t_2), u, post(t_1) \cup post(t_2)) |$$

$$t_1 \in \longrightarrow_1, t_2 \in \longrightarrow_2 \text{ and } act(t_1) = act(t_2) = u \in A\}.$$

By the First Compositionality Theorem 3.8.3

$$\mathcal{N}[\![P_1 \parallel P_2]\!] = \mathcal{N}[\![P_1]\!] \parallel_{\mathcal{N}} \mathcal{N}[\![P_2]\!] = [\mathcal{N}_1] \parallel_{\mathcal{N}} [\mathcal{N}_2] = [\mathcal{N}_0].$$

Thus it suffices to show

$$\mathcal{R}^*(\mathcal{N}_0) = \mathcal{R}^*(\mathcal{N}_1) \parallel_{\mathcal{R}} \mathcal{R}^*(\mathcal{N}_2).$$

To this end, we introduce an auxiliary operator

$$\parallel_A : Comm^* \times Comm^* \longrightarrow \mathcal{P}(Comm^*)$$

which for traces $tr_1$ and $tr_2$ yields $tr_1 \parallel_A tr_2$ , the set of successful interleavings of $tr_1$ and $tr_2$ which synchronise on all communications in $A$. This set is defined inductively as follows (cf. [OH86, Old86]) :

(1)  $\varepsilon \parallel_A \varepsilon = \{\varepsilon\}$

(2)  $\varepsilon \parallel_A a.tr = a.tr \parallel_A \varepsilon = \begin{cases} \{a\}.(\varepsilon \parallel_A tr) & \text{if } a \notin A \\ \emptyset & \text{otherwise} \end{cases}$

$$(3)\ a.tr_1{\underset{A}{\overset{\|}{}}}b.tr_2 = \begin{cases} \{a\}.(tr_1{\underset{A}{\overset{\|}{}}}b.tr_2) \cup \{b\}.(a.tr_1{\underset{A}{\overset{\|}{}}}tr_2) & \text{if } a,b \notin A \\[6pt] \{a\}.(tr_1{\underset{A}{\overset{\|}{}}}b.tr_2) & \text{if } a \notin A, b \in A \\[6pt] \{b\}.(a.tr_1{\underset{A}{\overset{\|}{}}}tr_2) & \text{if } a \in A, b \notin A \\[6pt] \{a\}.(tr_1{\underset{A}{\overset{\|}{}}}tr_2) & \text{if } a,b \in A \text{ and } a = b \\[6pt] \emptyset & \text{if } a,b \in A \text{ and } a \neq b \end{cases}$$

For example, $a.b.c{\underset{\{b\}}{\overset{\|}{}}}c.b.d = \{a.c.b.c.d, a.c.b.d.c, c.a.b.d.c, c.a.b.c.d\}$.

*Claim.* For all traces $tr_1 \in \alpha(P_1)$ and $tr_2 \in \alpha(P_2)$

$$tr_1{\underset{A}{\overset{\|}{}}}tr_2 = \{tr \in (\alpha(P_1) \cup \alpha(P_2))^* \mid tr{\downarrow}\alpha(P_1) = tr_1 \text{ and } tr{\downarrow}\alpha(P_2) = tr_2\}.$$

This claim is established by showing that the trace set on the right-hand side can be computed by the inductive definition of $tr_1{\overset{\|}{}}tr_2$. Thus we have two equivalent definitions of the set of successful interleavings of $tr_1$ and $tr_2$ at our disposal. The definition on the right-hand side appears in the operator $\|_{\mathcal{R}}$ of the denotational readiness semantics whereas the inductive definition of $tr_1{\underset{A}{\overset{\|}{}}}tr_2$ is closer to the operational net semantics.

The token games of the nets $\mathcal{N}_0$, $\mathcal{N}_1$ and $\mathcal{N}_2$ are related as follows:

(1) $M_{01} \cup M_{02}$ is unstable in $\mathcal{N}_0$ iff $M_{01}$ is unstable in $\mathcal{N}_1$ or $M_{02}$ is unstable in $\mathcal{N}_2$.

(2) For every trace $tr \in (\alpha(P_1) \cup \alpha(P_2))^*$ and $\mathcal{F} \subseteq \alpha(P_1) \cup \alpha(P_2)$ :

$$\exists M \in mark(\mathcal{N}_0) : M_{01} \cup M_{02} \overset{tr}{\Longrightarrow} M \text{ and } M \text{ is stable and } \mathcal{F} = next(M)$$

iff $\forall i \in \{1,2\}\ \exists M_i \in mark(\mathcal{N}_i)\ \exists tr_i \in \alpha(P_i)^*\ \exists \mathcal{G}_i \subseteq \alpha(P_i)$ :
$M_{0i} \overset{tr_i}{\Longrightarrow} M_i$ and $M_i$ is stable and $\mathcal{G}_i = next(M_i)$ and $tr \in tr_1{\underset{A}{\overset{\|}{}}}tr_2$ and
$\mathcal{F} = (\mathcal{G}_1 \cap \mathcal{G}_2 \cap A) \cup (\mathcal{G}_1 \cup \mathcal{G}_2 - A)$

(3) For every trace $tr \in (\alpha(P_1) \cup \alpha(P_2))^*$:

$$\exists M \in mark(\mathcal{N}_0) : M_{01} \cup M_{02} \overset{tr}{\Longrightarrow} M \text{ and } \mathcal{N}_0 \text{ can diverge from } M$$

iff $\exists M_1 \in mark(\mathcal{N}_1), M_2 \in mark(\mathcal{N}_2)$ :
$M_{01} \overset{tr_1}{\Longrightarrow} M_1$ and $M_{02} \overset{tr_2}{\Longrightarrow} M_2$ and
( $\mathcal{N}_1$ can diverge from $M_1$ or $\mathcal{N}_2$ can diverge from $M_2$)

The "if"-part of (2) and (3) is shown by induction on $l = |tr_1| + |tr_2|$ and the "only if" - part by induction on the length $|tr|$. By Lemma 4.4.11 and the claim above, properties (1)-(3) imply the desired equation $\mathcal{R}^*(\mathcal{N}_0) = \mathcal{R}^*(\mathcal{N}_1) +_{\mathcal{R}} \mathcal{R}^*(\mathcal{N}_2)$.

*Hiding: op = $\backslash b$*
We wish to show $\mathcal{R}^*[\![P_1\backslash b]\!] = \mathcal{R}^*[\![P_1]\!]\backslash b_{\mathcal{R}}$ for every $P_1 \in CProc$. Consider a net

$$\mathcal{N}_1 = (\alpha(P_1), Pl, \longrightarrow_1, M_0)$$

with $\mathcal{N}[\![P_1]\!] = [\mathcal{N}_1]$ and put

$$\mathcal{N}_0 = (\alpha(P_1) - \{b\}, Pl, \longrightarrow, M_0)$$

where

$$\longrightarrow = \qquad \{t | t \in \longrightarrow_1 \text{ and } act(t) \neq b\}$$

$$\cup \ \{(pre(t), \tau, post(t)) | t \in \longrightarrow_1 \text{ and } act(t) = b\},$$

Since by the First Compositionality Theorem 3.8.3

$$\mathcal{N}[\![\ P_1 \backslash b\ ]\!] = \mathcal{N}[\![\ P_1\ ]\!] \backslash b_{\mathcal{N}} = [\mathcal{N}_1] \backslash b_{\mathcal{N}} = [\mathcal{N}_0],$$

it suffices to show

$$\mathcal{R}^*(\mathcal{N}_0) = \mathcal{R}^*(\mathcal{N}_1) \backslash b_{\mathcal{R}}.$$

This equation follows from the subsequent relationships between the token games of $\mathcal{N}_0$ and $\mathcal{N}_1$, and from the chaotic closure built into the definition of $\backslash b_{\mathcal{R}}$.

(1)  $M_0$ is unstable in $\mathcal{N}_0$ iff $M_0$ is unstable in $\mathcal{N}_1$ or $b \in next(M_0)$ in $\mathcal{N}_1$ .

(2)  For every trace $tr \in (\alpha(P_1) - \{b\})^*$ and $\mathcal{F} \subseteq \alpha(P_1) - \{b\}$ :

$$\exists M \in mark(\mathcal{N}_0) : M_0 \overset{tr}{\Longrightarrow} M \text{ in } \mathcal{N}_0 \text{ and } M \text{ is stable and } \mathcal{F} = next(M)$$

> iff  $\exists M' \in mark(\mathcal{N}_1), tr' \in \alpha(P_1)^* : M_0 \overset{tr'}{\Longrightarrow} M'$ in $\mathcal{N}_1$ and
> $tr = tr' {\downarrow} (\alpha(P_1) - \{b\})$ and $M'$ is stable and $b \notin next(M') = \mathcal{F}$.

(3)  For every trace $tr \in (\alpha(P_1) - \{b\})^*$:

$$\exists tr' \leq tr \exists M \in mark(\mathcal{N}_0) : M_0 \overset{tr'}{\Longrightarrow} M \text{ in } \mathcal{N}_0 \text{ and } \mathcal{N}_0 \text{ can diverge from } M$$

> iff  $\exists tr' \in \alpha(P_1)^* : tr' {\downarrow} (\alpha(P_1) - \{b\}) \leq tr$ and
> $((\exists M' \in mark(\mathcal{N}_1) : M_0 \overset{tr'}{\Longrightarrow} M'$ in $\mathcal{N}_1$ and $\mathcal{N}_1$ can diverge from $M'$ )
> or $(\forall n \geq 0 \ \exists M'' \in mark(\mathcal{N}_1) : M_0 \overset{tr'.b^n}{\longrightarrow} M''))$.

The "if"-part follows from a variation of Proposition 4.3.5(4), with $b$ instead of $\tau$, and the "only if"-part is immediate from the definition of hiding on nets.

This completes the proof of the Second Compositionality Theorem.  □

An immediate consequence of the above theorem is that operational and denotational readiness semantics coincide on closed process terms without recursion. Formally:

**Corollary 4.6.4** For every non-recursive $P \in CProc$

$$\mathcal{R}^*[\![P]\!] = \mathcal{R}^{**}[\![P]\!].$$

*Proof.* By induction on the structure of $P$.  □

We wish to extend this result now to all closed process terms. Our plan is to represent the semantics of each recursive term as the semantic limit of its non-recursive approximations. For the denotational readiness semantics $\mathcal{R}^{**}$ this requires the continuity of its operators. Unfortunately, the hiding operator $\backslash b_{\mathcal{R}}$ lacks this property.

**Proposition 4.6.5** Hiding $\backslash b_{\mathcal{R}}$ is not $\sqsubseteq$-continuous on $DOM_{\mathcal{R}}$.

*Proof.* Consider a communication alphabet $A$ with $b \in A$ and define

$$\Gamma_n = \{(b^n.tr, A) | tr \in A^*\}$$

for $n \geq 0$. Then

$$(A, \Gamma_0) \sqsubseteq (A, \Gamma_1) \sqsubseteq \ldots \sqsubseteq (A, \Gamma_n) \sqsubseteq \ldots$$

is a chain in $DOM_{\mathcal{R}}$ with the limit

$$\bigsqcup_{n \geq 0} (A, \Gamma_n) = (A, \emptyset).$$

Hence

$$(\bigsqcup_{n \geq 0} (A, \Gamma_n)) \backslash b_{\mathcal{R}} = (A - \{b\}, \emptyset).$$

On the other hand,

$$(A, \Gamma_n) \backslash b_{\mathcal{R}} = (A - \{b\}, Info_{\mathcal{R}} : A - \{b\})$$

for every $n \geq 0$. Thus

$$(\bigsqcup_{n \geq 0} (A, \Gamma_n)) \backslash b_{\mathcal{R}} = (A - \{b\}, \emptyset) \neq (A - \{b\}, Info_{\mathcal{R}} : A - \{b\}) = \bigsqcup_{n \geq 0} ((A, \Gamma_n) \backslash b_{\mathcal{R}})$$

shows that $\backslash_{\mathcal{R}}$ is not $\sqsubseteq$-continuous on $DOM_{\mathcal{R}}$. □

Note that the information sets $\Gamma_n$ used in the above counterexample are not well-structured (indeed, not prefix closed: cf. property (2) of Definition 4.4.2). We can show that the hiding operator $\backslash b_{\mathcal{R}}$ and all the other operators $op_{\mathcal{R}}$ of Definition 4.5.6 are $\sqsubseteq$-continuous when their application is restricted to well-structured domain elements.

To this end, we introduce now a subdomain of $DOM_{\mathcal{R}}$. For a given alphabet $A$ let

$$ws\text{-}DOM_{\mathcal{R}} : A$$

consist of all well-structured elements $(A, \Gamma) \in DOM_{\mathcal{R}} : A$. Then the *well-structured readiness domain* is given by

$$ws\text{-}DOM_{\mathcal{R}} = \bigcup ws\text{-}DOM_{\mathcal{R}} : A$$

where the union is taken over all communication alphabets $A$. Note that for every fixed alphabet $A$ the subdomain $ws\text{-}DOM_{\mathcal{R}}:A$ is a complete partial order under the relation $\sqsubseteq$. Indeed, the least element $(A, Info_{\mathcal{R}} : A)$ of $DOM_{\mathcal{R}}$ is well-structured and the least upper bound of an ascending chain of well-structured elements is itself well-structured.

**Continuity Theorem 4.6.6** Every $n$-ary operator $op_{\mathcal{R}}$ of Definition 4.5.6, considered as a mapping

$$op_{\mathcal{R}} : \underbrace{ws\text{-}DOM_{\mathcal{R}} \times \ldots \times ws\text{-}DOM_{\mathcal{R}}}_{n \text{ times}} \longrightarrow ws\text{-}DOM_{\mathcal{R}},$$

is well defined, i.e. it preserves the conditions of being well-structured, and it is $\sqsubseteq$-continuous.

We first present a lemma that enables a uniform continuity proof for all operators except hiding. Consider an $(n + 1)$-ary relation $g \subseteq M_1 \times \ldots \times M_n \times M$ on sets $M_1, \ldots, M_n$ and $M$ with $n \geq 1$. The *image* of sets $X_1 \subseteq M_1, \ldots, X_n \subseteq M_n$ under $g$ is the set

$$g(X_1, \ldots, X_n) = \{y \in M \mid \exists x_1 \in X_1, \ldots, x_n \in X_n : (x_1, \ldots, x_n, y) \in g\}$$

and the *pre-image* of a set $Y \subseteq M$ under $g$ is the set

$$g^{-1}(Y) = \{(x_1, \ldots, x_n) \in M_1 \times \ldots \times M_n \mid \exists y \in Y : (x_1, \ldots, x_n, y) \in g\}$$

For singleton sets $Y = y$ we write $g^{-1}(y)$ instead of $g^{-1}(\{y\})$.

**Definition 4.6.7** A relation $g \subseteq M_1 \times \ldots \times M_n \times M$ as above is called *pre-image finite* if for every $y \in M$ the pre-image $g^{-1}(y)$ is a finite set. □

With this notion we can state the following continuity result for the reverse set inclusion.

**Continuity Lemma 4.6.8** Under a pre-image finite relation

$$g \subseteq M_1 \times \ldots \times M_n \times M,$$

the image is $\supseteq$-continuous.

*Proof.* The claim is that for all argument positions $i \in \{1, \ldots, n\}$, sets $X_1 \subseteq M_1, \ldots, X_{i-1} \subseteq M_{i-1}, X_{i+1} \subseteq M_{i+1}, \ldots, X_n \subseteq M_n$ and chains

$$M_i \supseteq X_{i,0} \supseteq X_{i,1} \supseteq \ldots$$

we have

$$g(X_1, \ldots, \bigcap_{j \geq 0} X_{i,j}, \ldots, X_n) = \bigcap_{j \geq 0} g(X_1, \ldots, X_{i,j}, \ldots, X_n).$$

The inclusion "$\subseteq$" follows from the fact that under *any* relation $g$ the image is always $\supseteq$-monotonic and the inclusion "$\supseteq$" exploits that $g$ is pre-image finite (cf. Proposition 5.2 of [OH86]). □

Since every operator except hiding can be represented as the image under a pre-image finite relation and since the partial order $\sqsubseteq$ on the readiness domain is essentially the reverse set inclusion $\supseteq$, the Continuity Lemma implies the $\sqsubseteq$-continuity of these operators. The details are given in the subsequent proof of the Continuity Theorem 4.6.6. For the hiding operator $\backslash b_{\mathcal{R}}$ this simple argument does not apply. For example, each of the infinitely many divergence points $(b^n, \uparrow)$, with $n \geq 0$, is in the pre-image of a single divergence point, viz. $(\varepsilon, \uparrow)$. Thus $\backslash b_{\mathcal{R}}$ cannot be represented as the image of a pre-image finite relation.

*Proof of Theorem 4.6.6.* We omit the details showing that all operators $op_{\mathcal{R}}$ preserve the properties of being well-structured. Now consider an $n$-ary operator symbol

$$op \in \{a. \, , \, + \, , \, \| \, , \, [b/a] \mid a, b \in Comm\},$$

$n \in \{1, 2\}$. Then for all alphabets $A_1, \ldots, A_n$ there exists an $(n+1)$-ary pre-image finite relation $g_{A_1, \ldots, A_n}$ on process information sets such that for all $(A, \Gamma_1), \ldots, (A_n, \Gamma_n) \in ws\text{-}DOM_{\mathcal{R}}$ the equation

$$op_{\mathcal{R}}((A_1, \Gamma_1), \ldots, (A_n, \Gamma_n)) = (op_\alpha(A_1, \ldots, A_n), g_{A_1, \ldots, A_n}(\Gamma_1, \ldots, \Gamma_n))$$

holds, where $op_\alpha$ is the corresponding set-theoretic operator on alphabets mentioned in Remark 3.1.4.

For example, for $op = a$, we have $n = 1$ and define $g_{A_1}$ as follows:

$$(\gamma_1, \delta) \in g_{A_1}$$

if $\quad (\exists \mathcal{X} : \gamma_1 = (\varepsilon, \mathcal{X}) \text{ and } \delta = (\varepsilon, \{a\}))$

or $\quad (\exists tr \, \exists \mathcal{X} : \gamma_1 = (tr, \mathcal{X}) \text{ and } \delta = (a.tr, \mathcal{X}))$

or $\quad (\gamma_1 = (\varepsilon, \uparrow) \text{ and } \delta = (\varepsilon, \emptyset))$

or $\quad (\exists tr \, \exists tr' \in (A_1 \cup \{a\})^* \, \exists \mathcal{F} \subseteq A_1 \cup \{a\} :$

$$\gamma_1 = (tr, \uparrow) \text{ and } tr \leq tr' \text{ and } \delta = (a.tr', \mathcal{F})).$$

Then $g_{A_1}$ is pre-image finite and satisfies

$$a._{\mathcal{R}}(A_1, \Gamma_1) = (A_1 \cup \{a\}, g_{A_1}(\Gamma_1)).$$

Returning to the general case consider an argument position $i \in \{1, \ldots, n\}$, arguments $(A_1, \Gamma_1), \ldots, (A_{i-1}, \Gamma_{i-1}), (A_{i+1}, \Gamma_{i+1}), \ldots, (A_n, \Gamma_n) \in ws\text{-}DOM_{\mathcal{R}}$ and a chain

$$(A_i, \Gamma_{i,0}) \sqsubseteq (A_i, \Gamma_{i,1}) \sqsubseteq (A_i, \Gamma_{i,2}) \sqsubseteq \ldots$$

in $ws\text{-}DOM_{\mathcal{R}}$. Then we calculate

$$op_{\mathcal{R}}((A_1, \Gamma_1), \ldots, \bigsqcup_{j \geq 0}(A_i, \Gamma_{i,j}), \ldots, (A_n, \Gamma_n))$$

$$= \quad op_{\mathcal{R}}((A_1, \Gamma_1), \ldots, (A_i, \bigcap_{j \geq 0} \Gamma_{i,j}), \ldots, (A_n, \Gamma_n))$$

$$= \quad (op_\alpha(A_1, \ldots, A_n), g_{A_1, \ldots, An}(\Gamma_1, \ldots, \bigcap_{j \geq 0} \Gamma_{i,j}, \ldots, \Gamma_n))$$

$$= \quad \{ \text{ Continuity Lemma 4.6.7 } \}$$
$$( op_\alpha(A_1, \ldots, A_n), \bigcap_{j \geq 0} g_{A_1, \ldots, A_n}(\Gamma_1, \ldots, \Gamma_{i,j}, \ldots, \Gamma_n))$$
$$= \quad \bigsqcup_{j \geq 0} ( op_\alpha(A_1, \ldots, A_n), g_{A_1, \ldots, A_n}(\Gamma_1, \ldots, \Gamma_{i,j}, \ldots, \Gamma_n))$$
$$= \quad \bigsqcup_{j \geq 0} op_\mathcal{R}((A_1, \Gamma_1), \ldots, (A_i, \Gamma_{i,j}), \ldots, (A_n, \Gamma_n)).$$

Thus $op_\mathcal{R}$ is $\sqsubseteq$-continuous on $DOM_\mathcal{R}$ and hence on $ws\text{-}DOM_\mathcal{R}$.

We now turn to the hiding operator $\backslash b_\mathcal{R}$, considered as a mapping on $ws\text{-}DOM_\mathcal{R}$. Since $\backslash b_\mathcal{R}$ is $\sqsubseteq$-monotonic (cf. Proposition 4.5.7), it suffices to show that for every chain

$$(A, \Gamma_0) \sqsubseteq (A, \Gamma_1) \sqsubseteq (A, \Gamma_2) \sqsubseteq \ldots \tag{4.16}$$

in $ws\text{-}DOM_\mathcal{R}$, the relationship

$$(\bigsqcup_{n \geq 0}(A, \Gamma_n))\backslash b_\mathcal{R} \sqsubseteq \bigsqcup_{n \geq 0}((A, \Gamma_n)\backslash b_\mathcal{R}) \tag{4.17}$$

holds. Recall that (4.16) is equivalent to

$$\Gamma_0 \supseteq \Gamma_1 \supseteq \Gamma_2 \supseteq \ldots \tag{4.18}$$

For convenience let us introduce the following abbreviations for sets of process information:

$$\Delta_n = \pi((A, \Gamma_n)\backslash b_\mathcal{R})$$

for $n \geq 0$ and

$$\Delta = \pi((A, \bigcap_{n \geq 0} \Gamma_n)\backslash b_\mathcal{R}).$$

Then (4.17) is equivalent to the inclusion

$$\bigcap_{n \geq 0} \Delta_n \subseteq \Delta. \tag{4.19}$$

Consider some process information $\delta = \bigcap_{n \geq 0} \Delta_n$.

*Case 1:* $\delta = \tau$

Then $\forall n \geq 0 : (\tau \in \Gamma_n$ or $\exists \mathcal{G} \subseteq A : (b, \mathcal{G}) \in \Gamma_n)$. By (4.18) and the finiteness of $A$, it follows that

$$\tau \in \bigcap_{n \geq 0} \Gamma_n \text{ or } \exists \mathcal{G} \subseteq A : (b, \mathcal{G}) \in \bigcap_{n \geq 0} \Gamma_n.$$

Thus $\tau \in \Delta$.

*Case 2:* $\delta = (tr, \mathcal{F})$

Consider the following condition :

$$C_n =_{df} \exists tr' \leq tr : (tr', \uparrow) \in \Delta_n \quad \text{or } \exists \mathcal{G} \subseteq \mathcal{F} : (tr, \mathcal{G}) \in \Delta_n$$
$$\text{or } \exists a \in Comm : (tr.a, \uparrow) \in \Delta_n.$$

Then $C_n$ lists all possibilities that $(tr, \mathcal{F})$ originates from the closure operator built into $\Delta_n$. Let us deal with the complementary situation first.

*Subcase 2.1:* $\exists n \geq 0 : \neg C_n$
Using (4.18), it follows that $\neg C_n$ holds for all but finitely many $n \geq 0$. Consequently, using (4.18) again, we have

$$\forall n \geq 0 \; \exists tr' : tr = tr'\downarrow(A - \{b\}) \text{ and } (tr', \mathcal{F}) \in \Gamma_n.$$

Clearly, if the quantifiers can be exchanged, i.e. if

$$\exists tr' \; \forall n \geq 0 : tr = tr'\downarrow(A - \{b\}) \text{ and } (tr', \mathcal{F}) \in \Gamma_n,$$

then $(tr, \mathcal{F}) \in \Delta$. Otherwise, by (4.18) and the prefix closure of $\Delta_n$,

$$\exists tr' \; \forall m \geq 0 \; \exists \mathcal{G} : tr'\downarrow(A - \{b\}) \leq tr \text{ and } (tr'.b_m, \mathcal{G}) \in \bigcap_{n \geq 0} \Gamma_n.$$

Thus $(tr'\downarrow(A - \{b\}), \uparrow) \in \Delta$. By the chaotic closure in $\Delta$, it follows that $(tr, \mathcal{F}) \in \Delta$.

*Subcase 2.2:* $\forall n \geq 0 : C_n$
By (4.18) and the chaotic closure in $\Delta$, this subcase can be inferred from Subcase 2.1 and Case 3 which we consider next.

*Case 3:* $\delta = (tr, \uparrow)$
Similarly to Case 2 we consider the condition

$$D_n =_{df} \exists tr' \leq tr : (tr', \uparrow) \in \Delta_n$$

which describes $(tr, \uparrow)$ originating from the closure operator built into $\Delta_n$ .

*Subcase 3.1 :* $\exists n \geq 0 : \neg D_n$
By (4.18), it follows that

$$\forall n \geq 0 \; \exists tr' : \quad tr = tr'\downarrow(A - \{b\}) \text{ and }$$
$$((tr', \uparrow) \in \Gamma_n \text{ or } \forall m \geq 0 \; \exists \mathcal{G} : (tr'.b^m, \mathcal{G}) \in \bigcap_{n \geq 0} \Gamma_n).$$

Then by arguments similar to Case 2

$$\exists tr' : \quad tr'\downarrow(A - \{b\}) \leq tr \text{ and }$$
$$((tr', \uparrow) \in \bigcap_{n \geq 0} \Gamma_n \text{ or } \forall m \geq 0 \; \exists \mathcal{G} : (tr'.b^m, \mathcal{G}) \in \bigcap_{n \geq 0} \Gamma_n).$$

Thus by the chaotic closure in $\Delta$, it follows that $(tr, \uparrow) \in \Delta$.

*Subcase 3.2 :* $\forall n \geq 0 : D_n$
By (4.18) and the chaotic closure in $\Delta$, this subcase can be inferred from Subcase 3.1
    Thus in all cases $\delta \in \Delta$. This shows (4.19) and hence completes the proof of the Continuity Theorem.                                                                                   $\square$

Given a recursive term $\mu X.P \in CProc$ and another term $R \in CProc$ with $\alpha(X) = \alpha(R)$, we define for $n \geq 0$ the term $P^n(R)$ inductively as follows :

$$P^0(R) = R \text{ and } P^{n+1}(R) = P\{P^n(R)/X\}.$$

With this notation, we can state the desired approximation property:

**Corollary 4.6.9** : **Fixed Point Approximation** For every recursive term $\mu X.P \in CProc$ the equation

$$\mathcal{R}^{**}[\![\,\mu X.P\,]\!] = \bigsqcup_{n \geq 0} \mathcal{R}^{**}[\![\,P^n(div{:}\alpha(X))\,]\!]$$

holds, i.e. the denotational readiness semantics of $\mu X.P$ can be represented as the semantic limit of its syntactic approximations $P^n(div{:}\alpha(X))$.

*Proof.* Use Kleene's Fixed Point Theorem 4.5.2, with the $\sqsubseteq$-continuity of the operators $op_{\mathcal{R}}$ on $ws\text{-}DOM_{\mathcal{R}}$ .                                  $\square$

Does this approximation property also hold for the operational readiness semantics $\mathcal{R}^*$ ? The answer is "yes", but we first prove it under the assumption that $\mathcal{R}^*$ is $\sqsubseteq$-monotonic.

**Lemma 4.6.10** Consider a recursive term $\mu X.P \in CProc$. If for all terms $Q, R \in CProc$ with $\alpha(X) = \alpha(Q) = \alpha(R)$

$$\mathcal{R}^*[\![Q]\!] \sqsubseteq \mathcal{R}^*[\![R]\!] \text{ always implies } \mathcal{R}^*[\![P\{Q/X\}]\!] \sqsubseteq \mathcal{R}^*[\![P\{R/X\}]\!] \qquad (4.20)$$

then

$$\mathcal{R}^*[\![\mu X.P]\!] = \bigsqcup_{n \geq 0} \mathcal{R}^*[\![P^n(div{:}\alpha(X))\,]\!]. \qquad (4.21)$$

*Proof.* Consider a recursive term $\mu X.P \in CProc$ and suppose that (4.20) is true. By Theorem 3.5.8, the operational net semantics satisfies the equation $\mathcal{N}[\![\mu X.P]\!] = \mathcal{N}[\![P\{\mu X.P/X\}]\!]$. Thus by the definition of $\mathcal{R}^*$, also

$$\mathcal{R}^*[\![\mu X.P\,]\!] = \mathcal{R}^*[\![P\{\mu X.P/X\}]\!]. \qquad (4.22)$$

Suppose now that (4.20) holds. Then by induction on $n \geq 0$, the assertions (4.20) and (4.22) imply that

$$\mathcal{R}^*[\![P^n(div{:}\alpha(X))]\!] \sqsubseteq \mathcal{R}^*[\![\mu X.P]\!]$$

for all $n \geq 0$. Hence

$$\bigsqcup_{n \geq 0} \mathcal{R}^*[\![P^n(div{:}\alpha(X))\,]\!] \sqsubseteq \mathcal{R}^*[\![\mu X.P\,]\!].$$

Thus to show (4.21), it remains to prove the reverse relationship:

$$\mathcal{R}^*[\![\mu X.P]\!] \sqsubseteq \bigsqcup_{n \geq 0} \mathcal{R}^*[\![P^n(div{:}\alpha(X))]\!]. \tag{4.23}$$

We start with preparatory remarks. Notice that by induction on $n \geq 0$, the assertions (4.20) and (4.22) imply that

$$\mathcal{R}^*[\![\mu X.P]\!] = \mathcal{R}^*[\![\,P^n(\mu X.P)]\!] \tag{4.24}$$

holds for every $n \geq 0$. (As an aside we remark that equation (4.24) would be false for the net semantics $\mathcal{N}$ because $\mathcal{N}[\![P^n(\mu X.P)]\!]$ can be an unfolded version of $\mathcal{N}[\![\mu X.P]\!]$.)

Now we wish to replace in $P^n(\mu X.P)$ the subterm $\mu X.P$ by $div{:}\alpha(X)$. To this end, we examine the token game of nets denoted by process terms of the form $P^n(R)$. Consider $k, n$ with $n > k \geq 0$ and $R, R' \in CProc$ with $\alpha(X) = \alpha(R) = \alpha(R')$. Since $\mu X.P$ is by definition action-guarded, no transition sequence consisting of $k$ transitions and starting in $dex(P^n(R))$ will decompose $R$ into $dex(R)$. Thus if $R$ is replaced by $R'$ there exists a corresponding transition sequence starting in $dex(P^n(R'))$. More precisely, we have the following property:

*Property 1.* For every transition sequence of the form

$$dex(P^n(R)) = M_0 \xrightarrow{t_1} \ldots \xrightarrow{t_k} M_k$$

there exists a transition sequence

$$dex(P^n(R')) = M_0' \xrightarrow{t_1'} \ldots \xrightarrow{t_k'} M_k'$$

such that

$$act(t_1) = act(t_1'), \ldots, act(t_n) = act(t_n')$$

and

$$next(M_0) = next(M_0'), \ldots, next(M_k) = next(M_{k'}).$$

Consequently, if a process information in $\mathcal{R}^*[\![\,P^n(R)]\!]$ does not require more than $k$ transition steps, it is also present in $\mathcal{R}^*[\![P^n(R')]\!]$ and in particular in $\mathcal{R}^*[\![\,P^n(\mu X.P)]\!]$, i.e. in $\mathcal{R}^*[\![\mu X.P]\!]$ by (4.24). This observation will be exploited to show (4.23).

Let us introduce the following abbreviations for the corresponding sets of process information on the right- and left-hand sides of (4.23):

$$\Delta_n = \pi(\mathcal{R}^*[\![P^n(div{:}\alpha(X))]\!])$$

for $n \geq 0$ and

$$\Delta = \pi(\mathcal{R}^*[\![\mu X.P]\!]).$$

Then Property 1 is equivalent to the inclusion

$$\bigcap_{n \geq 0} \Delta_n \subseteq \Delta. \tag{4.25}$$

When proving (4.25) we follow the overall structure of the continuity proof of $\backslash b_R$ in Theorem 4.6.5 though the details are of course different. Thus consider some process information $\delta \in \bigcap_{n \geq 0} \Delta_n$.

*Case 1:* $\delta = \tau$
Then $\forall n \geq 0 : \tau \in \textit{next}(\textit{dex}(P^n(\textit{div:}\alpha(X))))$. Take $n = 1$. By Property 1, $\tau \in \textit{next}(\textit{dex}(P^n(\mu X.P)))$ also. By (4.24), it follows that $\tau \in \Delta$.

*Case 2:* $\delta = (tr, \mathcal{F})$
Consider the following condition:

$$C_n =_{df} \exists tr' \leq tr : (tr', \uparrow) \in \Delta_n \quad \text{or } \exists \mathcal{G} \subseteq \mathcal{F} : (tr, \mathcal{G}) \in \Delta_n$$

$$\text{or } \exists a \in Comm : (tr.a, \uparrow) \in \Delta_n.$$

Then $C_n$ lists all possibilities that $(tr, \mathcal{F})$ originates from the closure operator built into $D_n$.

*Subcase 2.1:* $\exists n \geq 0 : \neg C_n$
Since $\Delta_0 \supseteq \Delta_1 \supseteq \Delta_2 \supseteq \ldots$, we have $\neg C_n$ for all but finitely many $n \geq 0$. Thus for all but finitely many $n$ there exists a transition sequence of the form

$$\textit{dex}(P^n(\textit{div:}\alpha(X))) = M_0 \xrightarrow{t_1} M_1 \ldots \xrightarrow{t_k} M_k \tag{4.26}$$

with $tr = (act(t_1) \ldots act(t_k)) \backslash \tau$ and $\mathcal{F} = \textit{next}(M_k)$. Then one of the following properties holds:

*Property 2.* There exists some $n$ and a transition sequence (4.26) of length $k < n$ and with $tr$ and $\mathcal{F}$ as above;

or

*Property 3.* There exists some prefix $tr' \leq tr$ such that for infinitely many $n$ there exists a transitive sequence (4.26) of length $k = n-1$ with $tr' = (act(t_1) \ldots act(t_k)) \backslash \tau$.

By Property 1, the above properties remain true if we replace $P^n(\textit{div:}\alpha(X))$ by $P^n(R)$ for an arbitrary $R \in \textit{CProc}$ with $\alpha(X) = \alpha(R)$, in particular for $R = \mu X.P$. By (4.24), Property 1 implies then that $(tr, \mathcal{F}) \in \Delta$. Property 2 implies that there exist infinitely many transitions sequences

$$\textit{dex}(\mu X.P) = M_0 \xrightarrow{t_1} M_1 \ldots \xrightarrow{t_k} M_k$$

with $tr'$ as above. By Proposition 4.3.5(4), it follows that $(tr'', \uparrow) \in \Delta$ for some prefix $tr'' \leq tr'$ so that, by the chaotic closure in $\Delta$, again $(tr, \mathcal{F}) \in \Delta$.

*Subcase 2.2:* $\forall n \geq 0 : C_n$
By the chaotic closure in $\Delta$, this subcase can be inferred from Subcase 2.1 and Case 3 below.

*Case 3:* $\delta = (tr, \uparrow)$
Consider the condition

$$D_n =_{df} \exists tr' \leq tr : (tr', \uparrow) \in \Delta_n$$

which describes $(tr, \uparrow)$ originating from the closure operator built into $\Delta_n$.

*Subcase 3.1:* $\forall n \geq 0 : \neg D_n$
Since $\Delta_0 \supseteq \Delta_1 \supseteq \Delta_2 \supseteq \ldots$, we have $\neg D_n$ for all but finitely many $n \geq 0$. Thus for all but finitely many $n$ there exists an infinite transition sequence of the form

$$dex(P^n(div{:}\alpha(X))) = M_0 \xrightarrow{t_1} M_1 \xrightarrow{t_2} M_2 \xrightarrow{t_3} \ldots$$

such that for some $k \geq 0$

$$tr = (act(t_1) \ldots act(t_k)) \backslash \tau$$

and

$$\tau = act(t_{k+1}) = act(t_{k+2}) = act(t_{k+3}) = \ldots$$

Then there exists some prefix $tr' \leq tr$ such that for infinitely many $n$ there exists a transition sequence

$$dex(P^n(div{:}\alpha(X))) = M_0 \xrightarrow{t_1} M_1 \ldots \xrightarrow{t_k} M_k$$

of length $k = n - 1$ with $tr' = (act(t_1) \ldots act(t_k)) \backslash \tau$. This is Property 3 above. As before, we conclude $(tr'', \uparrow) \in \Delta$ for some prefix $tr'' \leq tr'$. Thus by the chaotic closure in $\Delta$, we have $(tr, \uparrow) \in \Delta$.

*Subcase 3.2:* $\forall n \geq 0 : D_n$
By the chaotic closure in $\Delta$, this subcase can be inferred from Subcase 3.1. Thus in all cases $\delta \in \Delta$. This shows (4.23) and hence completes the proof of the lemma. $\square$

Next we discharge assumption (4.20) of Lemma 4.6.10, i.e. prove the monotonicity of $\mathcal{R}^*$. This proof employs a "bootstrap argument" where (4.21) is needed as well, and it uses the following corollary of the Second Compositionality Theorem 4.6.1.

**Corollary 4.6.11** For all non-recursive terms $P \in Proc$, all $X_1, \ldots, X_k \in Idf$ with $k \geq 0$ and $free(P) \subseteq \{X_1, \ldots, X_k\}$, all $Q_1, \ldots, Q_k \in CProc$ with $\alpha(X_1) = \alpha(Q_1), \ldots, \alpha(X_k) = \alpha(Q_k)$ and all environments $\rho$, the equation

$$\mathcal{R}^*[\![P\{Q_1, \ldots, Q_k / X_1, \ldots, X_k\}]\!]$$
$$= \mathcal{R}^{**}[\![P]\!](\rho[\mathcal{R}^*[\![Q_1]\!], \ldots, \mathcal{R}^*[\![Q_k]\!] / X_1, \ldots, X_k]).$$

holds. For $k = 0$, this reduces to Corollary 4.6.4.

*Proof.* We use induction on the structure of $P$. $\square$

**Lemma 4.6.12** For all terms $\mu X.P, Q, R \in CProc$ with $\alpha(X) = \alpha(Q) = \alpha(R)$

$$\mathcal{R}^*[\![\, Q \,]\!] \sqsubseteq \mathcal{R}^*[\![\, R \,]\!]$$

always implies

$$\mathcal{R}^*[\![P\{Q/X\} \,]\!] \sqsubseteq \mathcal{R}^*[\![P\{R/X\} \,]\!].$$

*Proof.* We proceed by induction on the number $m$ of occurrences of $\mu$ in $P$.

$m = 0$: We use Corollary 4.6.11 with $k = 1$, and the $\sqsubseteq$-monotonicity of the operators $op_{\mathcal{R}}$ in the denotational readiness semantics $\mathcal{R}^*[\![\, P \,]\!]$ (cf. Proposition 4.5.7).

$m \longrightarrow m + 1$: Suppose $P$ contains $m + 1$ occurrences of $\mu$. Then $P$ is of the form

$$P = P_0\{\mu Y.P_1, P_2, \dots, P_k/X_1, \dots, X_k\}$$

where $P_0 \in Proc$ is non-recursive and $P_1, \dots, P_k$ together contain $m$ occurrences of $\mu$. Then

$\qquad \mathcal{R}^*[\![P\{Q/X\} \,]\!]$

$= \quad \mathcal{R}^*[\![P_0\{\mu Y.P_1\{Q/X\}, P_2\{Q/X\}, \dots, P_k\{Q/X\}, Q/X_1, \dots, X_k, X\} \,]\!]$

$= \quad \{ \text{ Corollary 4.6.9 } \}$

$\qquad \mathcal{R}^{**}[\![P_0]\!](\rho[\mathcal{R}^*[\![\, \mu Y.P_1\{Q/X\} \,]\!],$
$\qquad\qquad\qquad \mathcal{R}^*[\![\, P_2\{Q/X\}]\!], \dots, \mathcal{R}^*[\![\, P_k\{Q/X\} \,]\!], \mathcal{R}^*[\![Q]\!]/X_1, \dots, X_k, X])$

$= \quad \{ \text{ (4.21) of Lemma 4.6.10 using the induction hypothesis to show (4.20) } \}$

$\qquad \mathcal{R}^{**}[\![P_0]\!](\rho[\bigsqcup_{n \geq 0} \mathcal{R}^*[\![(P_1\{Q/X\})^n(div{:}\alpha(Y)) \,]\!],$
$\qquad\qquad\qquad \mathcal{R}^*[\![P_2\{Q/X\} \,]\!], \dots, \mathcal{R}^*[\![P_k\{Q/X\} \,]\!], \mathcal{R}^*[\![\, Q \,]\!]/X_1, \dots, X_k, X])$

$\sqsubseteq \quad \{ \text{ induction hypothesis, Proposition 4.5.7 } \}$

$\qquad \mathcal{R}^{**}[\![P_0]\!](\rho[\bigsqcup_{n \geq 0} \mathcal{R}^*[\![(P_1\{R/X\})^n(div{:}\alpha(Y)) \,]\!],$
$\qquad\qquad\qquad \mathcal{R}^*[\![P_2\{R/X\}]\!], \dots, \mathcal{R}^*[\![P_k\{R/X\} \,]\!], \mathcal{R}^*[\![\, R \,]\!]/X_1, \dots, X_k, X])$

$= \quad \{ \text{ (4.21) of Lemma 4.6.10 using the induction hypothesis to show (4.20) } \}$

$\qquad \mathcal{R}^{**}[\![P_0]\!](\rho[\mathcal{R}^*[\![\mu Y.P_1\{R/X\}]\!],$
$\qquad\qquad\qquad \mathcal{R}^*[\![\, \mu Y.P_2\{R/X\}]\!], \dots, \mathcal{R}^*[\![\, \mu Y.P_k\{R/X\}]\!], \mathcal{R}^*[\![R]\!]/X_1, \dots, X_k, X])$

$= \quad \{ \text{ Corollary 4.6.11 } \}$

$\qquad \mathcal{R}^*[\![\, P_0\{\mu Y.P_1\{R/X\}, P_2\{R/X\}, \dots, P_k\{R/X\}, R/X_1, \dots, X_k, X\} \,]\!]$

$= \quad \mathcal{R}^*[\![P\{R/X\}]\!]$

as required.                                                                   $\square$

Combining Lemmas 4.6.9 and 4.6.10 yields:

**Corollary 4.6.13 : Operational Approximation.** For every recursive term $\mu X.P \in CProc$ the equation

$$\mathcal{R}^*[\![\mu X.P\,]\!] = \bigsqcup_{n \geq 0} \mathcal{R}^*[\![P^n(div{:}\alpha(X))\,]\!]$$

holds. □

Finally, with the help of Corollaries 4.6.4 and 4.6.11 of the Second Compositionality Theorem and Corollaries 4.6.9 and 4.6.13 on Fixed Point Approximation and Operational Approximation we can prove the main result of this section.

**Equivalence Theorem 4.6.14** For every closed process term $P$ the operational and denotational readiness semantics coincide:

$$\mathcal{R}^*[\![\,P\,]\!] = \mathcal{R}^{**}[\![\,P\,]\!].$$

*Proof.* As in the proof of Lemma 4.6.12, we proceed by induction on the number $m$ of occurences of $\mu$ in $P$.

$m = 0$: This is the statement of Corollary 4.4.12.

$m \longrightarrow m+1$: Suppose $P$ contains $m+1$ occurences of $\mu$. Then $P$ can be written as

$$P = P_0\{\mu Y.P_1, P_2, \ldots, P_k/X_1, \ldots, X_k\}$$

where $P_0 \in Proc$ is non-recursive and $P_1, \ldots, P_k$ together contain $m$ occurences of $\mu$. Then

$\mathcal{R}^*[\![P]\!]$

$=$ { Corollary 4.6.11 }

$\mathcal{R}^{**}[\![\,P_0\,]\!](\rho[\mathcal{R}^*[\![\mu Y.P_1]\!], \mathcal{R}^*[\![\,P_2]\!], \ldots, \mathcal{R}^*[\![P_k]\!]/X_1, \ldots, X_k])$

$=$ { Corollary 4.6.13 }

$\mathcal{R}^{**}[\![\,P_0\,]\!](\rho[\bigsqcup_{n \geq 0} \mathcal{R}^*[\![P_1{}^n(div{:}\alpha(Y))\,]\!], \mathcal{R}^*[\![P_2]\!], \ldots, \mathcal{R}^*[\![P_k]\!]/X_1, \ldots, X_k])$

$=$ { induction hypothesis }

$\mathcal{R}^{**}[\![\,P_0\,]\!](\rho[\bigsqcup_{n \geq 0} \mathcal{R}^{**}[\![P_1{}^n(div{:}\alpha(Y))]\!], \mathcal{R}^{**}[\![P_2]\!], \ldots, \mathcal{R}^{**}[\![P_k]\!]/X_1, \ldots, X_k])$

$=$ { Corollary 4.6.9 }

$\mathcal{R}^{**}[\![\,P_0\,]\!](\rho[\mathcal{R}^{**}[\![\mu Y.P_1\,]\!], \mathcal{R}^{**}[\![\,P_2]\!], \ldots, \mathcal{R}^{**}[\![P_k]\!]/X_1, \ldots, X_k])$

$=$ { $\mathcal{R}^{**}$ denotational }

$\mathcal{R}^{**}[\![P]\!]$

as required. □

As a consequence of the Equivalence Theorem we shall henceforth write $\mathcal{R}^*$ for both the operational and the denotational version of readiness semantics.

## 4.7   Full Abstraction

Process terms denote Petri nets describing all details of the process behaviour many of which are irrelevant from the viewpoint of trace specifications. We therefore investigate the following question:

> Under which circumstances can we replace a closed process term $P$ by a closed process term $Q$ without ever noticing this change by the satisfaction relation *sat*?

Since replacement can take place within a larger process term, we use the notion of a context to make this question precise. A *context* is a term $\mathcal{C}(X) \in Rec$ with one free identifier $X$. To simplify notation, we shall write $\mathcal{C}(R)$ instead of $\mathcal{C}(X)\{R\backslash X\}$ for the substitution of a process term $R$ for $X$ in $\mathcal{C}(X)$. For example, the "must" condition of $P$ *sat* $S$ in Definition 4.3.3 can be viewed as a condition on $\mathcal{C}(P)$ where the context is

$$\mathcal{C}(X) =_{df} X \parallel a \ldots a_n.stop{:}\alpha(P).$$

Equivalence under the satisfaction relation *sat* is covered by the following satisfaction equivalence $\equiv_{sat}$ on closed process terms:

$$P \equiv_{sat} Q$$

if for every trace specification $S$ the following holds:

$$P \ sat \ S \ \text{iff} \ Q \ sat \ S.$$

Now the above question becomes:

> Under which condition on $P$ and $Q$ do we have $\mathcal{C}(P) \equiv_{sat} \mathcal{C}(Q)$ for every context $\mathcal{C}(X)$ with $\mathcal{C}(P), \mathcal{C}(Q) \in CProc$ ?

Milner's notion of full abstraction [Mil77] (see also [Plo77, HP79]) can be seen as looking for a sufficient and necessary condition that solves this type of question.

**Definition 4.7.1** A semantics (or semantic model) $\mathcal{M} : CProc \longrightarrow DOM_{\mathcal{M}}$ is called *fully abstract* for an equivalence relation $\equiv$ on *CProc* if the following holds for all closed process terms $P$ and $Q$:

$$\mathcal{M}[\![P]\!] \ = \ \mathcal{M}[\![Q]\!] \ \text{iff} \quad \mathcal{C}(P) \equiv \mathcal{C}(Q) \text{ holds for every}$$
$$\text{context } \mathcal{C}(X) \text{ with } \mathcal{C}(P), \mathcal{C}(Q) \in CProc. \qquad \Box$$

Intuitively, a fully abstract model $\mathcal{M}$ optimally fits the equivalence $\equiv$ in the sense that $\mathcal{M}$ just makes the identifications on process terms that are forced by $\equiv$. For a given semantic model $\mathcal{M} : CProc \longrightarrow DOM_\mathcal{M}$ let the *model equivalence* $\equiv_\mathcal{M}$ be defined as follows:

$$P \equiv_\mathcal{M} Q \text{ if } \mathcal{M}[\![P]\!] = \mathcal{M}[\![Q]\!].$$

Then we can state the following consequences of the definition of full abstraction.

**Proposition 4.7.2**

(1) For every semantic model $\mathcal{M}$ which is fully abstract for an equivalence $\equiv$ the model equivalence $\equiv_\mathcal{M}$ is a congruence with respect to the process operators in *CProc* and $\equiv_\mathcal{M}$ is contained in $\equiv$.

(2) For every equivalence relation $\equiv$ on *CProc* there exists a fully abstract model $\mathcal{M}$ which is compositional with respect to the process operators in *CProc*. The model equivalence $\equiv_\mathcal{M}$ is independent of the choice of $\mathcal{M}$; it is uniquely determined by $\equiv$.

*Proof.* For a given equivalence on *CProc* define the following new equivalence $\equiv_{con}$ on *CProc*:

$$P \equiv_{con} Q \quad \text{if} \quad \mathcal{C}(P) \equiv \mathcal{C}(Q) \text{ for every context } \mathcal{C}(X)$$
$$\text{with } \mathcal{C}(P), \mathcal{C}(Q) \in CProc.$$

Then $\equiv_{con}$ is uniquely determined by $\equiv$; it is a congruence with respect to the process operators $op$ in *CProc*, i.e. for every such operator, $P_1 \equiv_{con} Q_1, \ldots, P_n \equiv_{con} Q_n$ always imply

$$op(P_1, \ldots, P_n) \equiv_{con} op(Q_1, \ldots, Q_n)$$

and it is contained in $\equiv$, i.e. $P \equiv_{con} Q$ implies $P \equiv Q$. By the definition of full abstraction, we conclude

$$\equiv_\mathcal{M} = \equiv_{con}.$$

This proves (1). Now (2) is an immediate consequence of (1). Just take $DOM_\mathcal{M}$ as the set of equivalence classes $[P]_{\equiv_{con}}$ of closed process term $P$ with respect to $\equiv_{con}$ and define $\mathcal{M} : CProc \longrightarrow DOM_\mathcal{M}$ as follows:

$$\mathcal{M}[\![P]\!] =_{df} [P]_{\equiv_{con}}.$$

Note that compositionality, i.e. the existence of semantic operators $op_\mathcal{M}$ on $DOM_\mathcal{M}$ satisfying the equation

$$\mathcal{M}[\![op(P_1, \ldots, P_n)]\!] = op_\mathcal{M}(\mathcal{M}[\![P_1]\!], \ldots, \mathcal{M}[\![P_n]\!])$$

for every $n$-ary operator symbol $op$ of *CProc* and all closed process terms, is only a reformulation of the fact that $\equiv_{con}$ is a congruence. Uniqueness of the model equivalence $\equiv_\mathcal{M}$ follows from the uniqueness of $\equiv_{con}$. $\square$

This proposition provides an attractive method of *specifying* the semantics of processes. Starting from an equivalence relation $\equiv$ that captures the kind of distinctions or observations on processes one is interested in, the proposition guarantees the existence of a compositional semantics $\mathcal{M}$ that is optimal for and unique up to model equivalence $\equiv_\mathcal{M}$. Then $\mathcal{M}$ is the semantics specified by $\equiv$. More generally, this specification method is used for programming languages with and without concurrency (see e.g. [Ast84]) and in the area of algebraic specification (see e.g. [ST87]).

The existence of a fully abstract semantics $\mathcal{M}$ is an interesting fact, but its implicit definition via contexts does not give us any ideas about the explicit structure of M. Often it is a very difficult or even unsolved problem to find such an explicit structure [Mil77, Plo77, HP79, MS88]. Fortunately, for the satisfaction equivalence $\equiv_{sat}$ we will be able to exhibit this structure: it is the modified readiness semantics $\mathcal{R}^*[\![\cdot]\!]$ discussed in the previous sections.

**Full Abstraction Theorem 4.7.3** The modified readiness semantics $\mathcal{R}^*[\![\cdot]\!] : CProc \longrightarrow DOM_\mathcal{R}$ is fully abstract for the satisfaction equivalence $\equiv_{sat}$, i.e. for all closed process terms $P$ and $Q$ the following holds

$$\mathcal{R}^*[\![P]\!] = \mathcal{R}^*[\![Q]\!]$$

if and only if for all contexts $\mathcal{C}(X)$ with $\mathcal{C}(P), \mathcal{C}(Q) \in CProc$ and all trace specifications $S$

$$\mathcal{C}(P) \text{ sat } S \text{ iff } \mathcal{C}(Q) \text{ sat } S.$$

*Proof.* "only if": Suppose $\mathcal{R}^*[\![P]\!] = \mathcal{R}^*[\![Q]\!]$ and consider a context $\mathcal{C}(X)$ with $\mathcal{C}(P), \mathcal{C}(Q) \in CProc$ and a trace specification $S$. Since $\mathcal{R}^*[\![\cdot]\!]$ is denotational, $\mathcal{R}^*[\![P]\!] = \mathcal{R}^*[\![Q]\!]$ implies $\mathcal{R}^*[\![\mathcal{C}(P)]\!] = \mathcal{R}^*[\![\mathcal{C}(Q)]\!]$. Thus

$$\mathcal{R}^*[\![\mathcal{C}(P)]\!] = \mathcal{R}^*[\![S]\!] \text{ iff } \mathcal{R}^*[\![\mathcal{C}(Q)]\!] = \mathcal{R}^*[\![S]\!]$$

Then $\mathcal{C}(P) \text{ sat } S \text{ iff } \mathcal{C}(Q) \text{ sat } S$ by the Correctness Theorem 4.4.7.

"if": Suppose $\mathcal{R}^*[\![P]\!] \neq \mathcal{R}^*[\![Q]\!]$, say $\mathcal{R}^*[\![P]\!] \not\sqsubseteq \mathcal{R}^*[\![Q]\!]$. Thus by the definition of $\sqsubseteq$, $\alpha(P) \neq \alpha(Q)$ or $\pi(\mathcal{R}^*[\![P]\!]) \not\supseteq \pi(\mathcal{R}^*[\![Q]\!])$. We will exhibit a context $\mathcal{C}(X)$ with $\mathcal{C}(P), \mathcal{C}(Q) \in CProc$ and a trace specification $S$ such that

$$\mathcal{C}(P) \text{ sat } S \text{ but not } \mathcal{C}(Q) \text{ sat } S.$$

Let $A = \alpha(P)$. If $\alpha(P) \neq \alpha(Q)$, say $\alpha(P) \not\supseteq \alpha(Q)$, take some fresh $d \notin \alpha(P) \cup \alpha(Q)$ and consider

$$\mathcal{C}(X) =_{df} d.(X \parallel stop{:}\{d\}) \parallel stop{:}A \cup \{d\}$$

and

$$S =_{df} h{\downarrow}(A \cup \{d\}) \leq \varepsilon.$$

The communication $d$ in $\mathcal{C}(X)$ serves to absorbe possible unstabilities of $P$ and $Q$ in $\mathcal{C}(P)$ and $\mathcal{C}(Q)$. The term $stop{:}\{d\}$ adds $d$ to the alphabet of $X$ in order to satisfy the alphabet constraints of the prefix operator. Synchronisation with $stop{:}A \cup \{d\}$

implies that $\mathcal{C}(P)$ deadlocks immediately. Since $\alpha(\mathcal{C}(P)) = A \cup \{d\} = \alpha(S)$, we have $\mathcal{C}(P)$ *sat* $S$. On the other hand, not $\mathcal{C}(Q)$ *sat* $S$ because $\alpha(\mathcal{C}(Q)) \neq \alpha(S)$.

If $\alpha(P) = \alpha(Q)$, we distinguish three cases depending on the structure of the process information in $\pi(\mathcal{R}^*[\![P]\!])$ and $\pi(\mathcal{R}^*[\![Q]\!])$.

*Case 1:* $\tau \in \pi(\mathcal{R}^*[\![Q]\!])$ and $\tau \notin \pi(\mathcal{R}^*[\![P]\!])$.
Then $P$ cannot diverge immediately. Take

$$\mathcal{C}(X) =_{df} X \parallel stop{:}A \text{ and } S =_{df} h{\downarrow}A \leq \varepsilon \ .$$

Then $\mathcal{C}(P), \mathcal{C}(Q) \in CProc$ and $\tau \in \pi(\mathcal{R}^*[\![\mathcal{C}(Q)]\!])$, but $\tau \notin \pi(\mathcal{R}^*[\![P]\!])$. In fact, $\mathcal{C}(P)$ is stable immediately, divergence free and can engage only in the empty trace. Thus $\mathcal{C}(P)$ *sat* $S$. On the other hand, not $\mathcal{C}(Q)$ *sat* $S$ because $\mathcal{C}(Q)$ is unstable as the $\tau$ in its readiness semantics indicates.

*Case 2:* $(tr, \mathcal{F}) \in \pi(\mathcal{R}^*[\![Q]\!])$ and $(tr, \mathcal{F}) \notin \pi(\mathcal{R}^*[\![P]\!])$.
Suppose $tr = a_1 \ldots a_n$ where $n \geq 0$ and $a_1, \ldots, a_n \in A$. Since $\mathcal{R}^*[\![P]\!]$ is well-structured (cf. Proposition 4.4.3), we conclude that

$$\neg \exists tr' \leq tr : (tr', \downarrow) \in \pi(\mathcal{R}^*[\![P]\!]) \tag{4.27}$$

because otherwise the chaotic closure would force $(tr, \mathcal{F}) \in \pi(\mathcal{R}^*[\![P]\!])$. Let $tr'$ be the longest prefix of $tr$ such that

$$\exists \mathcal{G} : (tr', \mathcal{G}) \in \pi(\mathcal{R}^*[\![P]\!]) . \tag{4.28}$$

Such a trace $tr'$ exists because there is an initial ready pair $(\varepsilon, \mathcal{G})$ in $\pi(\mathcal{R}^*[\![P]\!])$. Take some fresh $d \notin A$. Such a communication $d$ exists because *Comm* is infinite whereas $A \subseteq Comm$ is finite.

*Subcase 2.1:* $tr' < tr$
Then $tr' = a_1 \ldots a_n$ for some $k < n$. As context we consider the term

$$\begin{aligned}
\mathcal{C}(X) =_{df} d.(X & \\
\parallel\ & (d^k.stop{:}A \cup \{d\} \\
& +a_1.(d^{k-1}.stop{:}A \cup \{d\} \\
& \quad +a_2.(\ldots(d.stop{:}A \cup \{d\} \\
& \qquad\qquad +a_k.a_{k+1}.stop{:}A \cup \{d\})\ldots))) \\
)[\varphi] &
\end{aligned}$$

where the renaming morphism $\varphi : Act \longrightarrow Act$ is given by

$$\varphi(u) =_{df} \begin{cases} d & \text{if } u \in A \cup \{d\} \\ u & \text{otherwise} \end{cases}$$

For $m \geq 2$ the notation $d^m.stop{:}A \cup \{d\}$ abbreviates the prefix term

$$\underbrace{d.\ldots.d}_{m \text{ times}} .stop{:}A \cup \{d\} \ .$$

Clearly, $\mathcal{C}(P), \mathcal{C}(Q) \in CProc$. The initial communication $d$ of $\mathcal{C}(X)$ serves to absorb possible unstabilities of $P$ and $Q$ in $\mathcal{C}(P)$ and $\mathcal{C}(Q)$. Since $d \notin A$, the communications $d$ occuring in the right-hand operand of the parallel composition of $\mathcal{C}(P)$ and $\mathcal{C}(Q)$ do not require synchronisation with the left-hand operand $P$ or $Q$. Thus both $\mathcal{C}(P)$ and $\mathcal{C}(Q)$ can deadlock only after engaging in $k + 1$ communications.

In fact, $\mathcal{C}(P)$ must engage in $k + 1$ communications because, by property (4.27) above, $\mathcal{C}(P)$ is divergence free. Hence we consider as specification the trace formula

$$S =_{df} d\#h \leq k + 1$$

Then $\mathcal{C}(P)$ *sat* $S$, but not $\mathcal{C}(Q)$ *sat* $S$ because $\mathcal{C}(Q)$ may engage in the trace

$$(d.a_1 \ldots a_{k+1})\{\varphi\} = d.d \ldots d$$

of the length $k + 2$.

*Subcase 2.2:* $tr' = tr$ and $\mathcal{F} \not\subseteq succ(tr, P)$.
Thus we assume that the ready set $\mathcal{F}$ of $Q$ is not contained in the set of all successor communications of $tr$ in $P$. For simplicity we denote this set here by $succ(tr, P)$ instead of $succ(tr, \pi(\mathcal{R}^*[\![P]\!]))$ as required by Definition 4.4.1 . Take a communication

$$c \in \mathcal{F} - succ(tr, P)$$

and consider the context

$$
\begin{aligned}
\mathcal{C}(X) =_{df}\ &d.(X \\
&\| (d^{n+1}.stop{:}A \cup \{d\} \\
&\quad +a_1.(d^n.stop{:}A \cup \{d\} \\
&\qquad +a_2.(\ldots(d.d.stop{:}A \cup \{d\} \\
&\qquad\quad +a_n.(d.stop{:}A \cup \{d\} \\
&\qquad\qquad +c.div{:}A \cup \{d\}))\ldots))) \\
&)[\varphi]
\end{aligned}
$$

where the renaming morphism $\varphi$ is defined as in Subcase 2. Of course, $\mathcal{C}(P), \mathcal{C}(Q) \in CProc$. As before, the purpose of the extra commnication $d$ is to absorb unstabilities in $P$ or $Q$ and to avoid too early deadlocks in $\mathcal{C}(P)$ and $\mathcal{C}(Q)$. As a specification we take now

$$S =_{df} d\#h \leq n + 2.$$

Then $\mathcal{C}(P)$ *sat* $S$, but not $\mathcal{C}(Q)$ *sat* $S$ because $\mathcal{C}(Q)$ can diverge by engaging in the communication $c$ of $\mathcal{C}(X)$.

*Subcase 2.3:* $tr' = tr$ and $\mathcal{F} \subseteq succ(tr, P)$.
Since $\mathcal{R}^*[\![P]\!]$ is well-formed, we conclude that

$$\neg \exists \mathcal{G} \subseteq \mathcal{F} : (tr, \mathcal{G}) \in \pi(\mathcal{R}^*[\![P]\!]) \tag{4.29}$$

and

$$\neg \exists c \in A : (tr.c, \downarrow) \in \pi(\mathcal{R}^*[\![P]\!]). \tag{4.30}$$

Indeed, if (4.29) or (4.30) were wrong, the assumption that $\mathcal{F} \subseteq succ(tr, P)$ together with the acceptance closure or the radiation closure, respectively, would force $(tr, \mathcal{F}) \in \pi(\mathcal{R}^*[\![P]\!])$. As context consider now

$$
\begin{aligned}
\mathcal{C}(X) =_{df} d.(X \\
\| \ (d^{n+1}.stop{:}A \cup \{d\} \\
+ a_1.(d^n.stop{:}A \cup \{d\} \\
+ a_2.(\ldots (d.d.stop{:}A \cup \{d\} \\
+ a_n.(\textstyle\sum_{\ldots} c.stop{:}A \cup \{d\})) \ldots))) \\
)[\varphi]
\end{aligned}
$$

where $\varphi$ is as in Subcase 2 and where the sum $\sum_{\ldots}$ is taken over all communications $c \in A$ satisfying the condition

$$(tr.c, \downarrow) \in \pi(\mathcal{R}^*[\![Q]\!]) \tag{4.31}$$

$$\vee \ (\exists \mathcal{G} : (tr, \mathcal{G}) \in \pi(\mathcal{R}^*[\![P]\!]) \wedge c \in \mathcal{G} \cap (A - \mathcal{F})). \tag{4.32}$$

Since $tr' = tr$, property (4.28) above states that $\exists \mathcal{G} : (tr, \mathcal{G}) \in \pi(\mathcal{R}^*[\![P]\!])$, and (4.29) implies that

$$\forall \mathcal{G} : (tr, \mathcal{G}) \in \pi(\mathcal{R}^*[\![P]\!]) \longrightarrow \exists c \in \mathcal{G} \cap (A - \mathcal{F}).$$

Hence there exists a communication $c$ satisfying line (4.32) of the above condition.

Clearly, $\mathcal{C}(P), \mathcal{C}(Q) \in CProc$. Note that both $\mathcal{C}(P)$ and $\mathcal{C}(Q)$ are stable immediately and may engage only in $n + 2$ successive communications. By (4.27) and (4.30), the process term $\mathcal{C}(P)$ is divergence free. Thus by construction, $\mathcal{C}(P)$ must engage in $n + 2$ successive communications. Therefore we consider again the specification

$$S =_{df} d\#h \le n + 2.$$

Then $\mathcal{C}(P)$ *sat* $S$. On the other hand, not $\mathcal{C}(Q)$ *sat* $S$ because if (4.31) holds for some $c \in A$ then $\mathcal{C}(Q)$ can diverge after the trace

$$(d.a_1 \ldots a_n.c)\{\varphi\} = d.d \ldots d.d$$

of length $n + 2$ and otherwise $\mathcal{C}(Q)$ can deadlock after the trace

$$(d.a_1 \ldots a_n)\{\varphi\} = d.d \ldots d$$

of length $n + 1$.

*Case 3:* $(tr, \downarrow) \in \pi(\mathcal{R}^*[\![Q]\!])$ and $(tr, \downarrow) \notin \pi(\mathcal{R}^*[\![P]\!])$.
Suppose $tr = a_1 \ldots a_n$ where $n \le 0$ and $a_1, \ldots, a_n \in A$. Since $\mathcal{R}^*[\![P]\!]$ is well-structured, we conclude that

$$\neg \exists tr' \le tr : (tr', \downarrow) \in \pi(\mathcal{R}^*[\![P]\!]).$$

Take some fresh communication $d \notin A$ and consider

$$\mathcal{C}(X) =_{df} d.((X \parallel a_1 \ldots a_n.stop{:}A \cup \{d\})\backslash A)$$

and

$$S =_{df} d\#h \leq 1.$$

Then $\mathcal{C}(P), \mathcal{C}(Q) \in CProc$ and $\mathcal{C}(P)$ *sat* $S$, but not $\mathcal{C}(Q)$ *sat* $S$ because $\mathcal{C}(Q)$ is not divergence free.                                                                                     □

The full abstraction proof exploits that the modified readiness semantics $\mathcal{R}^*[\![\cdot]\!]$ incorporates three extra closure conditions:

- chaotic closure,

- acceptance closure, and

- radiation closure.

The chaotic closure, dealing with divergence, was introduced by Brookes, Hoare and Roscoe in their *failure semantics* $\mathcal{F}[\![\cdot]\!]$ for CSP [BHR84]. The acceptance closure on ready sets was introduced by DeNicola and Hennessy for a process semantics of CCS that is fully abstract for their "must" version of testing equivalence [DH84, Hen88]. For simplicity we call this semantics here *strong testing semantics* and denote it by $\mathcal{S}$. The radiation closure, however, is new.

To compare these semantics with $\mathcal{R}^*[\![\cdot]\!]$, consider the process terms

$$P = a.stop{:}\{a\} + Q \text{ and } Q = a.a.div{:}\{a\},$$

which are similar to the ones studied in Example 4.4.4 (5). Then $P$ and $Q$, or better, their syntactic equivalents in CSP and CCS, are distinguished by the failure and the strong testing semantics:

$$\mathcal{F}[\![P]\!] \neq \mathcal{F}[\![Q]\!] \text{ and } \mathcal{S}[\![P]\!] \neq \mathcal{S}[\![Q]\!].$$

But in the modified readiness semantics $\mathcal{R}^*[\![\cdot]\!]$ they are identified. Indeed, look at the abstract nets denoted by $P$ and $Q$:

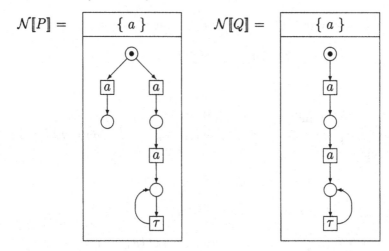

Then the ready pair $(a, \emptyset)$ belongs to $\mathcal{R}^*[\![P]\!]$ due to the token game of $\mathcal{N}[\![P]\!]$, but it also belongs to $\mathcal{R}^*[\![Q]\!]$ due to the radiation closure. Informally, the divergence point $(a.a, \downarrow)$ of $\mathcal{R}^*[\![Q]\!]$ "radiates up" and thus forces $(a, \emptyset)$ to be present in $\mathcal{R}^*[\![Q]\!]$. Hence

$$\mathcal{R}^*[\![P]\!] = \mathcal{R}^*[\![Q]\!].$$

The identification of $P$ and $Q$ is justified by the idea of full abstraction because for every context $\mathcal{C}(X)$, both $\mathcal{C}(P)$ and $\mathcal{C}(Q)$ satisfy exactly the same trace specification $S$.

This example demonstrates that the *modified readiness equivalence* $\equiv_{\mathcal{R}^*}$ on process terms, given by

$$P \equiv_{\mathcal{R}^*} Q \ \text{ if } \ \mathcal{R}^*[\![P]\!] = \mathcal{R}^*[\![Q]\!],$$

differs from the *failure equivalence* $\equiv_{\mathcal{F}}$ and *strong testing equivalence* $\equiv_{\mathcal{S}}$ defined likewise for the semantics $\mathcal{F}[\![\cdot]\!]$ and $\mathcal{S}[\![\cdot]\!]$. It has to be different because of the satisfaction relation *sat* which uniquely determines $\equiv_{\mathcal{R}^*}$ via the notion of full abstraction.

However, the differences appear only for processes which can diverge. On divergence free process terms $\equiv_{\mathcal{R}^*}$ and $\equiv_{\mathcal{S}}$ coincide and on divergence free process terms that are stable immediately $\equiv_{\mathcal{R}^*}$ and $\equiv_{\mathcal{F}}$ also coincide. This can be easily seen by comparing the definitions of the semantics $\mathcal{R}^*[\![\cdot]\!]$ with $\mathcal{S}[\![\cdot]\!]$ and $\mathcal{F}[\![\cdot]\!]$.

# 5

# PROCESS CONSTRUCTION

In this chapter we combine all three views of concurrent processes:

- the view of formulas describing the desired communication behaviour of the process,

- the view of terms decribing the architecture of the process, i.e. how it is composed from subprocesses,

- the view of nets describing all details of the operational machine behaviour of the process.

To this end, we present now an approach to the top-down construction of concurrent processes starting with formulas and ending in nets:

The bottom arrow in this diagram refers to the transition rules of the operational Petri net semantics of process terms, introduced in Chapter 3. The top arrow is the new contribution of this chapter: *transformation rules* that allow us to transform or *refine* a given trace specification $S$ *stepwise* into a process term $P$ satisfying $S$ in the sense of Chapter 4.

A stepwise refinement is here a sequence

$$S \ \equiv \ Q_1$$
$$|||$$
$$\vdots$$
$$|||$$
$$Q_n \ \equiv \ P$$

of equations in the modified readiness semantics $\mathcal{R}^*[\![\cdot]\!]$. Each equation $Q_i \equiv Q_{i+1}$, where $i=1,\ldots,n$-1, is obtained by applying one of the transformation rules; it represents a refinement step where a part of the original specification $S$ is replaced by a bit of process syntax. Therefore we take as terms $Q_i$ in between $S$ and $P$, so-called *mixed terms* (cf.[Old85, Old86]). These are syntactic constructs mixing process terms with trace specifications.

The idea of mixing programming notation (here represented by process terms) with specification parts stems from the work of Dijkstra and Wirth [Dij76, Wir71] on program development by stepwise refinement. It is well-known in the area of *transformational programming* [Bau85, Bau87], and has been formalised and utilised by many researchers, among them [Bac80, Heh84, Hoa85a, Mor88, Mor90, BW90a]. However, application of this idea to concurrent programming is only a recent activity (see e.g. [Heh84, Hoa85a, Old85, Old86, Bro87, Bak80]).

We use the transformation rules on mixed terms in a series of example process constructions. For each trace specification very different process terms can be constructed. To compare their operational behaviour, e.g. the possible concurrency or communication delays through internal actions, we study the Petri nets denoted by these process terms.

For each system of rules we can pose the question: are the rules complete? We distinguish two types of completeness. *Verification completeness* means that for every process term $P$ and every trace formula $S$, whenever $P$ *sat* $S$ holds, i.e. $P \equiv S$, then this equation can be deduced with the transformation rules. We observe that our rules are incomplete in this sense. The reason for this incompleteness is that some rules check semantic properties of processes dealing with liveness by sufficient, but not necessary, syntactic conditions.

In any case, we believe that verification completeness will provide little insight into how to do process construction. Therefore we also consider *construction completeness*. By this, we mean that for (a certain subset of) trace formulas $S$ there is a strategy describing *how to apply* the transformation rules to construct a process term $P$ (of a certain form) with $P \equiv S$. We present such a completeness result for the simplest strategy for process construction: the *expansion strategy*. We show that when starting with a formula $S$ specifying a regular set of traces this strategy will always, and under certain conditions mechanically, produce a process term $P$ satisfying $S$. This term $P$ denotes a finite Petri net, though one without any possible concurrency. In fact, the constructed net just corresponds to a deterministic automaton which satisfies the safety and liveness conditions required by $S$. This result resembles the synthesis of finite-state automata from formulas of propositional temporal logic [EC82, MW84].

# 5.1 Transformations on Mixed Terms

In this section we develop transformation rules for the verification and construction of concurrent processes with respect to our notion of process correctness *P sat S*. *Verification* means:

> Given a process term $P$ and a trace specification $S$, show that *P sat S*.

The customary approach to verification would develop a compositional proof system (cf. [Roe85]) for deducing correctness formulas *P sat S*. *Compositional* means here that for every $n$-ary operator symbol *op* on process terms there is a corresponding logical operator $op_{log}$ on trace specifications yielding a proof rule of the form

$$\frac{P_1 \; sat \; S_1, \ldots, P_n \; sat \; S_n}{op(P_1, \ldots, P_n) \; sat \; op_{log}(S_1, \ldots, S_n)} \text{ where } \ldots$$

Such a rule states that if $P_1 \; sat \; S_1, \ldots, P_n \; sat \; S_n$ are true correctness formulas satisfying the condition "..." then also $op(P_1, \ldots, P_n) \; sat \; op_{log}(S_1, \ldots, S_n)$ is a true correctness formula.

Compositionality is fine, but the use of correctness formulas *P sat S* is very inflexible: the letter $P$ before the symbol *sat* is always a process term and the letter $S$ after *sat* is always a trace specification. This is inconvenient for the more demanding task of constructing processes. *Construction* means:

> Given a trace specification $S$, find a process term $P$ with *P sat S*.

We shall view verification as a special case of construction where the result $P$ is known and only its correctness with respect to $S$ is left to be shown.

Our aim is a top-down construction (and hence verification) starting with a trace specification $S$ describing what the desired communication behaviour is and ending in a process term $P$ describing how this communication behaviour is realised. During the construction we wish to proceed by *stepwise refinement* as advocated by Dijkstra and Wirth [Dij76, Wir71]. Thus at each step of the construction we wish to replace a part of the specification by a bit of process syntax. To formalise this idea, we use so-called *mixed terms* (cf. [Old85, Old86]). These are syntactic constructs mixing process terms with trace specifications. An example of a mixed term is

$$a.(S \parallel T).$$

It describes a process where some parts are already constructed (prefix and parallel composition) whereas other parts are only specified ($S$ and $T$) and remain to be constructed in future refinement steps.

Formally, mixed terms are introduced by extending the syntax of process terms given in Definition 3.1.1 and 3.1.3 by the clause

$$P ::= S$$

where $S$ is a trace specification. Thus from now on letters $P$, $Q$, $R$ will range over mixed terms whereas letters $S$, $T$, $U$ continue to range over the set *Spec* of trace specifications.

**Definition 5.1.1** The set *Proc* + *Spec* of *mixed terms* consist of all terms $P$ that are generated by the context-free production rules

$$
\begin{array}{llll}
P ::= & S & (\text{ specification }) \\
& | & stop{:}A & (\text{ deadlock }) \\
& | & div{:}A & (\text{ divergence }) \\
& | & a.P & (\text{ prefix }) \\
& | & P + Q & (\text{ choice }) \\
& | & P \parallel Q & (\text{ parallelism }) \\
& | & P[\varphi] & (\text{ morphism }) \\
& | & X & (\text{ identifier }) \\
& | & \mu X.P & (\text{ recursion })
\end{array}
$$

and that satisfy the context-sensitive restrictions stated in Definition 3.1.3, i.e.

(1)  $P$ is action-guarded,

(2)  every subterm $a.Q$ of $P$ satisfies $a \in \alpha(Q)$,

(3)  every subterm $Q + R$ of $P$ satisfies $\alpha(Q) = \alpha(P)$,

(4)  every subterm $\mu X.Q$ of $P$ satisfies $\alpha(X) = \alpha(P)$.

The alphabet $\alpha(P)$ of a mixed term $P$ is defined as in Section 3.1 where in case of a trace specification $S$ the alphabet $\alpha(S)$ is as in Definition 4.2.1. Mixed terms without free process identifiers are called *closed*. The set of all closed mixed terms is denoted by *CProc* + *Spec*.                                                                        □

Semantically, mixed terms denote elements of the readiness domain $DOM_{\mathcal{R}}$. In fact, since trace specifications $S$ have a semantics $\mathcal{R}^*[\![S]\!]$ (cf. Definition 4.4.5) and since for every operator symbol $op$ of *Proc* there exists a corresponding semantic operator $op_{\mathcal{R}}$ on $DOM_{\mathcal{R}}$ (cf. Definition 4.5.6), we immediately obtain a denotational readiness semantics

$$
\mathcal{R}^*[\![\cdot]\!] : Proc + Spec \longrightarrow (Env_{\mathcal{R}} \longrightarrow DOM_{\mathcal{R}})
$$

for mixed terms which is defined according to the principles of Definition 4.5.3. As before, environments $\rho \in Env_{\mathcal{R}}$ assign values to the free identifiers in mixed terms. Thus for closed mixed terms the environment parameter $\rho$ of $\mathcal{R}^*[\![\cdot]\!]$ is not needed. We therefore write $\mathcal{R}^*[\![P]\!]$ instead of $\mathcal{R}^*[\![P]\!](\rho)$.

Since mixed terms $P$ may contain trace specifications, their semantics $\mathcal{R}^*[\![P]\!]$ need not be well-structured in the sense of Definition 4.4.2. Consequently, proofs about recursive mixed terms cannot rely on the continuity of the semantic operators and hence not on the usual fixed point approximation technique (cf. the Continuity

Lemma 4.6.7, Proposition 4.6.8 and Corrollary 4.6.9). In this sense, mixed terms are more difficult to cope with than ordinary process terms. Note also that the previous net semantics $\mathcal{N}[\![\cdot]\!]$ does not apply to mixed terms because it is not defined for the trace specifications contained in them. Indeed, trace specifications $S$ never stand for a single net, but rather for the set of all nets denoted by process terms $P$ with $P$ *sat* $S$.

Under the readiness semantics $\mathcal{R}^*[\![\cdot]\!]$, process terms, trace specifications and mixed terms are treated on an equal footing so that they are easy to compare. To do so, we introduce the following notation.

**Definition 5.1.2** For $P, Q \in CProc + Spec$ we write :

$$P \equiv >_{\mathcal{R}^*} Q \text{ if } \mathcal{R}^*[\![P]\!] \sqsupseteq \mathcal{R}^*[\![Q]\!],$$

$$P <\equiv_{\mathcal{R}^*} Q \text{ if } \mathcal{R}^*[\![P]\!] \sqsubseteq \mathcal{R}^*[\![Q]\!],$$

$$P \equiv_{\mathcal{R}^*} Q \text{ if } \mathcal{R}^*[\![P]\!] = \mathcal{R}^*[\![Q]\!],$$

We call $P \equiv >_{\mathcal{R}^*} Q$ a *semantic implication* and $P \equiv_{\mathcal{R}^*} Q$ a *semantic equation* in the readiness semantics. Since from now on we always refer to the readiness semantics, we shall drop the subscript $\mathcal{R}^*$ and write simply $P \equiv > Q, P <\equiv Q$ and $P \equiv Q$.  □

By the Correctness Theorem 4.4.6, our present definition of process correctness boils down to a semantic equation, i.e.

$$P \text{ } sat \text{ } S \text{ iff } P \equiv S$$

for all $P \in CProc$ and $S \in Spec$. Therefore a top-down construction of a process term $P$ from a trace specification $S$ will be presented as a sequence

$$S \equiv Q_1$$
$$|||$$
$$\vdots$$
$$|||$$
$$Q_n \equiv P$$

of semantics equations between mixed terms $Q_1, \ldots, Q_n$ where $Q_1$ is the given trace specification $S$ and $Q_n$ is the constructed process term $P$. The transitivity of $\equiv$ ensures $P \equiv S$, the desired result.

The sequence of equations is generated by applying the principles of *transformational programming* as e.g. advocated in the Munich Project CIP [Bau85, Bau87]. Thus each equation

$$Q_i \equiv Q_{i+1}$$

in the sequence is obtained by applying a *transformation rule* to a subterm of $Q_i$, usually a trace specification, say $S_i$. Most of the transformation rules to be introduced below state that under certain conditions a semantic equation of the form

$$S_i \equiv op(S_{i_1}, \ldots, S_{i_n})$$

holds, i.e. the trace specification $S_i$ can be refined into a mixed term consisting of an $n$-ary process operator op applied to trace specifications $S_{i_1}, \ldots, S_{i_n}$ that are logically related to $S_i$. Then $Q_{i+1}$ results from $Q_i$ by replacing its subterm $S_i$ by $op(S_{i_1}, \ldots, S_{i_n})$. Since the underlying readiness semantics is denotational, $S_i \equiv op(S_{i_1}, \ldots, S_{i_n})$ implies $Q_i \equiv Q_{i+1}$. In this way, the original trace specification $S$ is gradually transformed into a process term $P$.

Transformation rules are theorems about the readiness semantics of mixed terms that can be expressed as deduction rules of the form

$$(\mathcal{D}) \qquad \frac{\models S_1 \ , \ldots, \ \models S_m \qquad P_1 \equiv Q_1 \ , \ldots, \ P_n \equiv Q_n}{P \equiv Q} \qquad \text{where } \ldots$$

where $m, n \geq 0$ and "..." is a condition on the syntax of the trace specifications $S_1, \ldots, S_m$ and the mixed terms $P_1, Q_1, \ldots, P_n, Q_n, P, Q$. The rule $\mathcal{D}$ states that if the condition "..." is satisfied, the trace specifications $S_1, \ldots, S_m$ are valid and the semantic equations $P_1 \equiv Q_1, \ldots, P_n \equiv Q_n$ are true, then the semantic equation $P \equiv Q$ also holds. If $m = n = 0$, the notation simplies to

$$P \equiv Q \qquad \text{where } \ldots$$

We say that a deduction rule $\mathcal{D}$ is *sound* if the theorem denoted by $\mathcal{D}$ is true.

The syntactic condition "..." will always be a simple decidable property, e.g. concerning alphabets. By contrast, the validity of trace specifications is in general not decidable due to the Expressiveness Theorem 4.2.5. Thus in general the transformation rules $\mathcal{D}$ are effectively applicable only *relative* to the logical theory of trace specifications, i.e. the set

$$Th(Spec) \ = \ \{S \in Spec \mid \models S\}.$$

To enhance the readibility of transformation rules, we will sometimes deviate from the form $\mathcal{D}$ above and use equivalent ones. For example, we will often require that certain traces $tr$ satisfy a trace specification $S$, but this is of course equivalent to a validity condition:

$$tr \models S \text{ iff } \models S\{tr/h\}.$$

Depending on the syntactic form of the mixed terms $P$ and $Q$ in the conclusion of $\mathcal{D}$ we distinguish among several types of transformation rules:

(1) *Equation Rules: $P, Q$* are arbitrary mixed terms.

(2) *Specification Rules: $P, Q$* are trace specifications.

(3) *Construction Rules: $P$* is a mixed term involving one process operator *op* or one recursion symbol $\mu$ and $Q$ is a trace specification.

(4) *Algebraic Rules: $P, Q$* are mixed terms which both involve certain process operators or recursion symbols.

Some rules of type (1) - (4) will be classified as *derived rules* because they can be deduced from other rules. Their purpose is to organise the presentation of process constructions more clearly. We shall consider here only transformation rules of type (1) - (3); rules of type (4) are not used.

To state the semantic and syntactic conditions of our transformation rules, we need a few additional notions. The *prefix kernel* of a trace specification $S$ is given by the formula

$$kern(S) =_{df} \forall t : t \le h{\downarrow}\alpha(S) \longrightarrow S\{t/h\}$$

Thus $kern(S)$ is a trace specification which denotes the largest prefix closed set of traces satisfying $S$ (cf. [Zwi89]). We summarise its basic properties:

**Proposition 5.1.3** For all $S \in Spec$ and $tr \in Comm^*$

(1) $\alpha(kern(S)) = \alpha(S)$

(2) $\models kern(S) \longrightarrow S$

(3) $tr \models kern(S)$ iff *pref* $tr \models kern(S)$

(4) $tr \models kern(S)$ iff *pref* $tr \models S$

(5) *pref* $tr \models kern(S)$ iff *pref* $tr \models S$ □

By contrast, the *prefix closure* of a trace specification $S$ denotes the smallest prefix closed set of traces *containing* those which satisfy $S$. It can be expressed by the formula

$$\exists t : S\{h.\ t/h\}$$

(cf. Example 4.2.6 where prefix closure was defined for regular expressions).

The set of *initial communications* of a trace specification $S$ is given by

$$init(S) = \{a \in \alpha(S) \mid pref\ a \models S\}$$

Recall that *pref* $a \models S$ is equivalent to requiring $\varepsilon \models S$ and $a \models S$.

By Definition 5.1.1, every mixed term $P$ is action-guarded. We now introduce a stronger notion of communication-guardedness whereby the guarding communication may not be hidden. The purpose of this notion is a sufficient syntactic condition implying that every recursion in $P$ has a unique fixed point in the readiness semantics. In particular, if this fixed point is given by a trace specification, the recursion is divergence free. This observation gives rise to a corresponding recursion rule in Definition 5.1.6 whose soundness we prove in Theorem 5.1.7. Since uniqueness of fixed points is an undecidable property for the class of terms considered here (cf. Remark 3.5.6), no syntactic condition for it will be a necessary one.

**Definition 5.1.4** Let $A$ be a set of communications. A mixed term $P \in Proc + Spec$ is called *communication-guarded by $A$* if for every recursive subterm $\mu X.Q$ of $P$, every free occurrence of $X$ in $Q$ occurs within a subterm of $Q$ which is of the form

$$a.R$$

with $a \in A$, but not within a subterm of $Q$ which is of the form

$$R[b/a] \text{ or } R\backslash a$$

with $a \in A$ and $b \notin A$. $P$ is called *communication-guarded* if there exists a set $A$ of communications such that $P$ is communication-guarded by $A$.                              □

For example, the process term $\mu X.a.X$ studied in Example 4.5.8 is communication-guarded. More elaborate examples of communication-guarded (mixed) terms with $\alpha(X) = \alpha(Y) = \{up, dn\}$ are the following:

$$P_1 = \mu X. \ up. \ \mu Y. \ (\ dn. \ X + up. \ dn. \ Y),$$

$$P_2 = ((\mu X. \ up. \ dn. \ X)[lk/dn] \ \| \ 0 \le lk\#h - dn\#h \le 1)\backslash lk,$$

$$P_3 = \mu X. \ up. \ (X[lk/dn] \ \| \ dn. \ (dn\#h \le lk\#h))\backslash lk.$$

By contrast,
$$Q_1 = \mu X. \ up. \ ((X[lk/up])\backslash lk \ \| \ stop{:}\{up, dn\})$$

$$Q_2 = \mu X. \ up. \ (X[lk/dn] \ \| \ dn. \ X[lk/up])\backslash lk$$

are action-guarded, but not communication-guarded. The fixed point of the recursion in $Q_1$ is indeed not unique. For instance,

$$up.stop{:}\{up, dn\} \quad \text{and} \quad up.div{:}\{up, dn\}$$

are both solutions of the equation $X = up.((X[lk/up])\backslash lk \ \| \ stop{:}\{up, dn\})$. On the other hand, the semantic equation

$$Q_2 = P_3$$

implies that the recursion in $Q_2$ has a unique fixed point. This illustrates our remark that communication-guardedness is not a necessary condition for uniqueness.

**Proposition 5.1.5** Communication-guardedness is preserved under $\mu$-expansion. In other words: if a mixed term $P$ is communication-guarded by a communication set $A$, and $P'$ results from $P$ by replacing one recursion $\mu X.Q$ in $P$ by its expanded version $Q\{\mu X.Q/X\}$ then $P'$ also is communication-guarded.                              □

We can now introduce the announced transformation rules for mixed terms.

**Definition 5.1.6** In the following transformation rules, letters $P$, $Q$, $R$ range over *CProc + Spec* unless stated otherwise. As usual, letters $S$, $T$; $X$; $a$, $b$; $A$ range over *Spec*, *Idf*, *Comm*, and alphabets, respectively.

(1) Equation Rules:

   (Reflexivity)

$$P \equiv P$$

(Symmetry)

$$\frac{P \equiv Q}{Q \equiv P}$$

(Transitivity)

$$\frac{P \equiv Q, Q \equiv R}{P \equiv R}$$

(Context)

$$\frac{Q \equiv R}{P\{Q/X\} \equiv P\{R/X\}}$$

where $P \in Proc + Spec$ and $P\{Q/X\}, P\{R/X\} \in CProc + Spec$

(2) Specification Rules:

(Kernel)

$$S \equiv kern(S)$$

(Logic)

$$\frac{\models S \longleftrightarrow T}{S \equiv T} \quad \text{where } \alpha(S) = \alpha(T)$$

(3) Construction Rules:

(Deadlock)

$$stop{:}A \equiv h{\downarrow}A \leq \varepsilon$$

(Prefix)

$$\frac{init(S) = \{a\}}{a.S\{a.h/h\} \equiv S}$$

(Choice)

$$\frac{\varepsilon \models S \wedge T, \ init(S \wedge T) = \emptyset}{S + T \equiv S \vee T} \quad \text{where } \alpha(S) = \alpha(T)$$

(Parallelism)

$$S \parallel T \equiv S \wedge T$$

(Renaming)

- *same traces:*
  $$\forall \ tr' \in \alpha(T)^* :$$
  $$tr' \models T \text{ iff } \exists tr \in \alpha(S)^* : tr \models S$$
  $$\text{and } tr\{b_i/a_i\} = tr'$$
- *same liveness:*
  $$\forall \ tr_1, tr_2 \in \alpha(S)^* \ \forall c \in \alpha(S) :$$
  $$tr_1 \models S \text{ and } tr_2 \models S$$
  $$\text{and } tr_1\{b_i/a_i\} = tr_2\{b_i/a_i\} \text{ and } tr_1.c \models S$$
  $$\text{imply}$$
  $$\exists d \in \alpha(S) : tr_2.d \models S \text{ and } c\{b_i/a_i\} = d\{b_i/a_i\}$$

$$\overline{\qquad S[b_i/a_i] \equiv T \qquad}$$

where $\alpha(T) = \alpha(S)\{b_i/a_i\}$ and $b_i/a_i$ stands for a renaming
$b_1, \ldots, b_n/a_1, \ldots, a_n$ with $n \geq 1$

(Hiding)

- *empty trace:*
  $$\varepsilon \models S$$
- *logical implication:*
  $$\models S \longrightarrow T$$
- *stability:*
  $$\forall \ b \in B : b \models \neg S$$
- *divergence freedom:*
  $$\forall \ tr \in \alpha(S)^* \ \exists n \geq 0 \ \forall b_1, \ldots, b_n \in B :$$
  $$tr.b_1 \ldots b_n \models \neg S$$
- *same liveness:*
  $$\forall \ tr \in \alpha(S)^* \forall c \in \alpha(T) :$$
  $$tr \models S \text{ and } \forall b \in B : tr.b \models \neg S \text{ and } tr.c \models T$$
  $$\text{imply } tr.c \models S$$

$$\overline{\qquad S \backslash B \equiv T \qquad}$$

where $\alpha(T) = \alpha(S) - B$

(Recursion)

$$\frac{P\{S/X\} \equiv S}{\mu X. \ P \equiv S}$$

where $\mu X. \ P \in CProc + Spec$ is communication-guarded and $\alpha(S) = \alpha(X)$

(Expansion: derived)

$$\frac{init(S) = \{a_1, \ldots, a_n\}}{\sum_{i=1}^{n} a_i.\ S\{a_i.\ h/h\} \equiv S}$$

where $a_1, \ldots, a_n$ are $n \geq 2$ distinct communications

(Disjoint renaming: derived)

$$S[b_i/a_i] \equiv S\{b_i/a_i\}$$

where $b_i/a_i$ stands for a renaming $b_1, \ldots, b_n/a_1, \ldots, a_n$ with $n \geq 1$ and $b_1, \ldots, b_n \notin \alpha\alpha(S)$

□

The equation rules are standard for any type of equational reasoning. The kernel rule reflects a property of the process domain, i.e. that the set of traces in which a process may engage is prefix closed. Hence only the prefix kernel of a trace specification is relevant. The need for such a rule in trace-based reasoning has been observed in [Jon87, WGS87, Zwi89]. The logic rule provides the interface between trace logic and equality in the readiness domain. It allows the replacement of a trace specification $S$ by a logically equivalent specification $T$ and corresponds to the so-called consequence rule used in proof systems based on implications rather than equations.

Of the construction rules those for renaming and hiding are surprisingly complicated. The reason is that renaming and hiding can completely restructure the communication behaviour of a process. In particular, both operators can introduce externally observable nondeterminism and, additionally, hiding can introduce divergence and initial instability. We know from Proposition 4.3.6 that processes with such properties fail to satisfy the liveness conditions of any trace specification. To exclude such failure the rules for renaming and hiding have various semantic premises.

The difficult case of renaming is *aliasing*, i.e. when two originally different communications get the same name. For example, if

$$S \equiv h\!\downarrow\!\{a\} \leq a \wedge h\!\downarrow\!\{b\} \leq b.b$$

then

$$S[b/a] \equiv h\!\downarrow\!\{b\} \leq b.b.b$$

but if

$$S \equiv h\!\downarrow\!\{a,b\} \leq a \vee h\!\downarrow\!\{a,b\} \leq b.b$$

then $S[b/a]$ is externally nondeterministic (it either deadlocks after the first $b$ or accepts a second one) and hence not equivalent to any other trace specification. Fortunately, in most cases we are only interested in renamings $S[b_i/a_i]$ without aliasing. Then we can assume that the communications $b_i$ are not in the extended alphabet $\alpha\alpha(S)$ introduced in Definition 4.2.1 and apply the extremely simple rule for disjoint renaming. It states that the semantics of $S[b_i/a_i]$ is captured by a simple syntactic substitution on $S$, viz. $S\{b_i/a_i\}$.

For hiding we have not found a special case that would allow an equally simple treatment. Thus we always have to check all the premises of the hiding rule. In practical applications we found that the first four premises are easily established. Only the premise "same liveness" is more difficult; it is proven by a case analysis for all communications $c \in \alpha(T)$.

The remaining rules are all extremely simple. Parallel composition is just logical conjunction, choice is essentially logical disjunction, prefix is treated by logical substitution, the expansion rule combines prefix with (multiple) choice, and the recursion rule asks for a recursive semantic equation in its premise. Thus when applying the above transformation rules difficulties arise only when they are unavoidable: in the cases of renaming with aliasing and hiding.

We remark that the simple conjunction rule for parallelism was one of our aims when selecting the operators for process terms. That is why we have chosen COSY's version of parallel composition. By contrast, the parallel composition of CCS would be extremely difficult to deal with in our approach because it combines in a single operator the effect of COSY's parallelism, renaming with aliasing (to model *autoconcurrency*, i.e. concurrent communications with the same name) and hiding. Here we follow CSP and treat all these issues separately.

A simple disjunction rule for choice was another aim. It lead us to require that processes satisfying a trace specification should be stable initially. Indeed, if $S$ and $T$ would allow processes to have an initial unstability then $S+T$ would exhibit externally observable nondeterminism and hence not satisfy the liveness condition of any other trace specification. Of course, we could have avoided the problem of initial unstability altogether by selecting the external choice $\Box$ of CSP instead of the choice operator $+$ of CCS. Our reason for choosing $+$ is its simple net semantics in Chapter 3.

These two examples illustrate how our aim of bringing different views of concurrent processes together influenced certain design decisions in our approach.

## 5.2   Soundness

This section is devoted to the following theorem:

**Soundness Theorem 5.2.1** The transformation rules presented in Definition 5.1.6 are sound.

*Proof.* The equation rules for reflexivity, symmetry and transitivity are obviously sound. The soundness of the context rule follows from the fact that the readiness semantics $\mathcal{R}^*[\![\cdot]\!]$ is denotational. The soundness of the specification rules for logic and kernel is shown by using Definition 4.4.6 of the readiness semantics of trace specifications; for the kernel rule the argument is as follows:

$\mathcal{R}^*[\![S]\!]$

$=$    { Definition 4.4.6 and properties of $pref$ }

$(\alpha(S), \{tr, \mathcal{F}) \mid tr \in \alpha(S)^*$    and $pref\ tr \models S$ and

$\qquad\qquad\qquad \mathcal{F} = (a \in \alpha(S) \mid pref\ tr.a \models S\}\})$

$=$    { Proposition 5.1.3, (1) and (5) }

$(\alpha(kern(S)),$

$\{(tr, \mathcal{F}) \mid tr \in \alpha(kern(S))^*$    and $pref\ tr \models kern(S)$ and

$\qquad\qquad\qquad \mathcal{F} = \{a \in \alpha(kern(S)) \mid pref\ tr.a \models kern(S)\}\})$

$=$    { Definition 4.4.6 and properties of $pref$ }

$\mathcal{R}^*[\![kern(S)\,]\!]$.

The soundness of the construction rules is shown by exploiting the denotational definition of the readiness semantics, in particular Definition 4.5.6 of the semantic operators $op_{\mathcal{R}}$ on the readiness domain $DOM_{\mathcal{R}}$. Since these operators are applied here to trace specifications, we can skip over those clauses in their definition that deal with process information $\tau$ and $(tr, \uparrow)$ generated from their arguments. This simplifies matters considerably.

*Soundness of the deadlock rule:*

$$\mathcal{R}^*[\![stop{:}A]\!] = (A, \{(\varepsilon, \emptyset)\}) = \mathcal{R}^*[\![h{\downarrow}A \leq \varepsilon]\!]$$

*Soundness of the prefix rule:*

Suppose $init(S) = \{a\}$. Then

$\mathcal{R}^*[\![a.S\{a.h/h\}\,]\!]$

$=$    { $\mathcal{R}^*$ denotational }

$a._{\mathcal{R}}\mathcal{R}^*[\![S\{a.h/h\}]\!]$

$=$    { definition $._{\mathcal{R}}$ }

$close(\alpha(S), \{(\varepsilon, \{a\})\} \cup \{(a.tr, \mathcal{F}) \mid (tr, \mathcal{F}) \in \pi(\mathcal{R}^*[\![S\{a.h/h\}]\!])\})$

$=$    { definition $\mathcal{R}^*[\![S\{a.h/h\}]\!]$ and $\alpha(S\{a.h/h\}) = \alpha(S)$ }

$close(\alpha(S), \qquad \{(\varepsilon, \{a\})\}$

$\qquad\qquad\qquad \cup \quad \{(a.tr, \mathcal{F}) \mid tr \in \alpha(S)^*$ and $pref\ tr \models S\{a.h/h\}$ and

$\qquad\qquad\qquad\qquad\qquad \mathcal{F} = \{c \in \alpha(S) \mid tr.c \models S\{a.h/h\}\}\})$

$=$    { $\forall tr \in \alpha(S)^*:\ tr \models S\{a.h/h\}$ iff $\models S\{a.tr/h\}$

$\qquad\qquad$ iff $a.tr \models S$ and $\varepsilon \models S$ because of $init(S) = \{a\}\}$

$close(\alpha(S),\quad \{(\varepsilon,\{a\})\}$
$\qquad\qquad \cup\quad \{(a.tr,\mathcal{F}) \mid\ tr \in \alpha(S)^* \text{ and } pref\, a.tr \models S \text{ and}$
$\qquad\qquad\qquad\qquad \mathcal{F} = \{c \in \alpha(S) \mid a.tr.c \models S\}\})$

$=\quad \{init(S) = \{a\}\}$

$close(\alpha(S), \{(tr,\mathcal{F}) \mid\ tr \in \alpha(S)^* \text{ and } pref\, tr \models S \text{ and}$
$\qquad\qquad\qquad \mathcal{F} = \{c \in \alpha(S) \mid tr.c \models S\}\})$

$=\quad \{ \text{ definition and closedness of } \mathcal{R}^*[\![S]\!] \ \}$

$\mathcal{R}^*[\![S]\!].$

*Soundness of the choice rule:*
Let $A = \alpha(S) = \alpha(T)$ and suppose $\varepsilon \models S \cap T$ and $init(S \cap T) = \emptyset$. Then

$\mathcal{R}^*[\![S + T]\!]$

$=\quad \{\mathcal{R}^* \text{ denotational }\}$

$\mathcal{R}^*[\![S]\!] +_{\mathcal{R}} \mathcal{R}^*[\![T]\!]$

$=\quad \{ \text{ definition } +_{\mathcal{R}} \ \}$

$close(A,\quad \{(\varepsilon,\mathcal{F}\cup\mathcal{G}) \mid (\varepsilon,\mathcal{F}) \in \pi(\mathcal{R}^*[\![S]\!]) \text{ and } (\varepsilon,\mathcal{G}) \in \pi(\mathcal{R}^*[\![T]\!])\}$
$\qquad\qquad \cup\ \{(tr,\mathcal{F})\quad \mid tr \neq \varepsilon \text{ and } (tr,\mathcal{F}) \in \pi(\mathcal{R}^*[\![S]\!]) \cup \pi(\mathcal{R}^*[\![T]\!])\})$

$=\quad \{ \text{ definition } \mathcal{R}^*[\![S]\!] \text{ and } \mathcal{R}^*[\![T]\!] \ \}$

$close(A,\quad \{(\varepsilon,\mathcal{F}\cup\mathcal{G}) \mid \varepsilon \models S \text{ and } \mathcal{F} = \{a \in A \mid a \models S\} \text{ and}$
$\qquad\qquad\qquad\qquad \varepsilon \models T \text{ and } \mathcal{G} = \{a \in A \mid a \models T\}\qquad\quad \}$
$\qquad\qquad \cup\ \{(tr,\mathcal{F})\quad \mid tr \neq \varepsilon \text{ and } tr \in A^* \text{ and}$
$\qquad\qquad\qquad\qquad ((pref\, tr \models S \text{ and } \mathcal{F} = \{a \in A \mid tr.a \models S\}) \text{ or}$
$\qquad\qquad\qquad\qquad (pref\, tr \models T \text{ and } \mathcal{F} = \{a \in A \mid tr.a \models T\}))\})$

$=\quad \{ \ \varepsilon \models S \wedge T \text{ and } init(S \wedge T) = \emptyset \ \}$

$close(A,\quad \{(\varepsilon,\mathcal{F}\cup\mathcal{G}) \mid \ \varepsilon \models S \vee T \text{ and } \mathcal{F}\cup\mathcal{G} = \{a \in A \mid a \models S \vee T\}\}$
$\qquad\qquad \cup\ \{(tr,\mathcal{F})\quad \mid\ tr \neq \varepsilon \text{ and } tr \in A^* \text{ and } pref\, tr \models S \vee T \text{ and}$
$\qquad\qquad\qquad\qquad \mathcal{F} = \{a \in A \mid tr.a \models S \vee T\}\})$

$=\quad \{ \text{ definition and closedness of } \mathcal{R}^*[\![S \vee T]\!] \ \}$

$\mathcal{R}^*[\![S \vee T]\!].$

*Soundness of the parallelism rule:*
Let $A = \alpha(S)$ and $B = \alpha(T)$. Then

$\mathcal{R}^*[\![S \parallel T]\!]$

$=\quad \{\mathcal{R}^* \text{ denotational }\}$

$$\mathcal{R}^*[\![S]\!] \parallel_{\mathcal{R}} \mathcal{R}^*[\![T]\!]$$

$=$ { definition $\parallel_{\mathcal{R}}$}

$close(A \cup B, \quad \{(tr, \mathcal{F}) \,|\, tr^* \in (A \cup B)^*$ and

$\qquad pref \, tr{\downarrow}A \models S$ and $pref \, tr{\downarrow}B \models T$ and

$\qquad \mathcal{F} = \{a \in A \cap B \;\; | \;(tr{\downarrow}A).a \models S$ and $(tr{\downarrow}B).a \models T \;\}$

$\qquad \cup \; \{a \in A - B \;\; | \;(tr{\downarrow}A).a \models S \;\}$

$\qquad \cup \; \{a \in B - A \;\; | \;(tr{\downarrow}B).a \models T \;\}$ \hfill $\})$

$=$ { Projection Corollary 4.2.2 }

$close(A \cup B, \quad \{(tr, \mathcal{F}) \,|\, tr^* \in (A \cup B)^*$ and

$\qquad pref \, tr \models S$ and $pref \, tr \models T$ and

$\qquad \mathcal{F} = \{a \in A \cap B \,|\, tr.a \models S$ and $tr.a \models T\}$

$\qquad \cup \; \{a \in (A - B) \cup (B - A) \,|\, tr.a \models S$ or $tr.a \models T\}\})$

$=$ { definition and closedness of $\mathcal{R}^*[\![S \wedge T]\!]$ }

$\quad \mathcal{R}^*[\![S \wedge T]\!]$

*Soundness of the renaming rule:*
We treat only the case $b/a$ where a single communication is renamed, but the general case is equally simple. Let $A = \alpha(S)$ and $B = \alpha(T)$ and suppose that the premises "same traces" and "same liveness" hold. Then

$$\mathcal{R}^*[\![S[b/a]]\!]$$

$=$ {$\mathcal{R}^*$ denotational }

$\quad \mathcal{R}^*[\![S]\!][b/a]_{\mathcal{R}}$

$=$ { definition $[b/a]_{\mathcal{R}}$ }

$\quad close(B, \{(tr\{b/a\}, \mathcal{F}\{b/a\}) \,|\, (tr, \mathcal{F}) \in \pi(\mathcal{R}^*[\![S]\!])\})$

$=$ { definition $\mathcal{R}^*[\![S]\!]$}

$\quad close(B, \{(tr\{b/a\}, \mathcal{F}\{b/a\}) \,|\quad tr \in A^*$ and $pref \, tr \models S$ and

$\qquad\qquad\qquad\qquad \mathcal{F} = \{c \in A \,|\, tr.c \models S\}$ \hfill $\})$

$=$ { premise "same traces" for $tr'$ and $\mathcal{F}\{b/a\} \subseteq \mathcal{F}'$,

$\qquad$ and premise "same liveness" for $\mathcal{F}' \subseteq \mathcal{F}\{b/a\}$}

$\quad close(B, \{(tr', \mathcal{F}') \,|\quad tr' \in B^*$ and $pref \, tr' \models T$ and

$\qquad\qquad\qquad\qquad \mathcal{F}' = \{c' \in B \,|\, tr'.c' \models T\}$ \hfill $\})$

$=$ { definition and closedness of $\mathcal{R}^*[\![T]\!]$ }

$\quad \mathcal{R}^*[\![T]\!]$

*Soundness of the hiding rule:*

We treat only the case $B = \{b\}$ where a single communication is hidden. The soundness proof of the general case is similar. Let $A = \alpha(S)$ and $C = \alpha(T) = \alpha(S) - \{b\}$ and suppose that all premises of the rule hold. Then

$\mathcal{R}^*[\![S \backslash b]\!]$

$=$ $\{\mathcal{R}^*$ denotational $\}$

$\mathcal{R}^*[\![S]\!] \backslash b_{\mathcal{R}}$

$=$ $\{$ definition $\backslash b_{\mathcal{R}}\}$

$close(C, \quad \{ \qquad \tau \qquad | \; \exists \mathcal{G} \subseteq Comm : (b, \mathcal{G}) \in \pi(\mathcal{R}^*[\![S]\!])\}$
$\cup \{ \; (tr{\downarrow}C, \mathcal{F}) \; | \; (tr, \mathcal{F}) \in \pi(\mathcal{R}^*[\![S]\!]) \text{ and } b \notin \mathcal{F} \; \}$
$\cup \{ \; (tr{\downarrow}C, \uparrow) \; | \; \forall n \geq 0 \; \exists \mathcal{G} \subseteq Comm : (tr.b^n, \mathcal{G}) \in \pi(\mathcal{R}^*[\![S]\!])\})$

$=$ $\{$ definition $\mathcal{R}^*[\![S]\!]$ and premises "stability" and "divergence freedom" $\}$

$close(C, \{(tr{\downarrow}C, \mathcal{F}) \; | \quad tr \in A^* \text{ and } pref \; tr \models S \text{ and}$
$\qquad\qquad \mathcal{F} = \{c \in A \; | \; tr.c \models S\} \text{ and } tr.b \models \neg S\}$

$=$ $\{$ • inclusion " $\sqsupseteq$ ": Consider $tr \in A^*$ with $pref \; tr \models S$ and
$\qquad \mathcal{F} = \{c \in A \; | \; tr.c \models S\}$ and $tr.b \models \neg S$. By the premise
$\qquad$ "logical implication", $pref \; tr \models T$ and $\mathcal{F} \subseteq \{c \in C \; | \; tr.c \models T\}$.
$\qquad$ By the premise "same liveness", also $\mathcal{F} \supseteq \{c \in C \; | \; tr.c \models T\}$.

$\qquad$ • inclusion " $\sqsubseteq$ ": Given $tr \in A^*$ with $pref \; tr \models T$ and
$\qquad \mathcal{F} = \{c \in C \; | \; tr. \, c \models T\}$, consider the longest prefix $tr'$ of $tr$ such
$\qquad$ the $pref \; tr' \models S$ and $tr'. \, b \models \neg S$. Note that $tr'$ exists because of the
$\qquad$ premises "empty trace" and "divergence freedom". By the premise
$\qquad$ "same liveness", we conclude $tr' = tr$ and $\mathcal{F} \subseteq \{c \in C \; | \; tr. \, c \models S\}$.
$\qquad$ Furthermore, by the premise "logical implication",
$\qquad \mathcal{F} \supseteq \{c \in C \; | \; tr. \, c \models S\}$. $\qquad\qquad \}$

$\quad close(C, \{(tr{\downarrow}C, \mathcal{F}) \; | \quad tr \in A^* \text{ and } pref \; tr \models T \text{ and}$
$\qquad\qquad\qquad \mathcal{F} = \{c \in C \; | \; tr.c \models T\} \qquad \})$

$=$ $\{$ Projection Corollary 4.2.2 $\}$

$\quad close(C, \{(tr', \mathcal{F}) \; | \quad tr' \in C^* \text{ and } pref \; tr' \models T \text{ and}$
$\qquad\qquad\qquad \mathcal{F} = \{c \in C \; | \; tr'.c \models T\} \qquad \})$

$=$ $\{$ definition and closedness of $\mathcal{R}^*[\![T]\!]\}$

$\mathcal{R}^*[\![T]\!]\}.$

*Soundness of the recursion rule:*
Suppose $\mu X.P \in CProc + Spec$ is communication-guarded by a communication set $A$ and

$$P\{S/X\} \equiv S \tag{5.1}$$

for some $S \in Spec$ with $\alpha(S) = \alpha(X)$. To prove the conclusion of the rule, i.e.

$$\mu X.P \equiv S, \tag{5.2}$$

we show the two semantic implications "$<\equiv$" and "$\equiv>$". The implication "$<\equiv$" is easily established using a fixed point argument. Let $B = \alpha(S)$ and $\rho \in Env_{\mathcal{R}}$ be an arbitrary environment. Consider the mapping

$$\Phi_{P,\rho} : DOM_{\mathcal{R}} : B \longrightarrow DOM_{\mathcal{R}} : B$$

defined by

$$\Phi_{P,\rho}(B, \Gamma) = \mathcal{R}^*[\![P]\!](\rho[(B, \Gamma)/X]).$$

Since $\mathcal{R}^*$ is denotational, $\mathcal{R}^*[\![\mu X.P]\!]$ is the least fixed point of $\Phi_{P,\rho}$, "least" w.r.t. the partial ordering $\sqsubseteq$ on $DOM_{\mathcal{R}} : B$. By (5.1), $\mathcal{R}^*[\![S]\!]$ is a fixed point of $\Phi_{P,\rho}$. Hence

$$\mathcal{R}^*[\![\mu X.P]\!] \sqsubseteq \mathcal{R}^*[\![S]\!].$$

By definition, this is just the implication

$$\mu X.P <\equiv S. \tag{5.3}$$

Note that we have not yet exploited the fact that $\mu X.P$ is communication-guarded. This condition is needed only to show the reverse implication "$\equiv>$". Our aim is to show that every process information up to a certain depth $k \geq 0$ produced by $\mu X.P$ can also be produced by $S$. To this end, we consider expanded versions of $\mu X.P$ and use ideas on constructive and non-destructive operators due to Roscoe [Ros82, BHR84, Hoa85b].

The depth of a process information refers to the communication set $A$ by which $\mu X.P$ is communication-guarded. Formally, it is a mapping

$$\|\bullet\| : DOM_{\mathcal{R}} \longrightarrow \mathbb{N}_0$$

defined as follows:

$$
\begin{aligned}
\| \tau \| &= 0 \\
\| (tr, \mathcal{F}) \| &= |tr{\downarrow}A| + 1 \\
\| (tr, \uparrow) \| &= |tr{\downarrow}A|
\end{aligned}
$$

where $|tr{\downarrow}A|$ counts the number of communications $a \in A$ in the trace $tr$. Using $\|\bullet\|$, we introduce, for each $k \geq 0$, a *restriction operator*

$$\bullet{\downarrow}k : DOM_{\mathcal{R}} \longrightarrow DOM_{\mathcal{R}}$$

defined as follows:

$$(B,\Gamma){\downarrow}k = (B, \{\gamma \in \Gamma \mid \text{where } \parallel \gamma \parallel \leq k\})$$

Thus only process information $\gamma$ up to a depth $k$ are considered in $(B,\Gamma){\downarrow}k$.

The restriction operators enjoy the following inclusion properties for all $Q, R, Q_1, \ldots, Q_n \in CProc + Spec$, for all $k \geq 0$ and all $a \in Comm$, and for all $op \in \{+, \parallel, [b/a], \backslash c \mid (a \notin A \text{ or } b \in A) \text{ and } c \notin A\}$ :

$$\mathcal{R}^*[\![Q]\!] \sqsupseteq \mathcal{R}^*[\![R]\!] \text{ iff } \forall k \geq 0 : \mathcal{R}^*[\![Q]\!]{\downarrow}k \sqsupseteq \mathcal{R}^*[\![R]\!] \qquad (5.4)$$

$$\mathcal{R}^*[\![a.Q]\!]{\downarrow}0 \sqsupseteq \mathcal{R}^*[\![a.R]\!] \qquad\qquad\qquad \text{if } \alpha(Q) = \alpha(R) \qquad (5.5)$$

$$\mathcal{R}^*[\![a.Q]\!]{\downarrow}k+1 \sqsupseteq a._{\mathcal{R}}(\mathcal{R}^*[\![Q]\!]{\downarrow}k) \qquad\qquad \text{if } a \in A \qquad (5.6)$$

$$\mathcal{R}^*[\![a.Q]\!]{\downarrow}k+1 \sqsupseteq a._{\mathcal{R}}(\mathcal{R}^*[\![Q]\!]{\downarrow}k+1) \qquad\quad \text{if } a \notin A \qquad (5.7)$$

$$\mathcal{R}^*[\![op(Q_1, \ldots, Q_n)]\!]{\downarrow}k \sqsupseteq op_{\mathcal{R}}(\mathcal{R}^*[\![Q_1]\!]{\downarrow}k, \ldots, \mathcal{R}^*[\![Q_n]\!]{\downarrow}k) \qquad (5.8)$$

Property (5.4) is obvious; it will be used to show the implication $\mu X.\ P \equiv > S$. Properties (5.5) – (5.8) are easily established by looking at Definition 4.5.6 of the operators $a._{\mathcal{R}}$ and $op_{\mathcal{R}}$; these properties help to calculate the depth $k$ behaviour of mixed terms. Following Roscoe [Ros82], operators $op$ satisfying (5.8) are called non-destructive because the depth $k$ behaviour of $op(Q_1, \ldots, Q_n)$ can be calculated from the depth $k$ behaviour of its arguments $Q_1, \ldots, Q_n$; and operators like $a.$ in (5.6) are called constructive because the depth $k+1$ behaviour of $a.Q$ can be calculated already from the depth $k$ behaviour of $Q$. Note that (5.5) holds for any $R$ with $\alpha(Q) = \alpha(R)$. This is how we can finally replace "suitably guarded" occurrences of the term $\mu X.P$ by the trace specification $S$. Recursion, which is not listed among the above properties, will be dealt with by "sufficiently many" $\mu$-expansions.

We will now make precise the notions of "suitably guarded" and "sufficiently many". First we refine the notion of communication-guardedness. Let A be a set of communications and $k \geq 0$. An occurrence of a subterm $Q$ in a term $P_0$ is called *k-guarded by A in P* (respectively *k-guarded without $\mu$ by A in $P_0$*) if $Q$ occurs at the indicated position within a subterm of $P_0$ of the form

$$a_1.R_1(\ldots a_k.R_k(Q) \ldots)$$

of $P_0$ with $a_1, \ldots, a_k \in A$, but not within a subterm of $P_0$ of the form

$$R[b/a] \text{ or } R\backslash a$$

(respectively not of the form

$$\mu Y.R \text{ or } R[b/a] \text{ or } R\backslash a)$$

with $a \in A$ and $b \notin A$. Thus a term $P_0$ is communication-guarded by $A$ if for every recursive subterm $\mu X.Q$ of $P$ every free occurrence of $X$ in $Q$ is 1-guarded by $A$ in

$Q$. In particular, for $\mu X.P$ itself every free occurrence of $X$ in $P$ is 1-guarded by $A$ in $P$.

For a given $k \geq 0$ we wish to transform $\mu X.P$ into a term $P'$ where every occurrence of $\mu X.P$ lies within a subterm $Q$ of $P'$ which is $(k+1)$-guarded without $\mu$ by $A$ in $P'$. This transformation proceeds in two phases. First we show:

*Claim 1.* By zero or more $\mu$-expansions inside $P$, the term $\mu X.P$ can be transformed into a communication-guarded term $\mu X.\tilde{P}$ where every free occurrence of $X$ in $\tilde{P}$ is 1-guarded by $A$ and if it occurs within a recursion $\mu X.R$, then $\mu X.R$ and hence $X$ are $(k+1)$-guarded by $A$.

The proof of this claim is as follows. If no free occurrence of $X$ in $P$ occurs within a subterm of $P$ of the form $\mu Y.R$ then no $\mu$-expansion is necessary and hence $\mu X.\tilde{P} = \mu X.P$. Let now some free occurrence of $X$ in $P$ occur within a subterm of $P$ of the form $\mu Y.R$. Communication-guardedness of $\mu X.P$ implies that every free occurrence of $Y$ in $R$ is 1-guarded by $A$ in $R$. Let $\mu Y.R$ itself be $m$-guarded by $A$ in $P$ for some $m \geq 0$. Then replacing $\mu Y.R$ in $\mu X.P$ by its expanded version

$$R\{\mu Y.R/Y\}$$

results in a term

$$\mu X.P_1$$

which by Proposition 5.1.5 is communication-guarded in $A$ and in which all occurrences of $\mu Y.R$ in $R\{\mu Y.R/Y\}$ are $(m+1)$-guarded by $A$ in $P_1$ and all free occurrences of $X$ in $R\{\mu Y.R/Y\}$ outside $\mu Y.R$ are uncovered from the $\mu Y$-recursion. Note that $\mu Y.R$ in $R\{\mu Y.R/Y\}$ still contains free occurrences of $X$. However, by iterating the above $\mu Y$-expansion, we can push $\mu Y.R$ and all free occurrences of $X$ in it under more and more guarding communications of $A$. In fact, by a $(k+1)$-fold $\mu Y$-expansion, we obtain a term

$$\mu X.P_{k+1}$$

which by Proposition 5.1.5 is communication-guarded and in which every free occurrence of $X$ is 1-guarded by $A$ in $P_{k+1}$. Moreover if $X$ occurs within a $\mu Y$-recursion $\mu Y.R$ in $P_{k+1}$ then $\mu Y.R$ and hence $X$ are $(k+1)$-guarded by $A$ in $P_{k+1}$. We can repeat this expansion technique for every recursion in $P_{k+1}$ which is on top of a free occurrence of $X$. In this way we transform $\mu X.P$ by $\mu$-expansions into a term

$$\mu X.\tilde{P}$$

with the properties stated in Claim 1.

In a second transformation phase we simply expand the $\mu Y$-recursion in $\mu X.\tilde{P}$ sufficiently often. As in Section 4.6 we use the notation $\tilde{P}^k$ for $k \geq 0$ and $R \in CProc + Spec$ with $\alpha(X) = \alpha(R)$. Recall its inductive definition:

$$\tilde{P}^0(R) = R \text{ and } \tilde{P}^{k+1}(R) = \tilde{P}\{\tilde{P}^k(R)/X\}.$$

By Claim 1, the following claim is obviously true:

*Claim 2.* By $k + 1$ $\mu X$-expansions, the term $\mu X.\tilde{P}$ can be transformed into the term

$$P' = \tilde{P}^{k+1}(\mu X.\tilde{P})$$

where every occurrence of $\mu X.\tilde{P}$ occurs within a subterm $Q$ of $P'$ which is $(k+1)$-guarded without $\mu$ by $A$ in $P'$.

With all these preparations, we can quickly finish the soundness proof of the recursion rule. Take some $k \geq 0$. Then

$$\mathcal{R}^*[\![\mu X.P]\!]{\downarrow}k$$
$$=\quad \{ \ \mathcal{R}^* \text{ denotational and Claim 2 } \}$$
$$\mathcal{R}^*[\![\tilde{P}^{k+1}(\mu X.\tilde{P})]\!]{\downarrow}k$$
$$\sqsupseteq\quad \{ \text{ calculations using properties (5.5) – (5.8) } \}$$
$$\mathcal{R}^*[\![\ \tilde{P}^{k+1}(S)]\!]$$
$$=\quad \{ \ \mathcal{R}^* \text{ denotational and equation (5.1) } \}$$
$$\mathcal{R}^*[\![S]\!]$$

By (5.4), we conclude

$$\mathcal{R}^*[\![\mu X.P]\!] \sqsupseteq \mathcal{R}^*[\![S]\!]$$

By definition, this is just the implication

$$\mu X.P \implies S$$

which together with (5.3) establishes the desired equation (5.2).

*Derivation of the expansion rule:*

Suppose $init(S) = \{a_1, \ldots, a_n\}$ holds for $n \geq 2$ distinct communications $a_1, \ldots, a_n$. We show that the conclusion of the expansion rule can be derived using the rules for prefix, choice and logic. For $i = 1, \ldots, n$ define

$$S_i =_{df} S \wedge (h{\downarrow}A \leq \varepsilon \vee a_i \leq h{\downarrow}A)$$

where $A = \alpha(S)$. Then $\alpha(S_i) = A$ and $init(S) = \{a_i\}$. Thus by the prefix rule,

$$a_i.\, S_i\{a_i.h/h\} \equiv S_i$$

Moreover, if $i \neq j$ then $\varepsilon \models S_i \wedge S_j$ and $init(S_i \wedge S_j) = \emptyset$. Thus by successive applications of the choice rule and associativity of logical disjunction we arrive at

$$\sum_{i=1}^{n} a_i.S_i\{a_i.h/h\} \equiv \bigvee_{i=1}^{n} S_i$$

By the definition of $S_i$,

$$\models S_i\{a_i.h/h\} \longleftrightarrow S\{a_i.h/h\}$$

and by $init(S) = \{a_1, \ldots, a_n\}$ , also

$$\models \bigvee_{i=1}^{n} S_i \longleftrightarrow S.$$

Thus by the logic rule and the equation rules, we finally obtain

$$\sum_{n=1}^{n} a_i.S\{a_i.h/h\} \equiv S$$

as desired.

*Derivation of the rule for disjoint renaming:*
We treat only the case $b/a$ where a single communication is renamed, but the general case can be derived similarly. Suppose $b \notin \alpha\alpha(S)$. We show that the conclusion of the rule for disjoint renaming can be derived using the general renaming rule. To this end, we put

$$T =_{df} S\{b/a\}$$

By the Renaming Corollary 4.2.3,

$$\forall tr \in \alpha\alpha(S)^* : tr \models S \text{ iff } tr\{b/a\} \models T.$$

Since $b \notin \alpha\alpha(S) \supseteq \alpha(S)$, we can reverse this statement as follows:

$$\forall tr' \in \alpha(T)^* : tr' \models T \text{ iff } tr'\{a/b\} \models S.$$

Hence the first premise "same traces" of the renaming rule is satisfied. Note that the second premise "same liveness" is trivially satisfied because by $b \notin \alpha\alpha(S) \supseteq \alpha(S)$,

$$\forall tr_1, tr_2 \in \alpha(S)^* : tr_1\{b/a\} = tr_2\{b/a\} \text{ implies } tr_1 = tr_2$$

Thus the renaming rule yields

$$S[b/a] \equiv S\{b/a\},$$

the desired conclusion.                                                                        □

Let $\mu X.P \in CProc + Spec$ be communication-guarded. Then the recursion rule states that

$$P\{S/X\} \equiv P \text{ implies } \mu X.P \equiv S \qquad (5.9)$$

for every $S \in Spec$ with $\alpha(S) = \alpha(X)$. However, the above soundness proof of the recursion rule does not exploit the fact that the letter $S$ denotes a trace specification. The proof works just as well for any mixed term $Q$ with $\alpha(Q) = \alpha(X)$ instead of $S$.

In fact, the proof can easily be lifted to a purely semantic level. This yields the following result.

**Corollary 5.2.2 : Unique Fixed Points** Let $\mu X.P \in CProc + Spec$ be communication-guarded and $B = \alpha(X)$. Then for arbitrary environment $\rho$ the mapping

$$\Phi_{P,\rho} : DOM_{\mathcal{R}} : B \longrightarrow DOM_{\mathcal{R}} : B$$

defined by

$$\Phi_{P,\rho}(B,\Gamma) = \mathcal{R}^*[\![P]\!](\rho[(B,\Gamma)/X])$$

has a unique fixed point. Thus

$$\mathcal{R}^*[\![P]\!](\rho[(B,\Gamma)/X]) = (B,\Gamma)$$

implies

$$\mathcal{R}^*[\![\mu X.P]\!] = (B,\Gamma) \qquad\qquad \square$$

Insisting on trace specifications $S$ in the implication (5.9) of the recursion rule gives us an additional property of $\mu X.P$: its divergence freedom. This is needed for the application of the recursion rule to process construction.

## 5.3    Counters

In this section we begin a series of example process constructions. In each example we first use the transformation rules on mixed terms to transform a given trace specification stepwise in one or more process terms. Then we examine the operational behaviour of the constructed process terms by studying the Petri nets denoted by them.

Thus we are now at the heart of our approach where all three views of concurrent processes come together in a top-down fashion:

formulas

$\downarrow$

terms

$\downarrow$

nets

As a first illustration of this approach we shall construct *counters*, i.e. processes that can store a natural number which can be incremented and decremented with the help of communications *up* and *dn*. At first the size of the stored number is bounded as in Example 4.3.8.

**Example 5.3.1 1-Counter.** Consider the trace specification

$$S_1 =_{df} 0 \le up\#h - dn\#h \le 1.$$

We wish to construct a process term $P_1$ satisfying $S_1$, i.e. with

$$P_1 \equiv S_1,$$

and examine the net denoted by $P_1$. The idea of the construction is to use the prefix rule in order to discover a recursive semantic equation which can then be dealt with by the recursion rule.

We begin by determining the set of initial comunications of $S_1$. Since $\varepsilon \models S_1$ and $up \models S_1$ but not $dn \models S_1$ , we obtain:

$$init(S_1) = \{up\}.$$

Thus the prefix rule yields as the first construction step:

$$S_1 \qquad (5.10)$$

$$|||$$

$$up.S_1\{up.h/h\}.$$

We calculate the result of the substitution in $S_1$ using the logic rule:

$$S_1\{up.h/h\} \qquad (5.11)$$

$$||| \ \{\text{definition}\}$$

$$0 \le up\#(up.h) - dn\#(up.h) \le 1$$

$$||| \ \{\text{calculus}\}$$

$$0 \le 1 + up\#h - dn\#h \le 1.$$

Call the last trace specification $S_{1,up}$. Combining (5.10) and (5.11) by the transitivity and the context rule yields

$$S_1 \qquad (5.12)$$

$$|||$$

$$up.S_{1,up}.$$

We now examine the set of initial communications of $S_{1,up}$. Since $\varepsilon \models S_{1,up}$ and $dn \models S_{1,up}$ but not $up \models S_{1,up}$ , we obtain:

$$init(S_{1,up}) = \{dn\}.$$

Hence another application of the prefix rule yields the second construction step:

$$S_{1,up} \qquad (5.13)$$

$$|||$$

$$dn.S_{1,up}\{dn.h/h\}.$$

We calculate the result of the substitution in $S_{1,up}$ using the logic rule:

$$S_{1,up}\{dn.h/h\}$$ (5.14)

$$\text{||| \{definition\}}$$

$$0 < 1 + up\#(dn.h) - dn\#(dn.h) < 1$$

$$\text{||| \{calculus\}}$$

$$0 < 1 + up\#h - (1 + dn\#h) < 1$$

$$\text{||| \{calculus\}}$$

$$0 < up\#h - dn\#h < 1$$

$$\text{||| \{definition\}}$$

$$S_1.$$

Combining (5.12)–(5.14) by the transitivity and the context rule, we can summarize the two construction steps as follows:

$$S_1$$ (5.15)
$$\text{|||}$$
$$up.S_{1,up}$$
$$\text{|||}$$
$$up.dn.S_1.$$

Thus by two applications of the prefix rule, we have discovered the recursive semantic equation

$$up.dn.S_1 \equiv S_1.$$

Let $X$ be a process identifier with $\alpha(X) = \{up, dn\}$. Since $\mu X.up.dn.X$ is communication-guarded, the recursion rule is applicable and yields

$$\mu X.up.dn.X \equiv S_1.$$ (5.16)

Using the transitivity rule, we can write this down as the third and final step of our construction:

$$S_1$$ (5.17)
$$\text{|||}$$
$$up.S_{1,up}$$
$$\text{|||}$$
$$up.dn.S_1$$
$$\text{|||}$$
$$\mu X.up.dn.X.$$

Thus we can choose $P_1 = \mu X.up.dn.X$ to achieve $P_1 \equiv S_1$.

The abstract net denoted by $P_1$ is as follows:

$$\mathcal{N}[\![P_1]\!] =$$

Thus $P_1$ models a counter that can store only two values, viz. 0 and 1. In its initial state the value is 0. By engaging in a communication $up$, $P_1$ sets its value to 1, and by engaging in $dn$, $P_1$ resets its value to 0.                                                    □

**Example 5.3.2 2-Counter.** Next we wish to construct a process term satisfying the trace specification

$$S_2 =_{df} 0 < up\#h - dn\#h < 2$$

considered already in Example 4.3.7. Again we aim at recursive semantic equations which can be dealt with by the recursion rule, but this time we need both the prefix and the expansion rule to obtain these equations.

The set of initial communications of $S_2$ is

$$init(S_2) = up$$

so that the prefix rule yields as the first construction step

$$S_2 \qquad\qquad (5.18)$$
$$|||$$
$$up.S_2\{up.h/h\}.$$

The result of the substitution is equivalent to the trace specification

$$S_{2,up} = 0 < 1 + up\#h - dn\#h < 2.$$

Hence by the logic and context rule the first construction step can be rephrased as

$$S_2 \qquad\qquad (5.19)$$
$$|||$$
$$up.S_{2,up}.$$

In $S_{2,up}$ there are two initial communications possible:

$$init(S_{2,up}) = \{up, dn\}$$

Hence we apply the expansion rule to obtain

$$S_{2,up} \tag{5.20}$$
$$|||$$
$$dn.S_{2,up}\{dn.h/h\} + up.S_{2,up}\{up.h/h\}$$

as our second construction step. The two substitutions in $S_{2,up}$ are equivalent to the trace specifications $S_2$ and

$$S_{2,up.up} = 0 < 2 + up\#h - dn\#h < 2,$$

respectively. Thus by the logic and context rule the second construction step can be rephrased as

$$S_{2,up} \tag{5.21}$$
$$|||$$
$$dn.S_2 + up.S_{2,up.up}$$

Note that

$$init(S_{2,up.up}) = \{dn\}$$

Hence the prefix rule yields as third construction step

$$S_{2,up.up} \tag{5.22}$$
$$|||$$
$$dn.S_{2,up.up}\{dn.h/h\}$$

where the substitution in $S_{2,up.up}$ yields a formula which is equivalent to $S_{2,up}$. Thus by the logic and context rule this step can be rephrased as

$$S_{2,up.up} \tag{5.23}$$
$$|||$$
$$dn.S_{2,up}.$$

Combining (5.21) and (5.23) by the context rule yields the construction

$$S_{2,up} \tag{5.24}$$
$$|||$$
$$dn.S_2 + up.S_{2,up.up}$$
$$|||$$
$$dn.S_2 + up.dn.S_{2,up}.$$

Thus we have discovered a recursive semantic equation for $S_{2,up}$. Let $Y$ be a process identifier with $\alpha(Y)=\{up,dn\}$. Since $\mu Y.dn.S_2 + up.dn.Y$ is communication-guarded, the recursion and transitivity rule allow us to extend the construction (5.24) as follows:

$$S_{2,up} \tag{5.25}$$

$$|||$$

$$dn.S_2 + up.S_{2,up.up}$$

$$|||$$

$$dn.S_2 + up.dn.S_{2,up}$$

$$|||$$

$$\mu Y.(dn.S_2 + up.dn.Y).$$

Note that this last construction step has delivered a mixed term containing the original trace specification $S_2$. Hence combining (5.19) and (5.25) by the context and transitivity rule yields a second recursive equation, viz:

$$S_2 \tag{5.26}$$

$$|||$$

$$up.\mu Y.(dn.S_2 + up.dn.Y).$$

Let $X$ be a process identifier with alphabet $\alpha(X)=\{up,dn\}$. Then a final application of the recursion rule together with the transitivity rule yields:

$$S_2 \tag{5.27}$$

$$|||$$

$$up.\mu Y.(dn.S_2 + up.dn.Y)$$

$$|||$$

$$\mu X.up.\mu Y.(dn.X + up.dn.Y).$$

Thus starting from $S_2$ we have systematically constructed the process term

$$P =_{df} \mu X.up.\mu Y.(dn.X + up.dn.Y)$$

considered in Example 4.3.7.

   $P$ contains a nested recursion, but we can also construct a process term with a single recursion. Since our transformation rules are compositional, its construction can reuse large parts of the construction of $P$. In fact, until step (5.24) the construction is identical to that of $P$. But then we replace $S_2$ in (5.24) using the previous step (5.19). Hence we obtain the construction

$$S_{2,up} \tag{5.28}$$

$$|||$$

$$dn.S_2 + up.S_{2,up.up}$$

$$|||$$

$$dn.S_2 + up.dn.S_{2,up}$$

$$|||$$

$$dn.up.S_{2,up} + up.dn.S_{2,up}$$

resulting in another recursive equation for $S_{2,up}$. Using the recursion and transitivity rule we can extend this construction as follows:

$$S_{2,up} \tag{5.29}$$

$$|||$$

$$dn.S_2 + up.S_{2,up.up}$$

$$|||$$

$$dn.S_2 + up.dn.S_{2,up}$$

$$|||$$

$$dn.up.S_{2,up} + up.dn.S_{2,up}$$

$$|||$$

$$\mu X.(dn.up.X + up.dn.X).$$

Finally combining (5.19) and (5.29) delivers

$$S_2$$

$$|||$$

$$up.\mu X.(dn.up.X + up.dn.X).$$

Thus we have constructed the process term

$$R =_{df} up.\mu X.(dn.up.X + up.dn.X)$$

satisfying $S_2$.

Let us compare the processes $P$ and $R$ on the level of nets. Recall from Example 4.3.7 that $P$ denotes the following abstract net:

It thus consists of two copies of $\mathcal{N}[\![P_1]\!]$ of the previous example sharing a place. The abstract net of R contains one place more:

$$\mathcal{N}[\![R]\!] =$$

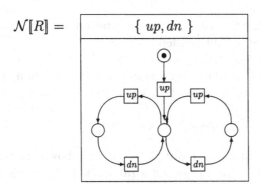

Thus as an implementation of $S_2$, the process term $P$ denoting $\mathcal{N}[\![P]\!]$ is preferable.

□

In the previous two examples process terms satisfying trace specifications were constructed in a rather mechanical way which we shall call the *expansion strategy*.

The basic idea of this strategy is as follows. Given a trace specification $S$ use the rules for deadlock, prefix and expansion to explore the initial communications of $S$ and generate an equation of the form

$$stop{:}A \equiv S \text{ or } \sum_{i=1}^{n} a_i.S_i \equiv S$$

Repeat this for all newly generated trace specifications $S_i$ until each of these new $S_i$ is semantically equivalent to a previously encountered specification. This repetition terminates provided the trace set of the original specification is *regular* in the sense of formal language theory [HU69]. Then we use the equation and specification rules to substitute the above equations into each other to obtain finitely many equations

$$P\{S/X\} \equiv S$$

which are solved one by one using the recursion rule. This yields a process term satisfying the original trace specification. We give full details of the expansion strategy in Section 5.7.

Here we make the following remark. Since every process term $P$ constructed by the expansion strategy involves only deadlock, prefix, choice and expansion, it is regular in the sense of Definition 3.5.3 and hence denotes a finite abstract net $\mathcal{N}[\![P]\!]$ by Theorem 3.5.5. Moreover, since $P$ does not involve parallelism, the net $\mathcal{N}[\![P]\!]$ is just an automaton in the sense of Remark 2.2.2. Hence there is no concurrency possible. Viewed as implementations process terms without parallelism are often undesirable, not only because they lack concurrency and hence run at reduced speed, but also because they lack modularity. By *modularity* we mean here that large process terms are constructed by combining sufficiently many copies of very few elementary component processes in parallel. Notice that modularity is also an essential aim in the construction of systolic VLSI systems.

In the following we shall see several examples of such modular constructions. The use of parallelism can even be necessary, viz. when constructing a process term for a specification of a non-regular trace set. As an illustration we shall consider in Example 5.3.4 the specification of an unbounded counter.

**Example 5.3.3** $k$-**Counters**. We explain now a systematic construction of bounded counters of capacity $k$. Recall from Example 4.3.7 that for $k \geq 1$ the specification is

$$S_k =_{df} 0 \leq up\#h - dn\#h \leq k.$$

For $k=1$ we take the process term $P_1$ of Example 5.3.1. As shown there, we have $P_1 \equiv S_1$ . For $k \geq 2$ we could use the expansion strategy as in Example 5.3.2 and produce for each $S_k$ a process term involving only prefix, choice and recursion.

However, we wish to proceed differently here and construct a process term $P_k$ with

$$P_k \equiv S_k$$

in a modular fashion from $k$ copies of $P_1$. We proceed by induction on $k$ where in the induction step $P_k$ is obtained from $P_{k-1}$ and $P_1$ by a *hierarchical construction* involving parallelism, disjoint renaming and hiding. The essence of the induction step can be conveniently expressed using mixed terms: we wish to deduce the equation

$$(S_{k-1}[lk/dn] \| S_1[lk/up]) \backslash lk \equiv S_k \tag{5.30}$$

with the transformation rules. The new communication $lk$ serves to synchronise the components $S_{k-1}$ and $S_1$ appropriately. Once its synchronisation purpose is fulfilled, $lk$ is turned into an internal action by the hiding operator. So let us fix some $k \geq 2$ . At first we look for a trace specification $S$ with

$$S_k = 0 \leq up\#h - dn\#h \leq k \tag{5.31}$$

$$\|\|$$

$$S\backslash lk \ .$$

We obtain $S$ by using the hidden communication $lk$ to split $S_k$ into a conjunction of two conditions:

$$S =_{df} \quad 0 \leq up\#h - lk\#h \leq k-1 \tag{5.32}$$

$$\wedge \quad 0 \leq lk\#h - dn\#h \leq 1. \tag{5.33}$$

To verify (5.31), we have to check the premises of the hiding rule. Obviously, $\varepsilon \models S$ and $\models S \longrightarrow S_k$ and $lk \models \neg S$. Thus the premises "empty trace", "logical implication" and "stability" are satisfied. By condition (5.33), it is not possible to extend a trace $tr \models S$ by arbitrarily many communications $lk$. Hence the premise "divergence freedom" is also satisfied. In most applications of the hiding rule the checking of these four premises is equally simple.

More tedious is the checking of the premise "same liveness". So consider a trace $tr \in \{up, lk, dn\}$ with $tr \models S$ and $tr.lk \models \neg S$. Then

$$lk\#tr = up\#tr \text{ or } lk\#tr = dn\#tr + 1. \tag{5.34}$$

We have to show that for every communication $c \in \alpha(S_k)$ whenever $tr.c \models S_k$ then also $tr.c \models S$. Since $\alpha(S_k) = \{up, dn\}$, this amounts to checking two cases.

*Case 1*: Suppose $tr.up \models S_k$. Then

$$up\#tr - dn\#tr < k. \tag{5.35}$$

If now $up\#tr - lk\#tr < k-1$ then clearly $tr.up \models S$ by condition (5.32) of $S$ and the assumption $tr \models S$. If, however, $up\#tr - lk\#tr = k-1$, then $lk\#tr = dn\#tr + 1$ by (5.34) and hence $up\#tr - dn\#tr = k$ which contradicts (5.35). Hence this subcase cannot arise.

*Case 2*: Suppose $tr.dn \models S_k$. Then

$$0 < up\#tr - dn\#tr. \tag{5.36}$$

If $0 < lk\#tr - dn\#tr$ then $tr.dn \models S$ by condition (5.33) of $S$ and $tr \models S$. If, however, $0 = lk\#tr - dn\#tr$, then $lk\#tr = up\#tr$ by (5.34) and hence $0 = up\#tr - dn\#tr$ which contradicts (5.36). Hence this subcase cannot arise either. Thus the construction step (5.31) is justified by the hiding rule.

For the subsequent step we introduce names for the two conditions of $S$:

$$
\begin{aligned}
T_{k-1} &=_{df} 0 \le up\#h - lk\#h \le k-1, \\
U_1 &=_{df} 0 \le lk\#h - dn\#h \le 1.
\end{aligned}
$$

Then by the parallelism rule we obtain

$$
\begin{array}{c}
S \\
||| \\
T_{k-1} \parallel U_1
\end{array}
\tag{5.37}
$$

and by the disjoint renaming rule

$$
\begin{array}{ccc}
T_{k-1} & & U_1 \\
||| & \text{and} & ||| \\
S_{k-1}[lk/dn] & & S_1[lk/up].
\end{array}
\tag{5.38}
$$

Combining (5.31) – (5.38) by the context rule we obtain

$$
\begin{array}{c}
S_k \\
||| \\
S \backslash lk \\
||| \\
(T_{k-1} \parallel U_1) \backslash lk \\
||| \\
(S_{k-1}[lk/dn] \parallel S_1[lk/up]) \backslash lk
\end{array}
\tag{5.39}
$$

and hence by the transitivity rule the desired equation (5.30).

Using (5.30) it is now a straightforward exercise to construct inductively the desired process terms $P_k$ with $P_k \equiv S_k$.

$k = 1$: $P_1 =_{df} \mu X.up.dn.X$ as in Example 5.3.1.

As induction hypothesis we suppose that $P_{k-1}$ has already been constructed. $k - 1 \longrightarrow k$: Then we construct $P_k$ as follows:

$$S_k$$
$$|||$$
$$(S_{k-1}[lk/dn] \parallel S_1[lk/up])\backslash lk$$
$$|||$$
$$(P_{k-1}[lk/dn] \parallel P_1[lk/up])\backslash lk.$$

Thus we define

$$P_k =_{df} (P_{k-1}[lk/dn] \parallel P_1[lk/up])\backslash lk.$$

For $k=2$, the process term $P_2$ is identical to the term $Q$ considered in Example 4.7.2. Hence the abstract net denoted by $P_2$ can be found there. For $k=3$, the abstract net denoted by $P_3$ is as follows:

$\mathcal{N}[\![P_3]\!] =$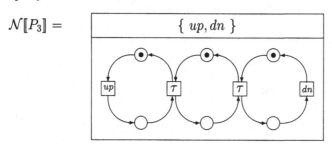

Thus in general, $P_k$ denotes a net consisting of $k$ copies of the net of $P_1$ which work in parallel and synchronise with each other by a hidden communication. At each reachable marking of the net at most two transitions are currently enabled.     □

**Example 5.3.4 Unbounded Counter.** This is our last example dealing with counters. We consider the trace specification

$$S_\infty =_{df} dn\#h \leq up\#h$$

of an unbounded counter. Already in Examples 3.5.2 and 4.3.8 we have seen the process term

$$P_\infty =_{df} \mu X.up.(X[lk/dn] \parallel \mu Y.dn.lk.Y)\backslash lk$$

of which we claimed that it models an unbounded counter. We verify this claim now by showing that indeed

$$P_\infty \equiv S_\infty.$$

Hence this is a verification example where the process term is known beforehand. As stated in Section 5.1, we view verification as a special case of construction where at each step it is clear which process operator should be extracted next from the trace specifications.

Since $init(S_\infty) = \{up\}$, the prefix rule together with the logic and context rule yields

$$S_\infty \tag{5.40}$$
$$|||$$
$$up.S_{up}$$

as the first construction step where

$$S_{up} =_{df} dn\#h \leq 1 + up\#h.$$

$S_{up}$ allows all the $up$'s and $dn$'s of $S_\infty$, but additionally requires one more $dn$. To deal with $S_{up}$, we split this specification into a conjunction of three conditions using $lk$ as an auxiliary communication. This leads us to consider the following trace specification $S$:

$$S =_{df} \quad lk\#h \leq up\#h \tag{5.41}$$
$$\wedge \quad dn\#h \leq 1 + lk\#h \tag{5.42}$$
$$\wedge \quad lk\#h \leq dn\#h. \tag{5.43}$$

Line (5.41) specifies a renamed copy of $S_\infty$. Line (5.42) specifies a renamed copy of $S_{up}$, however, one where the number of $lk$'s is bounded by the number of $dn$'s according to line (5.43).

By the hiding rule, we obtain

$$S_{up} \tag{5.44}$$
$$|||$$
$$S \backslash lk.$$

Indeed, the first four premises of the hiding rule are established easily (cf. Example 5.3.3). To check the premise "same liveness" consider a trace $tr \in \{up, lk, dn\}$ with $tr \models S$ and $tr.lk \models \neg S$. Then

$$lk\#tr = min\{up\#tr, dn\#tr\} \tag{5.45}$$

by condition (5.41) and (5.43) of $S$. We have to show that for every communication $c \in \alpha(S_{up})$ whenever $tr.c \models S_{up}$ then also $tr.c \models S$. Since $\alpha(S_{up}) = \{up, dn\}$, we have to check two cases.

*Case 1: $c = up$*
Since $tr \models S$ always implies $tr.up \models S$, the additional assumptions are not needed in this case.

*Case 2: $c = dn$*
If $tr.dn \models S_{up}$ then by definition

$$dn\#tr < 1 + up\#tr \tag{5.46}$$

If $dn\#tr < 1 + lk\#tr$ then also $tr.dn \models S$ by condition (5.42) of $S$ and $tr \models S$. If, however, $dn\#tr = 1 + lk\#tr$, then $lk\#tr = up\#tr$ by (5.45) and hence $dn\#tr = 1 + up\#tr$ which contradicts (5.46). Hence this subcase cannot arise.

Thus the application of the hiding rule in Step (5.44) is justified. Next we apply the parallelism rule to $S$ and obtain

$$S \tag{5.47}$$
$$|||$$
$$T \parallel U$$

where $T$ and $U$ denote the following parts of $S$:

$$\begin{aligned} T =_{df} \quad & lk\#h \leq up\#h, \\ U =_{df} \quad & dn\#h \leq 1 + lk\#h \\ \wedge \quad & lk\#h \leq dn\#h. \end{aligned}$$

Using the disjoint renaming rule and the logic rule we obtain

$$\begin{array}{ccc} T & & U \\ ||| & \text{and} & ||| \\ S_\infty[lk/dn] & & 0 \leq dn\#h - lk\#h \leq 1. \end{array} \tag{5.48}$$

Combining (5.40)–(5.48) with the context rule, we have the following construction:

$$S_\infty \tag{5.49}$$
$$|||$$
$$up.S_{up}$$
$$|||$$
$$up.S\backslash lk$$
$$|||$$
$$up.(T\|U)\backslash lk$$
$$|||$$
$$up.(S_\infty[lk/dn] \parallel 0 \leq dn\#h - lk\#h \leq 1)\backslash lk.$$

Thus we have deduced a recursive semantic equation for $S_\infty$. Since the condition of communication-guardedness is met, the recursion and the transitivity rule yield

$$S_\infty \tag{5.50}$$
$$|||$$
$$\mu X.up.(X[lk/dn] \parallel 0 \leq dn\#h - lk\#h \leq 1)\backslash lk.$$

Note that $0 \leq dn\#h - lk\#h \leq 1$ is a renamed copy of the 1-counter specification considered in Example 4.7.1. Hence we can deduce

$$0 \leq dn\#h - lk\#h \leq 1 \tag{5.51}$$
$$|||$$
$$\mu Y.dn.lk.Y$$

in the same way as in that example. Finally, combining (5.50) and (5.51) by the context rule proves that

$$P_\infty = \mu X.up.(X[lk/dn] \parallel \mu Y.dn.lk.Y)\backslash lk$$

satisfies the desired equation $P_\infty \equiv S_\infty$.

$P_\infty$ is a fairly elaborate process term due to Hoare where recursion is applied on top of a hierarchical construction involving parallelism, disjoint renaming and hiding. Such sophistication is needed here because $S_\infty$ describes a non-regular set of traces. In particular, the simple expansion strategy with prefix, choice and recursion as used in the first examples would not produce any process term for $S_\infty$. On the other hand, the actual manipulation with the non-regular trace specification $S_\infty$ was equally simple as with the previous regular specification $S_k$. As we have seen in Examples 3.5.2 and 4.3.8, $P_\infty$ denotes the following abstract net:

$$\mathcal{N}[\![P_\infty]\!] =$$
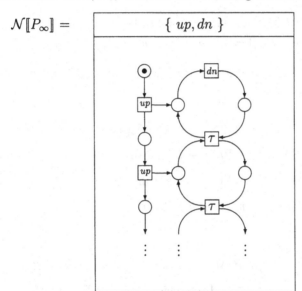

By successive activation of the transitions labelled with $up$, unboundedly many tokens are generated in this net. However, at most two transitions, viz. one $up$ and one $dn$ or one $up$ and one $\tau$, are concurrently enabled at each reachable marking. □

## 5.4   Binary Variable

A binary variable stores one of the values 0 or 1 at any moment of time. We assume that its initial value is 0. The current value can be read by testing whether it is 0 or 1. This is done by two read instructions $r0$ and $r1$. The instruction $r0$ is enabled only if the variable stores the value 0, and analogously for $r1$. The value of the variable can be changed by two write instructions $w0$ and $w1$. The instruction $w0$ sets the value to 0, and analogously for $w1$.

Viewing the instructions $r0$, $r1$, $w0$ and $w1$ as comunications, and using the abbreviations $RW = \{r0,r1,w0,w1\}$ and $W = \{w0,w1\}$, we can specify a binary variable in trace logic:

$$BIN0 =_{df} \qquad (last\ h{\downarrow}RW = r0 \longrightarrow last\ (w0.h{\downarrow}W) = w0) \qquad (5.52)$$
$$\wedge \quad (last\ h{\downarrow}RW = r1 \longrightarrow last\ h{\downarrow}W = w1). \qquad (5.53)$$

Thus if the last read is $r0$ then the last write must be $w0$. Note that the initialisation with 0 is represented in line (5.52) by the extra write $w0$ preceding $h{\downarrow}W$. If the last read is $r1$ then the last write must be $w1$. The write communications $w0$ and $w1$ are always possible. This specification is essentially due to Hoare [Hoa85b].

We now construct two different implementations of $BIN0$ using terms and nets, one sequential and the other concurrent. The sequential implementation is constructed simply by applying the expansion strategy. Let

$$BIN1 =_{df} \qquad (last\ h{\downarrow}RW = r0 \longrightarrow last\ h{\downarrow}W = w0)$$
$$\wedge \quad (last\ h{\downarrow}RW = r1 \longrightarrow last\ (w1.h{\downarrow}W) = w1)$$

by the trace specification of a binary variable with initial value 1. Then we obtain

$$BIN1$$

$$||| \ \{\text{expansion, logic and context}\}$$

$$r1.BIN1 + w1.BIN1 + w0.BIN0$$

$$||| \ \{\text{recursion and transitivity}\}$$

$$\mu Y.(r1.Y + w1.Y + w0.BIN0)$$

and hence

$$BIN0$$

$$||| \ \{\text{expansion, logic and context}\}$$

$$r0.BIN0 + w0.BIN0 + w1.BIN1$$

$$||| \ \{\text{context and transitivity}\}$$

$$r0.BIN0 + w0.BIN0$$

$$+ \ w1.\mu Y.(r1.Y + w1.Y + w0.BIN0)$$

$$||| \ \{\text{recursion and transitivity}\}$$

$$\mu X.(\ r0.X + w0.X$$

$$+ \ w1.\mu Y.(r1.Y + w1.Y + w0.X))$$

where $\alpha(X) = \alpha(Y) = RW$. Thus we have constructed

$$\mu X.(\ r0.X + w0.X$$
$$+ \ w1.\mu Y.(r1.Y + w1.Y + w0.X))$$

as a process term satisfying *BIN0*. This term denotes the following net:

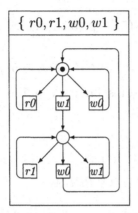

The marked place represents the value 0 and the other one the value 1. The dynamic behaviour of the net is purely sequential because every reachable marking has exactly one token.

We now present a second implementation of *BIN0* where some concurrency is possible. First note that a direct application of the parallelism rule to *BIN0* is possible and yields

$$(5.52) \parallel (5.53) \equiv BIN0$$

where (5.52) and (5.53) are the two conditions of *BIN0*. However, since (5.52) and (5.53) are trace specifications with the same alphabet, the definition of parallel composition enforces full synchrony and hence does not lead to any concurrency in the resulting net.

Nevertheless we can achieve a concurrent implementation of *BIN0* by a somewhat more elaborate construction using the general renaming rule. The idea is to distinguish between two different kinds of write communications: those which *change* the value stored by the variable and those which *preserve* the existing value. Then preserving writes can occur concurrently with read communications.

Thus we shall describe the internal behaviour of a binary variable in more detail. To this end, we introduce two new communications $c0$ and $c1$ for writes that change the value of the variable to 0 and 1, respectively. We abbreviate $C = \{c0,c1\}$, $CR = \{c0,c1,r0,r1\}$ and $CW = \{c0,c1,w0,w1\}$. The communications $w0$ and $w1$ are only used for preserving writes. Since changes occur alternatively, this leads to the following specification of the internal behaviour of a binary variable initialised with 0:

$$
\begin{aligned}
INTBIN0 =_{df} \quad & 0 \leq c1\#h - c0\#h \leq 1 & (5.54) \\
\wedge \quad & (last\ h{\downarrow}CR = r0 \longrightarrow last\ (c0.h{\downarrow}C) = c0) & (5.55) \\
\wedge \quad & (last\ h{\downarrow}CR = r1 \longrightarrow last\ h{\downarrow}C = c1) & (5.56) \\
\wedge \quad & (last\ h{\downarrow}CW = w0 \longrightarrow last\ (c0.h{\downarrow}C) = c0) & (5.57) \\
\wedge \quad & (last\ h{\downarrow}CW = w1 \longrightarrow last\ h{\downarrow}C = c1) & (5.58)
\end{aligned}
$$

The new specification *INTBIN0* can be successfully decomposed by the parallelism rule. Let

$$READ0 =_{df} (5.54) \wedge (5.55) \wedge (5.56)$$

and

$$PRES0 =_{df} (5.54) \wedge (5.57) \wedge (5.58)$$

with (5.54)–(5.58) referring to the corresponding conditions in *INTBIN0*. Then we obtain

$$INTBIN0 \tag{5.59}$$

$$|||$$

$$READ0 \parallel PRES0.$$

Process terms for *READ0* and *PRES0* can be easily constructed by the expansion strategy:

$$READ0 \tag{5.60}$$

$$|||$$

$$\mu XR.(r0.XR + c1.\mu YR.(r1.YR + c0.XR))$$

and

$$PRES0 \tag{5.61}$$

$$|||$$

$$\mu XW.(w0.XW + c1.\mu YW.(w1.YW + c0.XW))$$

where $\alpha(XR) = \alpha(YR) = CR$ and $\alpha(XW) = \alpha(YW) = CW$. Since the alphabets of *READ0* and *PRES0* intersect only on $C$, the parallel composition of *READ0* and *PRES0* allows asynchrony between $w0,w1$ and $r0,r1$ and thus concurrency in the resulting net. In this way we obtain a concurrent implementation for *INTBIN0*, but not for the original specification *BIN0*.

However, *BIN0* can be obtained from *INTBIN0* by just "forgetting" that some writes are called $c0$ and $c1$. Formally, this is done by renaming. We claim that

$$BIN0 \tag{5.62}$$

$$|||$$

$$INTBIN0[w0, w1/c0, c1].$$

Since this renaming is not disjoint, we have to check the more difficult premises of the general renaming rule. Fortunately, this is easily done once we have shown that the renaming is a bijection. To this end, we introduce the trace sets

$$\Gamma = \{tr \in (CR \cup CW)^* \mid tr \models INTBIN0\}$$

and

$$\Delta = \{tr' \in RW^* \mid tr' \models BIN0\}$$

and the mapping $\beta : \Gamma \longrightarrow \Delta$ by

$$\beta(tr) = tr\{w0, w1/c0, c1\}.$$

We show that $\beta$ is a bijection.

(i) $\beta$ *is well-defined*: For every $tr \in \Gamma$ the conditions (5.54)–(5.58) of *INTBIN0* imply that $\beta(tr)$ satisfies the conditions (5.52)–(5.53) of *BIN0*.

(ii) $\beta$ *is surjective*: Given a trace $tr' \in \Delta$ construct $tr$ by renaming every first write $w0$ or $w1$ of a new value in the extended trace $w0.tr'$ into $c0$ or $c1$, respectively, and then deleting the leading communication $c0$. For example,

$$tr' = r0.w0.w1.r1.w1.w1.w0.w0$$

yields

$$tr = r0.w0.c1.r1.w1.w1.c0.w0.$$

Then $tr \in \Gamma$ and $\beta(tr) = tr'$.

(iii) $\beta$ *is injective*: This follows from the fact that the pre-image $tr$ of a trace $tr'$ under $\beta$ is uniquely determined by $tr'$, viz. as explained in (ii).

Now the premises of the renaming rule are easily established. The premise "same traces" follows from the fact that $\beta$ is well-defined and surjective, and the premise "same liveness" follows from the fact that $\beta$ is injective. This verifies the chained relationship (5.62) between *BIN0* and *INTBIN0*.

Putting (5.59)–(5.62) together by the context rule yields our second construction of a process term satisfying *BIN0*:

$$BIN0$$
$$|||$$
$$INTBIN0[w0,w1/c0,c1]$$
$$|||$$
$$(READ0 \parallel PRES0) \, [w0,w1/c0,c1]$$
$$|||$$

$$\begin{aligned}
( \quad &\mu XR.(r0.XR + c1.\mu YR.(r1.YR + c0.XR)) \\
&\parallel \mu XW.(w0.XW + c1.\mu YW.(w1.YW + c0.XW)) \\
) \quad &[w0, w1/c0, c1].
\end{aligned}$$

This term denotes the following abstract net:

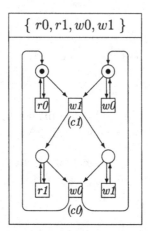

The transitions whose labels are introduced by the renaming are indicated by $(c1)$ and $(c0)$. This implementation allows the concurrent activation of reads and preserving writes.

## 5.5   Scheduling Problem

In his books on CCS, Milner considers a small scheduling problem ([Mil80], Chapter 3 and 10, and [Mil89], Sections 5.4, 5.5 and 11.3). Specification and implementation are described by CCS process terms; the proof that the implementation meets the specification is purely algebraic, i.e. by application of the algebraic rules of CCS. In [Mil80], Milner also gives an informal Petri net semantics of his implementation. Milner's example provides a very good illustration of our approach of relating three views of concurrent processes: we start from a trace specification and systematically construct three alternative process term implementations, one of them corresponding to Milner's solution in CCS. For each of the constructed process terms we examine its Petri net semantics.

Since we use COSY's parallel operator, our term construction and the resulting Petri net solution turns out to be simpler than Milner's CCS solution.

In trace logic Milner's scheduling problem can be stated as follows:

$$SPEC_k =_{df} \quad \bigwedge_{i=1}^{k} h{\downarrow}\{a_i, b_i\} \in pref(a_i.b_i)^*$$
$$\wedge \quad h{\downarrow}\{a_1, \ldots, a_k\} \in pref(a_1 \ldots a_k)^*$$

where $k \geq 1$. Thus we use here regular expressions to specify a process that can engage in communications $a_1, \ldots, a_k$ and $b_1, \ldots, b_k$. When observed through the window $\{a_i, b_i\}$ the process engages in a small cycle $a_i b_i$ and when observed through the window $\{a_1, \ldots, a_k\}$ it engages in a large cycle $a_1 \ldots a_k$. There are no further restrictions imposed on the communication behaviour of the process.

Recall that regular expressions are considered here as abbreviations. Given a regular expression $re$, we defined

$$tr \downarrow \alpha(re) \in re =_{df} TRACE(re)$$

where $TRACE(re)$ is the trace specification introduced in Section 4.2. However, for the simple type of regular expressions occuring in $SPEC_k$, the formula $TRACE(re)$ is much too cumbersome. We shall therefore use a simpler representation. Consider for distinct communications $c_1, \ldots, c_n$ the trace specification

$$S =_{df} tr\!\downarrow\!\{c_1, \ldots, c_n\} \in pref(c_1, \ldots, c_n)^*$$

and

$$T =_{df} c_n\#h \leq \ldots \leq c_1\#h \leq 1 + c_n\#h.$$

Since $\alpha(S) = \alpha(T)$ and $\models S \leftrightarrow kern(T)$, the kernel and logic rule yield

$$S \equiv T. \tag{5.63}$$

Thus we obtain

$$SPEC_k \equiv \bigwedge_{i=1}^{k} b_i\#h \leq a_i\#h \leq 1 + b_i\#h$$
$$\wedge \quad a_k\#h \leq \ldots \leq a_1\#h \leq 1 + a_k\#h.$$

We find regular expressions easier to read, but inequalities between the number of occurrences of certain communications easier to calculate with. We now present three different constructions of process terms from $SPEC_k$.

*First construction.* Since $SPEC_k$ describes a regular set of traces, the expansion strategy is succesful. For $k=1$ this strategy yields a copy of a 1-counter:

$$SPEC_1$$
$$|||$$
$$a_1.SPEC_1\{a_1.h/h\}$$
$$|||$$
$$a_1.b_1.SPEC_1$$
$$|||$$
$$\mu X_1.a_1.b_1.X_1.$$

This term denotes a simple cyclic net as in Example 5.3.1. However, already for $k=2$ things get much more complicated. As process term we obtain:

$$SPEC_2$$
$$|||$$
$$\mu X_2.a_1.\mu Y_2.(b_1.\mu Z_2.a_2.(b_2.X_2$$
$$+ a_1.(b_2.Y_2$$
$$+ b_1.b_2.Z_2)$$
$$)$$
$$+ a_2.(b_2.b_1.X_2$$
$$+ b_1.\mu V_2.(b_2.X_2$$
$$+ a_1.(b_2.Y_2$$
$$+ b_1.b_2.V_2)$$
$$)$$
$$)$$
$$).$$

Modulo strong bisimilarity the abstract net denoted this term is:

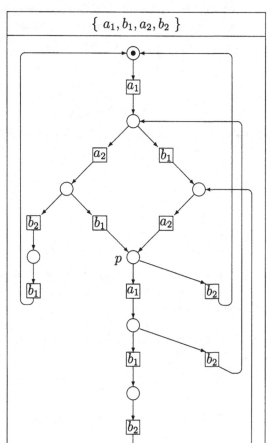

Strong bisimilarity allowed us to share two identical substructures starting in place $p$. This just simplifies the representation of the net.

In general, the expansion strategy leads to nets whose structure is difficult to grasp, but the number of places grows exponentially with $k$. To reduce this number, we consider another construction involving parallelism.

*Second construction.* Since $SPEC_k$ is given as a conjunction of several conditions, the application of the parallelism is straightforward. Define

$$PROC_i =_{df} h{\downarrow}\{a_i, b_i\} \in \mathit{pref}(a_i.b_i)^*$$

for $i=1,\dots,k$ and

$$SCH_k =_{df} h{\downarrow}\{a_1, \dots, a_k\} \in \mathit{pref}(a_1 \dots a_k)^*$$

standing for "process $i$" and "scheduler of size $k$". Then by successive applications of the parallelism rule, we obtain:

$$SPEC_k \tag{5.64}$$
$$|||$$
$$(\|_{i=1}^{k} PROC_i) \| SCH_k.$$

Process terms satisfying the specifications $PROC_i$ and $SCH_k$ are constructed by the expansion strategy. We record only the results of these constructions:

$$\begin{array}{ccc} PROC_i & & SCH_k \\ ||| & \text{and} & ||| \\ \mu XX_i.a_i.b_i.XX_i & & \mu YY_k.a_1\ldots a_k.YY_k \end{array} \tag{5.65}$$

where $\alpha(XX_i) = \{a_i,b_i\}$ and $\alpha(YY_i) = \{a_1,\ldots,a_k\}$.  Combining (5.64) and (5.65) completes the second construction:

$$SPEC_k$$
$$|||$$
$$(\ \|_{i=1}^{k} PROC_i\ ) \| SCH_k$$
$$|||$$
$$(\ \|_{i=1}^{k} \mu XX_i.a_i.b_i.XX_i) \| \mu YY_k.a_1\ldots a_k.YY_k.$$

For $k=3$, the constructed process term denotes the following abstract net:

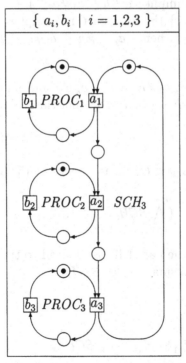

The annotation indicates which cycles in the net implement the specifications $PROC_i$ and $SCH_3$. Note that a concurrent activation of the transitions labeled by $b_i$ is possible. For arbitrary $k$, the net has only $3k$ places. The drawback of this implementation is that for each $k$ a new scheduler $SCH_k$ is needed. We overcome this drawback in our last construction yielding an implementation corresponding to Milner's own solution.

*Third construction.* Milner's aim was a *modular* scheduler which for arbitrary problem size could be built as a "ring of elementary identical components" [Mil80]. This idea can be realised very neatly using transformations on mixed terms. The point is to break down the large cycle $a_1 \ldots a_k$ of $SCH_k$ into $k+1$ cycles of size 2, viz. $a_1 a_2$, $a_2 a_3$, $\ldots$, $a_{k-1} a_k$ and $a_1 a_k$.

Formally, this idea is justified by simple calculations with inequalities based on the representation (5.63) of cyclic regular expressions. Represent the large cycle $a_1 \ldots a_k$ by

$$CYC_k =_{df} a_k \#h \leq \ldots \leq a_1 \#h \leq 1 + a_k \#h$$

and for $1 \leq i < j \leq k$ represent a cycle $a_i a_j$ by

$$SCH_{i,j} =_{df} a_j \#h \leq a_i \#h \leq 1 + a_j \#h.$$

We show the logical equivalence

$$\models CYC_k \leftrightarrow (\bigwedge_{i=1}^{k-1} SCH_{i,i+1}) \wedge SCH_{1,k}. \tag{5.66}$$

*Implication "→":* Clearly, $CYC_k$ implies $a_k \#h \leq a_1 \#h \leq 1 + a_k \#h$, which is $SCH_{1,k}$. Furthermore, for $i \in \{1,\ldots,k-1\}$ the formula $CYC_k$ implies $a_k \#h \leq a_{i+1} \#h$ and $a_{i+1} \#h \leq a_i \#h \leq 1 + a_k \#h$ and hence $a_{i+1} \#h \leq a_i \#h \leq 1 + a_{i+1} \#h$, which is $SCH_{i+1}$.

*Implication "←":* $SCH_{1,k}$ implies $a_1 \#h \leq 1 + a_k \#h$ and for $i \in \{1,\ldots,k-1\}$ the formula $SCH_{i,i+1}$ implies $a_{i+1} \#h \leq a_i \#h$. Together this yields the chain of inequalities in $CYC_k$.

By (5.63) above, we have $SCH_k \equiv CYC_k$ and hence by (5.66), the logic rule yields

$$SCH_k \equiv (\bigwedge_{i=1}^{k-1} SCH_{i,i+1}) \wedge SCH_{1,k}.$$

Thus successive applications of the parallelism rule lead to the following decomposition of the large cycle $SCH_k$ into small cycles $SCH_{i,j}$:

$$SCH_k \tag{5.67}$$
$$|||$$
$$(\|_{i=1}^{k} SCH_{i,i+1}) \| SCH_{1,k}.$$

Combining (5.67) with (5.64) of the previous construction we obtain:

$$SPEC_k \tag{5.68}$$
$$|||$$
$$(\|_{i=1}^{k} PROC_i) \| SCH_k$$
$$|||$$
$$(\|_{i=1}^{k} PROC_i) \| (\|_{i=1}^{k-1} SCH_{i,i+1}) \| SCH_{1,k}.$$

Note that each of the specifications $SCH_{i,j}$ is equivalent to

$$0 \le a_i \# h - a_j \# h \le 1.$$

Moreover, by (5.63) of the specifications $PROC_i$ is equivalent to

$$0 \le a_i \# h - b_i \# h \le 1$$

Thus $SCH_{i,j}$ and $PROC_i$ are all renamed copies of the 1-counter specified by

$$S_1 =_{df} 0 \le up\#h - dn\#h \le 1$$

in Example 4.7.1. Formally,

$$PROC_i \qquad\qquad SCH_{i,j}$$
$$||| \qquad \text{and} \qquad ||| \tag{5.69}$$
$$S_1[a_i, b_i/up, dn] \qquad S_1[a_i, a_j/up, dn]$$

by the logic and disjoint renaming rule. Recall from Example 4.7.1 that

$$\mu X.up.dn.X \equiv S_1. \tag{5.70}$$

Thus combining (5.68)–(5.70) we obtain the following process term satisfying $SPEC_k$:

$$(\|_{i=1}^{k} (\mu X.up.dn.X)[a_i, b_i/up, dn])$$
$$\| \quad (\|_{i=1}^{k-1} (\mu X.up.dn.X)[a_i, a_{i+1}/up, dn])$$
$$\| \quad (\mu X.up.dn.X)[a_1, a_k/up, dn].$$

It consists of the parallel composition of $2k$ copies of the 1-counter. For $k=4$ this term denotes the abstract net shown on the next page:

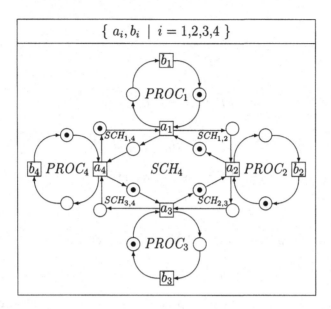

The annotation indicates the cycles that implement the specifications $PROC_i$. The rectangular part in the centre is the implementation of $SCH_4$ consisting of an appropriate synchronisation of the cycles $SCH_{1,2}$, $SCH_{2,3}$, $SCH_{3,4}$ and $SCH_{1,4}$. Note that the asymmetry in the initial token distribution is due to the cycle $SCH_{1,4}$. For arbitrary $k$ the net has $4k$ places. (The net given in [Mil80] needs $5k$ places.) Since only the part implementing the scheduler $SCH_k$ differs from the previous net implementation, concurrency of the $b_i$-transitions is still possible. We believe that this is an example where it is fairly difficult to get the net implementation right without the systematic guidance of formulas and terms.

## 5.6   Access Control

Consider a system consisting of readers and writers accessing a shared data structure. We wish to enforce certain access disciplines in this system. Verjus et al. have proposed solving this task in two steps [RV77, AHV85].

*Step 1:* Introduction of *FIFO* (first-in first-out) disciplines for readers and writers separately.

*Step 2:* Introduction of scheduling disciplines which define when the first reader in the *FIFO* queue is allowed to access the shared data structure.

Hence the whole system can be specified as a conjunction

$$SYS = READERS \land WRITERS \land FIFO \land SCH$$

of trace formulas describing the readers, the writers, the *FIFO* disciplines and the desired scheduling discipline separately. By the parallelism rule, a process term satisfying *SYS* can then be constructed as the parallel composition of process terms satisfying the individual conjuncts of *SYS*.

We shall treat here Step 2 dealing with the scheduler part *SCH*. Our presentation is based on [Old85] where also the rest of the system is dealt with (in a slightly extended syntax of trace formulas and process terms). In addition to [Old85], we study here the nets denoted by the constructed process terms.

Readers and writers are instances of a generic concept of a user. As far as the scheduling task is concerned, a user engages in the following three communications:

$$\left.\begin{array}{ll} r & \text{request} \\ a & \text{access} \\ t & \text{terminate} \end{array}\right\} \text{the use of the shared data.}$$

Whenever a user wants to access the shared data, it engages in the comunications $r,a$ and $t$ in that order. If the user is a reader, we write $rR$, $aR$ and $tR$ instead of $r,a$ and $t$, and if it is a writer, we write $rW,aW$ and $tW$. According to Step 1 above we imagine now that the names of readers and writers that have requested but not yet accessed the shared data are kept in two separate *FIFO* queues. For Step 2 we consider now three different scheduling disciplines for the case of $m>1$ readers and $n>1$ writers.

*First scheduler.* The first reader in the reader queue is allowed to access the shared data if no writer is active, and the first writer in the writer queue is allowed to access the shared data if no reader or writer is active. Thus any number of readers may access the shared data at a time, but only one writer.

In trace logic we express the number of active readers and writers by

$$\text{active}R =_{df} aR\#h - tR\#h$$

and

$$\text{active}W =_{df} aW\#h - tW\#h$$

and then consider the following specification:

$$
\begin{array}{llr}
SCH1_m =_{df} & 0 \leq \text{active}R \leq m & (5.71) \\
\wedge & 0 \leq \text{active}W \leq 1 & (5.72) \\
\wedge & (last\ h{\downarrow}\{aW,tW,aR\} = aR \longrightarrow \text{active}W = 0) & (5.73) \\
\wedge & (last\ h{\downarrow}\{aR,tR,aW\} = aW \longrightarrow \text{active}R = 0) & (5.74)
\end{array}
$$

Using the parallelism rule we decompose $SCH1_m$ as follows:

$$SCH1_m \qquad\qquad (5.75)$$
$$|||$$
$$A\_READ \parallel A\_WRITE$$

where $A\_READ =_{df}$ (5.71) $\wedge$ (5.74) deals with the active readers and $A\_WRITE =_{df}$ (5.72) $\wedge$ (5.73) deals with the active writers.

*A_READ* and *A_WRITE* are renamed copies of bounded counters with an additional test for zero. Using *up*, *dn* and *zero* as communications and $k>1$ as capacities, such a counter can be specified as follows:

$$COUNT_k =_{df} \quad 0 \le up\#h - dn\#h \le k$$
$$\wedge \quad (last\ h{\downarrow}\{up, dn, zero\} = zero \longrightarrow up\#h = dn\#h).$$

Thus by the logic and disjoint renaming rule, we obtain:

$$A\_READ \hspace{4cm} (5.76)$$
$$|||$$
$$COUNT_m[aR, tR, aW/up, dn, zero]$$

and

$$A\_WRITE \hspace{4cm} (5.77)$$
$$|||$$
$$COUNT_1[aW, tW, aR/up, dn, zero].$$

Next we obtain process terms for $COUNT_k$ using a hierarchical construction analogous to Example 5.3.3. For $k=1$ the expansion strategy yields that

$$Q_1 =_{df} \mu Z.(zero.Z + up.dn.Z)$$

satisfies $COUNT_1$. For $k>2$ we show inductively that

$$Q_k =_{df} (Q_{k-1}[lk/dn] \parallel Q_1[lk/up])\backslash lk \hspace{2cm} (5.78)$$

satisfies $COUNT_k$. Thus we have constructed a process term $Q_k$ with

$$Q_k \equiv COUNT_k \hspace{4cm} (5.79)$$

for each $k>1$. Combining the construction steps (5.75)–(5.77) and (5.79) we thus obtain

$$SCH1_m$$
$$|||$$
$$Q_m[aR, tW, aW/up, dn, zero]$$
$$\parallel Q_1[aW, tW, aR/up, dn, zero].$$

Thus using (5.78) the scheduler $SCH1_m$ is implemented in a modular fashion by $m+1$ copies of a 1-counter with zero-test.

For $m=2$ the net view of this implementation is as follows:

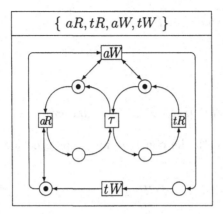

In this net double arrows $\leftrightarrow$ abbreviate cyclic transitions

 .

Note that the transitions $aR$ and $tR$ (of different readers) can be activated concurrently. For arbitrary $m$ the net consists of $2(m+1)$ places and $m+3$ transitions.

*Second Scheduler.* Now we wish to schedule readers and writers such that *priority* is given to the *readers*. Thus the first writer in the writer queue is allowed to access the shared data only if no reader is waiting in the reader queue.

Therefore we record the number of readers that have requested but not yet accessed the shared data by

$$requestR =_{df} rR\#h - aR\#h$$

and start from the following trace specification:

$$SCH2_m =_{df} \quad 0 \le requestR \le m \qquad\qquad (5.80)$$
$$\wedge \quad 0 \le activeR \le m \qquad\qquad (5.81)$$
$$\wedge \quad 0 \le activeW \le 1 \qquad\qquad (5.82)$$
$$\wedge \quad (last\ h{\downarrow}\{aW, tW, aR\} = aR \longrightarrow activeW = 0) \qquad (5.83)$$
$$\wedge \quad (last\ h{\downarrow}\{rR, aR, tR, aW\} = aW \longrightarrow$$
$$requestR = 0 \wedge activeR = 0). \qquad (5.84)$$

Note that condition (5.84) is logically equivalent to the conjunction of

$$last\ h{\downarrow}\{rR, aR, aW\} = aW \longrightarrow requestR = 0 \qquad (5.85)$$

and

$$last\ h{\downarrow}\{aR, tR, aW\} = aW \longrightarrow activeR = 0, \qquad (5.86)$$

each one with smaller projection alphabet than (5.84). Hence by using the logic and the parallelism rule we decompose $SCH2_m$ as follows:

$$SCH2_m \qquad\qquad (5.87)$$

$$|||$$

$$RREAD \parallel SCH1_m$$

where $R\_READ =_{df}$ (5.80) $\land$ (5.85). $RREAD$ is another copy of a bounded counter with zero-test. Formally, we have

$$R\_READ \tag{5.88}$$

$$|||$$

$$COUNT_m[rR, aR, aW/up, dn, zero].$$

Combining (5.87) and (5.88) with the construction steps used for $SCH1_m$ we finally obtain

$$SCH2_m$$

$$|||$$

$$Q_m[rR, aR, aW/up, dn, zero]$$
$$\|\quad Q_m[aR, tR, aW/up, dn, zero]$$
$$\|\quad Q_1[aW, tW, aR/up, dn, zero].$$

Thus using (5.78) above, $SCH2_m$ is implemented in a modular fashion by $2m+1$ copies of a 1-counter with zero-test.

For $m=2$ the net view of this implementation is as follows:

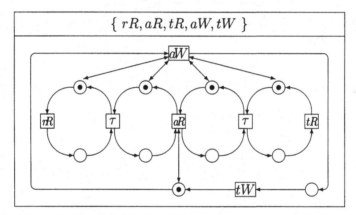

The transitions $rR, aR$ and $tR$ (of different writers) can be activated concurrently. For arbitrary $m$ the net consists of $4m+2$ places and $2m+3$ transitions.

*Third scheduler.* Finally, we wish to schedule readers and writers such that *priority* is given to the *writers*. Thus the first reader in the reader queue is allowed to access the shared data only if no writer is waiting in the writer queue.

Specification and construction of this scheduler is similar to that of the previous scheduler, but the resulting nets are quite different. We record the number of writers that have requested but not yet accessed the shared data by

$$requestW =_{df} rW\#h - aW\#h$$

and start from the following trace specification:

$$SCH3_{m,n} =_{df} \quad 0 \leq activeR \leq m \tag{5.89}$$
$$\wedge \quad 0 \leq requestW \leq n \tag{5.90}$$
$$\wedge \quad 0 \leq activeW \leq 1 \tag{5.91}$$
$$\wedge \quad (last\ h{\downarrow}\{rW, aW, tW, aR\} = aR \longrightarrow$$
$$requestW = 0 \wedge activeW = 0) \tag{5.92}$$
$$\wedge \quad (last\ h{\downarrow}\{aR, tR, aW\} = aW \longrightarrow activeR = 0). \tag{5.93}$$

Since condition (5.92) is logically equivalent to the conjunction of

$$last\ h{\downarrow}\{rW, aW, aR\} = aR \longrightarrow requestW = 0 \tag{5.94}$$

and

$$last\ h{\downarrow}\{aW, tW, aR\} = aR \longrightarrow activeW = 0, \tag{5.95}$$

the logic and parallelism rule yield

$$SCH3_{m,n}$$
$$|||$$
$$R\_WRITE \parallel SCH1_m$$

where $R\_WRITE =_{df}$ (5.90) $\wedge$ (5.94). Proceeding as in the previous construction, we finally obtain

$$SCH3_{m,n}$$
$$|||$$

$$Q_n[rW, aW, aR/up, dn, zero]$$
$$\parallel \quad Q_m[aR, tR, aW/up, dn, zero]$$
$$\parallel \quad Q_1[aW, tW, aR/up, dn, zero].$$

By referring to (5.78) above, $SCH3_m$ is thus implemented by $m+n+1$ copies of a 1-counter with zero-test.

For $m=n=2$ the net view of this implementation is shown on the next page. The transitions $rW$ can be activated concurrently to any other transition. As before, the transitions $aR$ and $tR$ (of different readers) can also be activated concurrently. For arbitrary $m$ and $n$ the net consists of $2(m+n+1)$ places and $m+n+4$ transitions. This example illustrates that by performing the same type of construction steps process terms denoting rather different nets can be constructed. By construction, these nets have all the safety and liveness properties required by the original specification. The nets themselves provide full information about the implementation details such as internal actions or the possible concurrency.

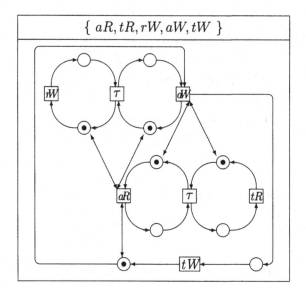

## 5.7   Completeness Issues

Based on the denotational readiness semantics $\mathcal{R}^*[\![\cdot]\!]$ we have developed sound transformation rules on mixed terms and demonstrated their applicability in a series of
example constructions and verifications. An important but difficult question is: were
we lucky in these examples or will we always be successful when attemping to verify
or construct processes with these transformation rules? In other words:

Are the transformation rules in some sense complete?

Let us first discuss *verification completeness*. This means that for every closed process
term $P$ and every trace specification $S$ whenever

$$P \equiv S$$

holds then this equation can be deduced with the transformation rules. Note that
in such a deduction we can make full use of the logical theory $Th(Spec)$ of trace
specifications (cf. Section 5.1).

J. Zwiers has shown verification completeness for a similar but simpler setting
where process correctness requires only the safety condition of Definition 4.3.1 [Zwi89].
Following Zwiers, one would prove more generally that for every process term $P$ with
$free(P) \subseteq \{X_1, \ldots, X_r\}$ and all trace specifications $S_1, \ldots, S_r$ and $S$, whenever

$$P\{S_1, \ldots, S_r / X_1, \ldots, X_r\} \equiv S$$

holds then this equation can be deduced with the transformation rules. The proof
would proceed by induction on $P$ and use (an extended version of) the Expressiveness
Theorem 4.2.5 for trace specifications.

We are unable to prove this result because three of our transformation rules exhibit
weaknesses:

(1) The choice rule is applicable only to specifications $S$ and $T$ with disjoint sets of initial communications although this is not necessary to ensure that $S + T \equiv S \vee T$.

(2) The hiding rule is applicable only if $S \setminus B$ is stable initially even if $S \setminus B$ occurs in the context of a prefix operation which would absorb an initial instability of $S \setminus B$.

(3) The recursion rule is applicable only to communication-guarded terms $\mu X.P$ although this is not necessary to ensure the uniqueness result $\mu X.P \equiv S$.

Indeed, it is not difficult to find a process term $P$ satisfying a trace specification $S$ although each of the conditions (1) – (3) above is violated by some subterm of $P$. Consequently, we cannot deduce $P \equiv S$ with our transformation rules. This shows that our transformation rules are incomplete for the full set of process terms. However, we conjecture that they are complete for a suitably restricted set of process terms. We leave statement and proof of such a completeness result as a topic for future research.

In any case, verification completeness will provide little insight into how to do process construction. This brings us to discuss *construction completeness*. By this we mean that for a certain subset of trace specifications $S$ we have a strategy describing *how to apply* the transformation rules in order to construct a process term $P$ (of a certain form) with

$$P \equiv S.$$

We illustrate this by proving now such a completeness result for the expansion strategy which we applied various times in the previous section.

As preparation we recall some elementary facts of regular languages (see e.g. [HU69]). For a communication alphabet $A$ and a language $L \subseteq A^*$ the *right congruence* of $L$ is the relation $\sim_L \subseteq A^* \times A^*$ defined as follows:

$$tr_1 \sim_L tr_2 \quad \text{if} \quad \forall tr \in A^* : tr_1.tr \in L \text{ iff } tr_2.tr \in L.$$

Then $L$ is regular if and only if $A^*/\sim_L$, the set of congruence classes under $\sim_L$, is finite. Moreover, if $L$ is regular then the questions of whether $tr \in L$ and $tr_1 \sim_L tr_2$ hold for given traces $tr$, $tr_1$ and $tr_2$ are decidable.

**Theorem 5.7.1 Expansion Strategy**. Let $S$ be a trace specification and $A = \alpha(S)$. If $\varepsilon \models S$ and the trace language

$$L = \{ tr \in A^* \mid tr \models kern(S) \}$$

is regular in the sense of formal language theory then a process term $P$ satisfying $S$ can be constructed from $S$. The construction involves the equation and specification rules and of the construction rules, only those for deadlock, prefix, expansion and recursion; it is effective if an algorithm for deciding membership and right congruence of $L$ is given.

*Proof.* First we introduce some auxiliary notation. For $tr \in A^*$ we use the abbreviation

$$S(tr) =_{df} S\{tr.h/h\}.$$

Every trace specification encountered in the construction of $P$ from $S$ will be semantically equivalent to a formula $S(tr)$. In particular, $S \equiv S(\varepsilon)$.

The following observations are immediate consequences of the definitions. For all traces $tr, tr_1, tr_2 \in A^*$:

$$tr \models S(tr_1) \text{ iff } tr_1.tr \in L \qquad\qquad (5.96)$$

$$S(tr_1) \equiv S(tr_2) \text{ iff } \models kern(S(tr_1)) \longleftrightarrow kern(S(tr_2)) \text{ iff } tr_1 \sim_L tr_2. \quad (5.97)$$

An *expansion equation (for S)* is a semantic equation $E$ of the form

$$E =_{df} P\{S(tr_1), \ldots, S(tr_n)/X_1, \ldots, X_n\} \equiv S(tr)$$

where $P$ is a process term with $free(P) = \{X_1, \ldots, X_n\}$ for $n \geq 0$ which is generated by the restricted syntax:

$$P ::= stop:A \mid a.X \mid P_1 + P_2 \mid \mu X.P.$$

Note that every such process term is communication-guarded. An expansion equation $E$ is called *elementary* if the term $P$ is of the form

$$P = stop:A$$

in case of $n = 0$ and

$$P = \sum_{i=1}^{n} a_i.X_i$$

otherwise. Elementary expansion equations for $S$ will be obtained by applying the rules for deadlock, prefix or expansion.

For an expansion equation $E$ as above we define

$$trace(E) = tr,$$

$$lhs(E) = \{S(tr_1), \ldots, S(tr_n)\},$$

$$rhs(E) = S(tr).$$

A set $\mathcal{E}$ of expansion equations is called *prefix closed* if the trace set

$$trace(\mathcal{E}) = \{trace(E) \mid E \in \mathcal{E}\}$$

is prefix closed and it is called *saturated* if the following condition holds:

$$\forall E \in \mathcal{E} \ \forall S(tr) \in lhs(E) \ \exists E' \in \mathcal{E} : rhs(E') = S(tr') \text{ and}$$

$$(tr' = tr \text{ or } (tr' < tr \text{ and } S(tr') \equiv S(tr))).$$

Thus each trace specification $S(tr)$ appearing on the left-hand side of equation $E$ is either explained by another equation or is semantically equivalent to a specification $S(tr')$ encountered earlier, i.e. with $tr' < tr$.

With this notation we can now give the construction of a process term $P$ from $S$. We proceed in two phases.

*Phase 1.* We first construct a *finite saturated* and prefix closed set $\mathcal{E}$ of *elementary* expansion equations for $S$. The construction proceeds top-down from $S$ and uses the equation and specification rules and of the construction rules, only those for deadlock, prefix and expansion. The set $\mathcal{E}$ is initalised by expanding $S(\varepsilon)$ as follows. If $init(S(\varepsilon)) = \emptyset$ then

$$\mathcal{E} := \{stop{:}A \equiv S(\varepsilon)\}.$$

Since $\varepsilon \models S$ and $S \equiv S(\varepsilon)$, this equation is justified by the rules of equation, specification and deadlock. If $init(S(\varepsilon)) = \{a_1, \ldots, a_n\}$ for $n \geq 1$ then

$$\mathcal{E} := \{\sum_{i=1}^{n} a_i.S(a_i) \equiv S(\varepsilon)\}$$

by the rules for equation, specification and prefix or expansion. Once $\mathcal{E}$ is thus initialised, the following step is repeated until no longer possible.

Scan the equations in $\mathcal{E}$. If there exists an equation $E \in \mathcal{E}$ such that for some specification $S(tr) \in lhs(E)$ there is no equation $E' \in \mathcal{E}$ with $rhs(E) = S(tr')$ and

$$tr' = tr \text{ or } (tr' < tr \text{ and } S(tr') \equiv S(tr)),$$

then $\mathcal{E}$ is augmented by expanding $S(tr)$ analogously to $S(\varepsilon)$. Thus if $init(S(tr)) = \emptyset$ then

$$\mathcal{E} := \mathcal{E} \cup \{stop{:}A \equiv S(tr)\}$$

because by the construction of $\mathcal{E}$ we have $\varepsilon \models S(tr)$, i.e. $tr \models S(\varepsilon)$. If $init(S(tr)) = \{a_1, \ldots, a_n\}$ for $n \geq 1$ then

$$\mathcal{E} := \mathcal{E} \cup \{\sum_{i=1}^{n} a_i.S(tr.a_i) \equiv S(tr)\}.$$

This repetition surely terminates with a finite set $\mathcal{E}$ because $L$ is regular. Indeed, suppose it does not terminate so that $\mathcal{E}$ is growing unboundedly. Since by construction of $\mathcal{E}$ the set $trace(\mathcal{E})$ is prefix closed, it can be organised as a finitely branching tree. By König's Infinity Lemma 4.3.4 and the observation (5.97) above, there exists an infinite sequence of traces

$$tr_1 < tr_2 < tr_3 < \ldots$$

such that for $i < j$,

$$tr_i \not\sim_L tr_j$$

holds, which is a contradiction because $L$ is regular. Clearly, $\mathcal{E}$ is saturated by the termination condition of the repetition.

*Phase 2.* Given a finite equation set $\mathcal{E}$ as delivered by Phase 1, we construct a possibly *nested recursive process term* $P$ satisfying $S$. The construction corresponds to a transformation of a system of parallel fixed points into a system of nested fixed points as known in denotational semantics (cf. e.g. [Bak80]); it uses the equation and specification rules and of the construction rules, only the recursion rule.

The construction marks more and more equations in $\mathcal{E}$ and maintains an initially empty set $\mathcal{P}$ of (general) expansion equations for $S$ which on termination contains $P \equiv S(\varepsilon)$ as its only equation. Initially, no equation in $\mathcal{E}$ is marked and $\mathcal{P}$ is empty. Then the following step is repeated until no longer possible.

Select an equation $E \in \mathcal{E}$ which is not yet marked and for which $trace(E)$ is maximal in $trace(\mathcal{E})$. Mark $E$ in $\mathcal{E}$ and update $\mathcal{P}$ as follows. If $E$ is of the form $stop\colon\! A \equiv S(tr)$ then

$$\mathcal{P} := \mathcal{P} \cup \{E\}.$$

Otherwise $E$ is of the form $\sum_{i=1}^{n} a_i.S(tr.a_i) \equiv S(tr)$. For some of the specifications $S(tr.a_i) \in lhs(E)$ there may exist expansion equations of the form

$$E_i =_{df} P_i \{S(tr_{i,1}), \ldots, S(tr_{i,n_i})/X_{i,1}, \ldots, X_{i,n_i}\} \equiv S(tr.a_i)$$

in $\mathcal{P}$. For simplicity we assume that this is the case for $i = 1, \ldots, m$ for some $m \leq n$. These equations will be removed from $\mathcal{P}$ and substituted into $E$.

More precisely, by using the context rule we produce the following new equation:

$$
\begin{aligned}
E' =_{df} \quad & \textstyle\sum_{i=1}^{m} a_i.P_i \{S(tr_{i,1}), \ldots, S(tr_{i,n_i})/X_{i,1}, \ldots, X_{i,n_i}\} \\
+ \quad & \textstyle\sum_{i=m+1}^{n} a_i.S(tr.a_i) \qquad\qquad\qquad\qquad\qquad\quad \equiv S(tr).
\end{aligned}
$$

To see that $E'$ is again an expansion equation, we reorganise the local substitutions into one global substitution. Note that this is not immediate because $S(tr_{i_1,j_1}) \neq S(tr_{i_2,j_2})$ is possible for $X_{i_1,j_1} = X_{i_2,j_2}$, but it is of course done very easily. Let $tr_1, \ldots, tr_r$ be distinct traces with

$$\{tr_1, \ldots, tr_r\} = \cup_{i=1}^{m}\{tr_{i,j} | j = 1, \ldots, n_i\} \cup \{tr.a_i | i = m+1, ..., n\}$$

and choose $r$ distinct identifiers $X_1, \ldots, X_r$ that do not occur bound in one of the terms $P_1, \ldots, P_m$ in $E'$. Then $E'$ can be represented as an expansion equation $E''$ of the form

$$E'' =_{df} Q\{S(tr_1), \ldots, S(tr_r)/X_1, \ldots, X_r\} \equiv S(tr)$$

with $free(Q) = \{X_1, \ldots, X_r\}$.

Now we apply the specification rules and observation (5.97) to check whether for some $i \in \{1, \ldots, r\}$

$$S(tr_i) \equiv S(tr). \tag{5.98}$$

Suppose this is the case, say for $i = 1,\ldots,q$ with $q \leq r$. Then we have discovered a recursive expansion equation. It can be dealt with by the recursion rule because expansion equations are always communication-guarded. Hence we update $\mathcal{P}$ as follows:

$$
\begin{aligned}
\mathcal{P} := \quad & (\mathcal{P} - \{E_1, \ldots, E_m\}) \\
\cup \quad & \{\mu X_1.Q\{X_1, \ldots, X_1, S(tr_{q+1}), \ldots, S(tr_r) \\
& \qquad /X_1, \ldots, X_q, X_{q+1}, \ldots, X_r\} \equiv S(tr)\}.
\end{aligned}
$$

If (5.98) does not hold for any $i \in \{1, \ldots, r\}$ then $\mathcal{P}$ is updated as follows:

$$\mathcal{P}_i := (\mathcal{P} - \{E_1, \ldots, E_m\}) \cup \{E''\}.$$

Since $\mathcal{E}$ is finite, this whole repetition terminates eventually. By construction and the properties of $\mathcal{E}$, the set $\mathcal{P}$ contains upon termination only one expansion equation, viz. of the form $P \equiv S(\varepsilon)$ with $P \in Proc$. Since $S(\varepsilon) \equiv S$, $P$ is the desired process term satisfying $S$.

Clearly, the construction of $P$ is effective modulo the logical theory $Th(Spec)$ of trace specifications. However, by examining the two construction phases, we find that apart from a few facts like $S \equiv S(\varepsilon)$, which can be looked up in a finite table, the only consultations of $Th(Spec)$ are of the form

$$tr \models S(tr_1),$$

e.g. to determine $init(S(tr_1))$, and

$$\models kern(S(tr_1)) \longleftrightarrow kern(S(tr_2)).$$

By the observations (5.96) and (5.97) above, this is equivalent to checking $tr_1.tr \in L$ and $tr_1 \sim_L tr_2$, respectively. Thus if the algorithm for deciding membership and right congruence of the regular language $L$ is given, the whole construction of $P$ is effective.

$\square$

Note that the conditions stated in the above theorem are necessary. If $\varepsilon \models S$ is false, $S$ is unsatisfiable by any process term and if $L$ is non-regular, the expansion strategy cannot by successful.

As observed in Section 5.3 any process term constructed by the expansion strategy denotes a net corresponding to an automaton. By construction, this automaton is deterministic. Hence it may and must engage in all the traces in the prefix kernel of the given specification. The "must" consition ensures that the interaction between user and process is deadlock free; it is absent in classical automata and language theory because the notion of deadlock is not considered there.

The strategy of expanding a given specification into a set of recursive equations is also basic in systems for the automatic design of sequential programs [BD77, MW80]. An objective for future research is to incorporate more process operators into this strategy, in particular parallel decomposition.

# 6

# EXTENSIONS

A crucial test for any theory of concurrent processes is case studies. These will clarify the application areas where this theory is particularly helpful but also reveal its shortcomings. Such shortcomings can be challenges for future research.

Considering all existing case studies based on Petri nets, algebraic process terms and logical formulas, it is obvious that these description methods are immensely helpful in specifying, constructing and verifying concurrent processes. We think in particular of protocol verification, e.g. [Vaa86, Bae90], the verification of VLSI algorithms, e.g. [Hen86], the design of computer architectures, e.g. [Klu87, DD89a, DD89b], and even of concurrent programming languages such as OCCAM [INM84, RH88] or POOL [Ame85, ABKR86, AR89, Vaa90]. However, these examples use one specific description method in each case.

Our overall aim is the smooth integration of description methods that cover different levels of abstraction in a top-down design of concurrent processes. This aim is similar to what Misra and Chandy have presented in their rich and beautiful book on UNITY [CM88]. However, we believe that their approach requires complementary work at the level of implementation, i.e. where UNITY programs are mapped onto architectures.

Our presentation of three different views of concurrent processes attempts to contribute to this overall aim. To obtain a coherent theory, we concentrated on a setting where simple classes of nets, terms and formulas are used. We demonstrated the applicability of this setting in a series of small but non-trivial process constructions. A case study applying our three view approach to the specification, construction and verification of communication protocols including a sliding window protocol can be found in [BDF88, DB89].

Another challenging area is the design of VLSI circuits. For example, one could first transform formulas into recursive terms which could then be transformed into circuit descriptions using an automatic system such as CADIC [BHK+87]. In such an application circuit descriptions would replace Petri nets. It is clear that in order to manage successfully with such realistic applications, the present theory needs to be extended. In this final chapter we outline possible extensions and directions for future research.

A part of the work described in this book has been extended in the ESPRIT project "ProCoS" (Provably Correct Systems) [Bjø89]. In this project trace specifications are extended to a specification languague $SL_0$ [JROR90] that covers also the description of communication values, and process terms are extended OCCAM-like programs [INM84], but Petri nets are replaced by the transputer machine languague. Using $SL_0$ several case studies have been performed: autopilot, gas burner, railway crossing, and lift system. Transformations on mixed terms for the construction of OCCAM-like programs from $SL_0$-specifications are under development [Rös90, RS91].

## 6.1   Nondeterminism

By the liveness condition of $P$ *sat* $S$, the process $P$ must engage in every trace satisfying (the prefix kernel of) $S$. As a consequence, $P$ is forced to be externally deterministic and process correctness boils down to a semantic equation:

$$P \text{ } sat \text{ } S \text{ iff } P \equiv S.$$

Thus a trace specification determines the communication behaviour of a process completely; we cannot leave certain aspects of this behaviour open. For example, we cannot specify a counter without fixing its capacity.

In this section we wish to be more flexible and allow nondeterminism at the level of specification. The idea is to use the ready sets, which so far were hidden in the underlying semantics, explicity in the specifications [Hoa81, Hoa85b]. Thus the readiness semantics is rich enough to accommodate this extension. The notion of process correctness is then captured by a semantic implication:

$$P \text{ } sat \text{ } S \text{ iff } P \Longrightarrow S.$$

Hence process constructions will now be sequences

$$S \equiv Q_1$$
$$\wedge$$
$$\parallel$$
$$\vdots$$
$$\wedge$$
$$\parallel$$
$$Q_n \equiv P$$

of semantic implications between mixed terms $Q_1, \ldots, Q_n$ where $Q_1$ is the given specification $S$ and $Q_n$ is the constructed process term $P$. In the following we give more details.

First we extend the trace logic of Section 4.1 to a *readiness logic* by introducing a new sort, viz.

$$set \qquad \text{(finite sets of communications)}.$$

With this sort comes a set *Var:set* of set variables $G$, $H$. Among the set variables there is a *distinguished set variable* called $F$; it will be used to specify ready sets. As constants of sort *set* we take all communication alphabets $A$.

The set *Exp: set of set expressions* consists then of the following expressions *se*:

$$se ::= A \mid G \mid se_1 \cup se_2 \mid se_1 \cap se_2 \mid se_1 - A \mid se[b/a].$$

The set *Exp:log of logical expressions* is now extended as follows:

$$le ::= \quad true \mid te_1 \leq te_2 \mid se_1 \subseteq se_2 \mid ne_1 \leq ne_2 \mid ce_1 = ce_2$$
$$\mid \ \neg le \mid le_1 \wedge le_2 \mid \exists t : le \mid \exists G : le \mid \exists n : le,$$

where trace expressions $te$, natural number expressions $ne$ and communication expressions $ce$ are defined as before. The elements of the so extended set *Exp:log* are also called *readiness formulas*.

The syntax of readiness logic is then given by the set *Exp* of all expressions of sort *trace*, *set*, *nat*, *comm* and *log*. In applications we may additionally use abbreviations such as

$$a \in se \quad =_{df} \quad \{a\} \subseteq se$$
$$se_1 = se_2 \quad =_{df} \quad se_1 \subseteq se_2 \wedge se_2 \subseteq se_1$$
$$se \neq \emptyset \quad =_{df} \quad \neg se \subseteq \emptyset.$$

As for trace logic the semantics of readiness logic is defined as a mapping

$$\Im : Exp \longrightarrow (Env_\Im \longrightarrow DOM_\Im)$$

where the expressions $se_1 \cup se_2, se_1 \cap se_2, se_1 - A, se[b/a], se_1 \subseteq se_2$ and $\exists G : se$ denote of course set-theoretic union, intersection, difference, renaming of $a$ into $b$, inclusion and existential quantification, respectively.

**Definition 6.1.1** A *readiness specification* is a readiness formula $S$ where at most the distinguished trace variable $h$ and the distinguished set variable $F$ are free and where the following restrictions hold:

- every positive occurrence of $F$ in $S$ is under an even number of negation symbols $\neg$,

- every negative occurrence of $F$ in $S$ is under an odd number of negation symbols $\neg$.

Here an occurrence of the variable $F$ in $S$ is called *positive* (resp. *negative*) if it occurs in $S$ within the $se_2$-part (resp. the $se_1$-part) of a subformula of the form $se_1 \subseteq se_2$.

□

From now on let *Spec*, with typical elements $S$, $T$, $U$, denote the set of all readiness specifications. We say that a ready pair $(tr, \mathcal{F})$ *satisfies* a specification $S$ and write

$$(tr, \mathcal{F}) \models S$$

if $\Im[\![S]\!](\rho) = \text{true}$ for $\rho(h) = tr$ and $\rho(F) = \mathcal{F}$. By the syntactic restrictions stated in Definition 6.1.1, every readiness specification $S$ is *monotonic in $F$*, i.e. for all traces $tr$ and ready sets $\mathcal{F}$ and $\mathcal{G}$

$$(tr, \mathcal{F}) \models S \text{ and } \mathcal{F} \subseteq \mathcal{G} \text{ imply } (tr, \mathcal{G}) \models S.$$

We find this property desirable because it leads to simpler transformation rules later in Definition 6.1.3. However, the restrictions also imply that readiness specifications are not closed under negation. It should be investigated whether this leads to any undesirable consequences.

As for trace specifications, the *projection alphabet*, or simply *alphabet* $\alpha(S)$, of a readiness specification $S$ gathers all communications that appear (after the normalisation of all trace expressions in $S$) in the set $A$ of any projection operator $\bullet \downarrow A$. In particular, set expressions in $S$ do not matter here. They matter only when determining the *extended alphabet* $\alpha\alpha(S)$ which gathers all communications appearing somewhere in $S$, and also in set expressions. With these definitions the Projection Corollary 4.2.2 and the Renaming Corollary 4.2.3 remain true for readiness specifications.

Next we extend the notion of process correctness. A closed process term $P$ *satisfies* a readiness specification $S$, abbreviated

$$P \text{ sat } S,$$

if $\alpha(P) = \alpha(S)$ and the following conditions hold:

(1) *Safety.* If $P$ may engage in a trace $tr$ then there exists some ready set $\mathcal{F}$ with $(tr, \mathcal{F}) \models S$.

(2) *Liveness.* After every trace $tr$ the process $P$ must engage in one of the ready sets $\mathcal{F}$ with $(tr, \mathcal{F}) \models S$.

(3) *Stability.* $P$ is stable immediately.

The new liveness condition can be defined by looking at the Petri net denoted by $P$. We omit this definition here, but remark that it implies the eventual stability of $P$ after every trace $tr$ and hence divergence freedom of $P$. We explain instead the idea of the extended notion of process correctness by an example.

Consider the following readiness specification of a counter:

$$S =_{df} \quad dn\#h \leq up\#h \tag{6.1}$$
$$\wedge \quad (dn\#h = up\#h \longrightarrow up \in F) \tag{6.2}$$
$$\wedge \quad (dn\#h < up\#h \longrightarrow dn \in F). \tag{6.3}$$

Line (6.1) specifies the desired safety property: the number of $dn$'s must never exceed the number of $up$'s. Lines (6.2) and (6.3) specify the desired liveness properties: if the number of $dn$'s equals the number of $up$'s, the process must engage in another communication $up$; if the number of $dn$'s is smaller than the number of $up$'s, the process must engage in another $dn$.

This specification leaves certain aspects of the counter behaviour open: after every trace $tr$ with $dn\#tr < up\#tr$ a process satisfying $S$ may either be ready to engage only in another $dn$, as required by (6.3), or in both $up$ and $dn$, as allowed by (6.1). These two possibilities may depend on the trace $tr$. As a consequence, counters of any capacity satisfy $S$, in particular all the process terms constructed in the Section 5.3. For example,

$$P_1 = \mu X.up.dn.X \qquad\qquad sat \quad S\ ,$$
$$P_k = (P_{k-1}[lk/dn] \parallel P_1[lk/up]) \backslash lk \qquad sat \quad S\ ,$$
$$P_\infty = \mu X.up.(X[lk/dn] \parallel \mu Y.dn.lk.Y) \backslash lk \quad sat \quad S\ .$$

Thus a single readiness specification can describe even an infinite set of different communication behaviours.

As a special case, we can use readiness specifications without any free occurence of $F$ to describe only safety and divergence freedom, but no specific readiness for communications. Consider for example the divergence free process term

$$MUTEX = CYCLE1 \parallel SEM \parallel CYCLE2$$

discussed in Section 3.2. How can we express that $MUTEX$ satisfies the mutual exclusion property ? If $CYCLE1$ is in its critical section $b_1.e_1$, the difference between the number of communications $b_1$ and the number of communications $e_1$ is 1; otherwise it is 0. Analogously for $CYCLE2$ and its critical section $b_2.e_2$. Thus at most one cycle is in its critical section if

$$MUTEX \ sat \ SPEC$$

where

$$SPEC =_{df} \quad b_1\#h - e_1\#h + b_2\#h - e_2\#h \leq 1 \tag{6.4}$$
$$\wedge \quad \varepsilon \leq h \downarrow \{n_i, p_i, v_i \mid i = 1, 2\}. \tag{6.5}$$

Note that line (6.5) is a tautology with the sole purpose of extending the alphabet of $SPEC$ to that of $MUTEX$.

Since *SPEC* requires no specific liveness, process terms with various other communication behaviours also satisfy *SPEC*. One extreme is deadlock:

$$stop{:}A \; sat \; SPEC$$

for $A = \{n_i, p_i, b_i, e_i, v_i \mid i = 1, 2\}$. Clearly, a process that does nothing at all trivially satisfies *SPEC*.

Let us now be a bit more formal and explain how the extended notion of process correctness can be interpreted in the readiness semantics.

**Definition 6.1.2** The *(readiness) semantics of a readiness specification* is as follows:

$$\mathcal{R}^*[\![S]\!] = (\alpha(S), \{(tr, \mathcal{F}) \mid tr \in \alpha(S)^* \text{ and } \mathcal{F} \subseteq \alpha(S) \text{ and } (tr, \mathcal{F}) \models S\}). \qquad \Box$$

Had we defined the relationship $P \; sat \; S$ rigorously then we could now prove the following correctness theorem:

$$P \; sat \; S \text{ iff } \mathcal{R}^*[\![P]\!] \sqsupseteq \mathcal{R}^*[\![S]\!]$$

for every closed process term $P$ and readiness specification $S$. Using the symbol $\Rightarrow$ for semantic implication introduced in Definition 5.1.2, this can be stated more conveniently as follows:

$$P \; sat \; S \text{ iff } P \Rightarrow S.$$

With Definition 6.1.2 it is straightforward to extend the readiness semantics to all mixed terms:

$$\mathcal{R}^*[\![\cdot]\!] : Proc + Spec \longrightarrow (Env_{\mathcal{R}} \longrightarrow DOM_{\mathcal{R}}).$$

This is the semantic basis for transformation rules on mixed terms.

**Definition 6.1.3** In the following transformation rules, letters $P$, $Q$, $R$ range over *CProc+ Spec* unless stated otherwise. As before, letters $S$, $T$; $X$; $a$, $b$; $A$ range over *Spec*, *Idf*, *Comm* and alphabets, respectively.

(1) Implication Rules:
    (Reflexivity)

$$P \Rightarrow P$$

(Transitivity)

$$\frac{P \Rightarrow Q, \; Q \Rightarrow R}{P \Rightarrow R}$$

(Context)

$$\frac{Q \Rightarrow R}{P\{Q/X\} \Rightarrow P\{R/X\}}$$

where $P \in Proc + Spec$ and $P\{Q/X\}, P\{R/X\} \in CProc + Spec$

(2) Specification Rule:
(Consequence)

$$\frac{\models S \longrightarrow T}{S \Rrightarrow T} \qquad \text{where } \alpha(S) = \alpha(T)$$

(3) Construction Rules:
(Deadlock)

$$stop{:}A \Rrightarrow h{\downarrow}A \leq \varepsilon$$

(Prefix)

$$\frac{(\varepsilon, \{a\}) \models S}{a.S\{a.h/h\} \Rrightarrow S} \qquad \text{where } a \in \alpha(S)$$

(Choice)

$$S + T \Rrightarrow (h{\downarrow}A = \varepsilon \longrightarrow S \wedge T) \wedge (h{\downarrow}A \neq \varepsilon \longrightarrow S \vee T)$$

where $A = \alpha(S) = \alpha(T)$

(Parallelism)

$$S \parallel T \Rrightarrow \exists G \; \exists H : (S\{G/F\} \wedge T\{H/F\} \wedge (G \cap H) \cup ((G \cup H) - A) \subseteq F)$$

where $A = \alpha(S) = \alpha(T)$

(Renaming)

$$S[b_i/a_i] \Rrightarrow \exists t \; \exists G : (S\{t, G/h, F\} \wedge t[b_i/a_i] = h{\downarrow}A \wedge G[b_i/a_i] \subseteq F)$$

where $A = \alpha(S)\{b_i/a_i\}$ and $b_i/a_i$ stands for a renaming
$b_1, \ldots, b_n/a_1, \ldots, a_n$ with $n \geq 1$

(Hiding)

- *logical implication:*
  $\models S\{F - B/F\} \longrightarrow T$
- *stability:*
  $\forall b \in B : b \models \neg \exists F.S$
- *divergence freedom:*

$$\frac{\forall tr \in \alpha(S)^* \; \exists n \geq 0 \; \forall b_1, \ldots, b_n \in B : tr.b_1 \ldots b_n \models \neg \exists F : S}{S \backslash B \Rrightarrow T}$$

where $\alpha(T) = \alpha(S) - B$

(Recursion)

$$\frac{P\{S/X\} \Rrightarrow S}{\mu X.P \Rrightarrow S}$$

where $\mu X.P \in CProc + Spec$ is communication-guarded and $\alpha(S) = \alpha(X)$

(Expansion: derived)

$$\frac{(\varepsilon, \{a_1, \ldots, a_n\}) \models S}{\sum_{i=1}^{n} a_i.S\{a_i.h/h\} \Rrightarrow S} \quad \text{where } a_1, \ldots, a_n \in \alpha(S)$$

(Disjoint renaming: derived)

$$S[b_i/a_i] \Rrightarrow S\{b_i/a_i\}$$

where $b_i/a_i$ stands for a renaming $b_1, \ldots, b_n/a_1, \ldots, a_n$ with $n \geq 1$ and $b_1, \ldots, b_n \notin \alpha\alpha(S)$. □

Rules with existential quantifiers over ready sets are difficult to use in practice. This is the case for the general renaming rule and, unfortunately, also for the parallelism rule. On the other hand, the hiding rule is simpler now because $S \backslash b$ need not be deterministic any more. Note that the formulas $\neg \exists F.S$ in the premises of this rule need not be readiness specifications because of the extra negation symbol. But since these formulas do not appear in the refinement steps of process constructions, this does not matter.

Missing in these transformation rules is an analogue to the kernel rule for trace specifications. It should allow us to replace a given readiness specification $S$ by a stronger specification which denotes the "well-structured kernel" of $S$. We have not yet found such a rule. Finally, we remark that in the rules for choice, parallelism, renaming and disjoint renaming the reverse semantic implication $\Lleftarrow$ also holds and hence so does $\equiv$. The rules for deadlock, prefix and expansion cannot be strengthened. Of course, implications $\Rrightarrow$ suffice for the purpose of establishing process correctness $P \Rrightarrow S$.

**Soundness Theorem 6.1.4** The transformation rules presented in Definition 6.1.3 are sound.

*Proof.* We have to show that every rule states a true theorem about the readiness semantics. Mostly, this can be done similarly as in the proof of the Soundness Theorem 5.2.1. Only the construction rules deserve extra comment. These rules exploit that the semantics of readiness specifications $S$ is *closed*, i.e.

$$close(\mathcal{R}^*[\![S]\!]) = \mathcal{R}^*[\![S]\!],$$

where *close* is the closure operator of Definition 4.4.1. This is an immediate consequence of the fact that readiness specifications are monotonic in the variable $F$.

The soundness proof of the choice rule uses the *monotonicity* and the initial stability of $S$ and $T$ to show that for the *empty* trace $S+T$ boils down to the conjunction $S \wedge T$; otherwise it amounts to the disjunction $S \vee T$. The soundness proofs of the rules for parallelism and hiding use the *projection corollary*. The general renaming rule is a straightforward reformulation of the semantics. From this rule the disjoint renaming rule is derived by using the *renaming corollary*. The expansion rule is derived from the prefix and choice rule with the help of the consequence and context rule.

More interesting is the soundness proof of the recursion rule. It uses *Park's fixed point induction* [Par70, LS84] for the *reverse* order $\sqsupseteq$ on the readiness domain and exploits the uniqueness of fixed points of communication-guarded recursions shown in Section 5.2. The details are as follows.

Suppose $\mu X.P \in CProc + Spec$ is communication-guarded and

$$P\{S/X\} \Longrightarrow S \tag{6.6}$$

for some $S \in Spec$ with $\alpha(S) = \alpha(X)$. Let $B = \alpha(S)$ and consider the mapping

$$\Phi_{P,\rho} : DOM_{\mathcal{R}} : B \longrightarrow DOM_{\mathcal{R}} : B$$

defined by

$$\Phi_{P,\rho}(B,\Gamma) = \mathcal{R}^*[\![P]\!](\rho[(B,\Gamma)/X]).$$

By (6.6) and the definition of $\mathcal{R}^*[\![\mu X.P]\!]$, we have

$$\Phi_{P,\rho}(\mathcal{R}^*[\![\mu X.P]\!]) = \mathcal{R}^*[\![\mu X.P]\!] \tag{6.7}$$

and

$$\Phi_{P,\rho}(\mathcal{R}^*[\![S]\!]) \sqsupseteq \mathcal{R}^*[\![S]\!]. \tag{6.8}$$

The reverse order $\sqsupseteq$ is ordinary set inclusion on the sets of process information, i.e.

$$(A,\Gamma) \sqsupseteq (B,\Delta) \quad \text{iff} \quad A = B \text{ and } \Gamma \subseteq \Delta$$

for all $(A,\Gamma),(B,\Delta) \in DOM_{\mathcal{R}}$. Therefore it is straightforward to see that all semantic operators $op_{\mathcal{R}}$ and hence $\Phi_{p,\rho}$ are $\sqsupseteq$-continuous on $DOM_{\mathcal{R}}$. (Of course, they are not all $\sqsubseteq$-continuous as we know from Proposition 4.6.8.)

Park's fixed point induction – applied to the reverse order $\sqsupseteq$ on $DOM_{\mathcal{R}} : B$ – states the following: for every $\sqsupseteq$-continuous mapping $\Phi : DOM_{\mathcal{R}} : B \longrightarrow DOM_{\mathcal{R}} : B$ and every domain element $d \in DOM_{\mathcal{R}} : B$,

$$\Phi(d) \sqsupseteq d$$

implies

$$FIX\ \Phi \sqsupseteq d$$

where $FIX\ \Phi$ is the least fixed point of $\Phi$ w.r.t. $\sqsupseteq$.

Thus taking $\Phi = \Phi_{P,\rho}$ and $d = \mathcal{R}^*[\![S]\!]$, line (6.8) yields

$$FIX\ \Phi_{P,\rho} \sqsupseteq \mathcal{R}^*[\![S]\!] \tag{6.9}$$

Note that $FIX\,\Phi_{P,\rho}$ is the greatest fixed point of $\Phi_{P,\rho}$ w.r.t. to the partial order $\sqsubseteq$ on $DOM_{\mathcal{R}}$. In particular, we obtain

$$\Phi_{P,\rho}(FIX\,\Phi_{P,\rho}) = FIX\,\Phi_{P,\rho}. \tag{6.10}$$

By the communication-guardedness of $\mu X.P$ and Corollary 5.2.2, the mapping $\Phi_{P,\rho}$ has a unique fixed point. Thus

$$\mathcal{R}^*[\![\mu X.P]\!] = FIX\,\Phi_{P,\rho} \tag{6.11}$$

from (6.7) and (6.10). Now (6.11) and (6.9) yield

$$\mathcal{R}^*[\![\mu X.P]\!] \sqsupseteq \mathcal{R}^*[\![S]\!] \tag{6.12}$$

which by definition is just

$$\mu X.P \Longrightarrow S, \tag{6.13}$$

the conclusion of the recursion rule.                                    $\square$

## 6.2   Fairness

A process term satisfying a readiness specification can, after every finite trace, non-deterministically choose between one of the ready sets offered by the specification. Sometimes we wish to restrict this nondeterminism to a *fair* one, i.e. ready sets which are offered sufficiently often should also be chosen eventually.

As an example from the area of communication protocols consider a very simple *transmission medium* that can input data and either output them correctly or yield a transmission error. We can model such a medium as a process that can engage in communications in, out and err. Viewed as a net the behaviour of this process is given as follows:

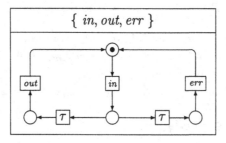

The two internal $\tau$-transitions express the fact that after every communication *in* the process can nondeterministically choose between the ready sets $\{out\}$ and $\{err\}$. Such a transmission medium is unreliable because an input might never have a corresponding output. If it is used as part of a communication protocol then the protocol will not satisfy any liveness property. To achieve liveness, all transmission media in the protocol must be reliable, i.e. each input must be output eventually. This is just a fairness requirement stating that after every communication *in*, the ready set $\{out\}$ should be chosen eventually.

Fairness requirements are not properties of finite traces, but *infinite traces*, also known as *streams* [Bro83]. In our example, we require that a reliable transmission medium may not engage in any infinite trace ending in

$$\ldots in.err.in.err.in.err\ldots \tag{6.14}$$

Fairness has been the topic of enormously many papers (see [Fra86] for an overview), but an integration into the present framework is not yet solved.

We plan to extend the readiness specifications of the previous section by letting the variable $h$ range over finite and infinite traces. The variables $F$ continues to range over finite ready sets. The reliable transmission medium could then be specified as follows:

$$
\begin{aligned}
\text{MSPEC} \;=\; & out\#h + err\#h \le in\#h & (6.15)\\
\wedge\; & in\#h \le 1 + out\#h + err\#h & (6.16)\\
\wedge\; & (out\#h + err\#h = in\#h \longrightarrow in \in F) & (6.17)\\
\wedge\; & (out\#h + err\#h < in\#h \longrightarrow out \in F) & (6.18)\\
\wedge\; & (in\#h = \infty \longrightarrow out\#h = \infty) & (6.19)
\end{aligned}
$$

where lines (6.15) and (6.16) specify safety, lines (6.17) and (6.18) specify liveness via ready sets and line (6.19) specifies fairness by disallowing infinite traces of the form (6.14) above. The idea is that MSPEC describes an infinite set of different transmission behaviours all satisfying line (6.19).

Providing the right semantic foundation and transformation rules for this kind of specifications is an interesting topic for further research. This work might benefit from ideas of [Hen85, Par85, BKO87].

## 6.3 Concurrency

So far our notions of process correctness are insensitive to concurrency. For example, the trace specification

$$S_2 = 0 \le up\#h - dn\#h \le 2$$

of a 2-counter can be implemented by the purely sequential net

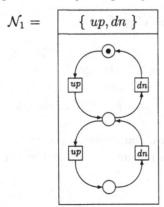

$\mathcal{N}_1 =$   $\{\, up, dn \,\}$

or the net

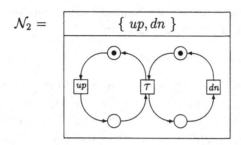

$$\mathcal{N}_2 = \boxed{\{\, up, dn\,\}}$$

allowing concurrency. At the moment we cannot express in our specification language which of these implementations is preferred, but it seems desirable to be able to do so.

In the following we outline a first idea how this could be done. Inspired by the theory of Mazurkiewicz-traces initiated in [Maz77] we propose specifying the required concurrency by an independence relation (cf. the introduction to Chapter 4). This is a symmetric and irreflexive binary relation on the alphabet of a specification. The idea is that whenever two communications are independent according to this relation then the process should allow them to occur concurrently.

We suggest the independence relation be calculated from the specification syntax.

**Definition 6.3.1** Let $S$ be a trace specification. The *independence relation* of $S$ is the relation $I(S) \subseteq \alpha(S) \times \alpha(S)$ where

$$a\ I(S)\ b$$

holds for all communications $a$, $b \in \alpha(S)$ that do not appear in the same projection set $A$ of a trace projection $\bullet{\downarrow}A$ in the normal form of $S$ (cf. Section 4.1). $\qquad\square$

Process correctness $P$ *sat* $S$ would now additionally require that for every ready pair $(tr, \mathcal{F})$ of $P$, any two communications $a$, $b \in \mathcal{F}$ with $a\ I(S)\ b$ can occur concurrently in $P$ after $tr$. Note that this is a very simple approach where concurrency is required only for two communications at a time.

In the example of the trace specification $S_2$ above we calculate

$$up\ I(S_2)\ dn$$

because $S_2$ abbreviates $0 \le |h{\downarrow}\{up\}| - |h{\downarrow}\{dn\}| \le 2$. Thus $S_2$ is satisfied only by process terms $P$, where after every trace $tr$ with $up\#tr = dn\#tr + 1$, the communications $up$ and $dn$ can occur concurrently. Hence any term $P$ denoting the concurrent net $\mathcal{N}_2$ above would satisfy $S_2$, but any term $P$ denoting the sequential net $\mathcal{N}_1$ would not.

Perhaps these ideas can help utilise the growing theory around Mazurkiewicz-traces (see e.g. [Aal87, Bed87]) for the purposes of process construction.

# 6.4 Structured Communications

The key to realistic applications of process theory is the introduction of structured communications. For example, to describe message-passing along communication channels, one introduces communications with a *channel structure*. These are pairs (*ch, m*) consisting of a channel name *ch* and a message *m* taken from a possibly infinite message set [Hoa78, Mil80, INM84].

In principle, every process term with message-passing can be translated into an equivalent term using only atomic communications [Mil80, Mil83, Hoa85b]. However, in case of infinite message sets this translation yields terms using infinite choices and infinite recursion schemes. Thus the point of using a channel structure is to manipulate finite representations of infinite objects. But even if the message set is finite, a channel structure allows us to describe processes more concisely.

There are various proposals how to do this for each of the three views of processes discussed here, e.g. [HI90], but more research is needed to find good transformations from formulas to terms and from terms to nets in this case. Some steps in this direction are done in the ESPRIT project "ProCoS" [Rös90, RS91].

# 6.5 Further Research Topics

*Bisimulations on Nets Based on Places.* Investigate the idea of defining bisimulations on nets by lifting relations on places. See also [ABS91]

*Finite Nets for Non-Regular Process Terms.* Prove Conjecture 3.5.7, i.e. define a new operational Petri net semantics where only the interaction of recursion with parallelism yields infinite nets, but the use of action morphisms is harmless. See also [Tau89].

*Denotational Net Semantics.* In Section 3.8 we defined composition operators for Petri nets, but recursion was treated only by the $\mu$-expansion law. A denotational net semantics requires that recursion is dealt with by using fixed points (cf. Definition 4.4.1). Define a denotational net semantics for process terms similar to Winskel's event structure semantics in [Win82]. Prove that modulo strong bismilarity it agrees with the operational sematics. Does the denotational net semantics simplify the proof of the Equivalence Theorem 4.6.14 for the more abstract readiness semantics? Can one define a denotational net semantics that yields finite nets whenever the operational semantics does ?

*Characterisation Theorem.* Characterise the class of nets denoted by process terms.

*Process Correctness and Temporal Logic.* Pursue the relationship between process correctness $P \ sat \ S$ and temporal logic indicated in Section 4.3.

*The Algebra of the Readiness Semantics.* Find the algebraic laws of the modified readiness semantics. The aim is a set of laws which is complete for non-recursive mixed terms. However, there should also be derived laws which are helpful for a purely algebraic process verification as e.g. advocated in [BK86]. Together with the transformation rules given in Section 5.1 these laws allow more flexible process constructions. Based on the rich work on process algebra by Bergstra, Klop et al. and also DeNicola and Hennessy [DH84, Hen88], this should not be too difficult. The laws would also exhibit the subtle differences between modified readiness equivalence and testing and failure equivalence (cf. Section 4.7).

*Completeness Theorem.* State and prove a completeness theorem for the transformation rules of Section 5.7. Proof techniques from Zwiers [Zwi89] will be helpful here.

*Strategies for Process Construction.* Compare the expansion strategy of Section 5.7 with the automatic synthesis of finite-state automata from formulas of propositional temporal logic as described e.g. by Emerson and Clarke [EC82] or Manna and Wolper [MW84]. Develop new strategies incorporating parallel decomposition. What is the connection of this to the recent work on compositional model checking for temporal logic formulas? Find subclasses of trace formulas which allow an automatic approach.

*Process Construction and Logic Programming.* Can Logic Programming and the search strategy built into PROLOG be succesfully used to express verification rules for process correctness and to program strategies for process construction?

*Relationship to Net-Based Verification.* Explore the relationship of net-based verification, using e.g. linear algebra techniques [Rei85], to process verification based on transformation rules. Do structure theorems of net theory, e.g. [Ber87], imply the success of certain strategies for process verification and construction?

*More Flexible Specification Language.* Develop the general format of a more flexible specification language extending trace logic. Such an extension could incorporate user defined symbols for relations and functions on traces.

# BIBLIOGRAPHY

[Aal87]   I.H. Aalbersberg. *Studies in trace theory*. PhD thesis, Univ. of Leiden, Dept. Comput. Sci., 1987.

[ABKR86] P. America, J.W. de Bakker, J.N. Kok, and J. Rutten. Operational semantics of a parallel object-oriented language. In *Proc. 13th ACM Symp. Principles of Progr. Languages, St. Petersburg*, Florida, 1986.

[ABS91]  C. Autant, Z. Belmesk, and P. Schnoebelen. Strong bisimilarity on nets revisted. Technical report, Lab. d'Inform. Fond. et d'Intelligence Artif., Institut Imag – CNRS, Grenoble, 1991. (It appears in: *Proc. PARLE 91, Lecture Notes in Computer Science*, Springer-Verlag).

[AHV85]  F. André, D. Herman, and J.-P. Verjus. *Synchronization of Parallel Programs*. MIT Press, Cambridge, Mass., 1985.

[Ame85]  P. America. Definition of the programming language POOL-T. Technical Report ESPRIT Project 415, Doc. Nr. 0091, Philips Research Lab., Eindhoven, 1985.

[Apt83]  K.R. Apt. Formal justification of a proof system for communicating sequential processes. *J. ACM*, pages 197–216, 1983.

[AR89]   P. Amerika and J. Rutten. *A parallel object-oriented language: design and semantic foundations*. PhD thesis, Free University, Amsterdam, 1989.

[AS85]   B. Alpern and F.B. Schneider. Defining liveness. *Inform. Proc. Letters*, 21:181–185, 1985.

[Ast84]  E. Astesiano. Combining an operational with an algebraic approach to the specification of concurrency. In D. Bjørner, editor, *Proc. Workshop on Combining Methods*, Nyborg, Denmark, 1984.

[Bac80]   R.J.R. Back. Correctness preserving refinements: proof theory and applications. Technical Report Mathematical Centre Tracts 131, Mathematical
          Centre, Amsterdam, 1980.

[Bae90]   J.C.M. Baeten, editor. *Applications of Process Algebra*. Cambridge University Press, 1990.

[Bak80]   J.W. de Bakker. *Mathematical Theory of Program Correctness*. Prentice-
          Hall, London, 1980.

[Bau85]   F.L. Bauer et al. The Munich Project CIP, Vol. I: The Wide Spectrum
          Language CIP-L. In *Lecture Notes in Computer Science 183*. Springer-
          Verlag, 1985.

[Bau87]   F.L. Bauer et al. The Munich Project CIP, Vol. II: The Program Transformation System CIP-S. In *Lecture Notes in Computer Science 292*. Springer-
          Verlag, 1987.

[BBK87]   J.C.M. Baeten, J.A. Bergstra, and J.W. Klop. On the consistency of
          Koomen's fair abstraction rule. *Theoret. Comput. Sci.*, 51:129–176, 1987.

[BD77]    R.M. Burstall and J. Darlington. A transformation system for developing
          recursive programs. *J. ACM*, 24:44–67, 1977.

[BDF88]   M. Bretschneider, M. Duque Antón, and A. Fink. Constructing and verifying protocols using TCSP. In K. Sabnani S. Aggarwal, editor, *Proc.
          IFIP Working Conference on Protocol Specification, Testing and Verification*. North-Holland, 1988.

[Bed87]   M. Bednarczyk. *Categories of asynchronous systems*. PhD thesis, Univ. of
          Sussex, Dept. Comput. Sci., 1987.

[Ber87]   G. Berthelot. Transformations and decompositions of nets. In W. Brauer,
          W. Reisig, and G. Rozenberg, editors, *Petri Nets: Central Models and
          Their Properties, Lecture Notes in Computer Science 254*, pages 359–376.
          Springer-Verlag, 1987.

[Bes87]   E. Best. COSY: its relation to nets and CSP. In W. Brauer, W. Reisig, and
          G. Rozenberg, editors, *Petri Nets: Applications and Relationships to Other
          Models of Concurrency, Lecture Notes in Computer Science 255*, pages 416–
          440. Springer-Verlag, 1987.

[BF86]    E. Best and C. Fernandez. Notations and terminology on Petri nets. Technical Report Arbeitspapiere der GMD 195, Gesellschaft Math. Datenverarb.,
          St. Augustin, 1986.

[BHK+87]  B. Becker, G. Hotz, R. Kolla, P. Molitor, and H.G. Osthof. CADIC – a
          system for hierarchical design of integrated circuits. Technical Report SFB
          124, Univ. Saarbrücken, Fachbereich Angew. Math. u. Inform., 1987.

[BHR84] S.D. Brookes, C.A.R. Hoare, and A.W. Roscoe. A theory of communicating sequential processes. *J. ACM*, 31:560–599, 1984.

[Bjø89] D. Bjørner et al. A ProCoS project description – ESPRIT BRA 3104. *EATCS Bulletin*, 39:60–73, 1989.

[BK86] J.A. Bergstra and J.W. Klop. Algebra of communicating processes. In J.W. de Bakker, M. Hazewinkel, and J.K. Lenstra, editors, *Proc. CWI Symposium on Mathematics and Computer Science, CWI Monograph I*, pages 89–138, Amsterdam, 1986. North-Holland.

[BKO87] J.A. Bergstra, J.W. Klop, and E.-R. Olderog. Failures without chaos: a new process semantics for fair abstraction. In M. Wirsing, editor, *Proc. IFIP Working Conference on Formal Description of Programming Concepts III*, pages 77–101. North-Holland, 1987.

[BMOZ88] J.W. de Bakker, J.-J.Ch. Meyer, E.-R. Olderog, and J.I. Zucker. Transition systems, metric spaces and ready sets in the semantics of uniform concurrency. *J. Comput. System Sci.*, 36:158–224, 1988.

[Bro83] M. Broy. Fixed point theory for communication and concurrency. In D. Bjørner, editor, *Proc. IFIP Working Conference on Formal Description of Programming Concepts II*, pages 125–147, Amsterdam, 1983. North-Holland.

[Bro86] M. Broy. Process semantics of communicating concurrent programs. Technical Report Bericht MIP-8602, Univ. Passau, Fak. Math. u. Inform., 1986.

[Bro87] M. Broy. Specification and top-down design of distributed systems. *J. Comput. System Sci.*, 34:236–265, 1987.

[BS90] J. Bradfield and C. Stirling. Verifying temporal properties of processes. In J.C.M. Baeten and J.W. Klop, editors, *Proc. CONCUR '90 Theories of Concurrency: Unification and Extension, Lecture Notes in Computer Science 458*, pages 115–125. Springer-Verlag, 1990.

[BW90a] R.J.R. Back and J. van Wright. Refinement calculus, Part I: sequential nondeterministic programs. In J.W. de Bakker, W.P. de Roever, and G. Rozenberg, editors, *Stepwise Refinement of Distributed Systems – Models, Formalisms, Correctness, Lecture Notes in Computer Science 430*, pages 42–66. Springer-Verlag, 1990.

[BW90b] J.C.M. Baeten and P. Weijland. *Process Algebra*. Cambridge University Press, 1990.

[CH74] R.H. Campbell and A.N. Habermann. The specification of process synchronisation by path expressions. In *Lecture Notes in Computer Science 16*. Springer-Verlag, 1974.

[CH81]   Z. Chaochen and C.A.R. Hoare. Partial correctness of communicating processes. In *Proc. 2nd Intern. Conf. on Distributed Comput. Systems*, Paris, 1981.

[CM88]   K.M. Chandy and J. Misra. *Parallel Program Design – A Foundation*. Addison-Wesley, 1988.

[Cza85]   L. Czaja. Making nets structured and abstract. In G. Rozenberg, editor, *Advances in Petri Nets 1985, Lecture Notes in Computer Science 222*, pages 181–202. Springer-Verlag, 1985.

[DB89]   M. Duque Antòn and M. Bretschneider. Formulas, processes and petri-nets applied to the specification and verification of a HDLC protocol. In J. Diaz and F. Orejas, editors, *Proc. TAPSOFT '89, Vol.2, Lecture Notes in Computer Science 352*, pages 140–154. Springer-Verlag, 1989.

[DD89a]   W. Damm and G. Döhmen. AADL: A net-based specification method for computer architecture design. In J.W. de Bakker, editor, *Languages for Parallel Architectures - Design, Semantics, Implementation Models*, Chichester, 1989. John Wiley & Sons.

[DD89b]   W. Damm and G. Döhmen. Specifying distributed computer architectures in AADL. *Parallel Computing*, 9:193–211, 1989.

[DDM87]   P. Degano, R. DeNicola, and U. Montanari. CCS is an (augmented) contact-free C/E system. In M. Venturini Zilli, editor, *Math. Models for the Semantics of Parallelism, Lecture Notes in Computer Science 280*, pages 144–165. Springer-Verlag, 1987.

[DDM88a]   P. Degano, R. DeNicola, and U. Montanari. A distributed operational semantics for CCS based on condition/event systems. *Acta Inform.*, 26:59–91, 1988.

[DDM88b]   P. Degano, R. DeNicola, and U. Montanari. On the consistency of "truly concurrent" operational and denotational semantics. In IEEE, editor, *Proc. 3rd Annual Symp. on Logics in Computer Science '88*, pages 133–141, Edinburgh, 1988.

[DDPS83]   F. DeCindio, G. DeMichelis, L. Pomello, and C. Simone. Milner's communicating systems and Petri nets. In G. Rozenberg A. Pagnoni, editor, *Applications and Theory of Petri Nets, Inform.-Fachberichte 66*. Springer Verlag, 1983.

[DH84]   R. DeNicola and M. Hennessy. Testing equivalences for processes. *Theoret. Comput. Sci.*, 34:83–134, 1984.

[Dij76]   E.W. Dijkstra. *A Discipline of Programming*. Prentice-Hall, Englewood Cliffs, NJ, 1976.

[DM87]   P. Degano and U. Montanari. Concurrent histories: a basis for observing distributed systems. *J. Comput. System Sci.*, 34:442–461, 1987.

[EC82]   E.A. Emerson and E.M. Clarke. Using branching time temporal logic to synthesize synchronization skeletons. *Sci. Comput. Progr.*, 2:241–266, 1982. publ. 1983.

[FLP84]  N. Francez, D. Lehmann, and A. Pnueli. A linear history semantics for languages for distributed programming. *Theoret. Comput. Sci.*, 32:25–46, 1984.

[Fra86]  N. Francez. *Fairness.* Springer-Verlag, New York, 1986.

[Gen87]  H. Genrich. Predicate/transition nets. In W. Brauer, W. Reisig, and G. Rozenberg, editors, *Petri Nets: Central Models and Their Properties, Lecture Notes in Computer Science 254*, pages 207–247. Springer-Verlag, 1987.

[GM84]   U. Goltz and A. Mycroft. On the relationship of CCS and Petri nets. In J. Paredaens, editor, *Proc. 11th Coll. Automata, Languages and Programming, Lecture Notes in Computer Science 172*, pages 196–208. Springer-Verlag, 1984.

[GMS89]  C.A. Gunter, P.D. Mosses, and D.S. Scott. Semantic domains and denotational semantics. Technical Report DAIMI PB-276, Comput. Sci. Dept., Aarhus Univ., 1989.

[Gol88a] U. Goltz. On representing CCS programs by finite Petri nets. In M.P. Chytil, L. Janiga, and V. Koubek, editors, *Proc. Math. Found. of Comput. Sci. 1988, Lecture Notes in Computer Science 324*, pages 339–350. Springer-Verlag, 1988.

[Gol88b] U. Goltz. *Über die Darstellung von CCS-Programmen durch Petrinetze.* PhD thesis, RWTH Aachen, 1988.

[GS86]   S. Graf and J. Sifakis. A logic for the specification and proof of regular controllable processes of CCS. *Acta Inform.*, 23:507–527, 1986.

[GV87]   R.J. van Glabbeek and F.W. Vaandrager. Petri net models for algebraic theories of concurrency. In J.W. de Bakker, A.J. Nijman, and P.C. Treleaven, editors, *Proc. PARLE Conf., Eindhoven, Vol. II, Lecture Notes in Computer Science 259*, pages 224–242. Springer-Verlag, 1987.

[Har87]  D. Harel. Statecharts: a visual formalism for complex systems. *Sci. Comput. Progr.*, 8:231–274, 1987.

[Heh84]  E.C.R. Hehner. Predicative programming, Part I and II. *Comm. ACM*, 27:134–151, 1984.

[Hen85]  M. Hennessy. An algebraic theory of fair asynchronous communicating processes. In W. Brauer, editor, *Proc. 12th Coll. Automata, Languages and Programming, Lecture Notes in Computer Science 194*, pages 260–269. Springer-Verlag, 1985.

[Hen86]  M. Hennessy. Proving systolic systems correct. *ACM TOPLAS*, 8:344–387, 1986.

[Hen88]  M. Hennessy. *Algebraic Theory of Processes*. MIT Press, Cambridge, Mass., 1988.

[HI90]  M. Hennessy and A. Ingólfsdóttir. A theory of communicating processes with value-passing. In M.S. Paterson, editor, *Proc. 17th Coll. Automata, Languages and Programming, Lecture Notes in Computer Science 443*, pages 209–219. Springer-Verlag, 1990.

[HM85]  M. Hennessy and R. Milner. Algebraic laws for nondeterminism and concurrency. *J. ACM*, 32:137–161, 1985.

[Hoa78]  C.A R. Hoare. Communicating sequential processes. *Comm. ACM*, 21:666–677, 1978.

[Hoa80]  C.A.R. Hoare. A model for communicating sequential processes. In R.M. McKeag and A.M. McNaghton, editors, *On the Construction of Programs*, pages 229–243. Cambridge University Press, 1980.

[Hoa81]  C.A.R. Hoare. A calculus of total correctness for communicating processes. *Sci. Comput. Progr.*, 1:44–72, 1981.

[Hoa85a]  C.A.R. Hoare. *Communicating Sequential Processes*. Prentice-Hall, London, 1985.

[Hoa85b]  C.A.R. Hoare. Programs are predicates. In C.A.R. Hoare and J.C. Shepherdson, editors, *Mathematical Logic and Programming Languages*, pages 141–155, London, 1985. Prentice-Hall.

[HP79]  M. Hennessy and G.D. Plotkin. Full abstraction for a simple programming language. In J. Becvar, editor, *8th Symp. on Math. Found. of Comput. Sci., Lecture Notes in Computer Science 74*, pages 108–120. Springer-Verlag, 1979.

[HU69]  J.E. Hopcroft and J.D. Ullman. *Formal Languages and Their Relation to Automata Theory*. Addison-Wesley, Reading, Mass., 1969.

[INM84]  INMOS Ltd. *OCCAM Programming Manual*. Prentice-Hall, London, 1984.

[Jon87]  B. Jonsson. *Compositional Verification of Distributed Systems*. PhD thesis, Uppsala Univ., Dept. Comput. Sci., 1987.

[JROR90] K.M. Jensen, H. Rischel, E.-R. Olderog, and S. Rössig. Syntax and informal semantics of the ProCoS specification language level 0. Technical Report ESPRIT Basic Research Action ProCoS, ID/DTH KMJ 4/2, Technical University of Denmark, Lyngby, Dept. Comput. Sci., 1990.

[Kel76] R.M. Keller. Formal verification of parallel programs. *Comm. ACM*, 19:371–384, 1976.

[Kle52] S.C. Kleene. *Introduction to Meta-Mathematics*. Van Nostrand, New York, 1952.

[Klu87] W. Kluge. Reduction, data flow and control flow models of computation. In W. Brauer, W. Reisig, and G. Rozenberg, editors, *Petri Nets: Applications and Relationships to Other Models of Concurrency, Lecture Notes in Computer Science 255*, pages 466–498. Springer-Verlag, 1987.

[Knu68] D.E. Knuth. *The Art of Computer Programming. Vol.1: Fundamental Algorithms*. Addison - Wesley, Reading, Mass., 1968.

[Kön27] D. König. Über eine Schlußweise aus dem Endlichen ins Unendliche. *Acta Litt. ac. sci.*, 3:121–130, 1927.

[LC75] P.E. Lauer and R.H. Campbell. Formal semantics of a class of high-level primitives for coordinating concurrent processes. *Acta Inform.*, 5:297–332, 1975.

[LS84] J. Loeckx and K. Sieber. *The Foundation of Program Verification*. Teubner-Wiley, Stuttgart, 1984.

[LTS79] P.E. Lauer, P.R. Torrigiani, and M.W. Shields. COSY – A system specification language based on paths and processes. *Acta Inform.*, 12:109–158, 1979.

[May84] E.W. Mayr. An algorithm for the general Petri net reachability problem. *SIAM J. Comput.*, 13:441–460, 1984.

[Maz77] A. Mazurkiewicz. Concurrent program schemes and their interpretations. Technical Report DAIMI PB-78, Aarhus Univ., 1977.

[MC81] J. Misra and K.M. Chandy. Proofs of networks of processes. *IEEE Trans. Software Eng.*, 7:417–426, 1981.

[Mil77] R. Milner. Fully abstract models of typed $\lambda$-calculi. *Theoret. Comput. Sci.*, 4:1–22, 1977.

[Mil80] R. Milner. A calculus of communicating systems. In *Lecture Notes in Computer Science 92*. Springer-Verlag, 1980.

[Mil83] R. Milner. Calculi for synchrony and asynchrony. *Theoret. Comput. Sci.*, 25:267–310, 1983.

[Mil84]   R. Milner. A complete inference system for a class of regular behaviours. *J. Comput. System Sci.*, 28:439–466, 1984.

[Mil86]   R. Milner. Process constructors and interpretations. In H.-J. Kugler, editor, *Information Processing 86*, pages 507–514, Amsterdam, 1986. North-Holland.

[Mil89]   R. Milner. *Communication and Concurrency*. Prentice-Hall, London, 1989.

[Min67]   M.L. Minsky. *Computation: Finite and Infinite Machines*. Prentice-Hall, Englewood Cliffs, NJ, 1967.

[Mor88]   C. Morgan. The specification statement. *ACM TOPLAS*, 10, 1988.

[Mor90]   C. Morgan. *Programming from Specifications*. Prentice-Hall, London, 1990.

[MS88]    A.R. Meyer and K. Sieber. Towards fully abstract semantics for local variables, Preliminary Report. In *Proc. 15th ACM Symp. Principles of Program. Lang.*, pages 191–203, San Diego, California, 1988.

[MW80]    Z. Manna and R. Waldinger. A deductive approach to program synthesis. *ACM TOPLAS*, 2:90–121, 1980.

[MW84]    Z. Manna and P. Wolper. Synthesis of communicating processes from temporal logic specifications. *ACM TOPLAS*, 6:68–93, 1984.

[Niv79]   M. Nivat. Infinite words, infinite trees, infinite computations. In J.W. de Bakker, editor, *Foundations of Computer Science III.2, Math. Centre Tracts 109*, pages 3–52, Amsterdam, 1979.

[NPW81]   M. Nielsen, G.D. Plotkin, and G. Winskel. Petri nets, event structures and domains, Part 1. *Theoret. Comput. Sci.*, 13:85–108, 1981.

[OH86]    E.-R. Olderog and C.A.R. Hoare. Specification-oriented semantics for communicating processes. *Acta Inform.*, 23:9–66, 1986.

[OL82]    S. Owicki and L. Lamport. Proving liveness properties of concurrent programs. *ACM TOPLAS*, 4:199–223, 1982.

[Old85]   E.-R. Olderog. Specification-oriented programming in TCSP. In K.R. Apt, editor, *Logics and Models of Concurrent Systems*, pages 397–435. Springer-Verlag, 1985.

[Old86]   E.-R. Olderog. Process theory: semantics, specification and verification. In J.W. de Bakker, W.P. de Roever, and G. Rozenberg, editors, *Current Trends in Concurrency, Lecture Notes in Computer Science 224*, pages 442–509. Springer-Verlag, 1986.

[Old87]   E.-R. Olderog. Operational Petri net semantics for CCSP. In G. Rozenberg, editor, *Advances in Petri Nets 1987, Lecture Notes in Computer Science 266*, pages 196–223. Springer-Verlag, 1987.

[Old89]  E.-R. Olderog. Correctness of concurrent processes. In A. Kreczmar and
         G. Mirkowska, editors, *Proc. Mathematical Foundations of Computer Sci-
         ence 1989, Lecture Notes in Computer Science 379*, pages 107–132. Springer-
         Verlag, 1989.

[Oss83]  M. Ossefort. Correctness proofs of communicating processes: three illustra-
         tive examples from the literature. *ACM TOPLAS*, 5:620–640, 1983.

[Par70]  D. Park. Fixpoint induction and proofs of program properties. In D. Michie
         B. Metzer, editor, *Machine Intelligence 5*, pages 59–78. Edinburgh Univ.
         Press, 1970.

[Par76]  D. Park. Finiteness is mu-ineffable. *Theoret. Comput. Sci.*, 3:173–181, 1976.

[Par81]  D. Park. Concurrency and automata on infinite sequences. In P. Deussen,
         editor, *Proc. 5th GI Conf. on Theoret. Comput. Sci., Lecture Notes in Com-
         puter Science 104*, pages 196–223. Springer-Verlag, 1981.

[Par85]  J. Parrow. *Fairness properties in process algebra*. PhD thesis, Uppsala
         Univ., Dept. Comput. Sci., 1985.

[Pet62]  C.A. Petri. *Kommunikation mit Automaten*. PhD thesis, Univ. Bonn, 1962.
         Schriften des Inst. für Instrumentelle Math.

[Pet77]  C.A. Petri. Non-sequential processes. Technical Report Internal Report
         GMD-ISF-77-5, Gesellschaft Math. Datenverarb., St. Augustin, 1977.

[Plo77]  G.D. Plotkin. LCF considered as a programming language. *Theoret. Com-
         put. Sci.*, 5:223–255, 1977.

[Plo81]  G.D. Plotkin. Structured approach to operational semantics. Technical
         Report DAIMI FN-19, Aarhus Univ., Comput. Sci. Dept., 1981.

[Plo82]  G.D. Plotkin. An operational semantics for CSP. In D. Bjørner, editor, *For-
         mal Description of Programming Concepts II*, pages 199–225, Amsterdam,
         1982. North-Holland.

[Pnu77]  A. Pnueli. The temporal logic of programs. In *18th IEEE Symposium on
         Foundations of Computer Science*, pages 46–57, 1977.

[Pnu86]  A. Pnueli. Applications of temporal logic to the specification and verification
         of reactive systems: a survey of current trends. In J.W. de Bakker, W.-P.
         de Roever, and G. Rozenberg, editors, *Current Trends in Concurrency,
         Lecture Notes in Computer Science 224*, pages 510–584. Springer-Verlag,
         1986.

[Pom85]  L. Pomello. Some equivalence notions for concurrent systems – an overview.
         In G. Rozenberg, editor, *Advances in Petri Nets 1985, Lecture Notes in
         Computer Science 222*, pages 381–400. Springer-Verlag, 1985.

[Rei84]  W. Reisig. Partial order semantics versus interleaving semantics for CSP-
         like languages and its impact on fairness. In J. Paredaens, editor, *Proc. 11th
         Coll. Automata, Languages and Programming, Lecture Notes in Computer
         Science 172*, pages 403–413. Springer-Verlag, 1984.

[Rei85]  W. Reisig. *Petri Nets, An Introduction, EATCS Monographs on Theoret.
         Comput. Sci.* Springer-Verlag, 1985.

[Rem87]  M. Rem. Trace theory and systolic computation. In J.W. de Bakker, A.J.
         Nijman, and P.C. Treleaven, editors, *Proc. PARLE Conf., Eindhoven, Vol.
         I, Lecture Notes in Computer Science 258*, pages 14–33. Springer-Verlag,
         1987.

[RH88]   A.W. Roscoe and C.A.R. Hoare. The laws of OCCAM programming. *The-
         oret. Comput. Sci.*, 60:177–229, 1988.

[Roe85]  W.P. de Roever. The quest for compositionality – a survey of assertion-
         based proof systems for concurrent programs, Part 1. In E.J. Neuhold and
         G. Chroust, editors, *Proc. IFIP Conf. on Formal Models in Programming*,
         Amsterdam, 1985. North-Holland.

[Ros82]  A.W. Roscoe. *A mathematical theory of communicating processes.* PhD
         thesis, Oxford Univ., Progr. Research Group, 1982.

[Rös90]  S. Rössig. Transformation of $SL_0$ specifications into PL programs. Technical
         Report ESPRIT Basic Research Action ProCoS, OLD SR 1/4, University
         of Oldenburg, FB Informatik, 1990.

[RS59]   M.O. Rabin and D.S. Scott. Finite automata and their decision problems.
         *IBM J. Research*, 3(2), 1959.

[RS91]   S. Rössig and M. Schenke. Specification and stepwise development of com-
         municating systems. Technical Report ESPRIT Basic Research Action Pro-
         CoS, OLD SR 6/1, University of Oldenburg, FB Informatik, 1991.

[RV77]   P. Robert and J.-P. Verjus. Toward autonomous descriptions of synchro-
         nization modules. In B. Gilchrist, editor, *Proc. IFIP Information Processing
         77*, pages 981–986, Amsterdam, 1977. North-Holland.

[Sco70]  D.S. Scott. Outline of a mathematical theory of computation. Technical
         Report Tech. Monograph PRG-2, Oxford Univ., Progr. Research Group,
         1970.

[Sho67]  J.R. Shoenfield. *Mathematical Logic.* Addison-Wesley, 1967.

[Sne85]  J.L.A. van de Snepscheut. Trace theory and and VLSI design. In *Lecture
         Notes in Computer Science 200*. Springer-Verlag, 1985.

[ST87]   D.T. Sanella and A. Tarlecki. On observational equivalence and algebraic
         specification. *J. Comput. System Sci.*, 34:150–178, 1987.

[Ste89]  B. Steffen. Characteristic formulae. In G. Ausiello, M. Dezani-Ciancaglini, and S. Ronchi Della Roccha, editors, *Proc. 16th Coll. Automata, Languages and Programming, Lecture Notes in Computer Science 372*, pages 723–732. Springer-Verlag, 1989.

[Sti87]  C. Stirling. Modal logics for communicating systems. *Theoret. Comput. Sci.*, 49:311–347, 1987.

[Sto77]  J.E. Stoy. *Denotational Semantics: The Scott-Strachey Approach to Programming Language Theory*. MIT Press, Cambridge, Mass., 1977.

[Tar55]  A. Tarski. A lattice-theoretic fixpoint theorem and its applications. *Pacific J. Math*, 5:285–309, 1955.

[Tau85]  D. Taubner. Two net oriented semantics for TCSP. Technical Report Bericht Nr. 116/85, Univ. Hamburg, Fachbereich Inform., 1985.

[Tau87]  D. Taubner. Theoretical CSP and formal languages. Technical Report Bericht TUM-18706, TU München, Inst. f. Inform., 1987.

[Tau89]  D. Taubner. Finite Representations of CCS and TCSP Programs by Automata and Petri Nets. In *Lecture Notes in Computer Science 369*. Springer-Verlag, 1989.

[Vaa86]  F.W. Vaandrager. Verification of two communication protocol by means of process algebra. Technical Report CS-R8608, CWI, Amsterdam, 1986.

[Vaa90]  F.W. Vaandrager. *Algebraic Techniques for Concurrency and their Application*. PhD thesis, University of Amsterdam, 1990.

[WGS87]  J. Widom, D. Gries, and F.B. Schneider. Completeness and incompleteness of trace-based network proof systems. In *Proc. 14th ACM Symp. on Principles of Progr. Languages*, pages 27–38, München, 1987.

[Win80]  G. Winskel. *Events in computation*. PhD thesis, Univ. of Edinburgh, Dept. Comput. Sci., 1980.

[Win82]  G. Winskel. Event structure semantics of CCS and related languages. In E.M. Schmidt, editor, *Proc. 9th Coll. Automata, Languages and Programming, Lecture Notes in Computer Science 140*. Springer-Verlag, 1982.

[Win84]  G. Winskel. A new definition of morphism on Petri nets. In E.M. Schmidt, editor, *Proc. 1th Symp. Theoret. Aspects of Comput., Lecture Notes in Computer Science 140*. Springer-Verlag, 1984.

[Win87]  G. Winskel. Event structures. In W. Brauer, W. Reisig, and G. Rozenberg, editors, *Petri Nets: Applications and Relationships to Other Models of Concurrency, Lecture Notes in Computer Science 255*, pages 325–392. Springer-Verlag, 1987.

[Wir71]  N. Wirth. Program development by stepwise refinement. *Comm. ACM*, 14:221–227, 1971.

[ZRE85]  J. Zwiers, W.P. de Roever, and P. van Emde-Boas. Compositionalty and concurrent networks. In W. Brauer, editor, *Proc. 12th Coll. Automata, Languages and Programming, Lecture Notes in Computer Science 194*, pages 509–519. Springer-Verlag, 1985.

[Zwi89]  J. Zwiers. Compositionalty, Concurrency and Partial Correctness – Proof Theories for Networks of Processes and Their Relationship. In W. Brauer, W. Reisig, and G. Rozenberg, editors, *Lecture Notes in Computer Science 321*. Springer-Verlag, 1989.

# AUTHOR INDEX

# SUBJECT INDEX

# SYMBOL INDEX

In this book various sets of syntactic and semantic objects are defined. For each set we introduce some typical elements ranging over this set. For example, we introduce $re$ as a typical element of $Reg$, the set of regular expressions. In this symbol index we record this by writing $re \in Reg$. In applications these typical elements may be decorated by subscripts or dashes.

## SETS AND MULTISETS

## FUNCTIONS

For a function $f : A \longrightarrow B$ and a set $M \subseteq A$ we use the following notation:

261

# Petri Nets

# Process Terms

## Net Semantics

## Logical Formulas

# TRACE SPECIFICATIONS AND MIXED TERMS

| | | |
|---|---|---|
| $S, T, U \in Spec$ | trace specifications | 110 |
| $\alpha(S)$ | (projection) alphabet | 110 |
| $\alpha\alpha(S)$ | extended alphabet | 110 |
| $tr \models S$ | satisfaction relation for traces | 110 |
| $pref\ tr \models S$ | ... and all their prefixes | 116 |
| $P\ sat\ S$ | satisfaction relation for process terms | 115 |
| $kern(S)$ | kernel | 175 |
| $init(S)$ | initial communications | 175 |
| $Th(Spec)$ | theory of trace specifications | 174 |
| $P, Q, R \in Proc + Spec$ | mixed terms | 172 |
| $CProc + Spec$ | closed mixed terms | 172 |

# READINESS SEMANTICS

| | | |
|---|---|---|
| $\mathcal{R}$ | readiness semantics | 124 |
| $\mathcal{R}^*$ | modified readiness semantics | 124 |
| $\gamma, \delta \in Info_{\mathcal{R}} : A$ | process information | 125 |
| $\Gamma, \Delta \in Info_{\mathcal{R}} : A$ | sets of process information | 125 |
| $(A, \Gamma), (B, \Delta) \in DOM_{\mathcal{R}}$ | readiness domain | 125 |
| $ws\text{-}DOM_{\mathcal{R}}$ | well-structured readiness domain | 149 |
| $\alpha(A, \Gamma)$ | alphabet part | 125 |
| $\pi(A, \Gamma)$ | process information part | 125 |
| $close(A, \Gamma)$ | closure operator | 126 |
| $succ(tr, \Gamma)$ | successor communications | 126 |
| $\mathcal{F}, \mathcal{G}, \mathcal{H}$ | ready sets | 125 |
| $\mathcal{X} \subseteq Comm \cup \{\uparrow\}$ | ready sets or divergence symbol | 125 |
| $\mathcal{R}^*(\mathcal{N})$ | readiness semantics of nets | 125 |
| $\mathcal{R}^*[\![P]\!]$ | (operational) readiness semantics of process terms | 126 |
| $\mathcal{R}^*[\![S]\!]$ | readiness semantics of trace specifications | 134 |
| $x \sqsubseteq y$ | partial order | 136 |
| $\bot$ | least element (*bottom*) | 138 |
| $\bigsqcup D$ | least upper bound | 136 |
| $\bigsqcup_{x \geq 0} x_n$ | limit of a chain | 137 |
| $fix\ \Phi$ | fixed point of $\Phi$ | 137 |
| $\Phi^n$ | $n$-fold iteration of $\Phi$ | 138 |
| $\rho \in Env_{\mathcal{M}}$ | environments | 138 |
| $\mathcal{R}^{**}[\![P]\!](\rho)$ | denotational readiness semantics of process terms | 142 |
| $op_{\mathcal{R}}$ | readiness operators for | 140 |
| $stop{:}A_{\mathcal{R}}$ | ... deadlock | 140 |
| $div{:}A_{\mathcal{R}}$ | ... divergence | 140 |

Printed in the United States
By Bookmasters